Twin ★ Star Exorcists
ONMYOJI

2

STORY & ART
YOSHIAKI SUKENO

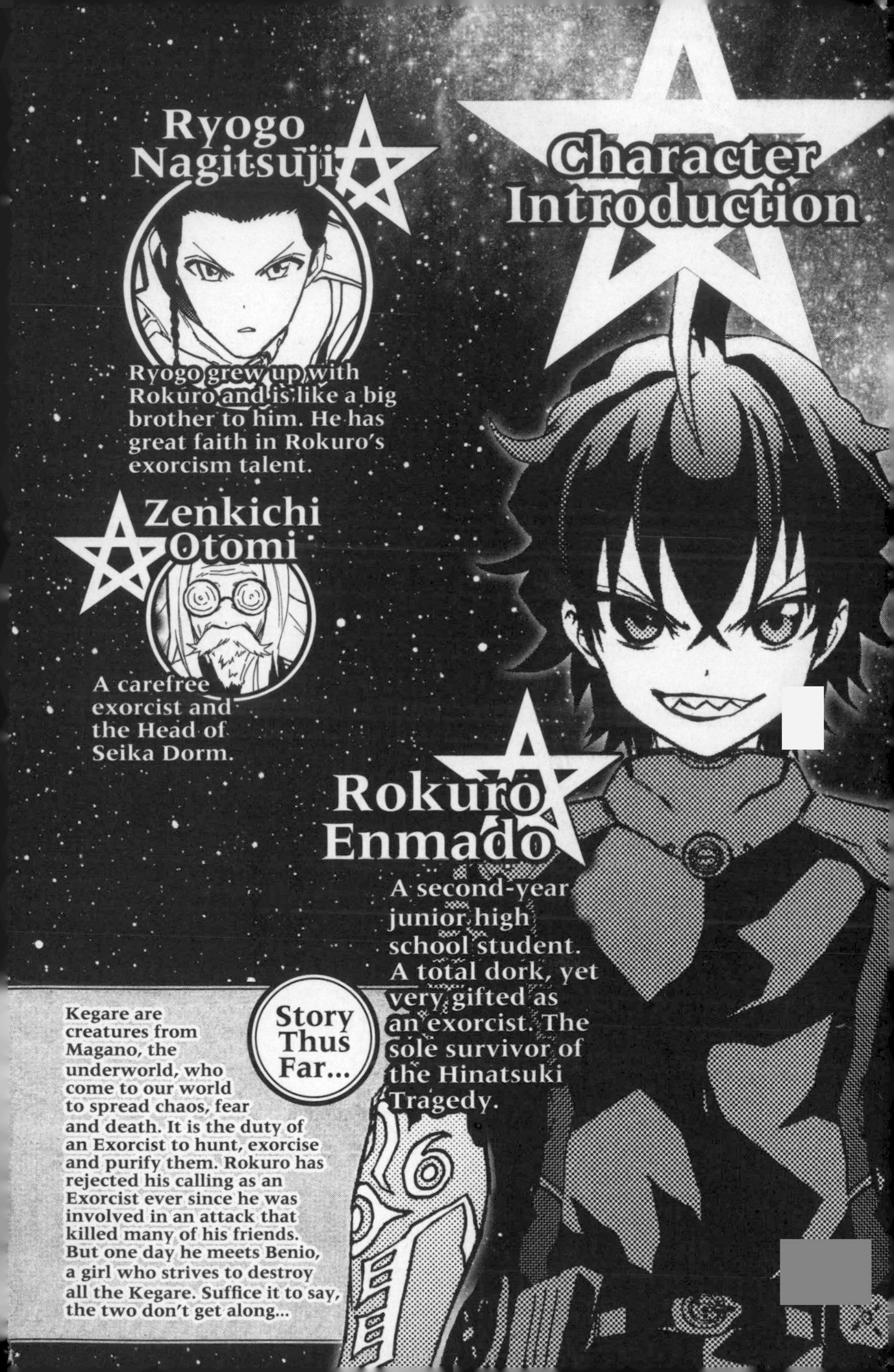

Character Introduction
Rokuro Enmado
A second-year junior high school student. A total dork, yet very gifted as an exorcist. The sole survivor of the Hinatsuki Tragedy.
Ryogo Nagitsuji
Ryogo grew up with Rokuro and is like a big brother to him. He has great faith in Rokuro's exorcism talent.
Zenkichi Otomi
A carefree exorcist and the Head of Seika Dorm.
Story Thus Far...
Kegare are creatures from Magano, the underworld, who come to our world to spread chaos, fear and death. It is the duty of an Exorcist to hunt, exorcise and purify them. Rokuro has rejected his calling as an Exorcist ever since he was involved in an attack that killed many of his friends. But one day he meets Benio, a girl who strives to destroy all the Kegare. Suffice it to say, the two don't get along...

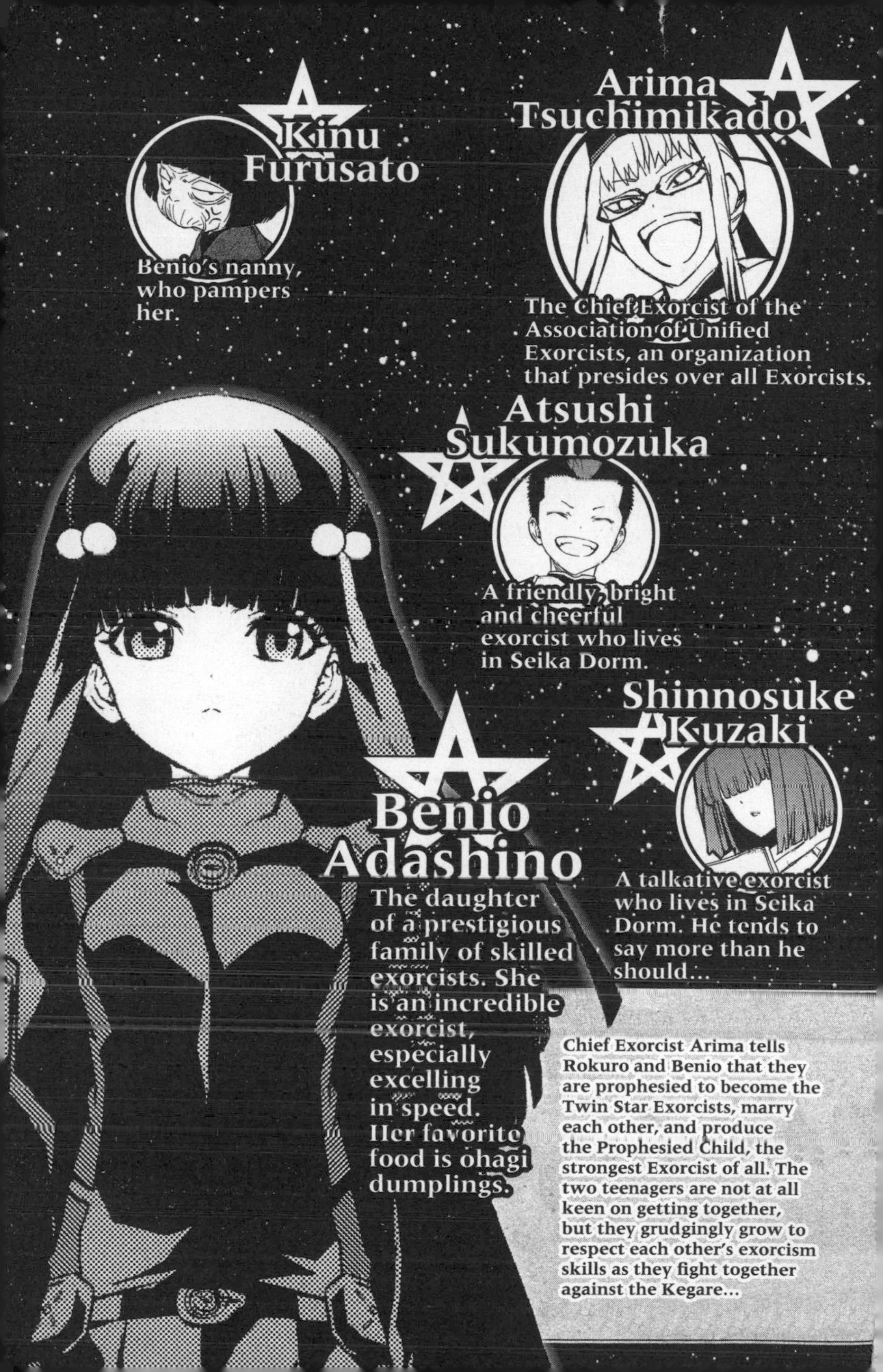
Kinu Furusato
Benio's nanny, who pampers her.
Arima Tsuchimikado
The Chief Exorcist of the Association of Unified Exorcists, an organization that presides over all Exorcists.
Atsushi Sukumozuka
A friendly, bright and cheerful exorcist who lives in Seika Dorm.
Shinnosuke Kuzaki
A talkative exorcist who lives in Seika Dorm. He tends to say more than he should...
Benio Adashino
The daughter of a prestigious family of skilled exorcists. She is an incredible exorcist, especially excelling in speed. Her favorite food is ohagi dumplings.
Chief Exorcist Arima tells Rokuro and Benio that they are prophesied to become the Twin Star Exorcists, marry each other, and produce the Prophesied Child, the strongest Exorcist of all. The two teenagers are not at all keen on getting together, but they grudgingly grow to respect each other's exorcism skills as they fight together against the Kegare...

ONMYOJI

EXORCISMS

ONMYOJI have worked for the Imperial Court since the Heian era.
In addition to exorcising evil spirits, as civil servants they performed a
variety of roles, including advising nobles by foretelling the future, creating
the calendar, observing the movements of the stars, measuring time…

#4 Who Are You?

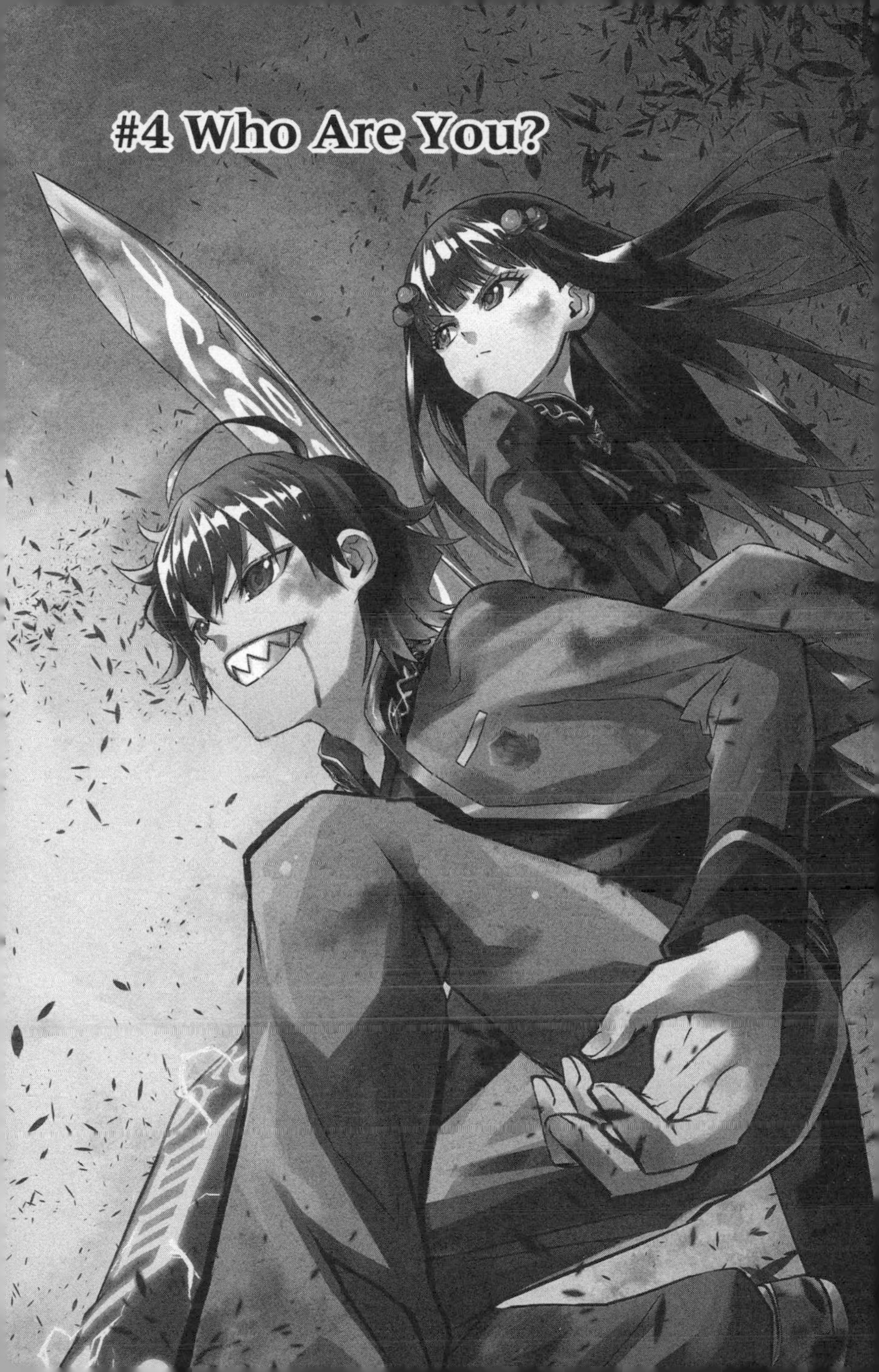

Twin Star Exorcists

ONMYOJI

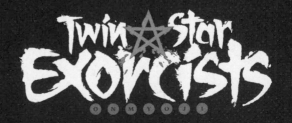

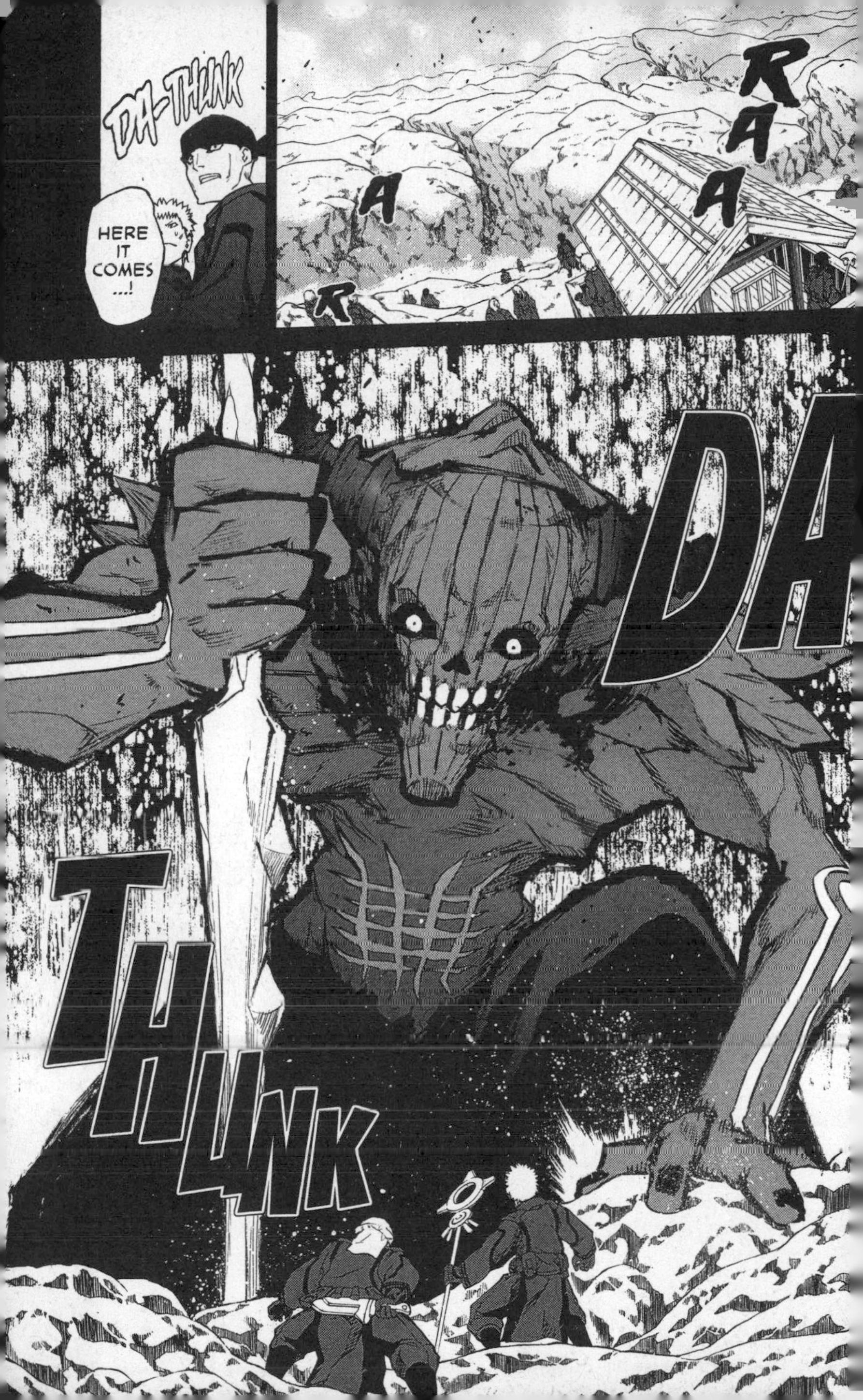
RAAAR
DA-THUNK
HERE IT COMES ....!
DA
THUNK

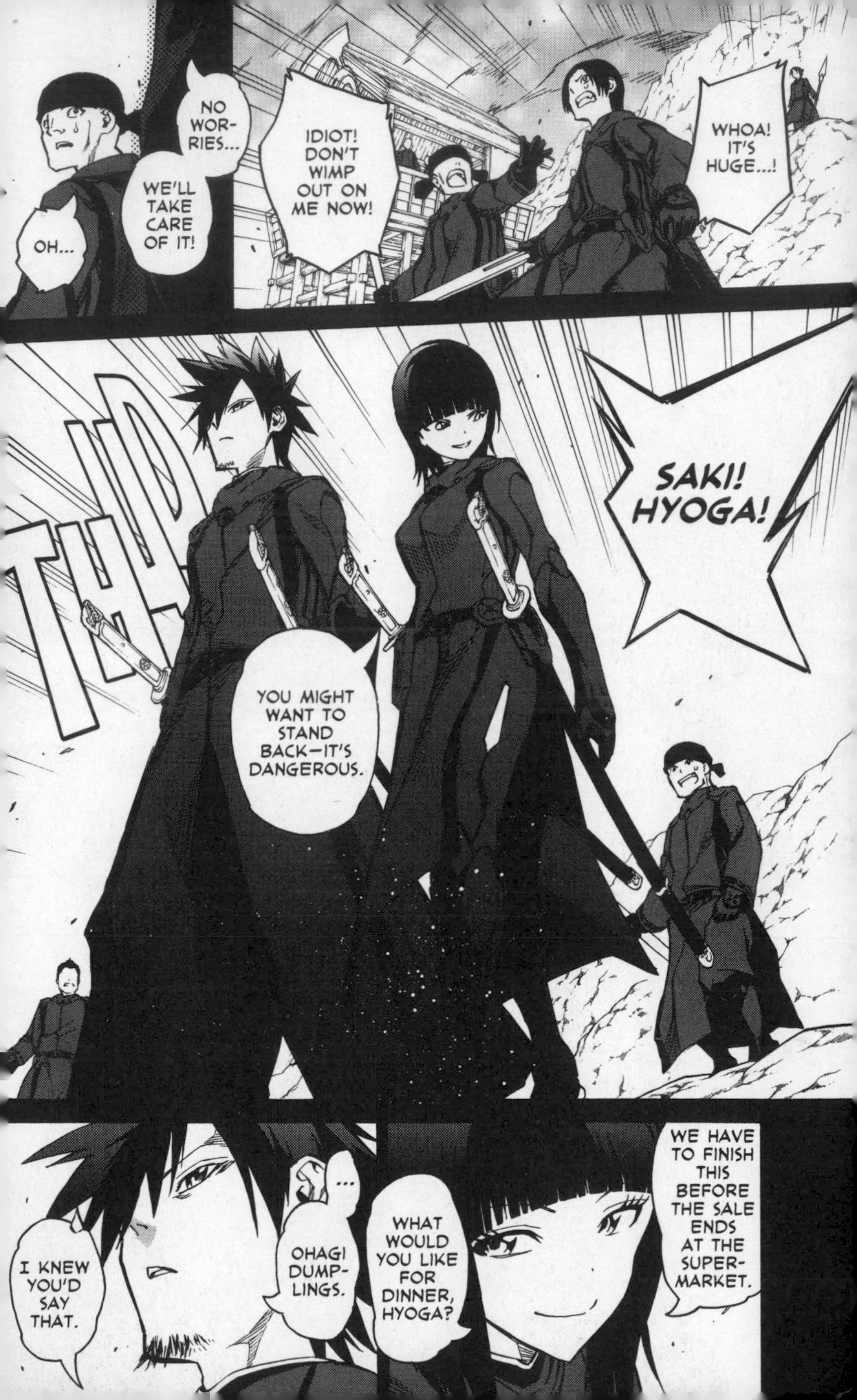
WHOA! IT'S HUGE...!
IDIOT! DON'T WIMP OUT ON ME NOW!
NO WORRIES...
WE'LL TAKE CARE OF IT!
OH...
SAKI! HYOGA!
THP
YOU MIGHT WANT TO STAND BACK—IT'S DANGEROUS.
WE HAVE TO FINISH THIS BEFORE THE SALE ENDS AT THE SUPERMARKET.
WHAT WOULD YOU LIKE FOR DINNER, HYOGA?
...
OHAGI DUMPLINGS.
I KNEW YOU'D SAY THAT.

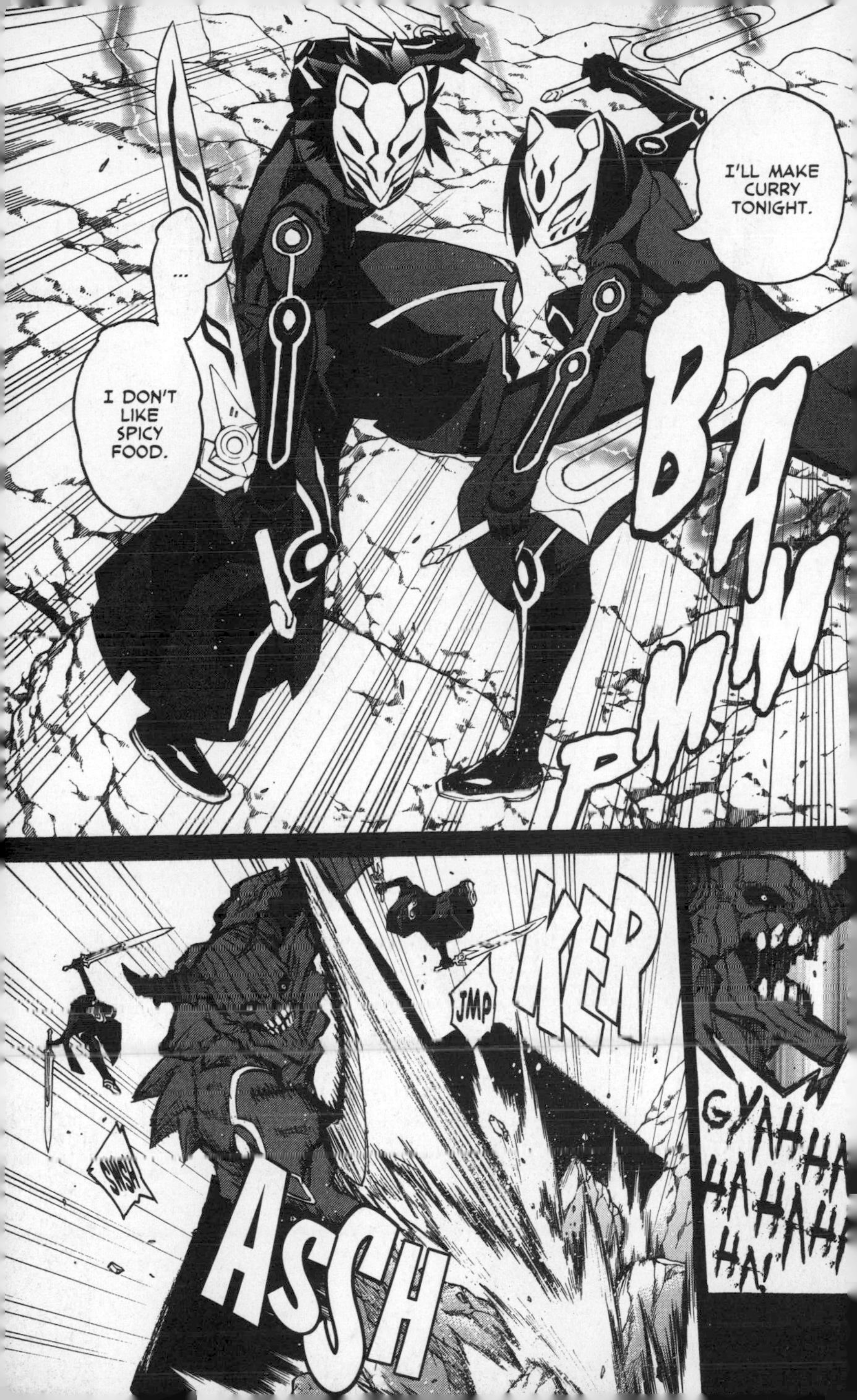
I'LL MAKE CURRY TONIGHT.
...
I DON'T LIKE SPICY FOOD.
BAMMP
GYAHHAHAHAHAHA!
KER
JMP
ASSH
SMSH

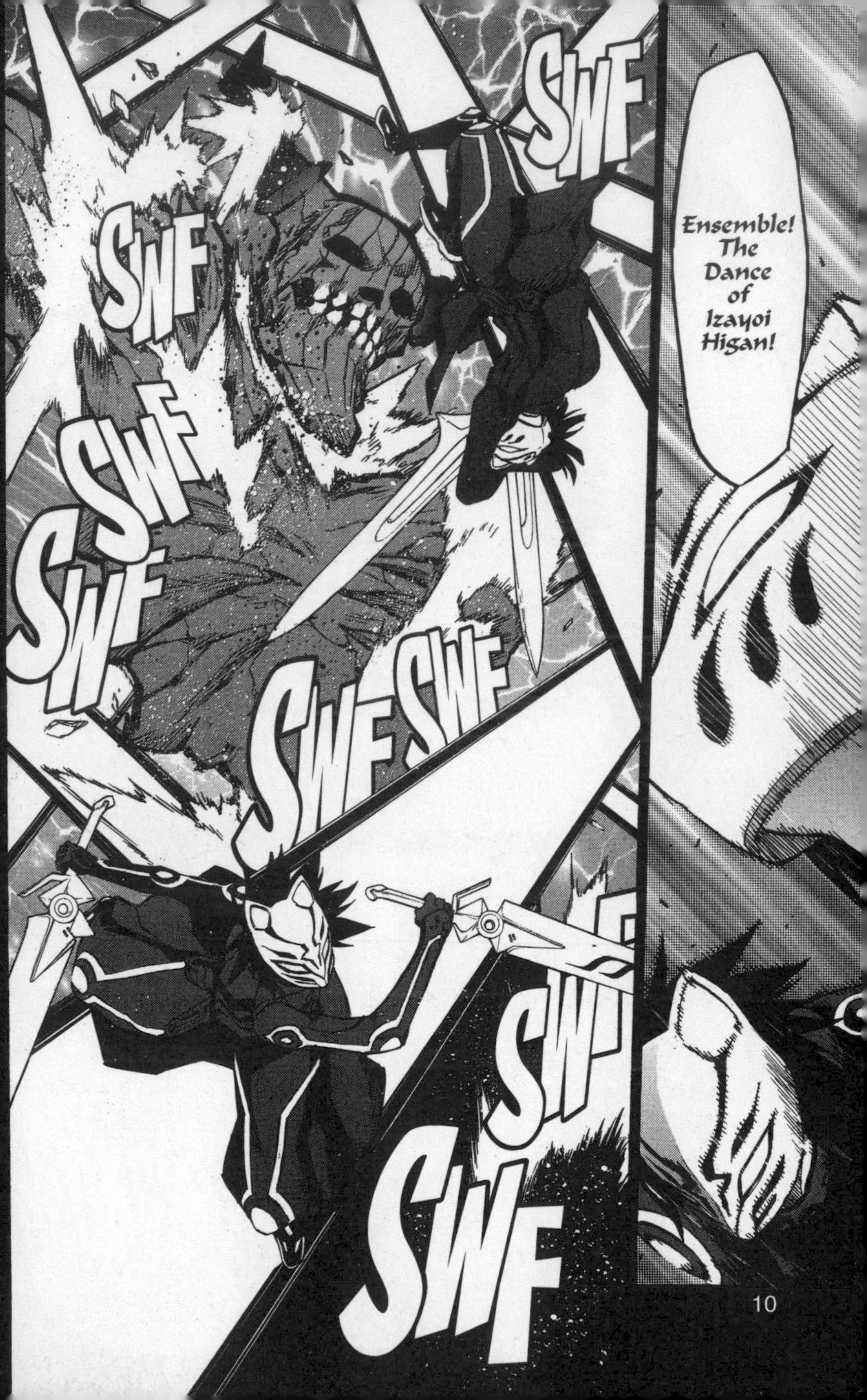
Ensemble! The Dance of Izayoi Higan!
SWF
SWF
SWF
SWF
SWF SWF
SWF
SWF
SWF

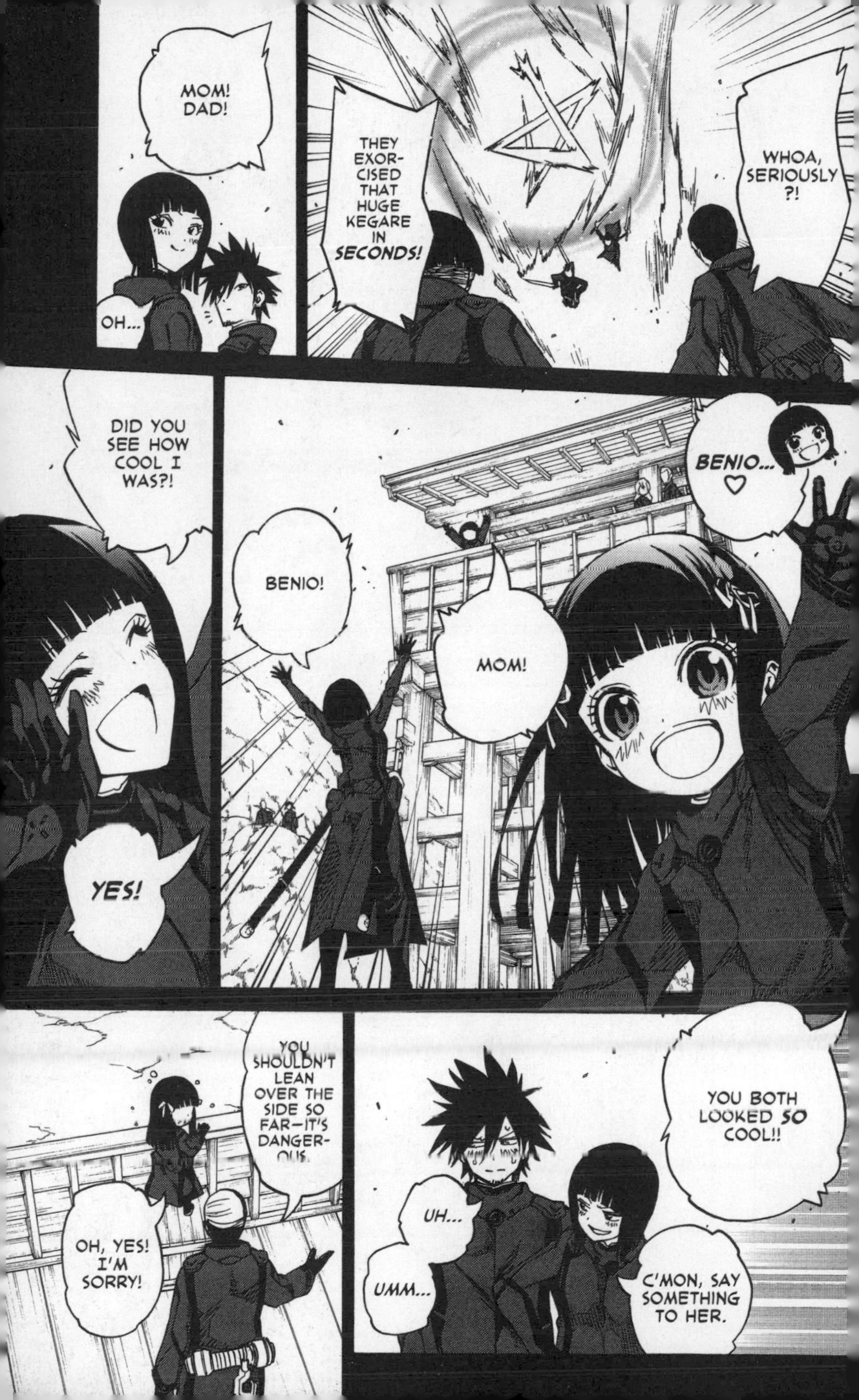
WHOA, SERIOUSLY?!
THEY EXORCISED THAT HUGE KEGARE IN SECONDS!
MOM! DAD!
OH...
BENIO... ♡
MOM!
BENIO!
DID YOU SEE HOW COOL I WAS?!
YES!
YOU BOTH LOOKED SO COOL!!
UH...
C'MON, SAY SOMETHING TO HER.
UMM...
YOU SHOULDN'T LEAN OVER THE SIDE SO FAR—IT'S DANGEROUS.
OH, YES! I'M SORRY!

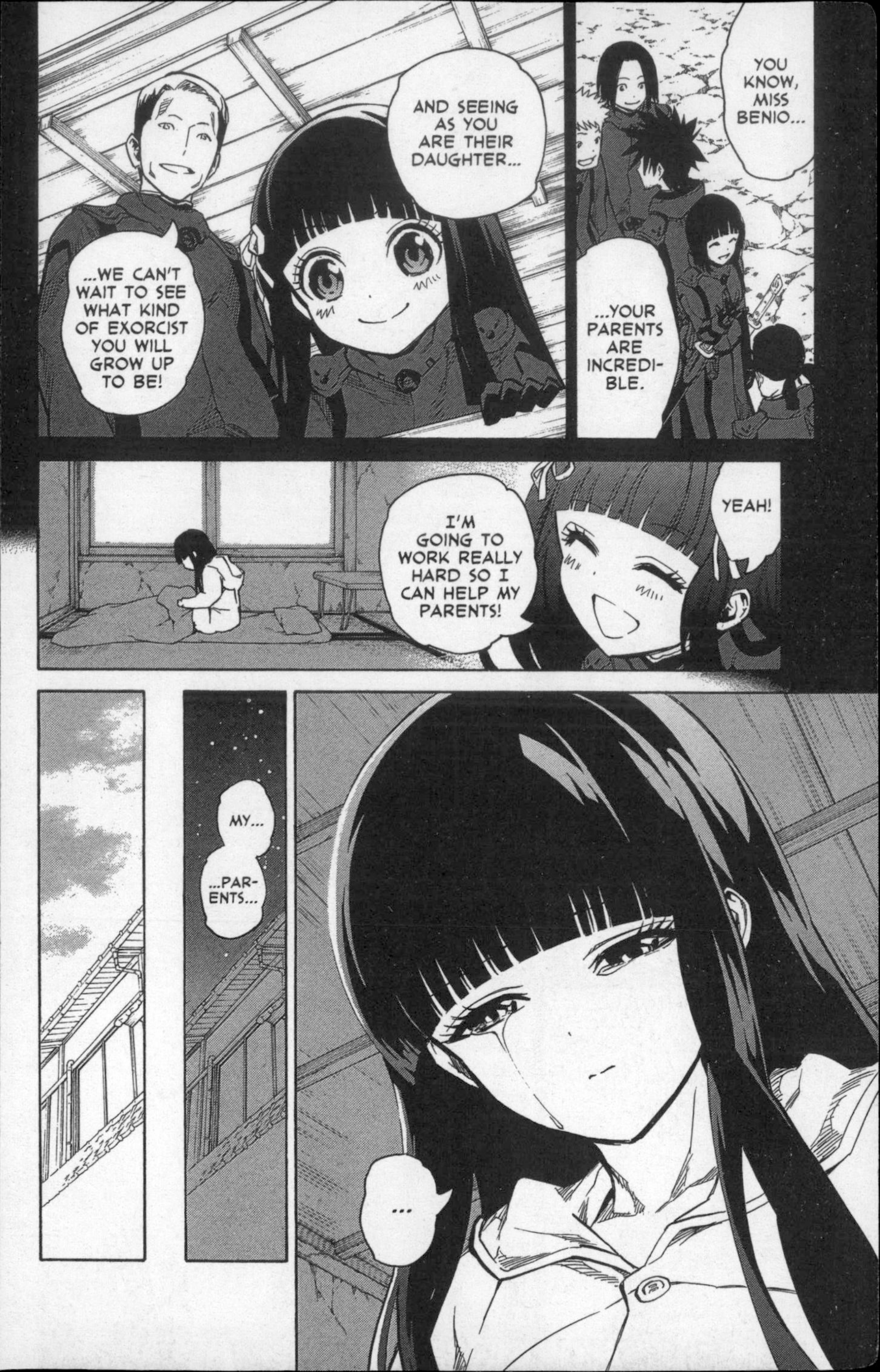
YOU KNOW, MISS BENIO...
...YOUR PARENTS ARE INCREDI-BLE.
AND SEEING AS YOU ARE THEIR DAUGHTER...
...WE CAN'T WAIT TO SEE WHAT KIND OF EXORCIST YOU WILL GROW UP TO BE!
YEAH!
I'M GOING TO WORK REALLY HARD SO I CAN HELP MY PARENTS!
...
MY...
...PAR-ENTS...

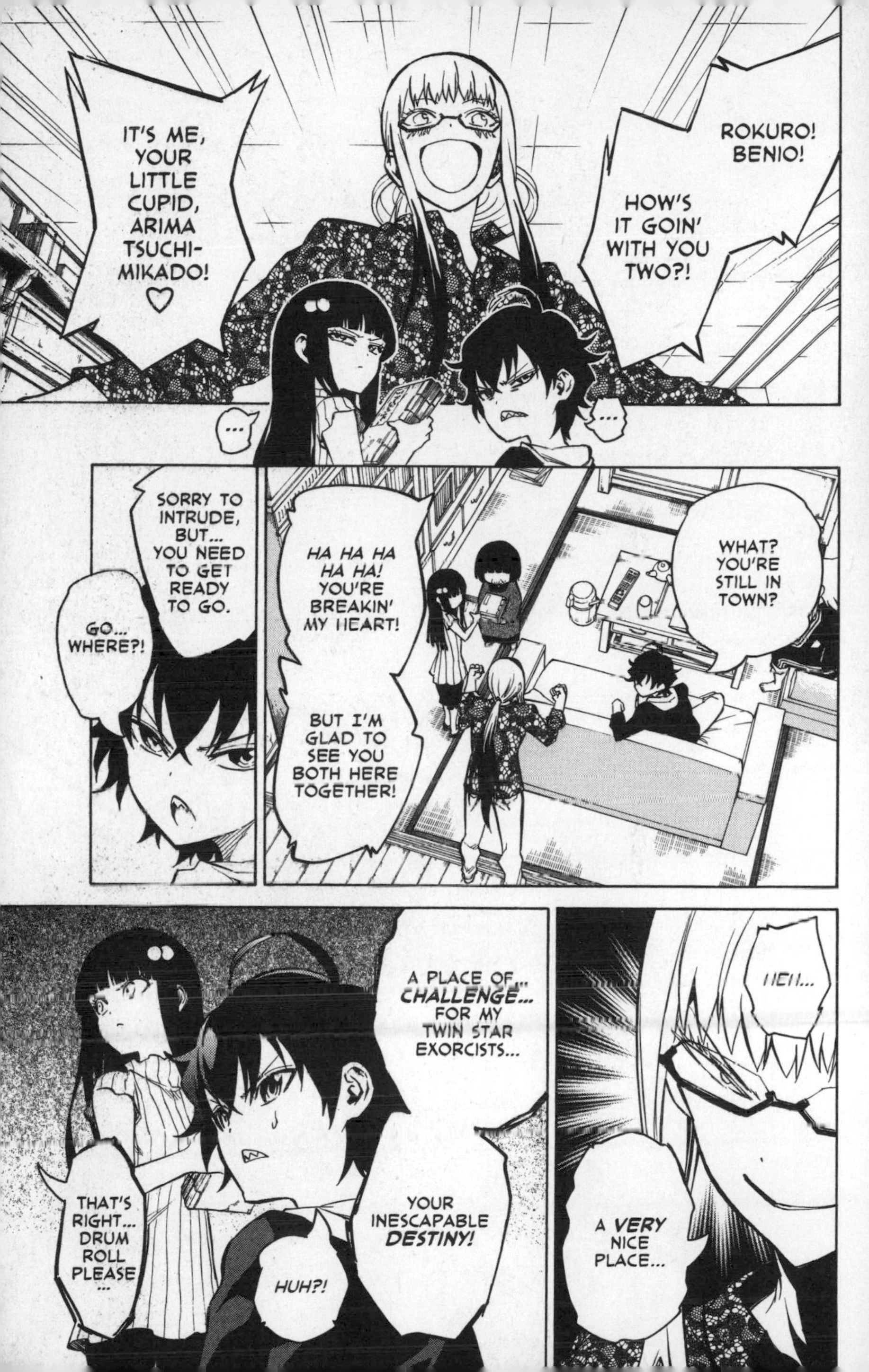
ROKURO! BENIO!
HOW'S IT GOIN' WITH YOU TWO?!
IT'S ME, YOUR LITTLE CUPID, ARIMA TSUCHI-MIKADO! ♡
...
...
WHAT? YOU'RE STILL IN TOWN?
HA HA HA HA HA! YOU'RE BREAKIN' MY HEART!
BUT I'M GLAD TO SEE YOU BOTH HERE TOGETHER!
SORRY TO INTRUDE, BUT... YOU NEED TO GET READY TO GO.
GO... WHERE?!
HEH...
A VERY NICE PLACE...
A PLACE OF... CHALLENGE... FOR MY TWIN STAR EXORCISTS...
YOUR INESCAPABLE DESTINY!
THAT'S RIGHT... DRUM ROLL PLEASE ...
HUH?!

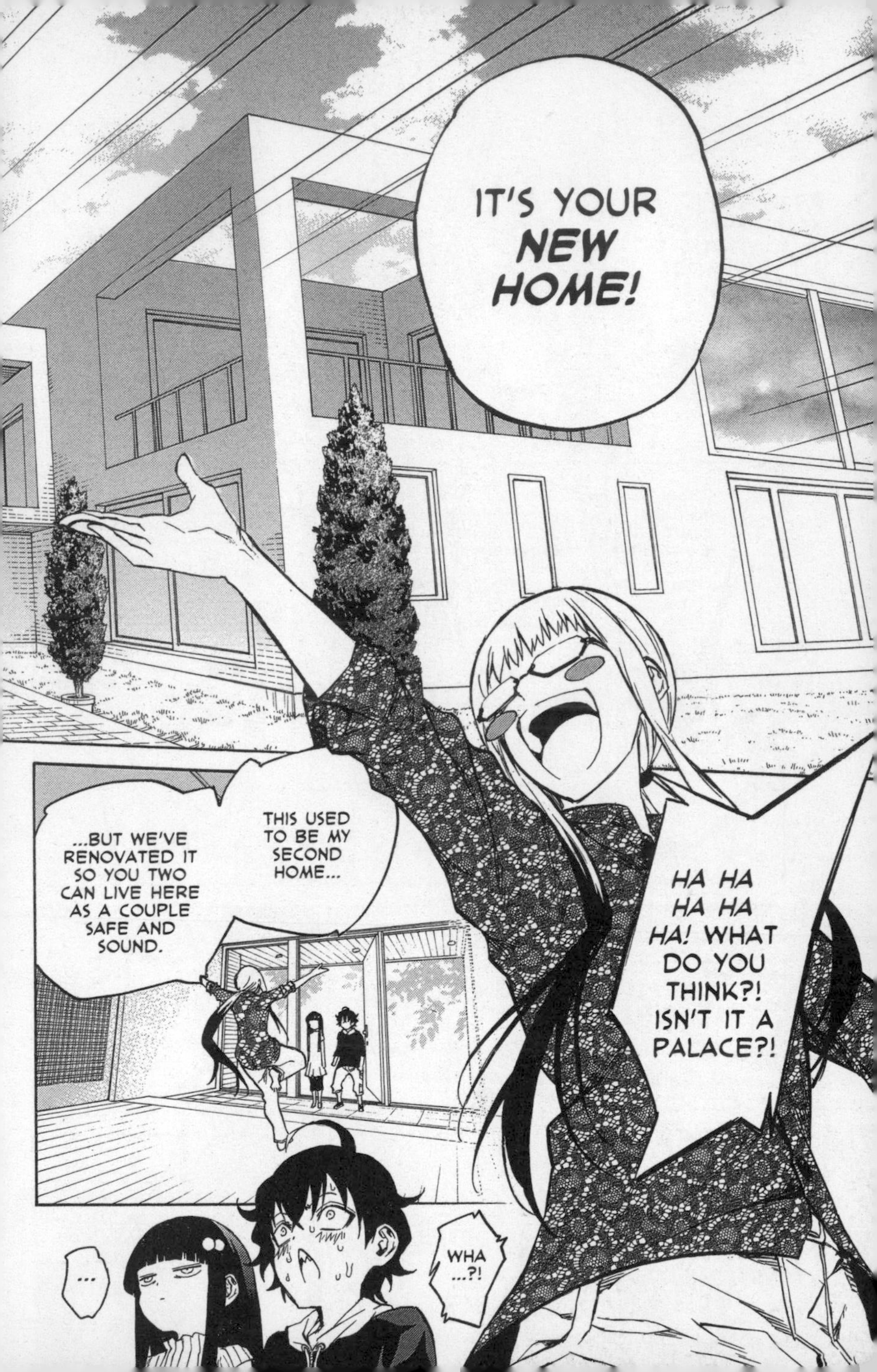
IT'S YOUR *NEW HOME!*
HA HA HA HA HA! WHAT DO YOU THINK?! ISN'T IT A PALACE?!
THIS USED TO BE MY SECOND HOME...
...BUT WE'VE RENOVATED IT SO YOU TWO CAN LIVE HERE AS A COUPLE SAFE AND SOUND.
WHA ...?!
...

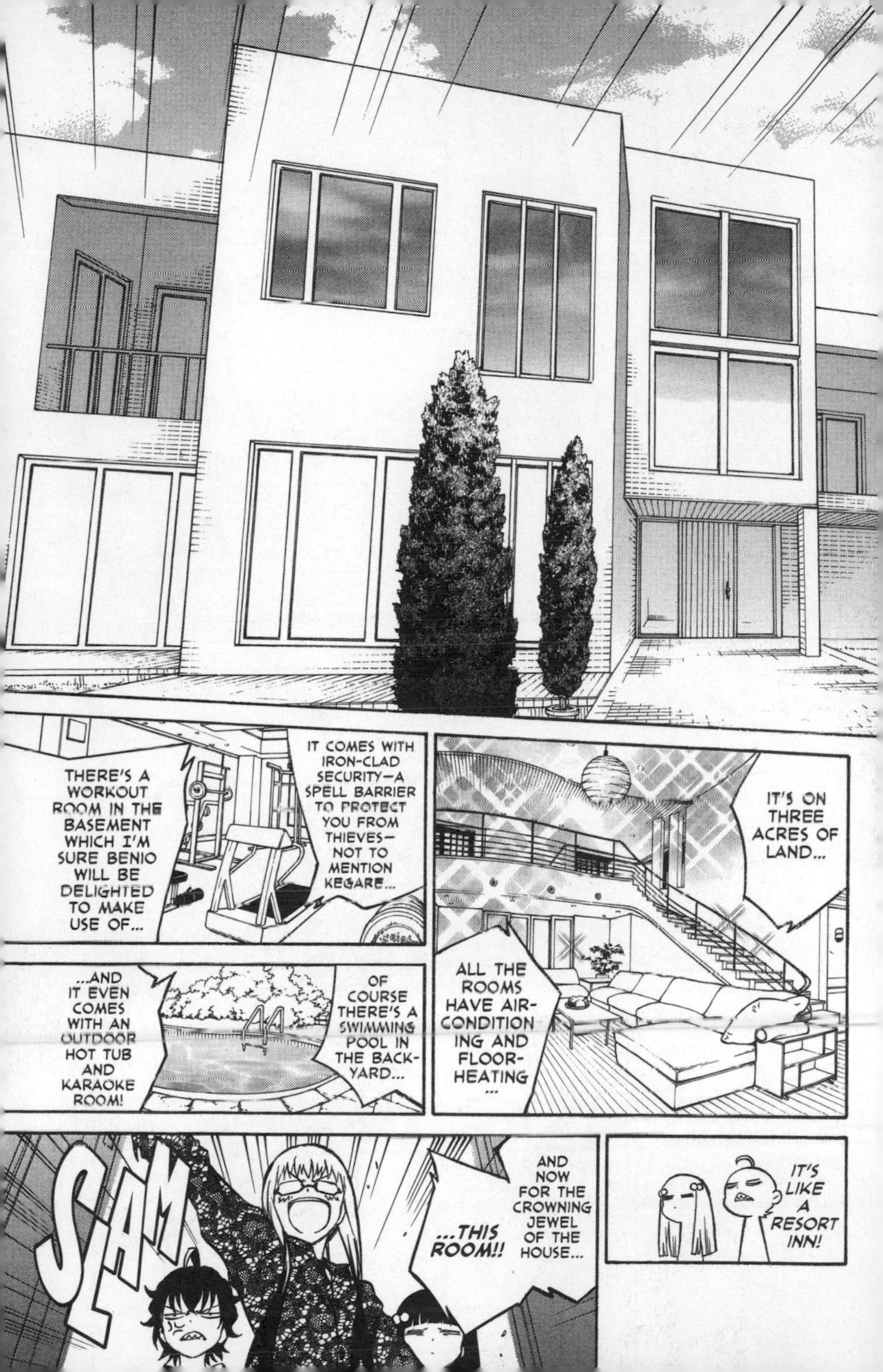
IT'S ON THREE ACRES OF LAND...
ALL THE ROOMS HAVE AIR-CONDITIONING AND FLOOR-HEATING...
IT COMES WITH IRON-CLAD SECURITY—A SPELL BARRIER TO PROTECT YOU FROM THIEVES—NOT TO MENTION KEGARE...
THERE'S A WORKOUT ROOM IN THE BASEMENT WHICH I'M SURE BENIO WILL BE DELIGHTED TO MAKE USE OF...
OF COURSE THERE'S A SWIMMING POOL IN THE BACKYARD...
...AND IT EVEN COMES WITH AN OUTDOOR HOT TUB AND KARAOKE ROOM!
IT'S LIKE A RESORT INN!
AND NOW FOR THE CROWNING JEWEL OF THE HOUSE...
...THIS ROOM!!
SLAM

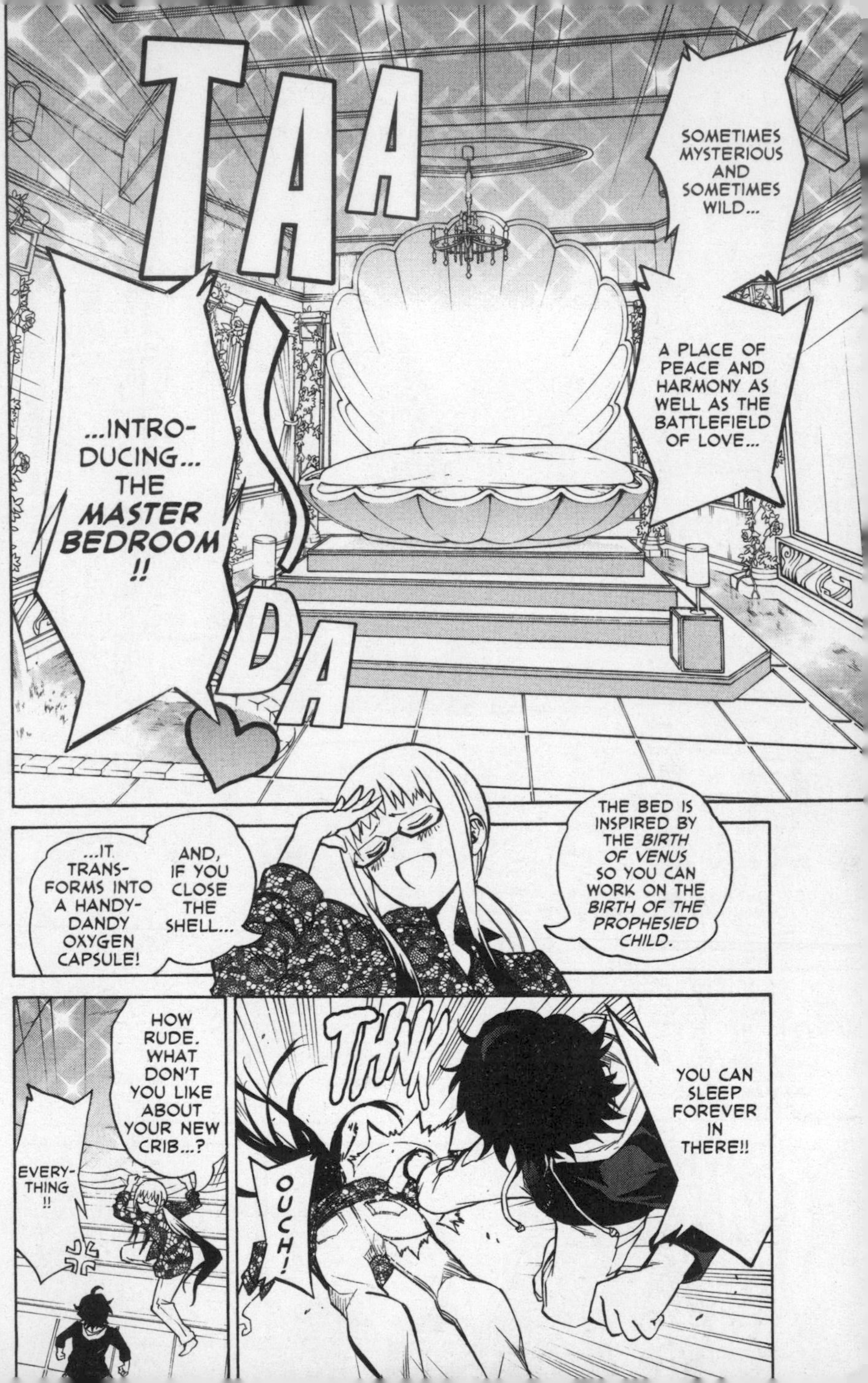
SOMETIMES MYSTERIOUS AND SOMETIMES WILD...
A PLACE OF PEACE AND HARMONY AS WELL AS THE BATTLEFIELD OF LOVE...
TAA DA
...INTRO-DUCING... THE *MASTER BEDROOM* !!
THE BED IS INSPIRED BY THE *BIRTH OF VENUS* SO YOU CAN WORK ON THE *BIRTH OF THE PROPHESIED CHILD.*
AND, IF YOU CLOSE THE SHELL...
...IT TRANS-FORMS INTO A HANDY-DANDY OXYGEN CAPSULE!
YOU CAN SLEEP FOREVER IN THERE!!
THNK
OUCH!
HOW RUDE. WHAT DON'T YOU LIKE ABOUT YOUR NEW CRIB...?
EVERY-THING !!

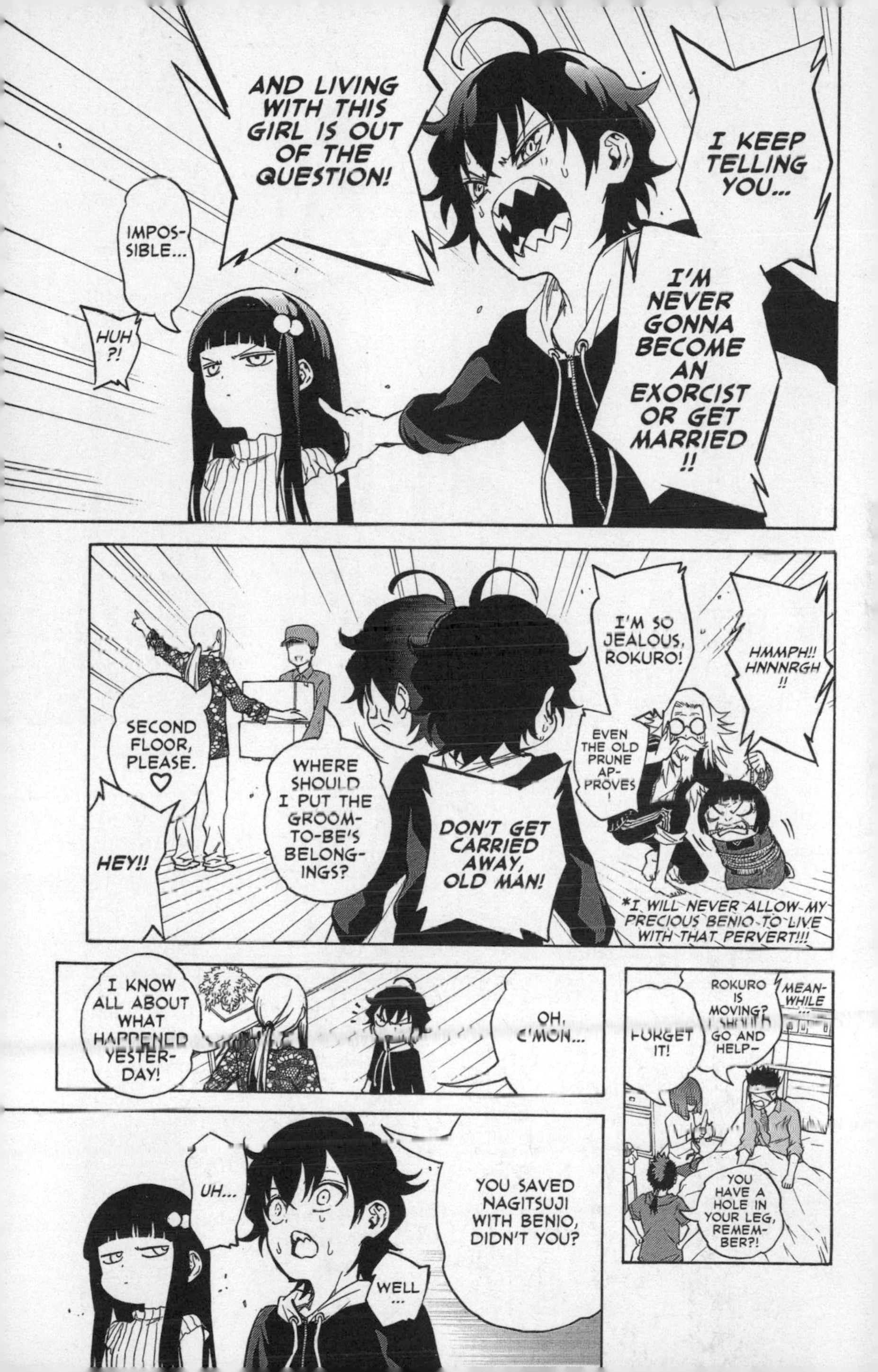
I KEEP TELLING YOU...
I'M NEVER GONNA BECOME AN EXORCIST OR GET MARRIED!!
AND LIVING WITH THIS GIRL IS OUT OF THE QUESTION!
IMPOSSIBLE...
HUH?!
HMMPH!! HNNNRGH!!
I'M SO JEALOUS, ROKURO!
EVEN THE OLD PRUNE APPROVES!
*I WILL NEVER ALLOW MY PRECIOUS BENIO TO LIVE WITH THAT PERVERT!!!
DON'T GET CARRIED AWAY, OLD MAN!
WHERE SHOULD I PUT THE GROOM-TO-BE'S BELONGINGS?
SECOND FLOOR, PLEASE. ♡
HEY!!
MEANWHILE...
ROKURO IS MOVING? I SHOULD GO AND HELP—
FORGET IT!
YOU HAVE A HOLE IN YOUR LEG, REMEMBER?!
OH, C'MON...
I KNOW ALL ABOUT WHAT HAPPENED YESTERDAY!
YOU SAVED NAGITSUJI WITH BENIO, DIDN'T YOU?
UH...
WELL...

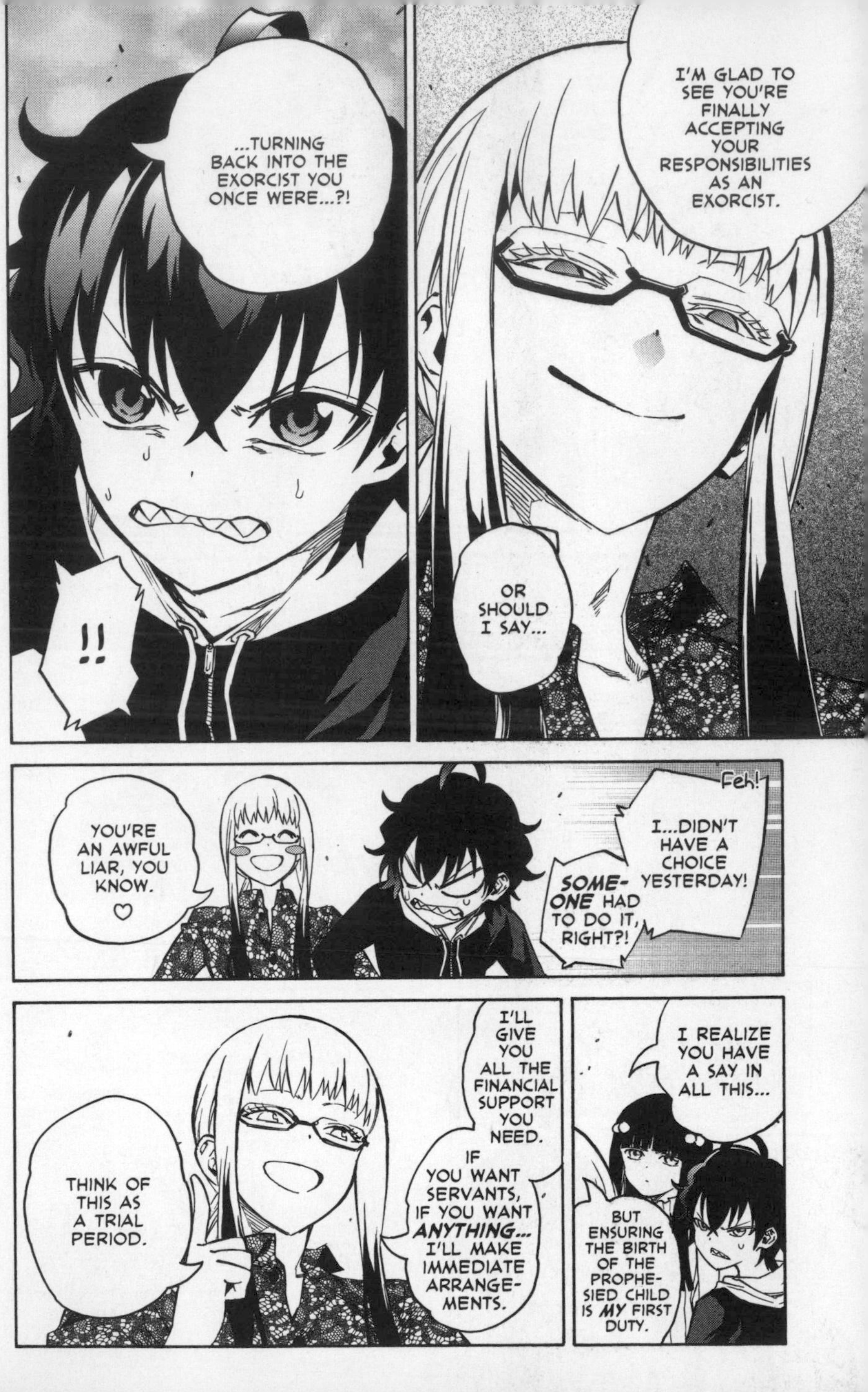
I'M GLAD TO SEE YOU'RE FINALLY ACCEPTING YOUR RESPONSIBILITIES AS AN EXORCIST.
OR SHOULD I SAY...
...TURNING BACK INTO THE EXORCIST YOU ONCE WERE...?!
!!
Feh!
I...DIDN'T HAVE A CHOICE YESTERDAY!
SOME-ONE HAD TO DO IT, RIGHT?!
YOU'RE AN AWFUL LIAR, YOU KNOW. ♡
I REALIZE YOU HAVE A SAY IN ALL THIS...
BUT ENSURING THE BIRTH OF THE PROPHE-SIED CHILD IS MY FIRST DUTY.
I'LL GIVE YOU ALL THE FINANCIAL SUPPORT YOU NEED.
IF YOU WANT SERVANTS, IF YOU WANT ANYTHING... I'LL MAKE IMMEDIATE ARRANGE-MENTS.
THINK OF THIS AS A TRIAL PERIOD.

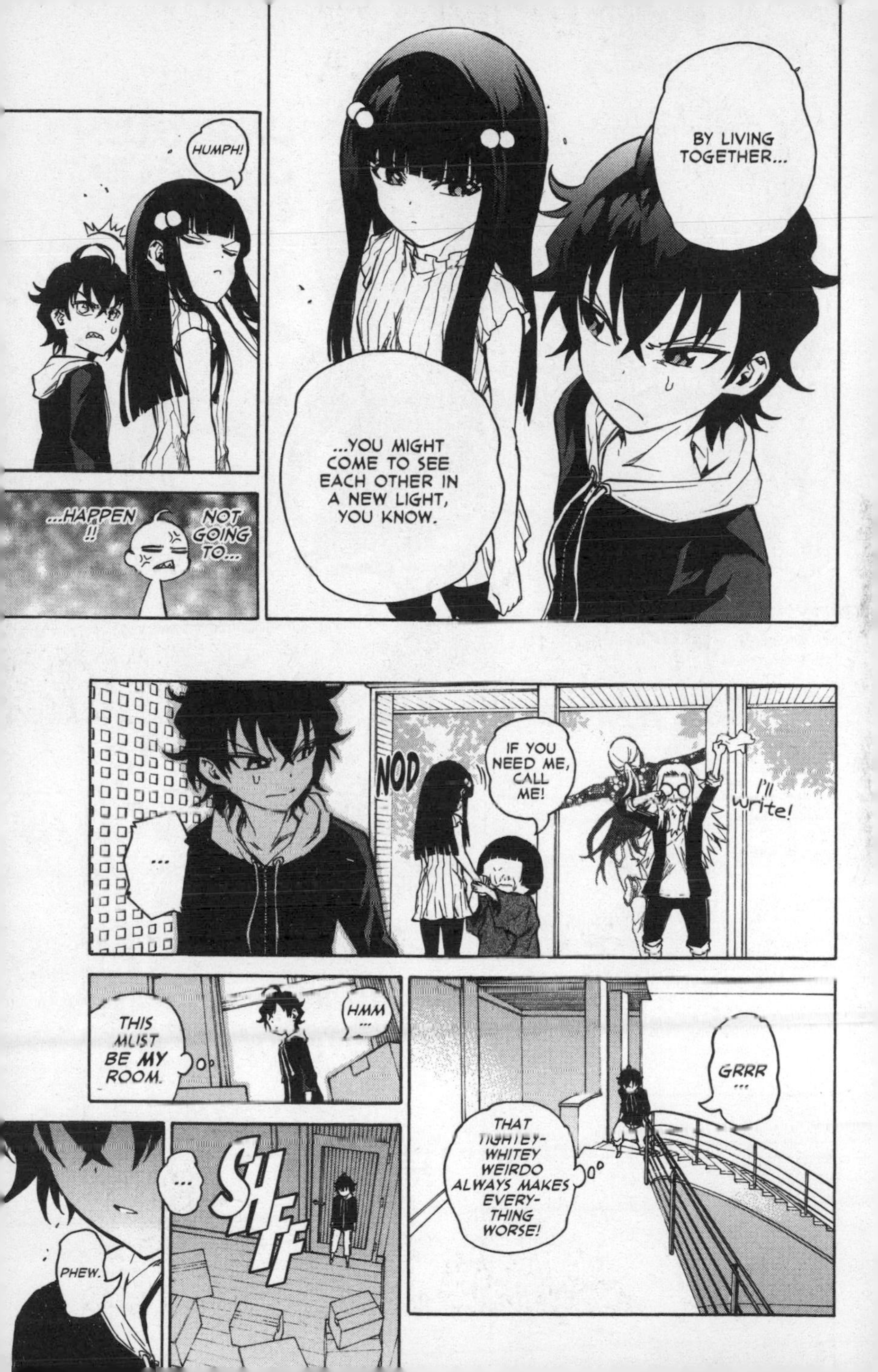
BY LIVING TOGETHER...
...YOU MIGHT COME TO SEE EACH OTHER IN A NEW LIGHT, YOU KNOW.
HUMPH!
NOT GOING TO...
...HAPPEN!!
I'll write!
IF YOU NEED ME, CALL ME!
NOD
...
GRRR...
THAT TIGHTEY-WHITEY WEIRDO ALWAYS MAKES EVERYTHING WORSE!
HMM...
THIS MUST BE MY ROOM.
SHFF
...
PHEW.

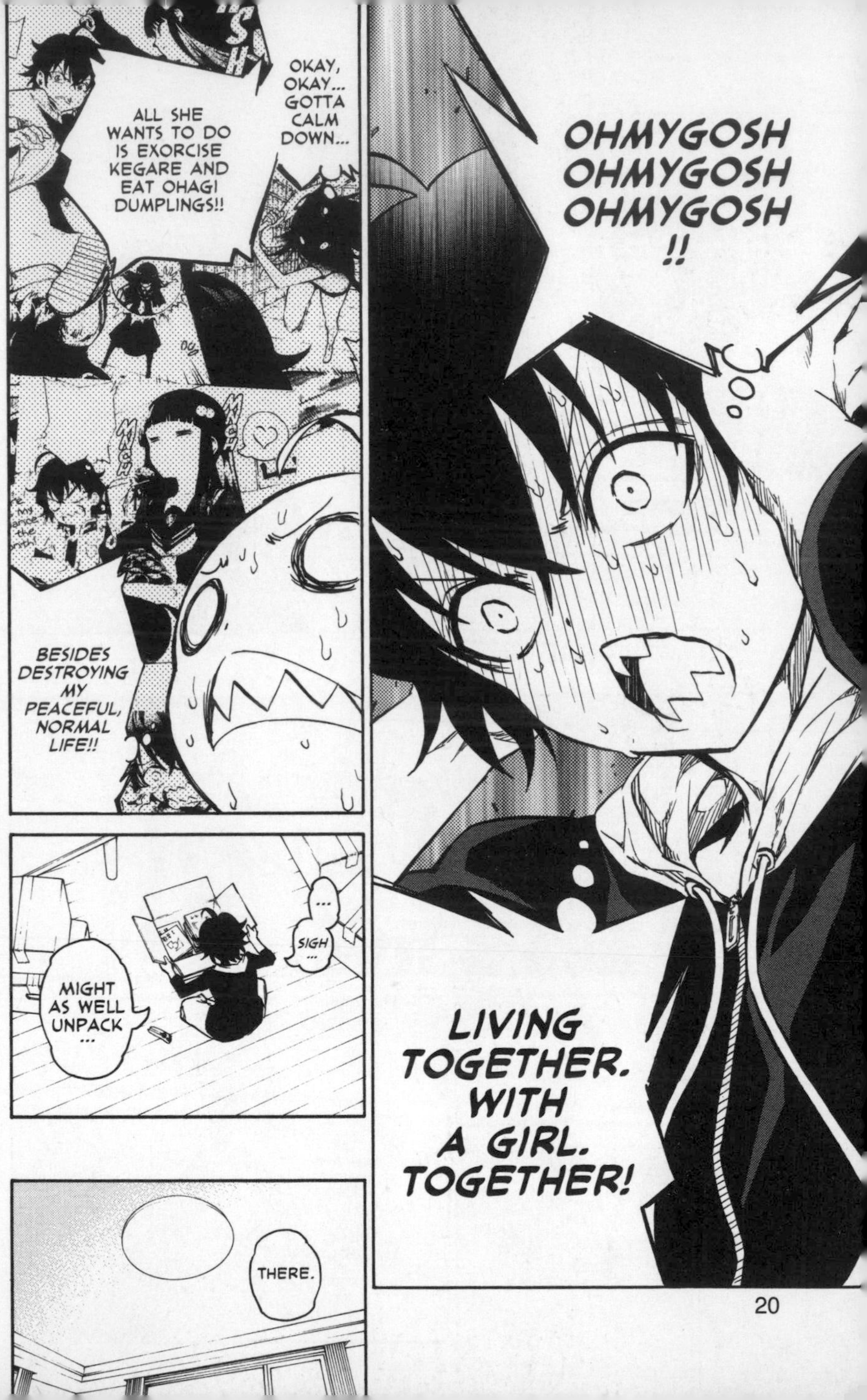
OHMYGOSH OHMYGOSH OHMYGOSH !!
LIVING TOGETHER. WITH A GIRL. TOGETHER!
OKAY, OKAY... GOTTA CALM DOWN...
ALL SHE WANTS TO DO IS EXORCISE KEGARE AND EAT OHAGI DUMPLINGS!!
BESIDES DESTROYING MY PEACEFUL, NORMAL LIFE!!
...
SIGH ...
MIGHT AS WELL UNPACK ...
THERE.

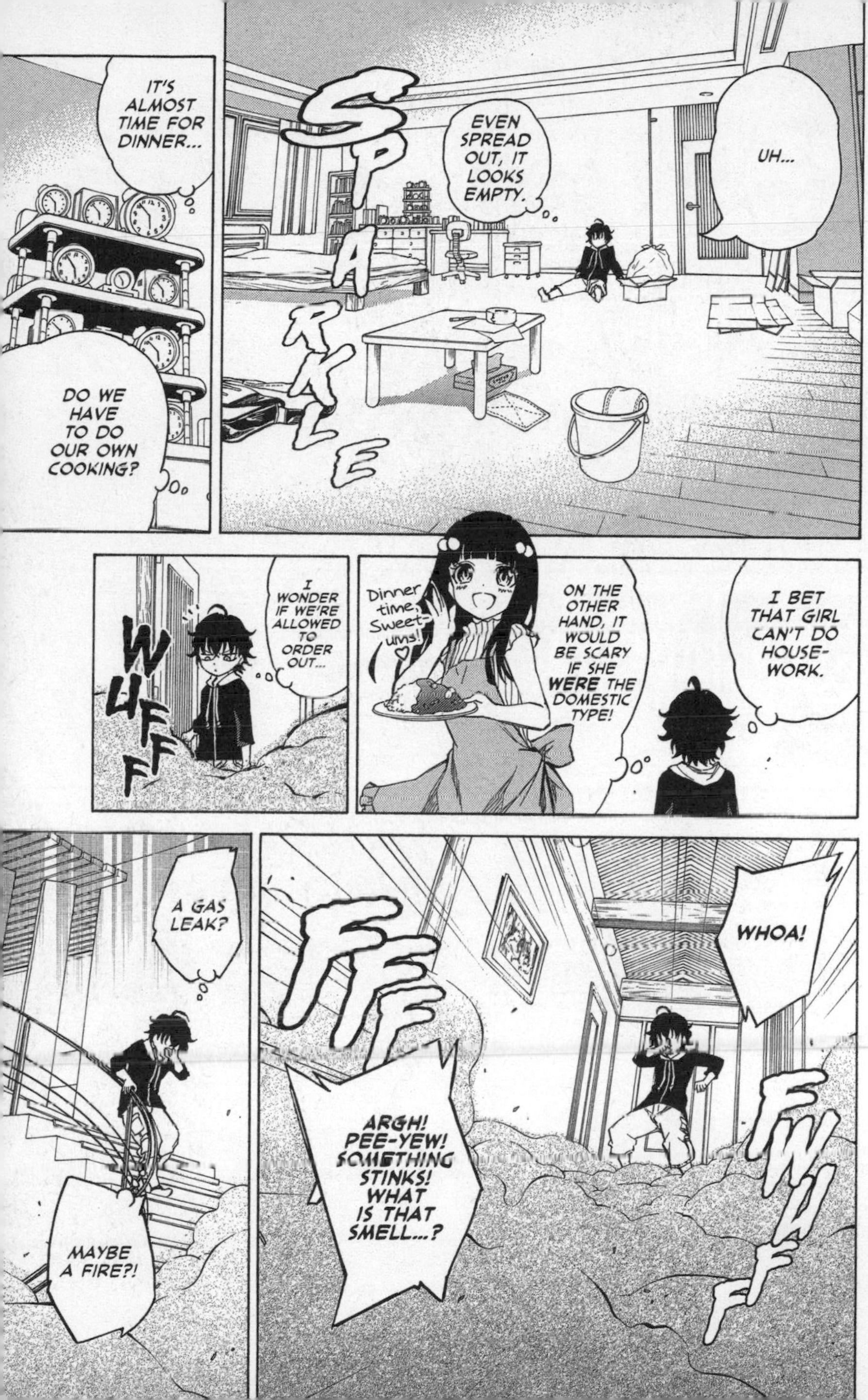
UH...
EVEN SPREAD OUT, IT LOOKS EMPTY.
SPARKLE
IT'S ALMOST TIME FOR DINNER...
DO WE HAVE TO DO OUR OWN COOKING?
I BET THAT GIRL CAN'T DO HOUSEWORK.
ON THE OTHER HAND, IT WOULD BE SCARY IF SHE WERE THE DOMESTIC TYPE!
Dinner time, Sweet-ums! ♥
I WONDER IF WE'RE ALLOWED TO ORDER OUT...
WUFFF
WHOA!
FWUFF
ARGH! PEE-YEW! SOMETHING STINKS! WHAT IS THAT SMELL...?
FFF
A GAS LEAK?
MAYBE A FIRE?!

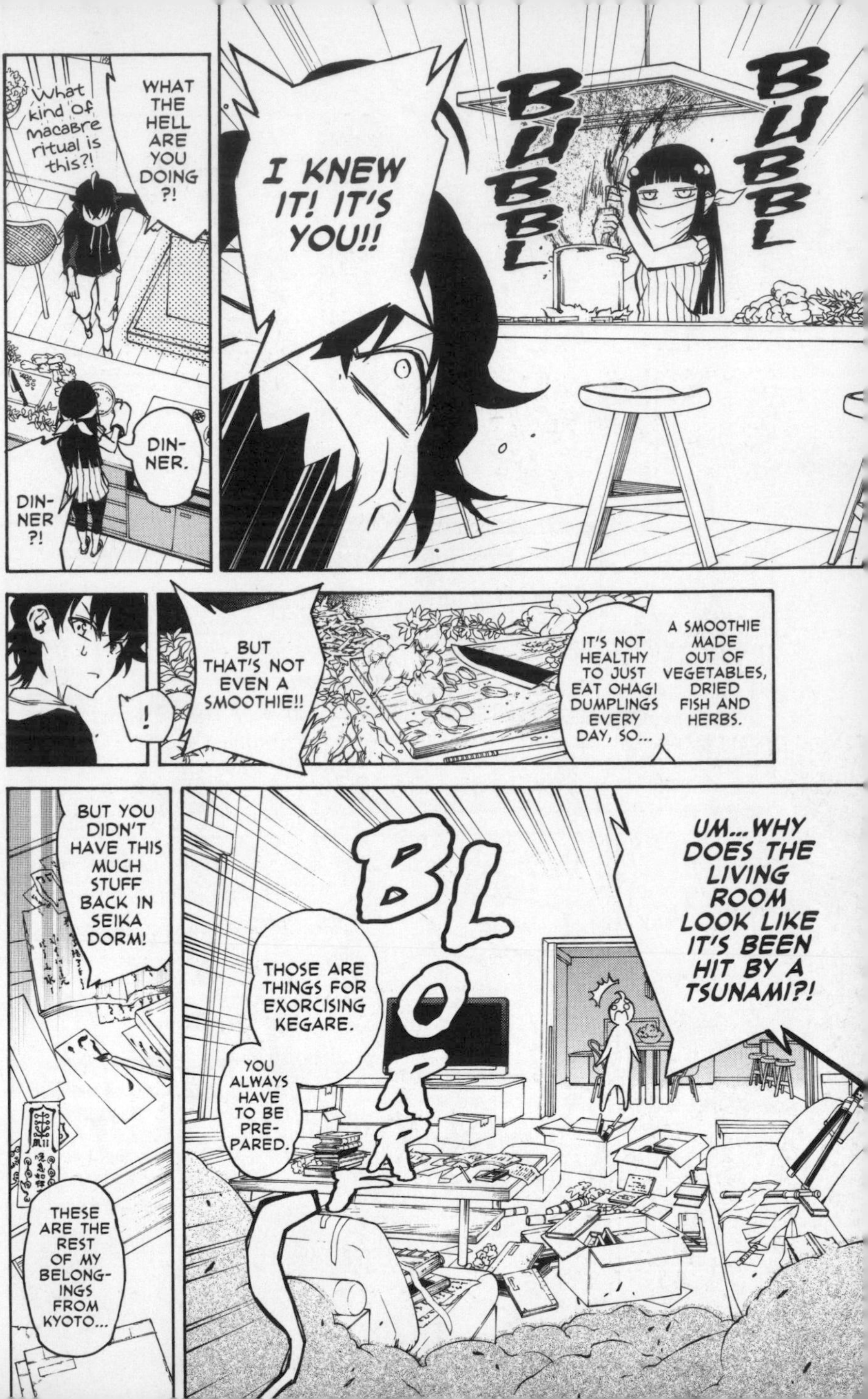
BUBBL
BUBBL
I KNEW IT! IT'S YOU!!
WHAT THE HELL ARE YOU DOING ?!
What kind of macabre ritual is this?!
DIN-NER.
DIN-NER ?!
A SMOOTHIE MADE OUT OF VEGETABLES, DRIED FISH AND HERBS.
IT'S NOT HEALTHY TO JUST EAT OHAGI DUMPLINGS EVERY DAY, SO...
BUT THAT'S NOT EVEN A SMOOTHIE!!
!
UM...WHY DOES THE LIVING ROOM LOOK LIKE IT'S BEEN HIT BY A TSUNAMI?!
BLORRF
THOSE ARE THINGS FOR EXORCISING KEGARE.
YOU ALWAYS HAVE TO BE PRE-PARED.
BUT YOU DIDN'T HAVE THIS MUCH STUFF BACK IN SEIKA DORM!
THESE ARE THE REST OF MY BELONG-INGS FROM KYOTO...

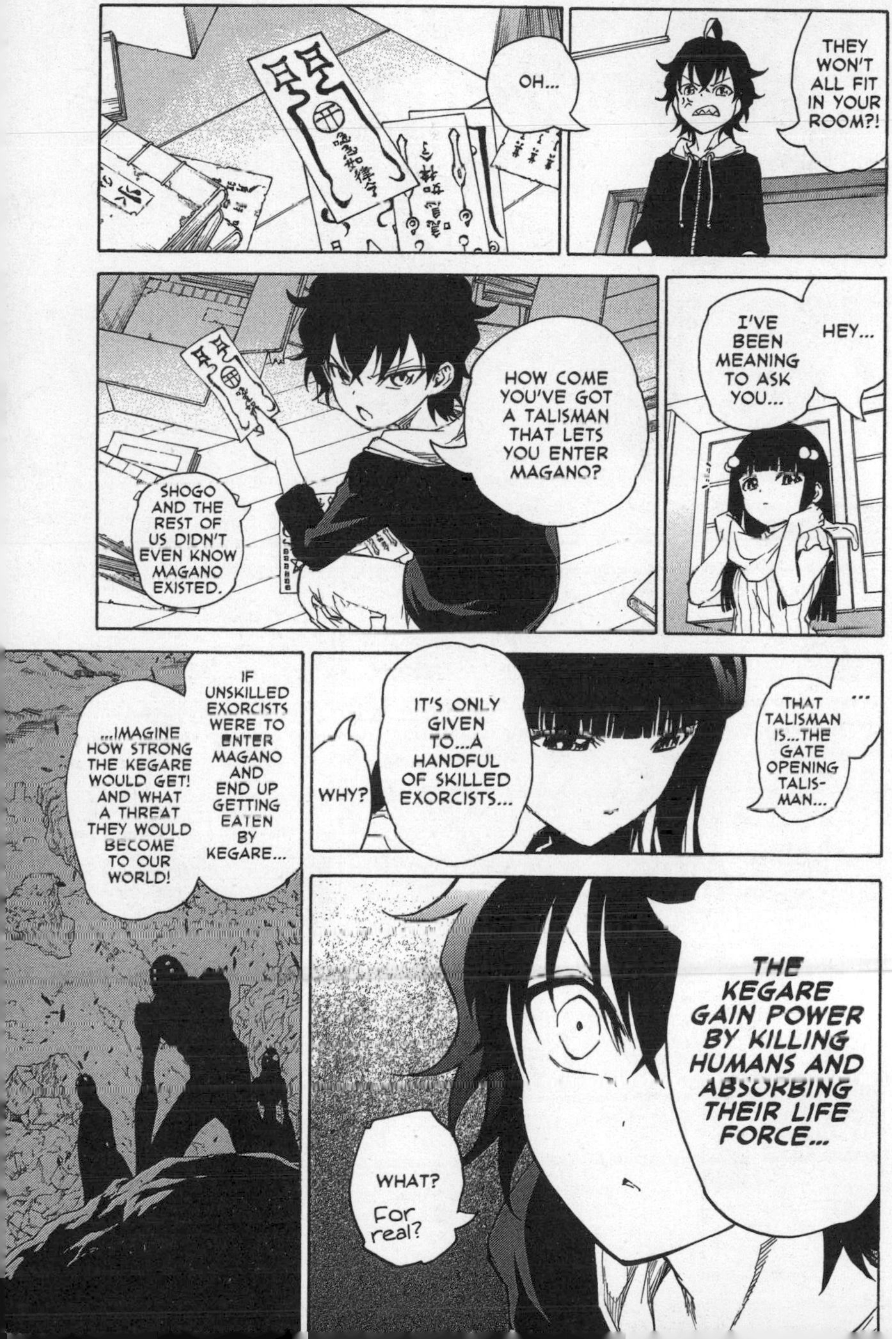
THEY WON'T ALL FIT IN YOUR ROOM?!
OH...
HEY...
I'VE BEEN MEANING TO ASK YOU...
HOW COME YOU'VE GOT A TALISMAN THAT LETS YOU ENTER MAGANO?
SHOGO AND THE REST OF US DIDN'T EVEN KNOW MAGANO EXISTED.
...
THAT TALISMAN IS...THE GATE OPENING TALIS-MAN...
IT'S ONLY GIVEN TO...A HANDFUL OF SKILLED EXORCISTS...
WHY?
THE KEGARE GAIN POWER BY KILLING HUMANS AND ABSORBING THEIR LIFE FORCE...
WHAT?
For real?
IF UNSKILLED EXORCISTS WERE TO ENTER MAGANO AND END UP GETTING EATEN BY KEGARE...
...IMAGINE HOW STRONG THE KEGARE WOULD GET! AND WHAT A THREAT THEY WOULD BECOME TO OUR WORLD!

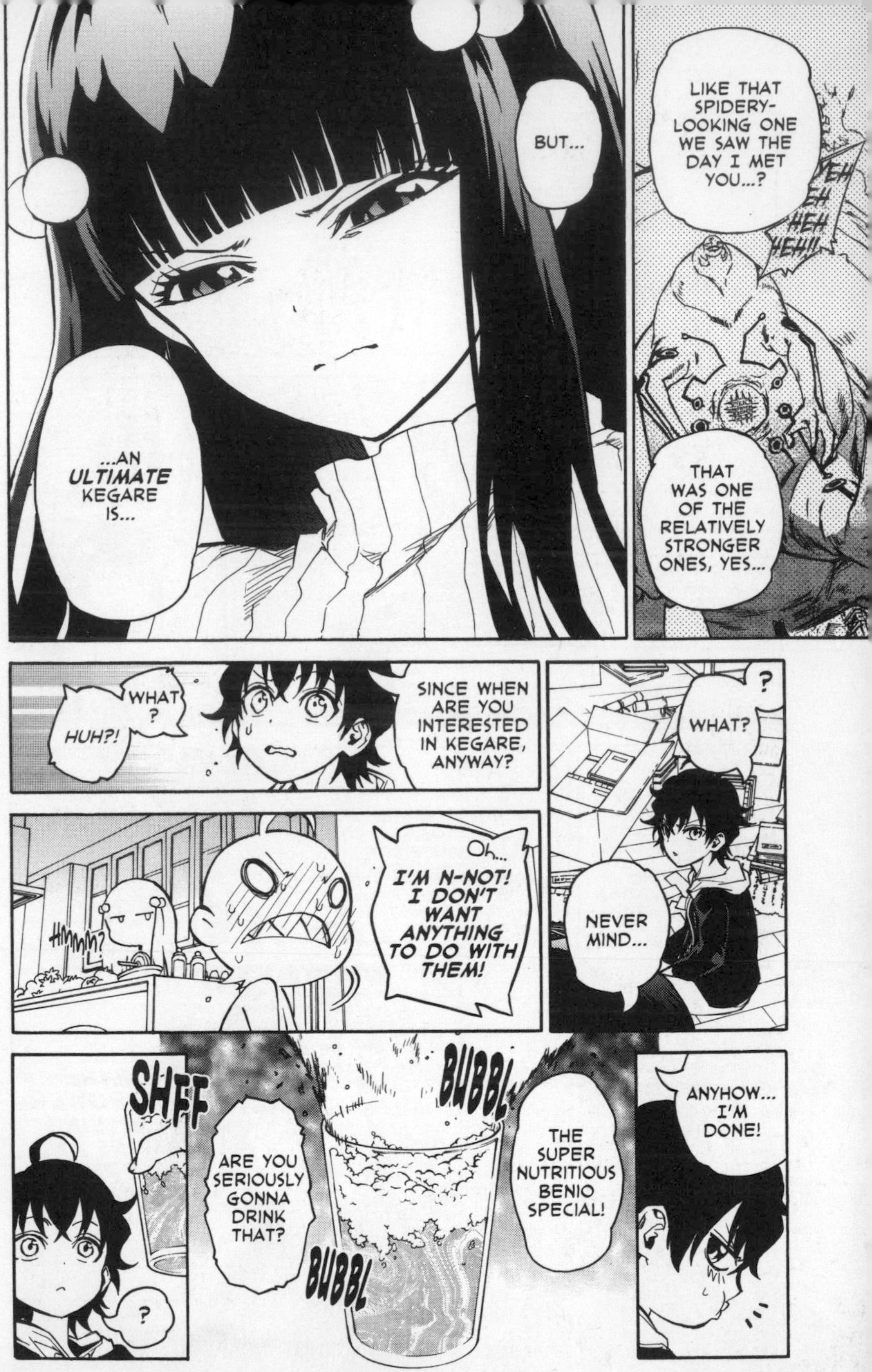
LIKE THAT SPIDERY-LOOKING ONE WE SAW THE DAY I MET YOU...?
THAT WAS ONE OF THE RELATIVELY STRONGER ONES, YES...
BUT...
...AN *ULTIMATE* KEGARE IS...
?
WHAT?
NEVER MIND...
SINCE WHEN ARE YOU INTERESTED IN KEGARE, ANYWAY?
WHAT?
HUH?!
Oh...
I'M N-NOT! I DON'T WANT ANYTHING TO DO WITH THEM!
Hmmm?
ANYHOW... I'M DONE!
BUBBL
THE SUPER NUTRITIOUS BENIO SPECIAL!
ARE YOU SERIOUSLY GONNA DRINK THAT?
BUBBL
SHFF
?

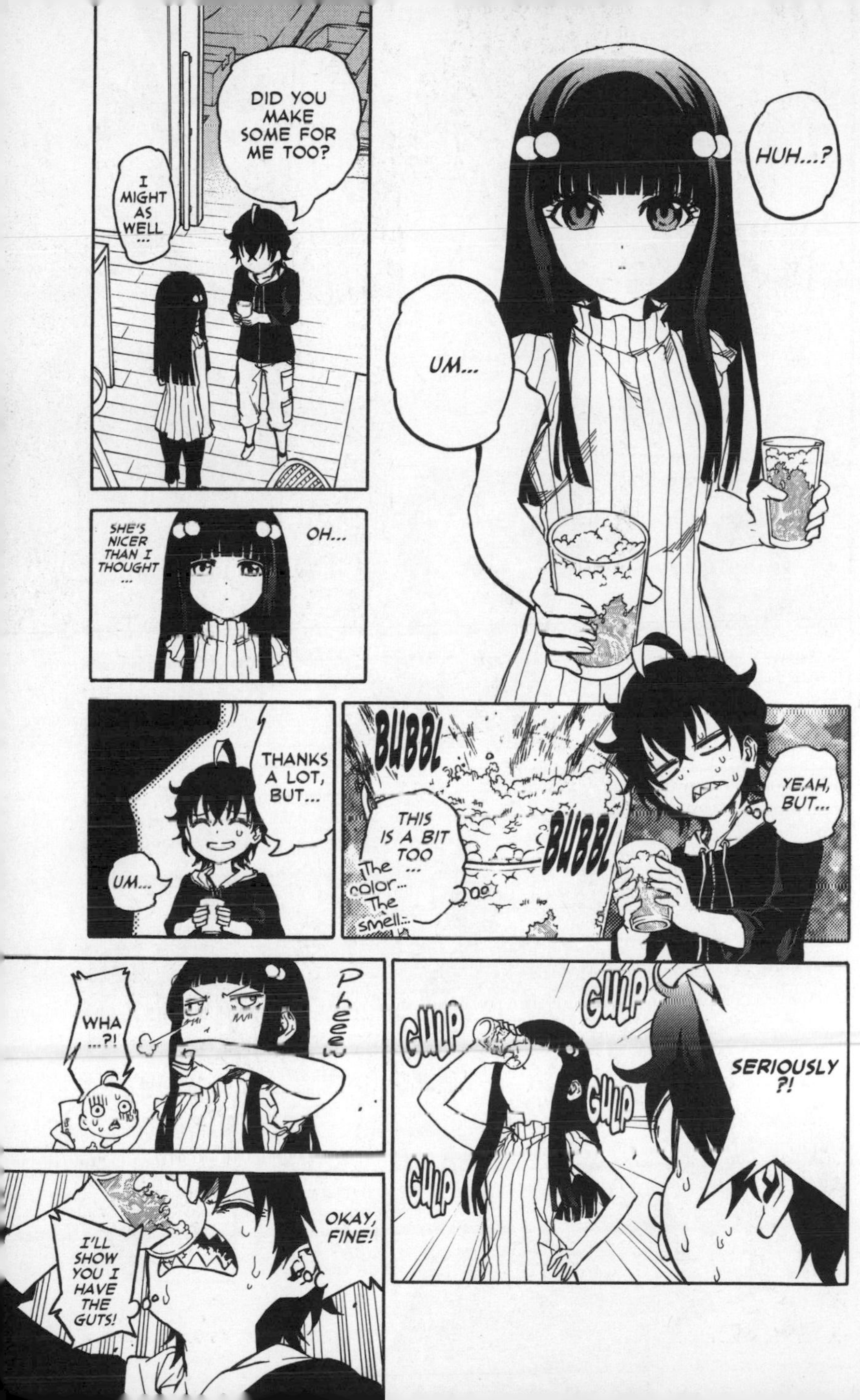
HUH...?
UM...
DID YOU MAKE SOME FOR ME TOO?
I MIGHT AS WELL...
OH...
SHE'S NICER THAN I THOUGHT...
YEAH, BUT...
BUBBL
BUBBL
THIS IS A BIT TOO...
The color... The smell...
THANKS A LOT, BUT...
UM...
SERIOUSLY?!
GULP
GULP
GULP
GULP
Pheeew
WHA...?!
OKAY, FINE!
I'LL SHOW YOU I HAVE THE GUTS!

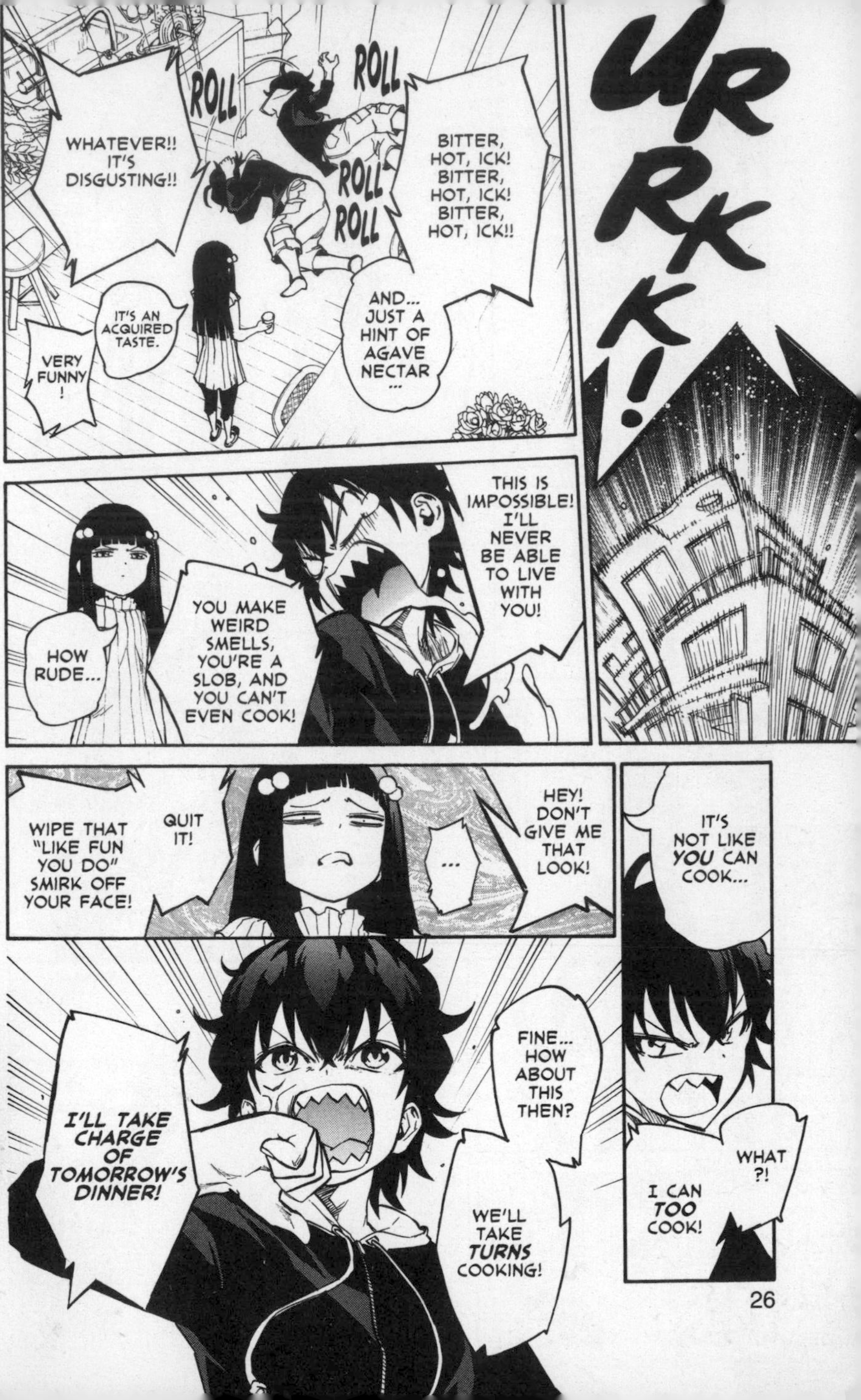
URRKK!
BITTER, HOT, ICK! BITTER, HOT, ICK! BITTER, HOT, ICK!!
ROLL
ROLL
ROLL
ROLL
AND... JUST A HINT OF AGAVE NECTAR...
WHATEVER!! IT'S DISGUSTING!!
IT'S AN ACQUIRED TASTE.
VERY FUNNY!
THIS IS IMPOSSIBLE! I'LL NEVER BE ABLE TO LIVE WITH YOU!
YOU MAKE WEIRD SMELLS, YOU'RE A SLOB, AND YOU CAN'T EVEN COOK!
HOW RUDE...
IT'S NOT LIKE *YOU* CAN COOK...
WHAT?!
I CAN *TOO* COOK!
HEY! DON'T GIVE ME THAT LOOK!
...
QUIT IT!
WIPE THAT "LIKE FUN YOU DO" SMIRK OFF YOUR FACE!
FINE... HOW ABOUT THIS THEN?
WE'LL TAKE *TURNS* COOKING!
I'LL TAKE CHARGE OF TOMORROW'S DINNER!

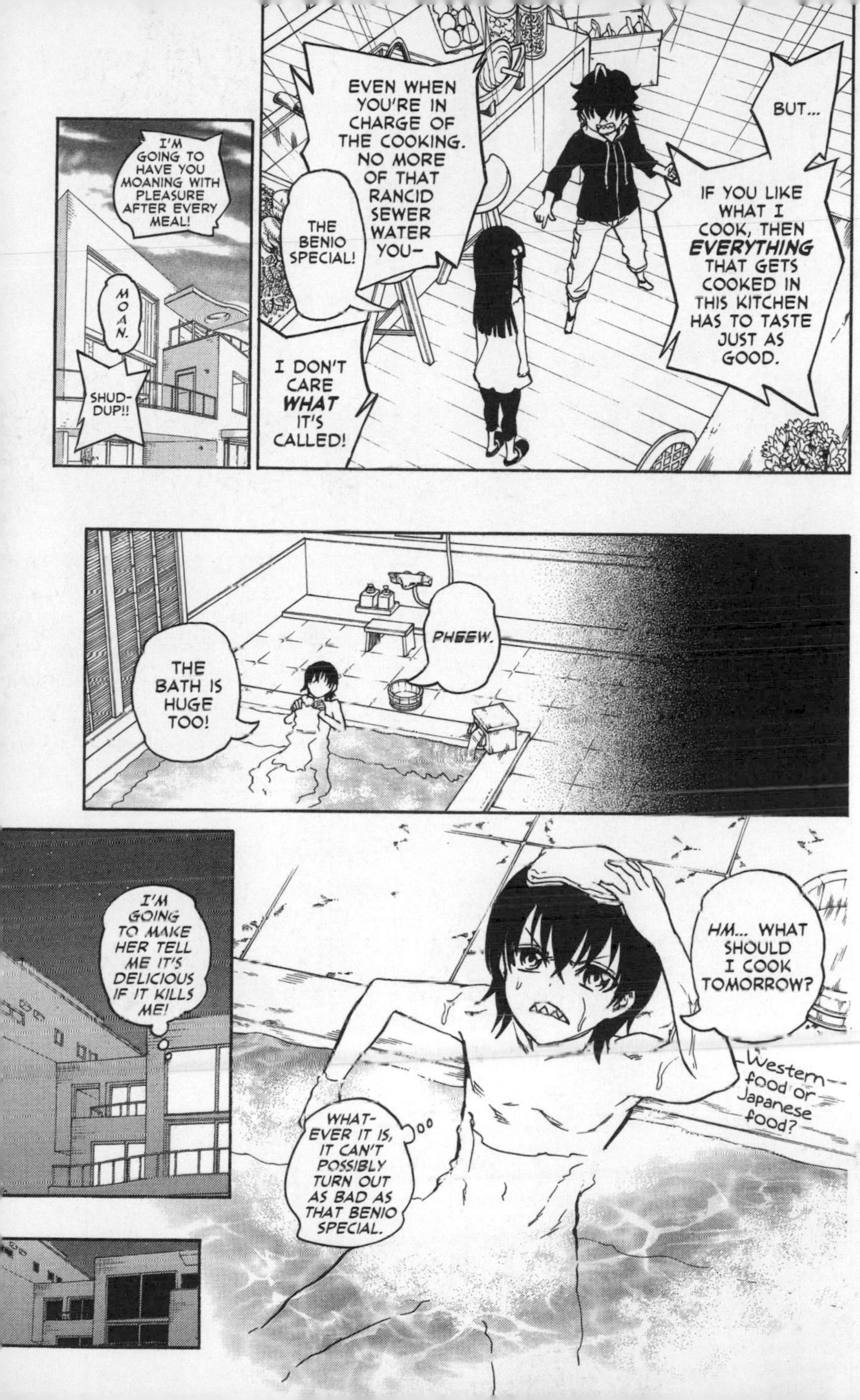
BUT...
IF YOU LIKE WHAT I COOK, THEN **EVERYTHING** THAT GETS COOKED IN THIS KITCHEN HAS TO TASTE JUST AS GOOD.
EVEN WHEN YOU'RE IN CHARGE OF THE COOKING. NO MORE OF THAT RANCID SEWER WATER YOU—
THE BENIO SPECIAL!
I DON'T CARE **WHAT** IT'S CALLED!
I'M GOING TO HAVE YOU MOANING WITH PLEASURE AFTER EVERY MEAL!
MOAN.
SHUD-DUP!!
PHEEW.
THE BATH IS HUGE TOO!
HM... WHAT SHOULD I COOK TOMORROW?
Western food or Japanese food?
WHATEVER IT IS, IT CAN'T POSSIBLY TURN OUT AS BAD AS THAT BENIO SPECIAL.
I'M GOING TO MAKE HER TELL ME IT'S DELICIOUS IF IT KILLS ME!

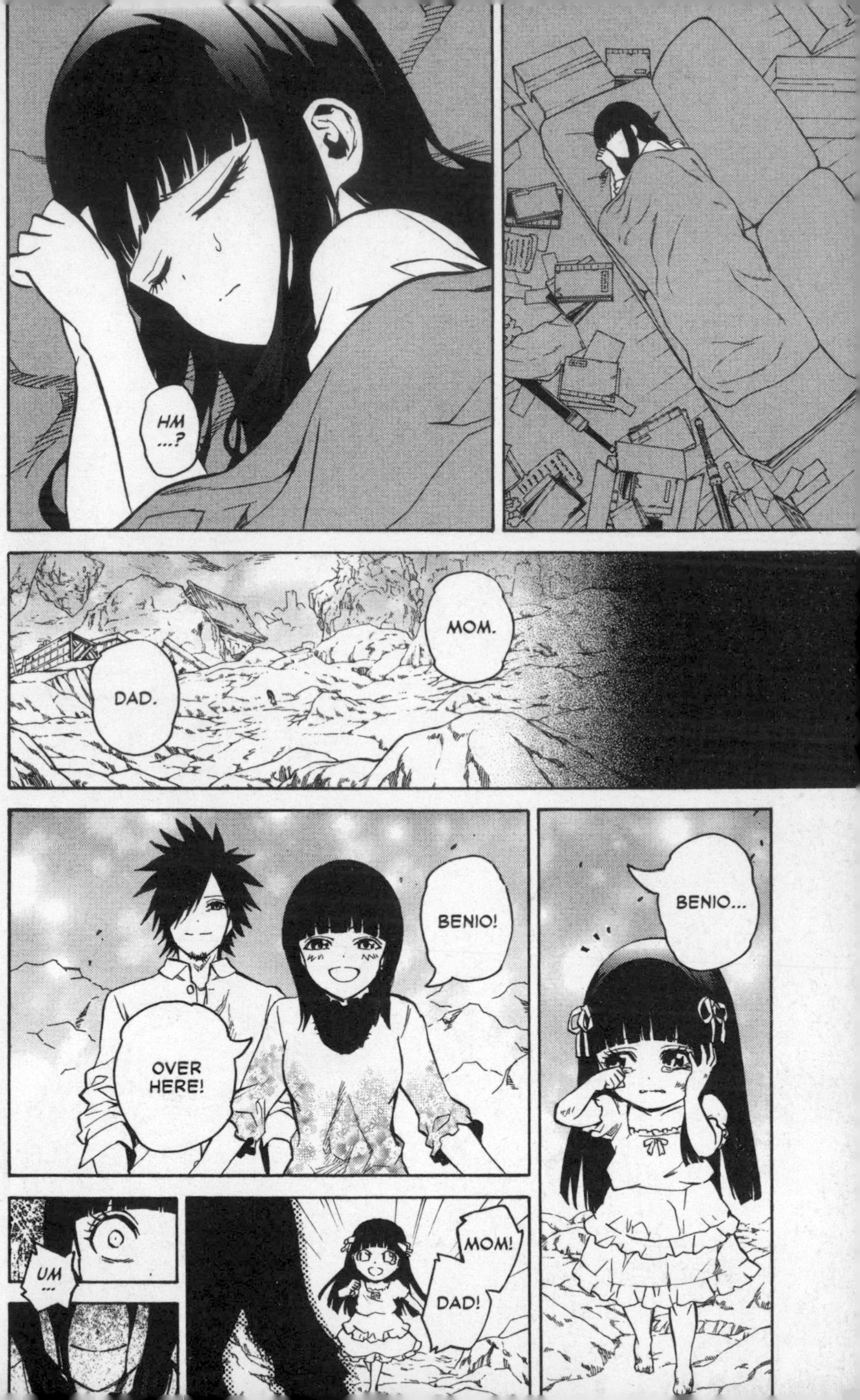
HM ...?
MOM.
DAD.
BENIO...
BENIO!
OVER HERE!
MOM!
DAD!
UM ...

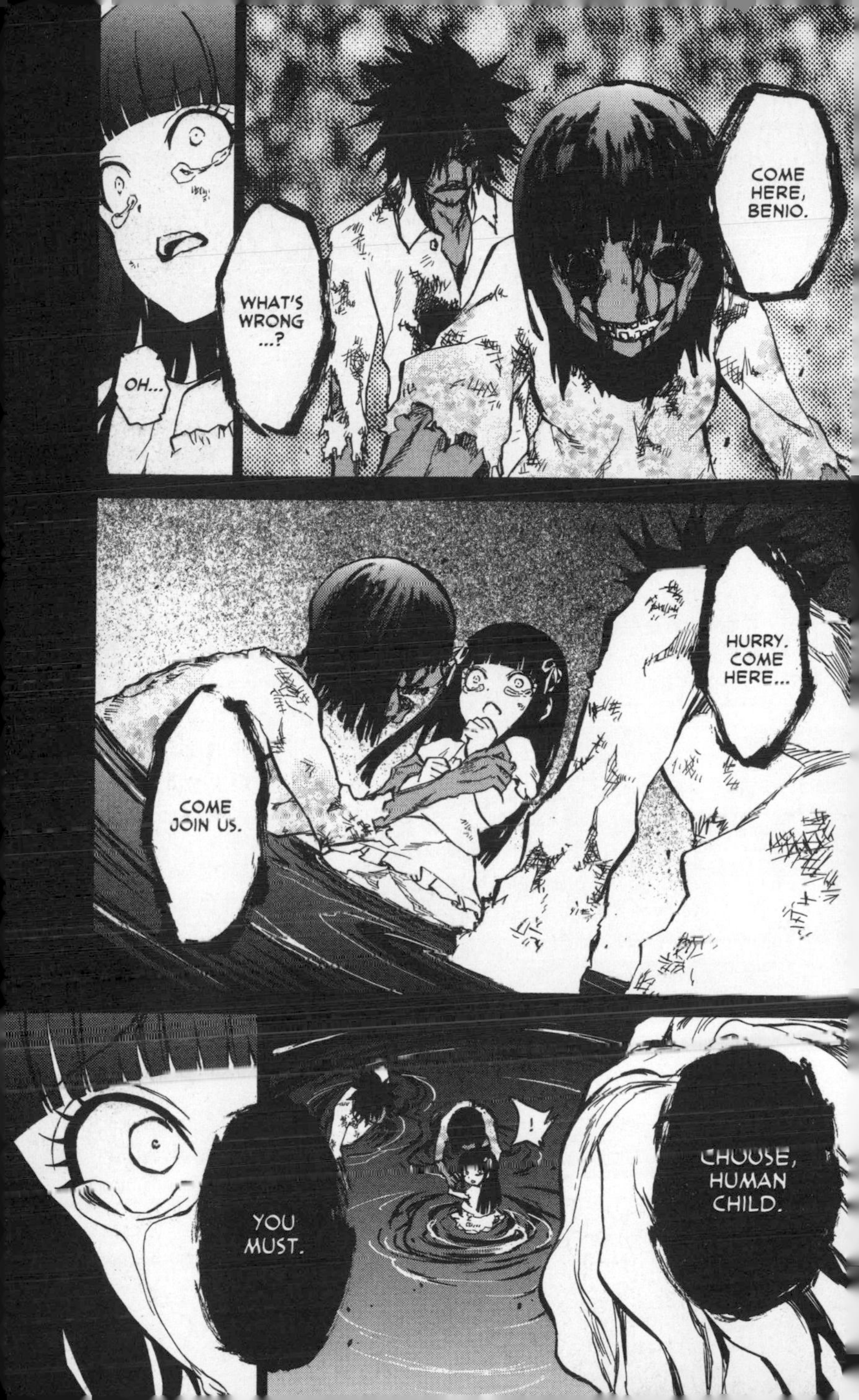
COME HERE, BENIO.
WHAT'S WRONG ...?
OH...
HURRY. COME HERE...
COME JOIN US.
CHOOSE, HUMAN CHILD.
!
YOU MUST.

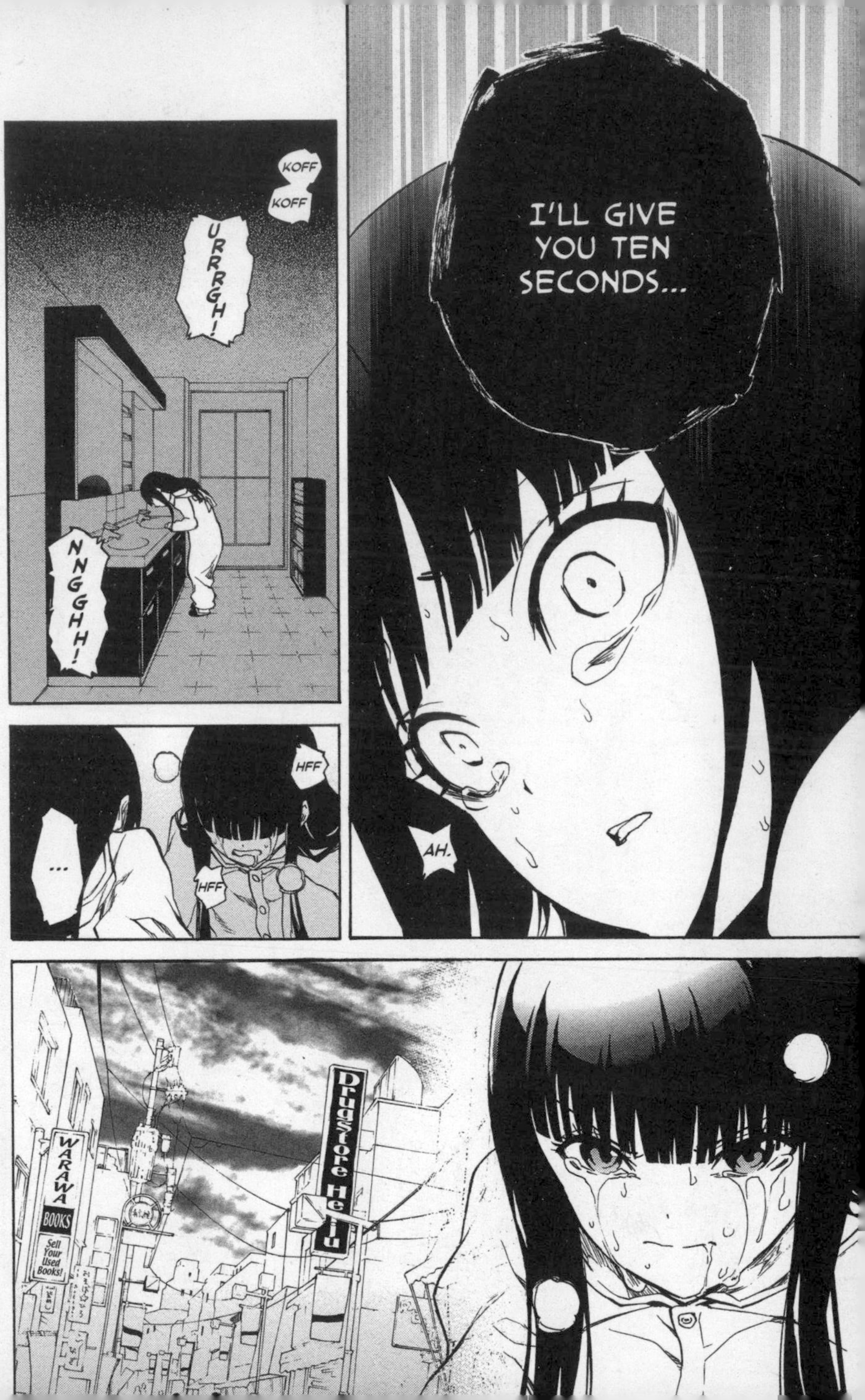
I'LL GIVE YOU TEN SECONDS...
AH.
KOFF
KOFF
URRGH!
NNGGHH!
HFF
HFF
...
WARAWA
BOOKS
Sell Your Used Books!
Drugstore

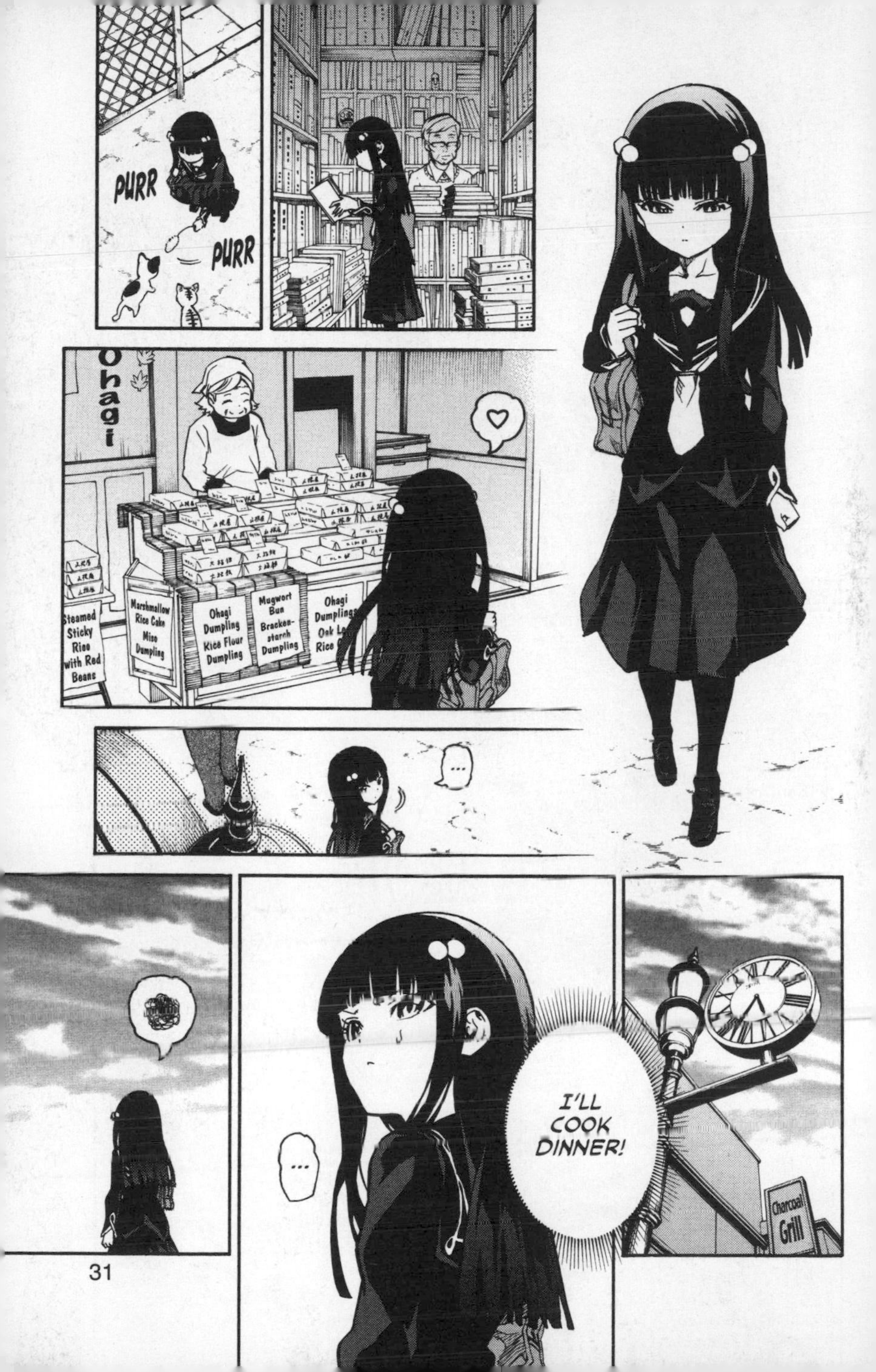
PURR
PURR
Ohagi Dumplings
Mugwort Bun
Bracken-starch Dumpling
Ohagi Dumpling
Rice Flour Dumpling
Marshmallow Rice Cake
Miso Dumpling
Steamed Sticky Rice with Red Beans
Ohagi
...
Charcoal Grill
I'LL COOK DINNER!
...

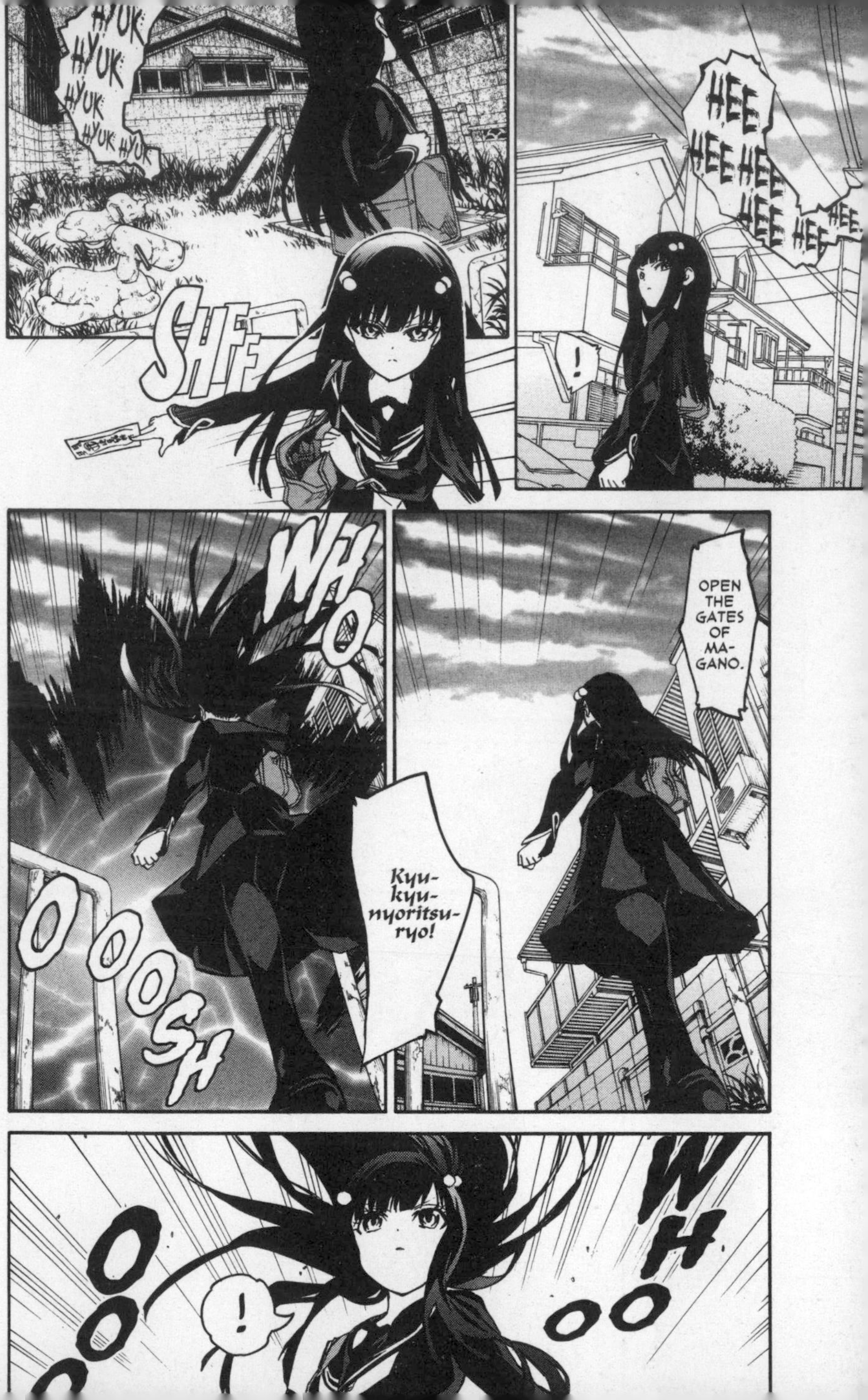
HEE HEE HEE HEE HEE HEE HEE
!
HYUK HYUK HYUK HYUK HYUK HYUK
SHFF
OPEN THE GATES OF MA-GANO.
WHO
OOOOSH
Kyu-kyu-nyoritsu-ryo!
WHOO
!
OOO

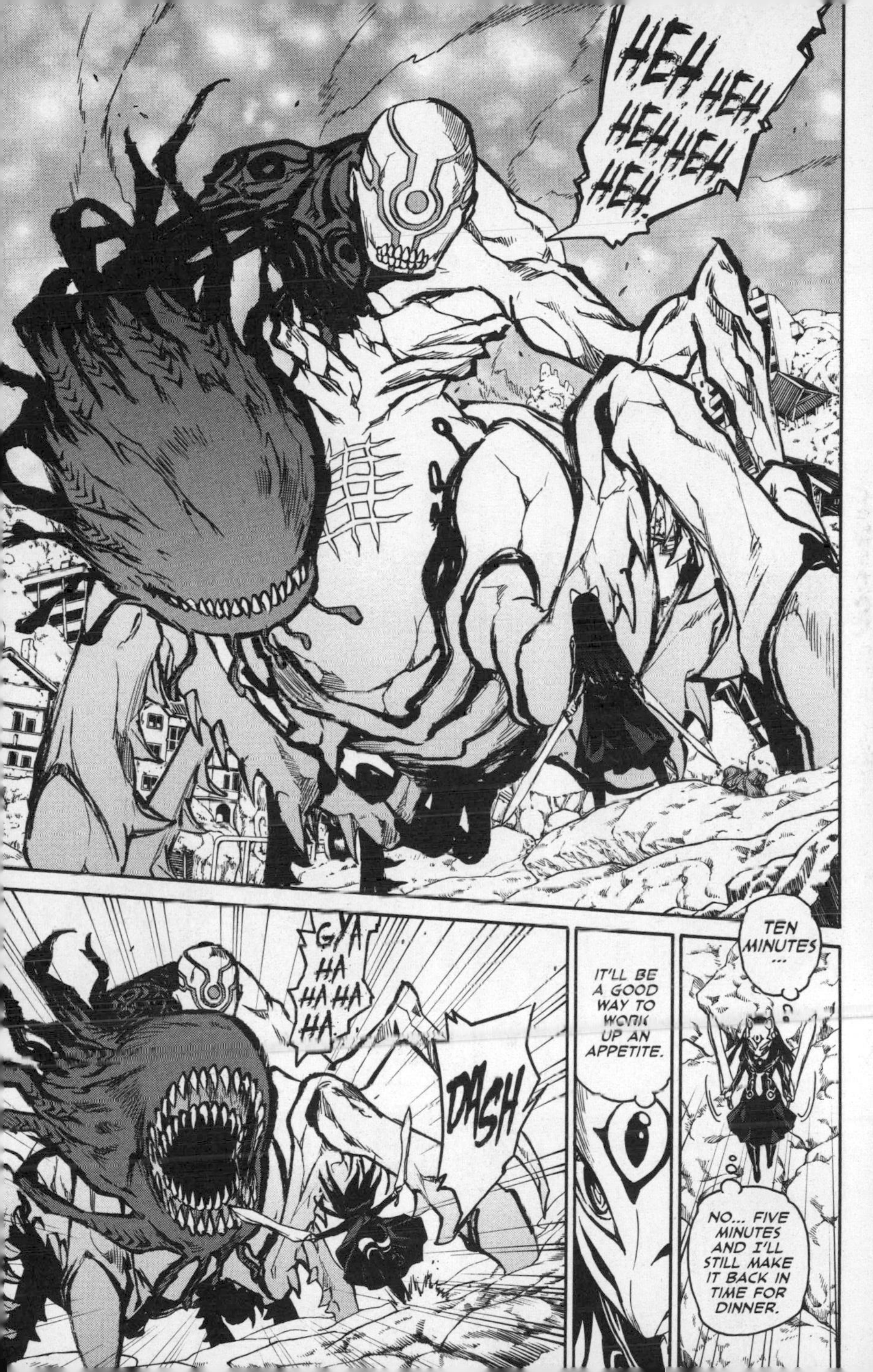
HEH HEH HEH HEH HEH HEH.
TEN MINUTES...
NO... FIVE MINUTES AND I'LL STILL MAKE IT BACK IN TIME FOR DINNER.
IT'LL BE A GOOD WAY TO WORK UP AN APPETITE.
GYA HA HA HA HA.
DASH

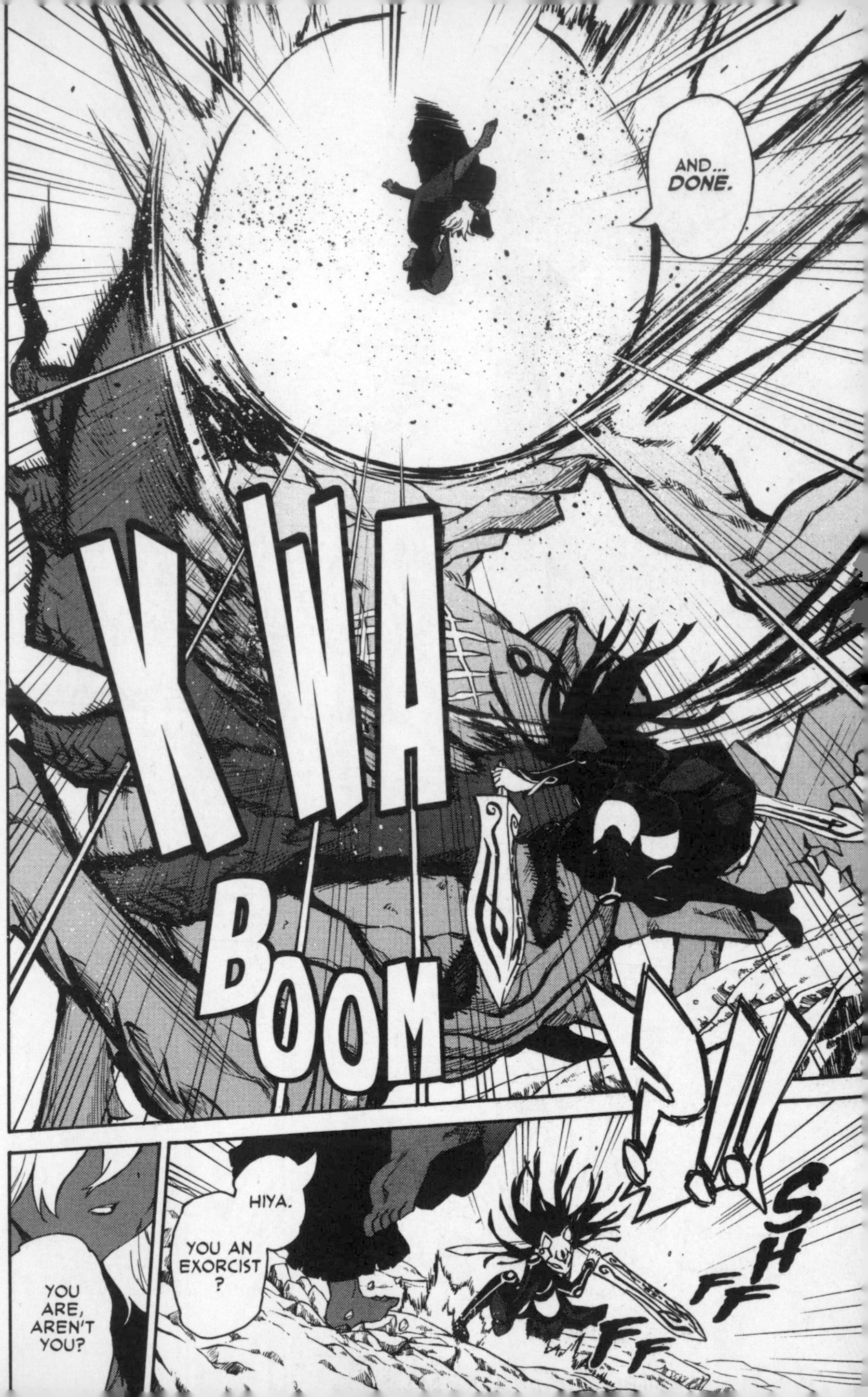
AND... DONE.
KWA
BOOM
SHFF
FF
HIYA.
YOU AN EXORCIST?
YOU ARE, AREN'T YOU?

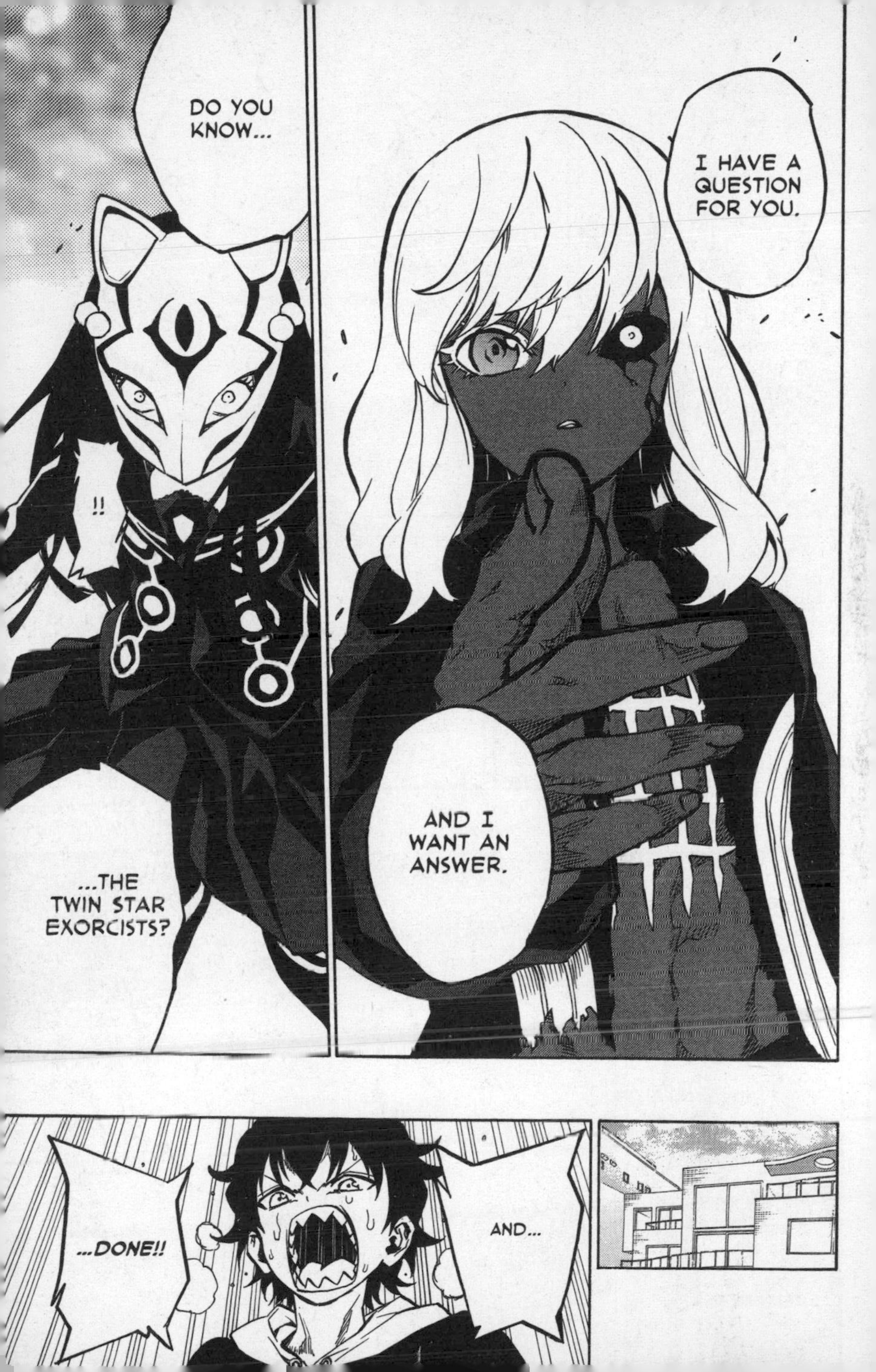
I HAVE A QUESTION FOR YOU.
AND I WANT AN ANSWER.
DO YOU KNOW...
!!
...THE TWIN STAR EXORCISTS?
AND...
...DONE!!

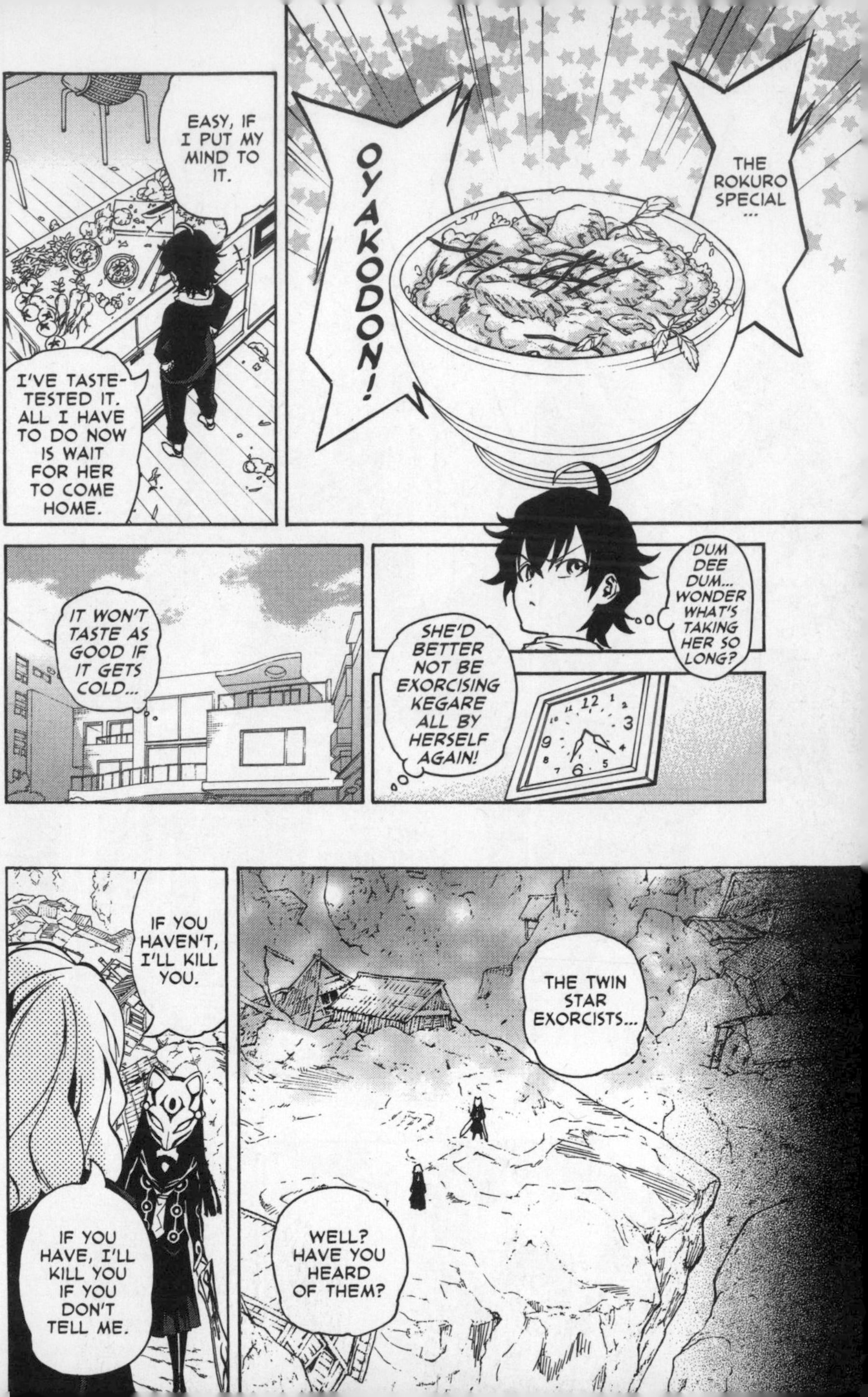
THE ROKURO SPECIAL...
OYAKODON!
EASY, IF I PUT MY MIND TO IT.
I'VE TASTE-TESTED IT. ALL I HAVE TO DO NOW IS WAIT FOR HER TO COME HOME.
DUM DEE DUM... WONDER WHAT'S TAKING HER SO LONG?
SHE'D BETTER NOT BE EXORCISING KEGARE ALL BY HERSELF AGAIN!
IT WON'T TASTE AS GOOD IF IT GETS COLD...
THE TWIN STAR EXORCISTS...
WELL? HAVE YOU HEARD OF THEM?
IF YOU HAVEN'T, I'LL KILL YOU.
IF YOU HAVE, I'LL KILL YOU IF YOU DON'T TELL ME.

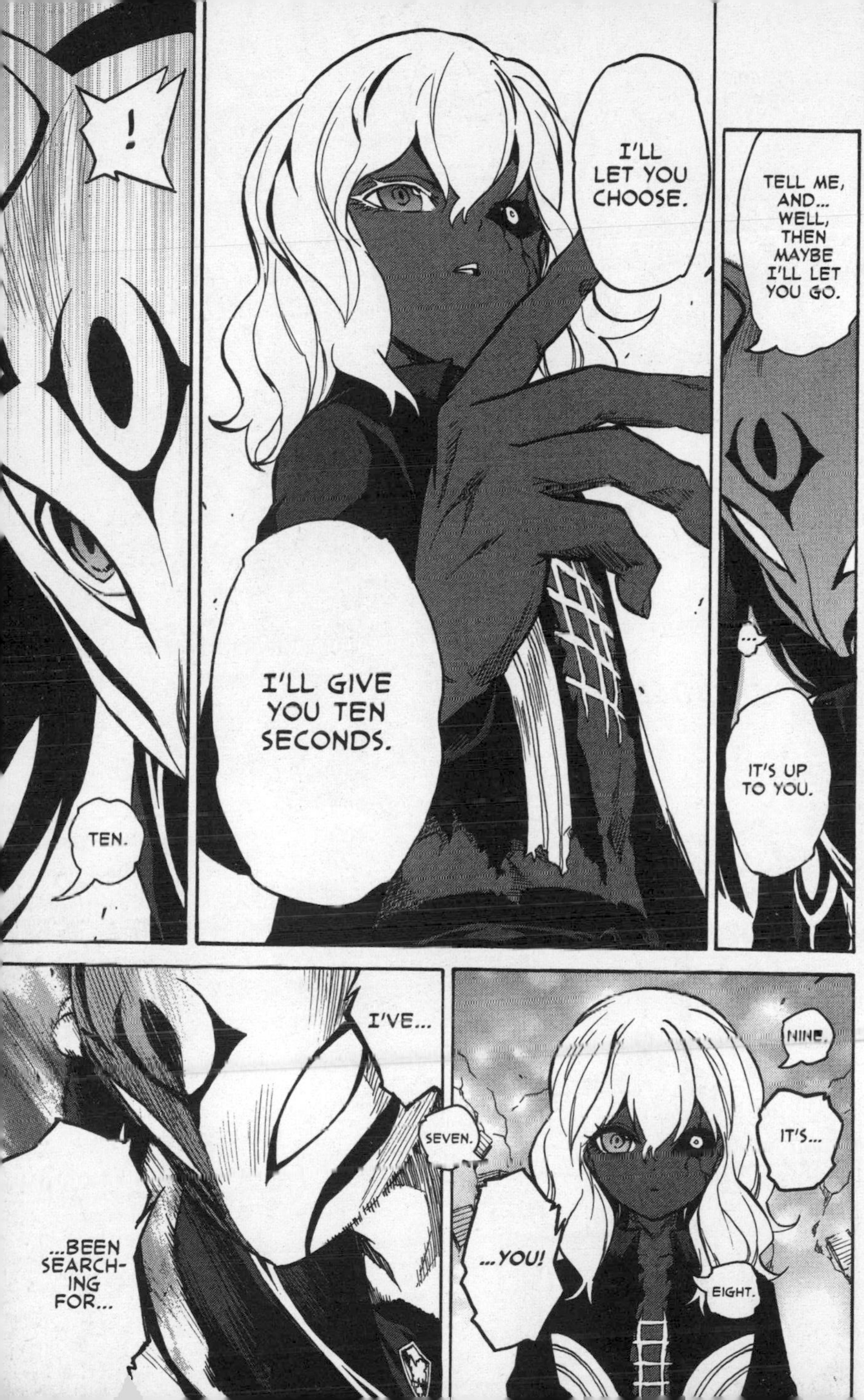
TELL ME, AND... WELL, THEN MAYBE I'LL LET YOU GO.
...
IT'S UP TO YOU.
I'LL LET YOU CHOOSE.
I'LL GIVE YOU TEN SECONDS.
!
TEN.
NINE.
IT'S...
...YOU!
EIGHT.
I'VE...
SEVEN.
...BEEN SEARCH-ING FOR...

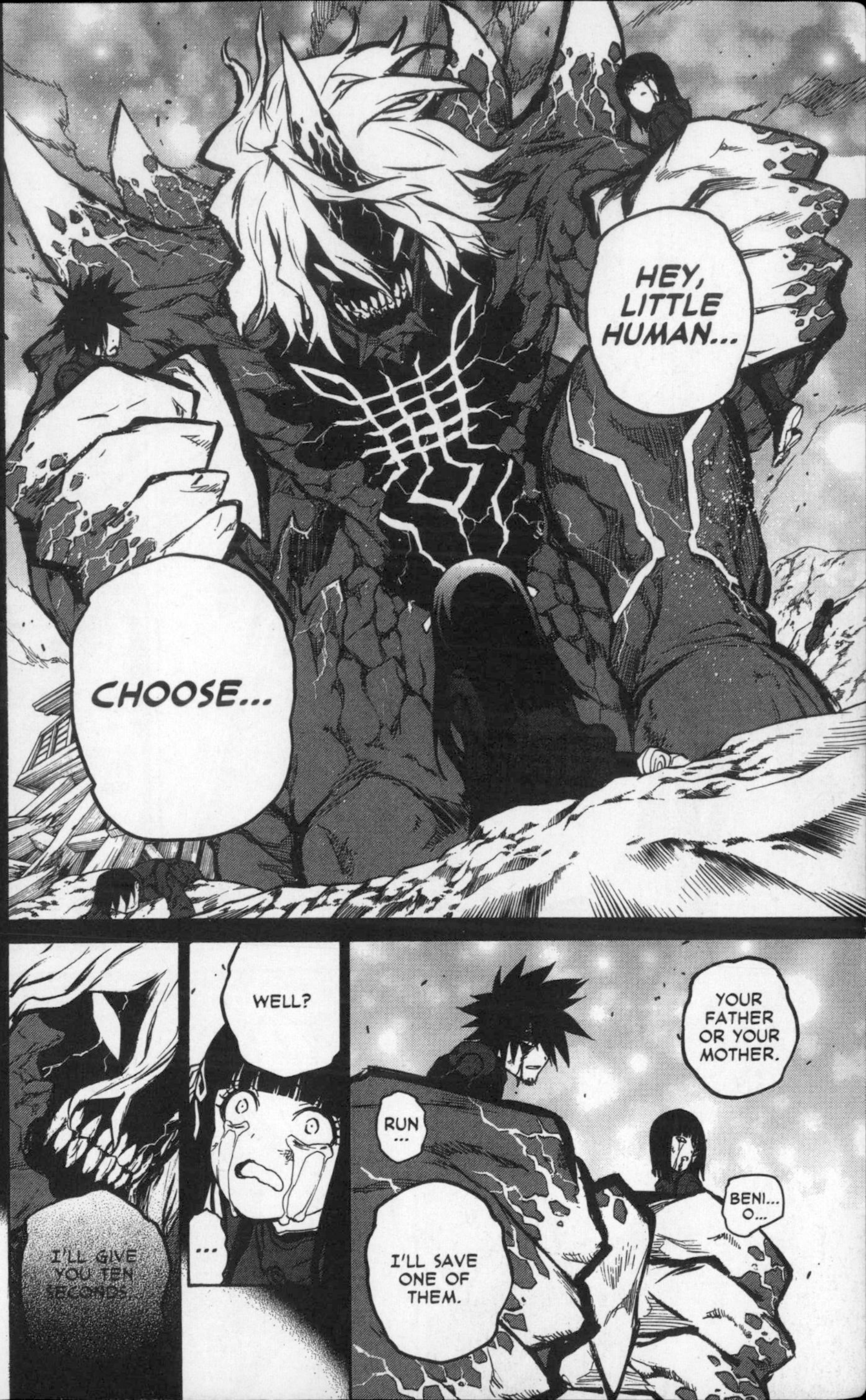
HEY, LITTLE HUMAN...
CHOOSE...
YOUR FATHER OR YOUR MOTHER.
RUN ...
BENI... O...
I'LL SAVE ONE OF THEM.
WELL?
...
I'LL GIVE YOU TEN SECONDS.

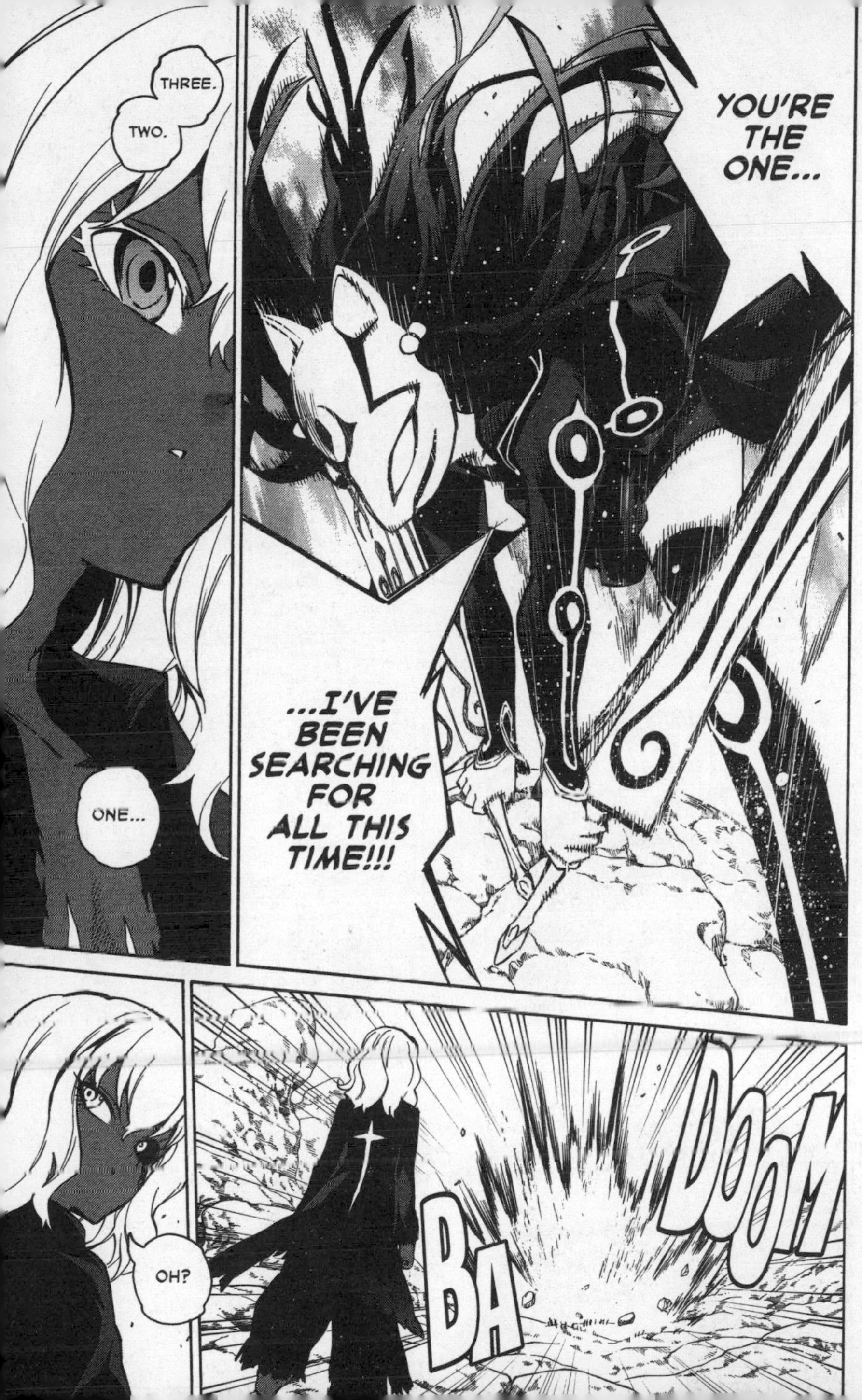
YOU'RE THE ONE...
...I'VE BEEN SEARCHING FOR ALL THIS TIME!!!
THREE.
TWO.
ONE...
BA DOOM
OH?

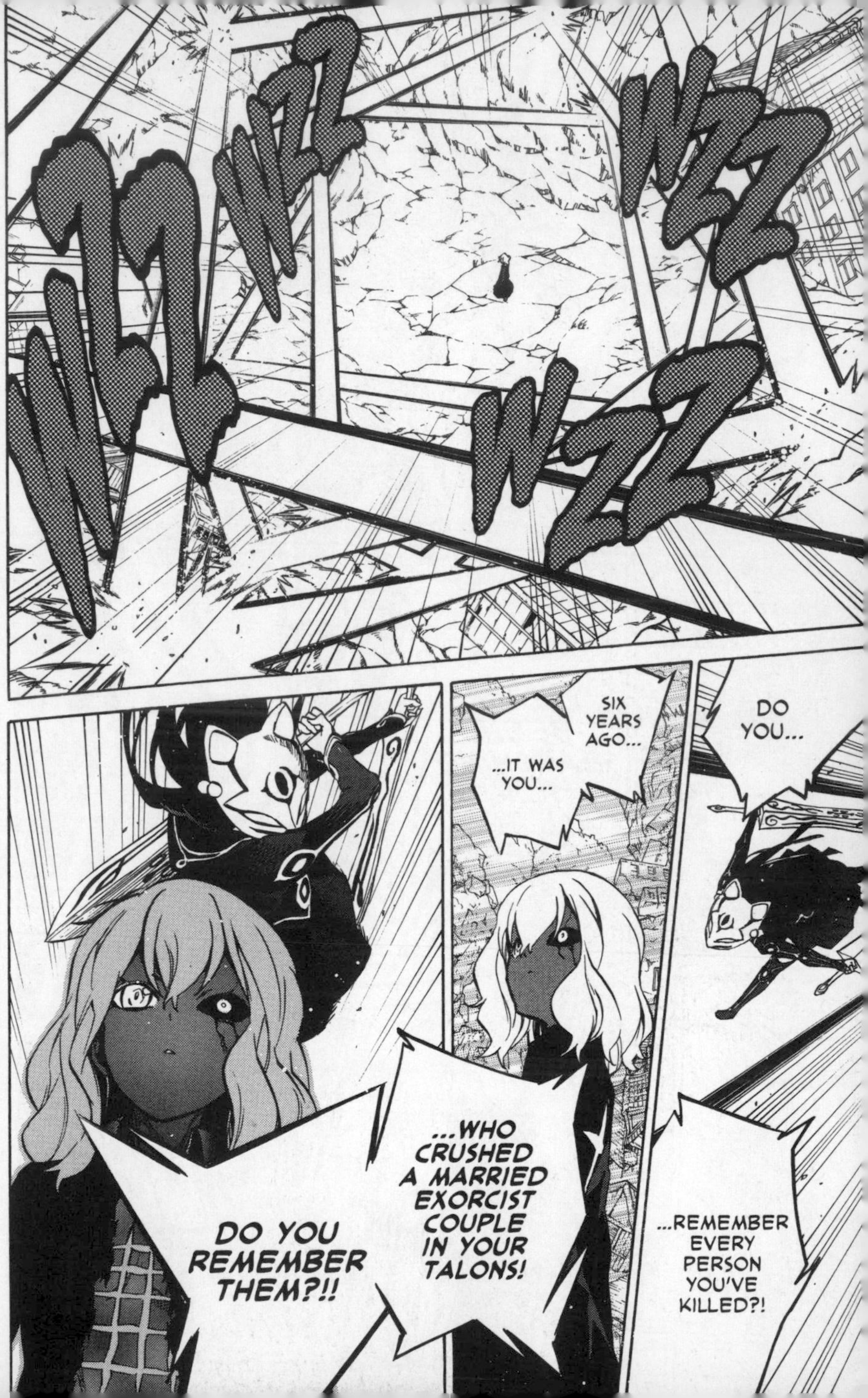
WZZ
WZZ
WZZ
WZZ
DO YOU...
...REMEMBER EVERY PERSON YOU'VE KILLED?!
SIX YEARS AGO...
...IT WAS YOU...
...WHO CRUSHED A MARRIED EXORCIST COUPLE IN YOUR TALONS!
DO YOU REMEMBER THEM?!!

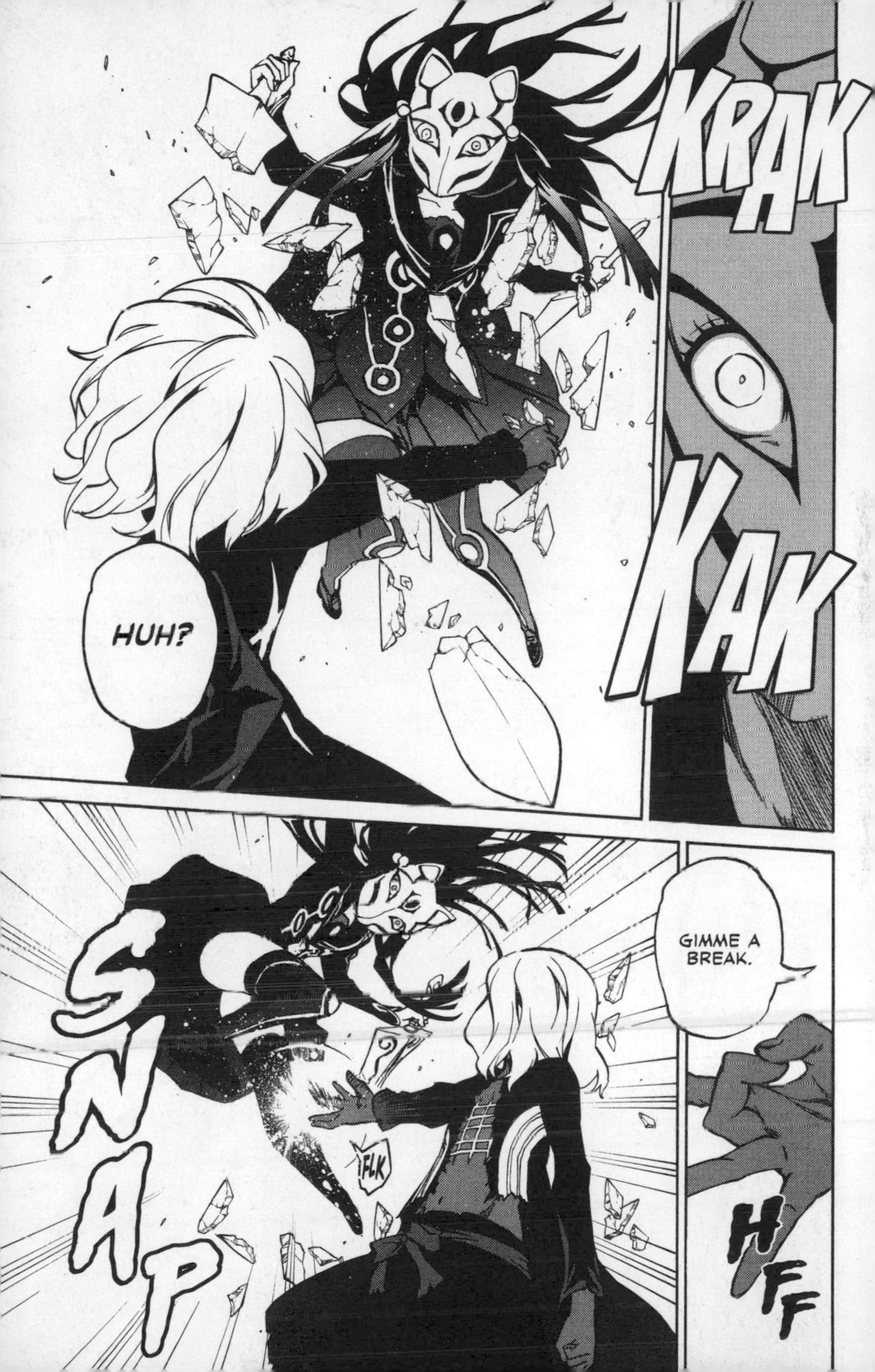
KRAK
KAK
HUH?
GIMME A BREAK.
HFF
SNAP
FLK

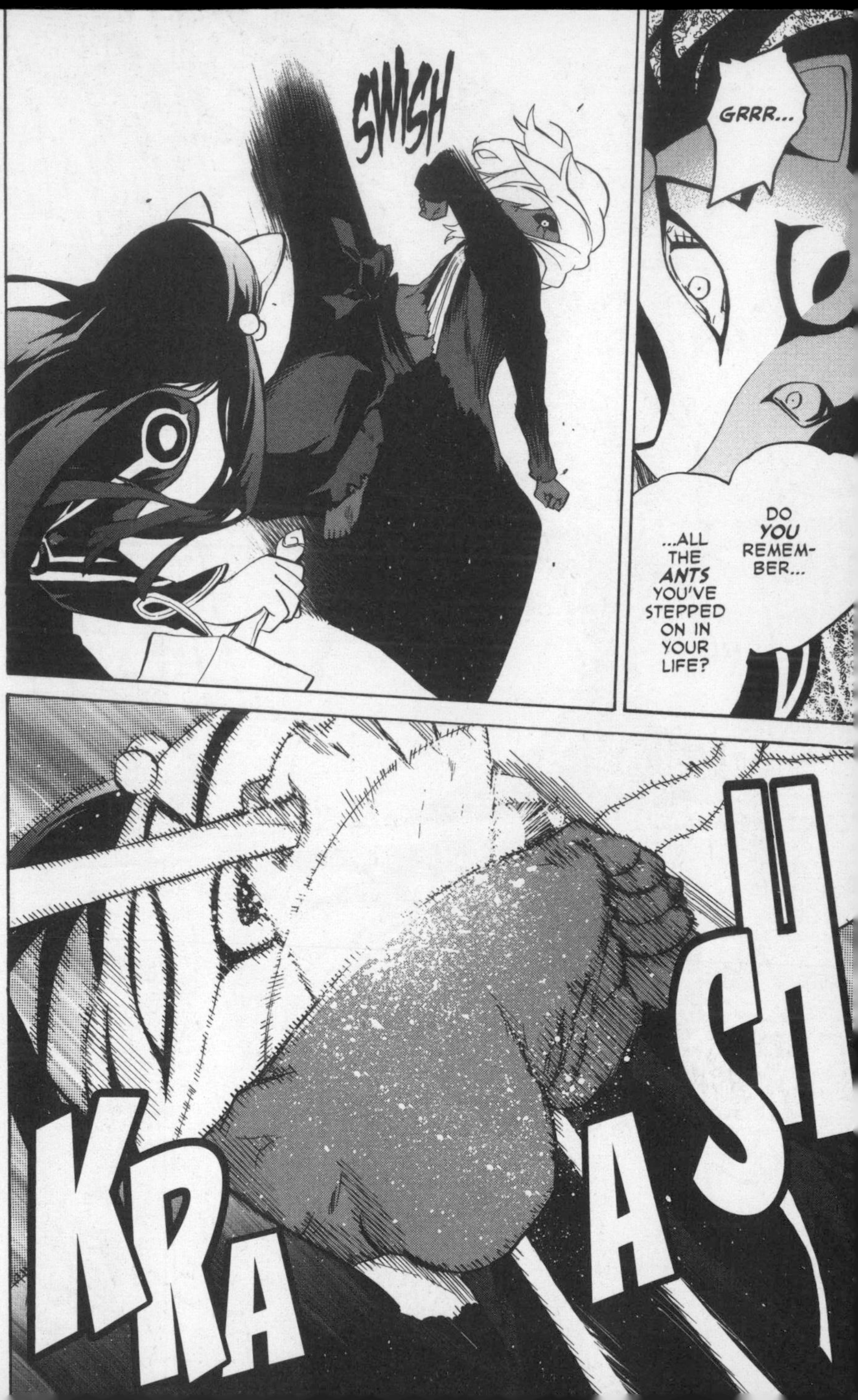
GRRR...
DO YOU REMEMBER...
...ALL THE ANTS YOU'VE STEPPED ON IN YOUR LIFE?
SWISH
KRAASH

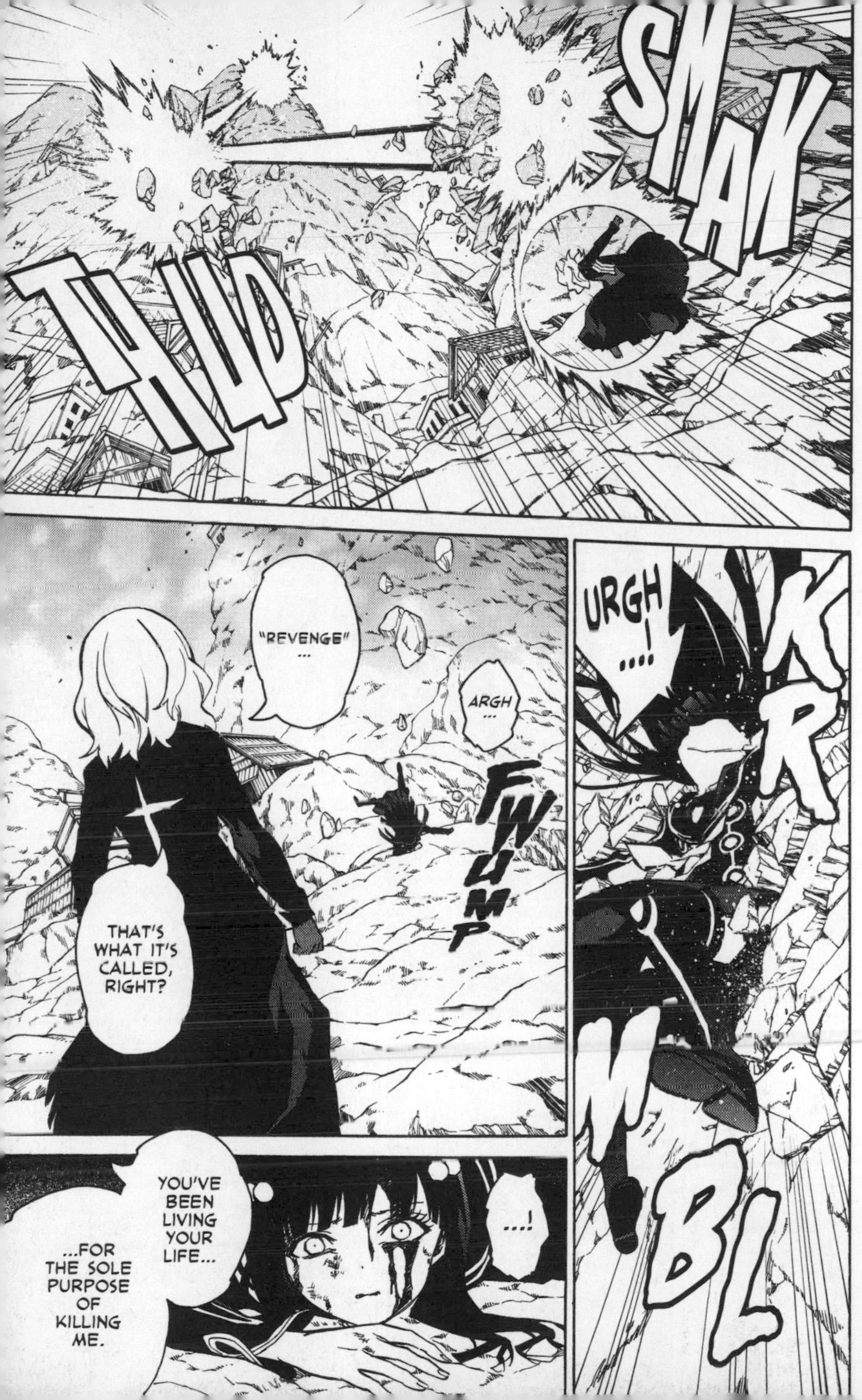
SHAK
THUD
URGH ...!
KR
MBL
FWUMP
ARGH ...
"REVENGE" ...
THAT'S WHAT IT'S CALLED, RIGHT?
...!
YOU'VE BEEN LIVING YOUR LIFE...
...FOR THE SOLE PURPOSE OF KILLING ME.

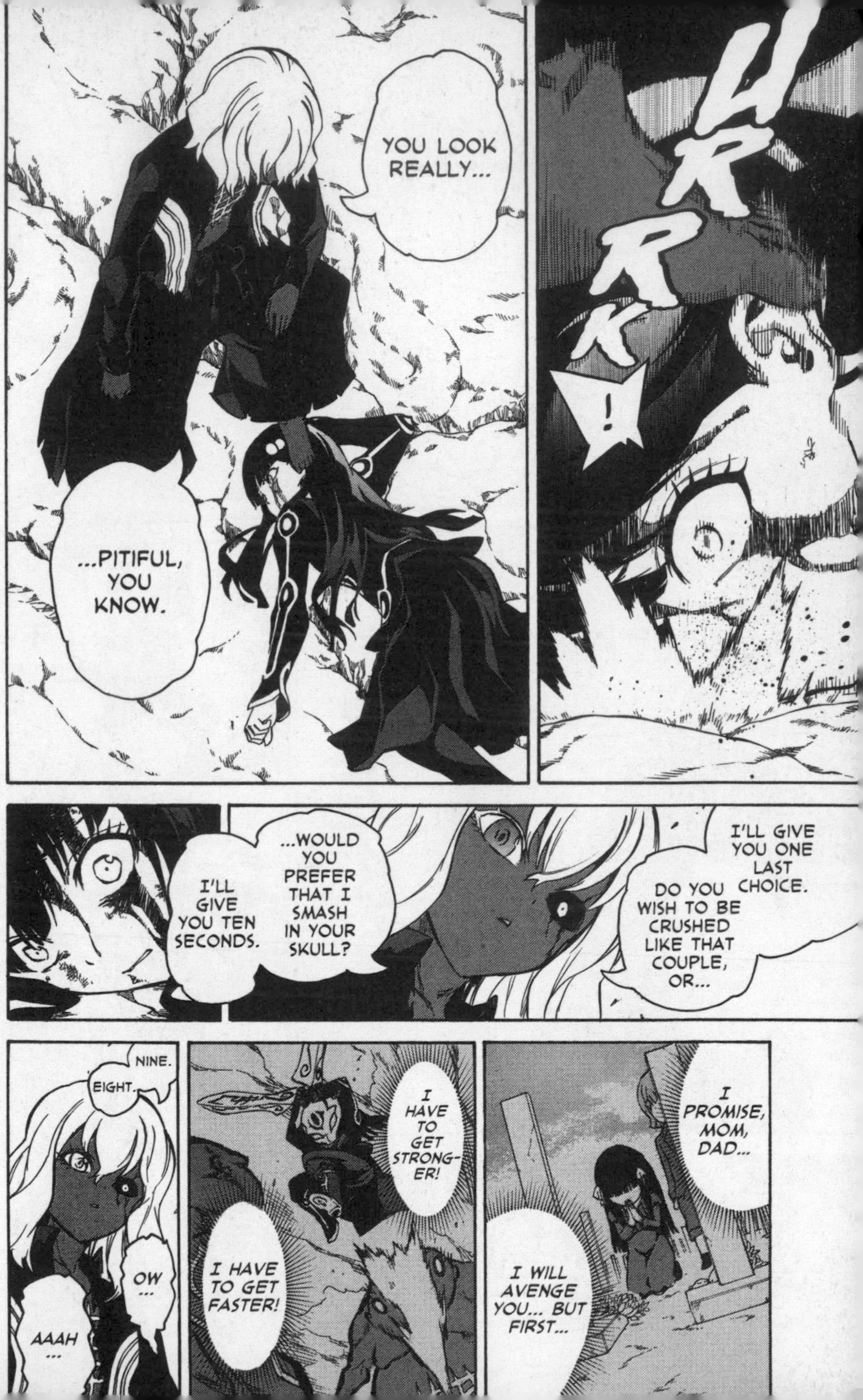
URRK
!
YOU LOOK REALLY...
...PITIFUL, YOU KNOW.
I'LL GIVE YOU ONE LAST CHOICE.
DO YOU WISH TO BE CRUSHED LIKE THAT COUPLE, OR...
...WOULD YOU PREFER THAT I SMASH IN YOUR SKULL?
I'LL GIVE YOU TEN SECONDS.
I PROMISE, MOM, DAD...
I WILL AVENGE YOU... BUT FIRST...
I HAVE TO GET STRONGER!
I HAVE TO GET FASTER!
NINE.
EIGHT.
OW...
AAAH...

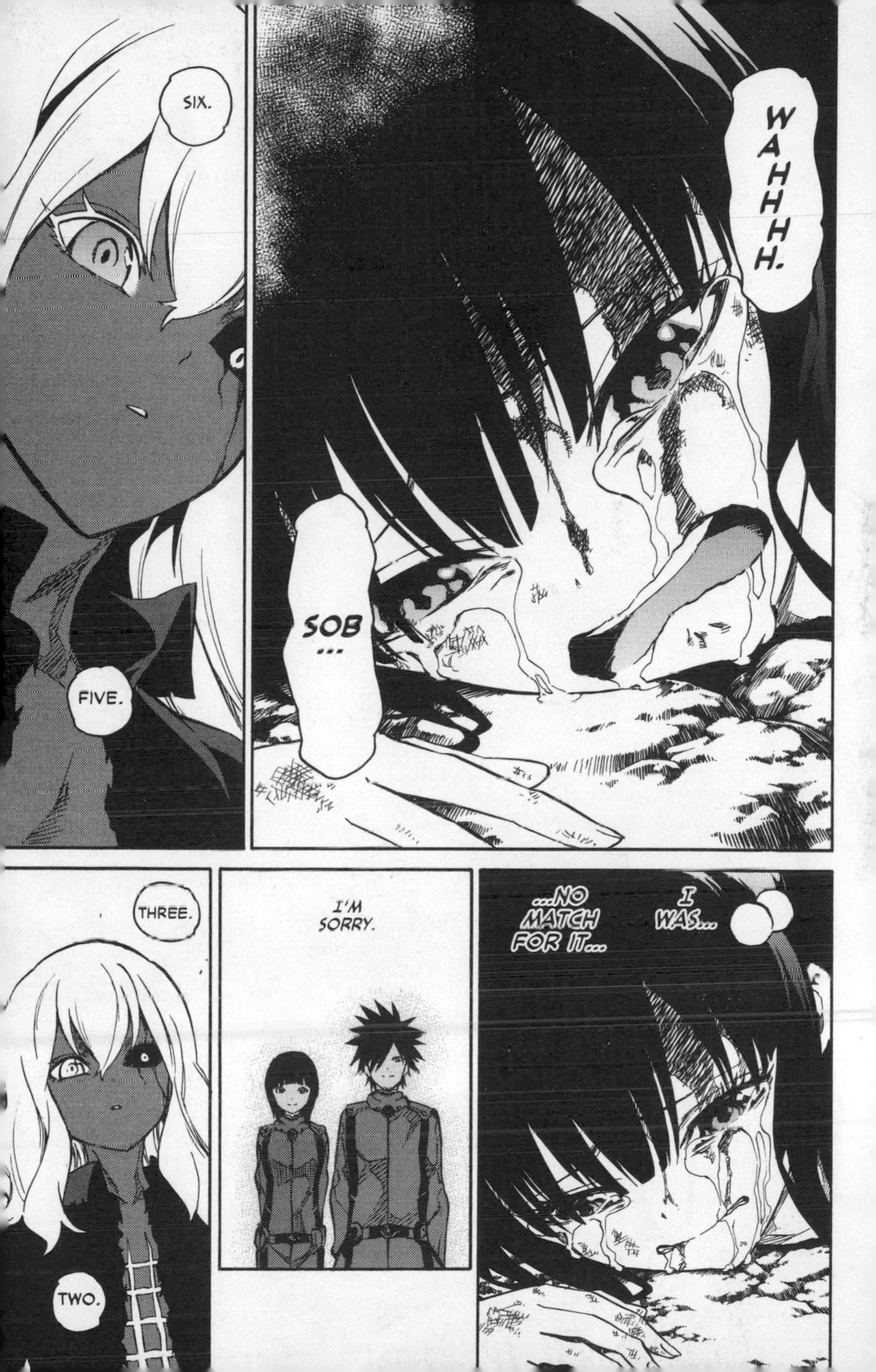
WAHHHH.
SOB...
SIX.
FIVE.
I WAS...
...NO MATCH FOR IT...
I'M SORRY.
THREE.
TWO.

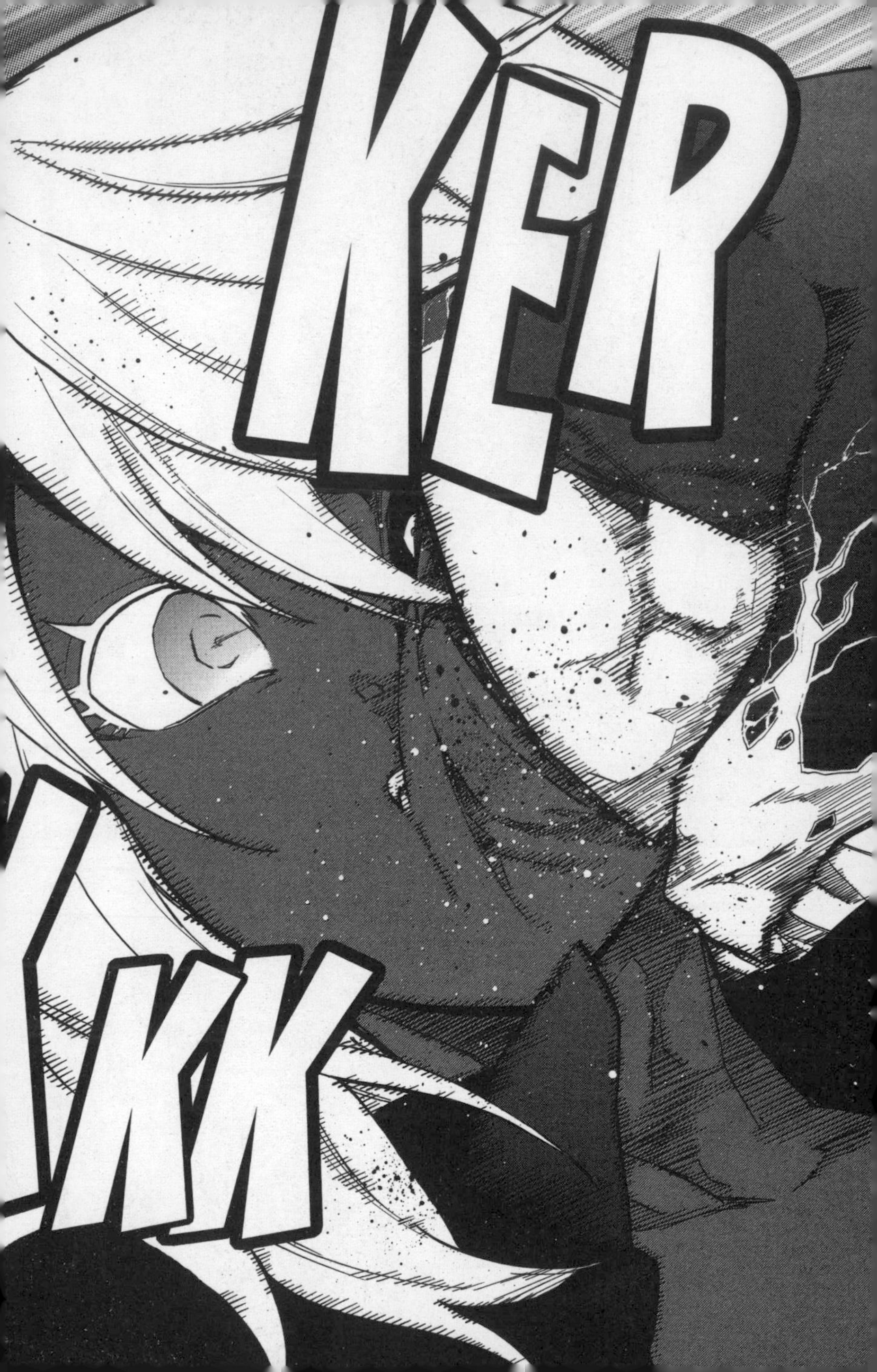
KER
KK

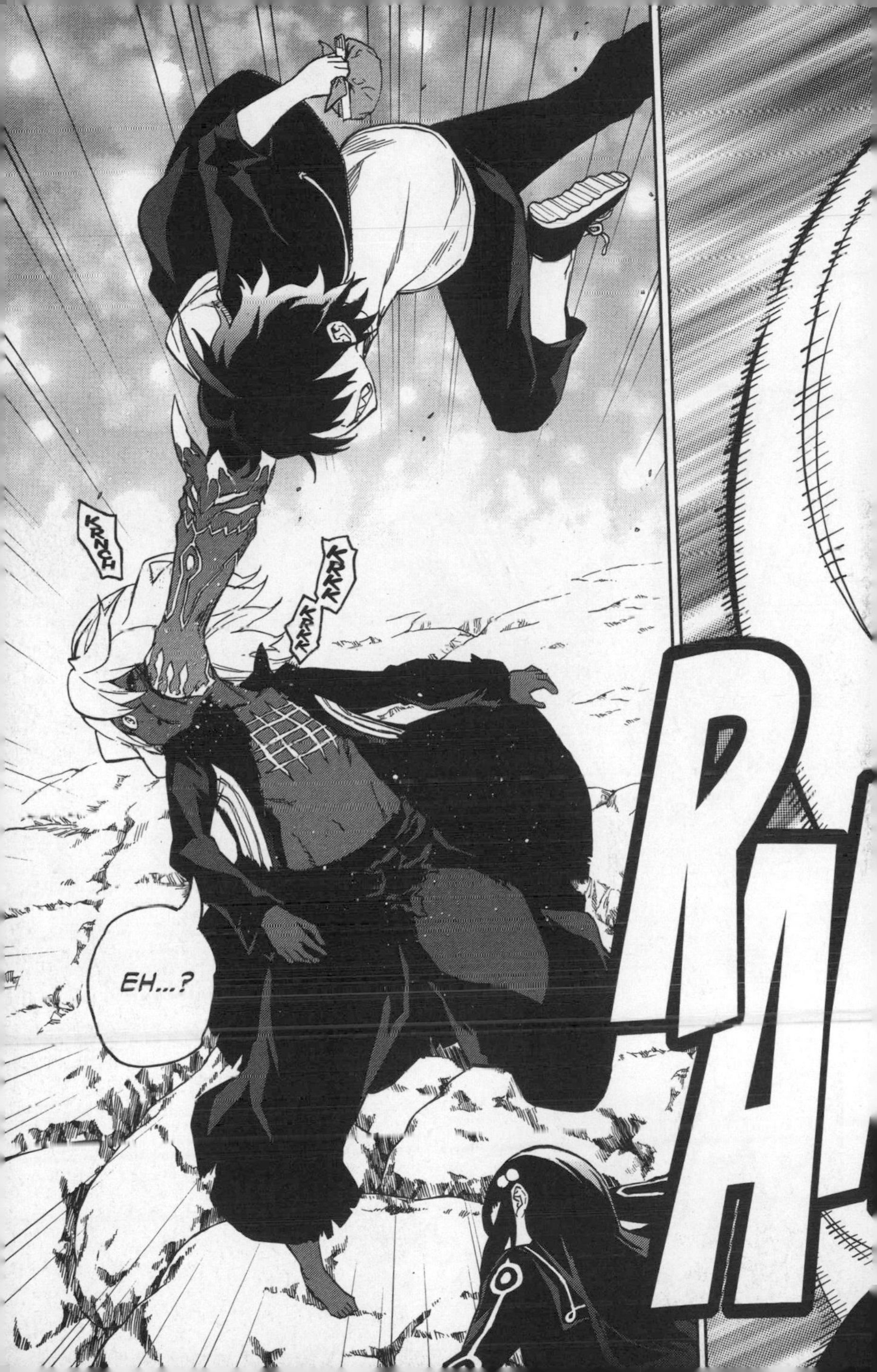
KRKKK
KRKKK
KRNCH
EH...?
RA

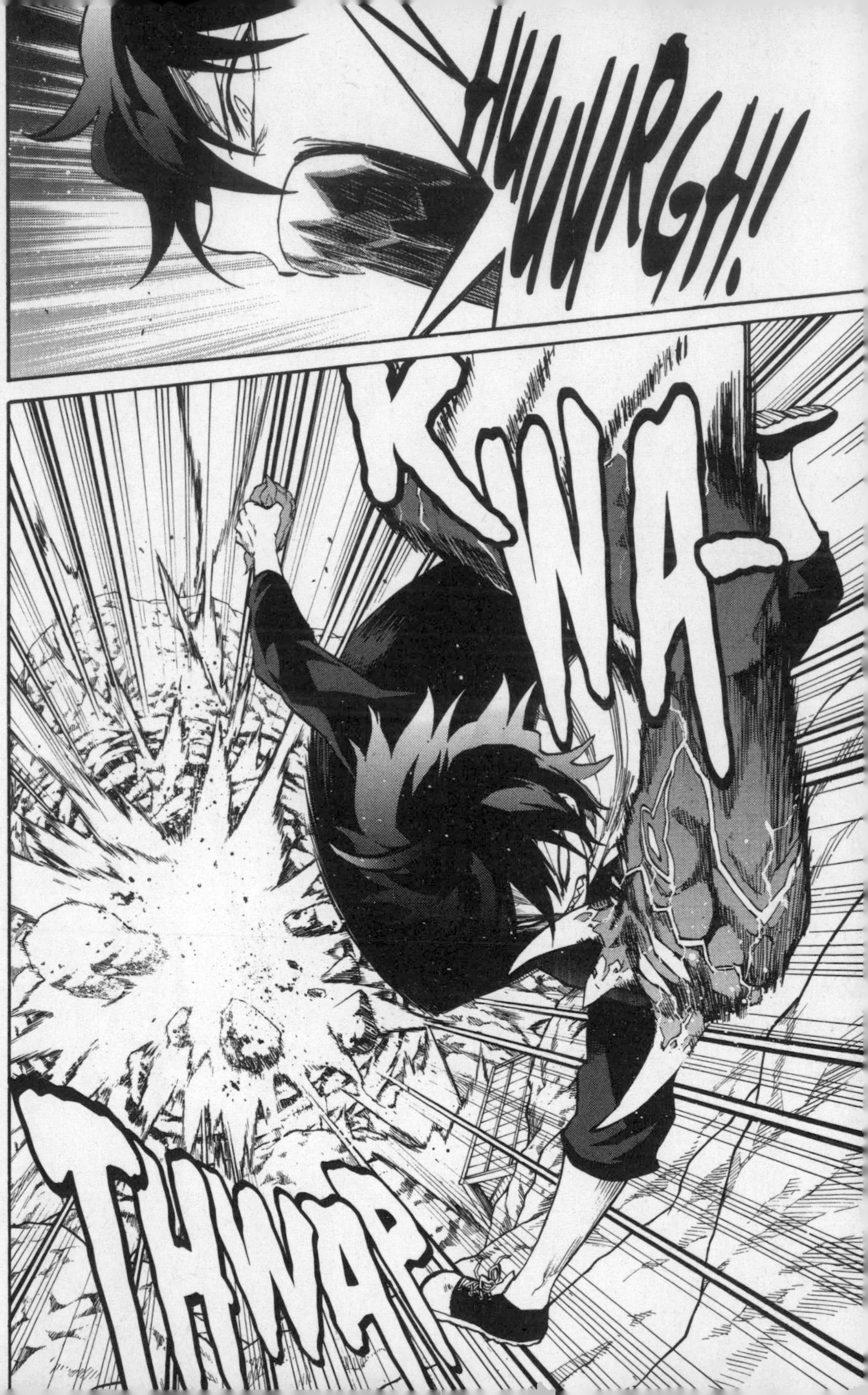
HUUURGH!!
KWA
THWAP

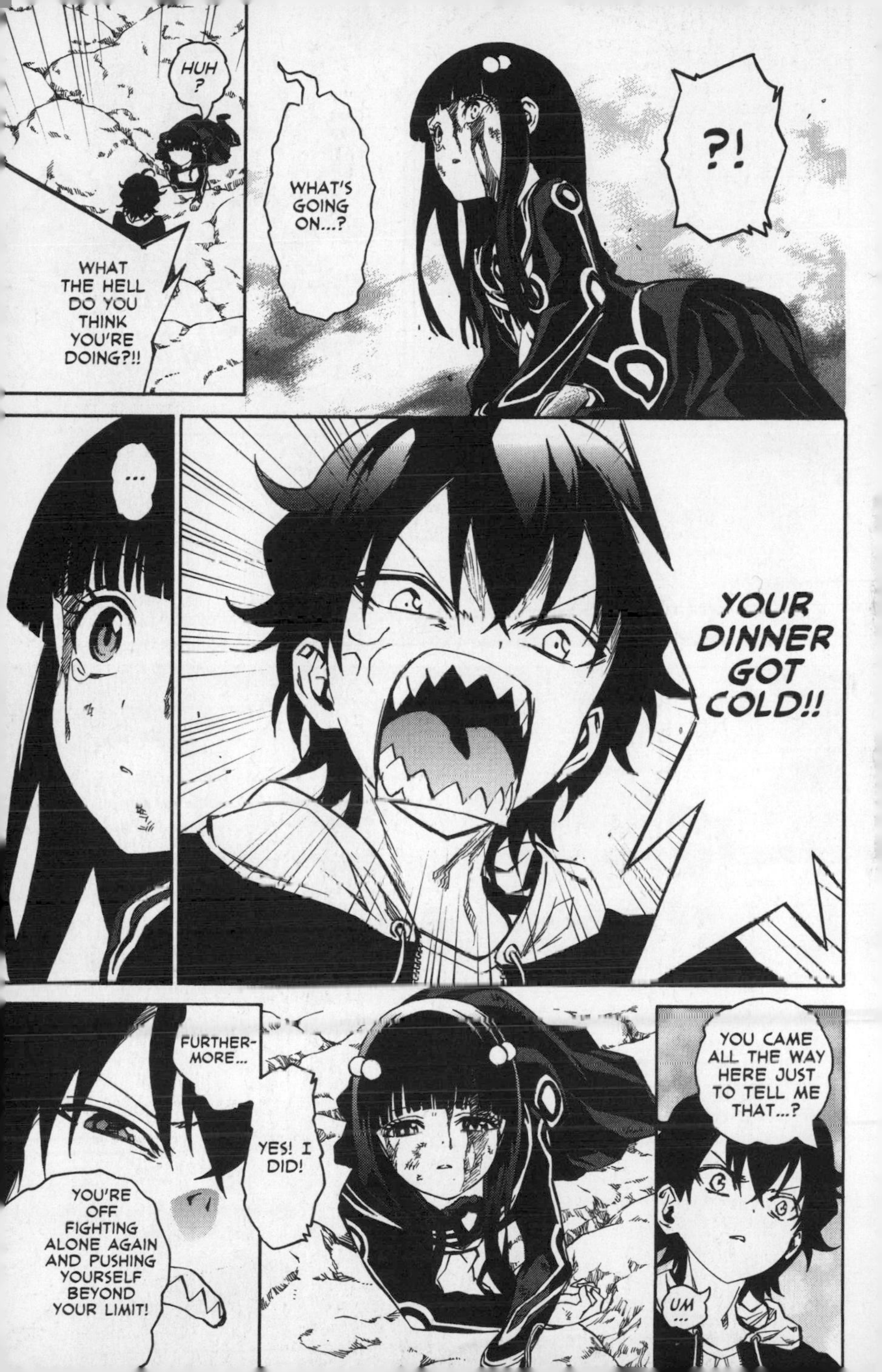
?!
WHAT'S GOING ON...?
HUH ?
WHAT THE HELL DO YOU THINK YOU'RE DOING?!!
YOUR DINNER GOT COLD!!
...
YOU CAME ALL THE WAY HERE JUST TO TELL ME THAT...?
UM ...
YES! I DID!
FURTHER- MORE...
YOU'RE OFF FIGHTING ALONE AGAIN AND PUSHING YOURSELF BEYOND YOUR LIMIT!

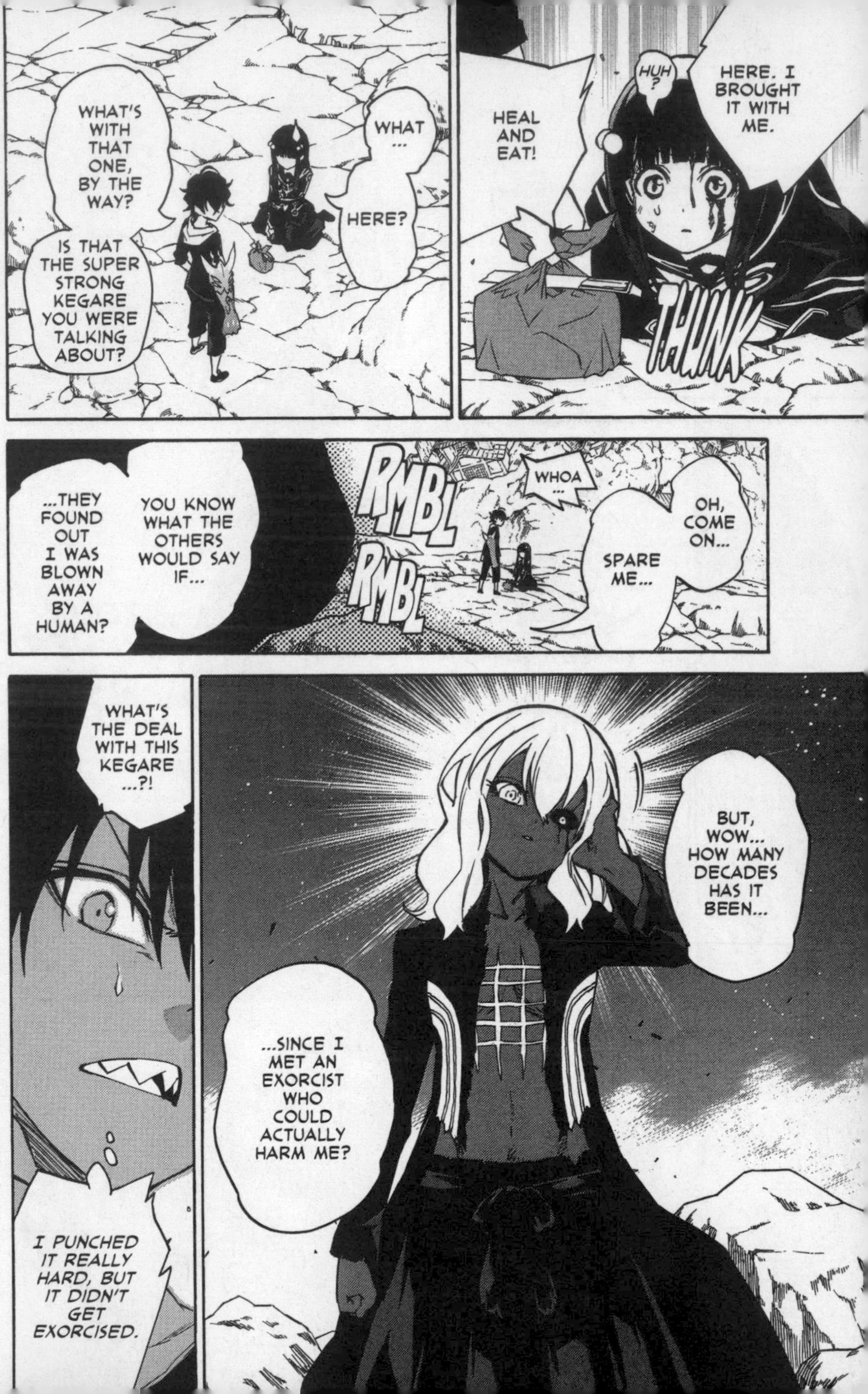
HERE. I BROUGHT IT WITH ME.
HUH?
HEAL AND EAT!
THUNK
WHAT...
HERE?
WHAT'S WITH THAT ONE, BY THE WAY?
IS THAT THE SUPER STRONG KEGARE YOU WERE TALKING ABOUT?
OH, COME ON...
SPARE ME...
WHOA...
RMBL
RMBL
YOU KNOW WHAT THE OTHERS WOULD SAY IF...
...THEY FOUND OUT I WAS BLOWN AWAY BY A HUMAN?
BUT, WOW... HOW MANY DECADES HAS IT BEEN...
...SINCE I MET AN EXORCIST WHO COULD ACTUALLY HARM ME?
WHAT'S THE DEAL WITH THIS KEGARE ...?!
I PUNCHED IT REALLY HARD, BUT IT DIDN'T GET EXORCISED.

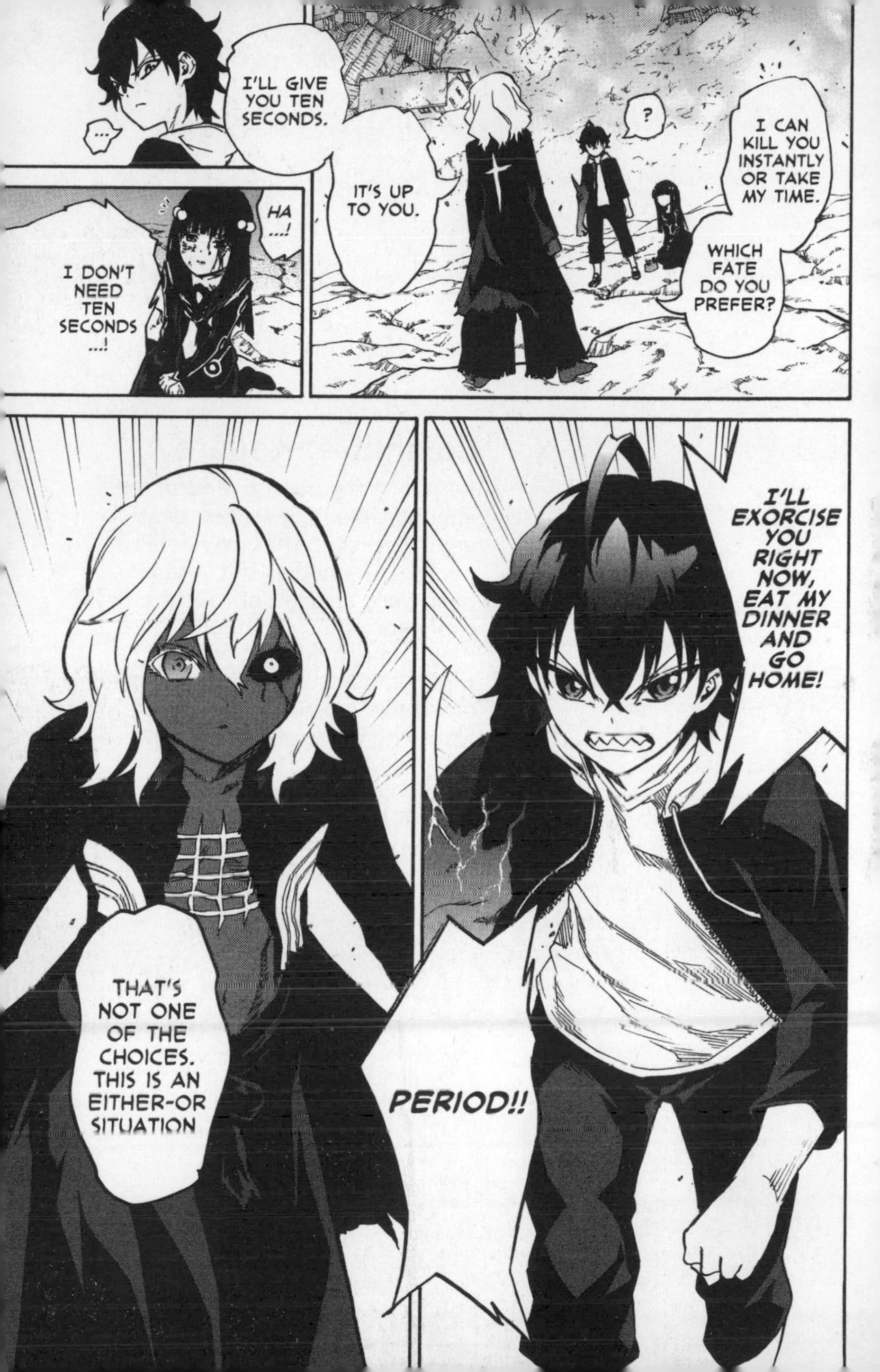
I CAN KILL YOU INSTANTLY OR TAKE MY TIME.
?
WHICH FATE DO YOU PREFER?
IT'S UP TO YOU.
I'LL GIVE YOU TEN SECONDS.
...
HA ...!
I DON'T NEED TEN SECONDS ...!
I'LL EXORCISE YOU RIGHT NOW, EAT MY DINNER AND GO HOME!
PERIOD!!
THAT'S NOT ONE OF THE CHOICES. THIS IS AN EITHER-OR SITUATION

Column 4: Kegare

Kegare is the collective term for impurity, blood, diseases, death... any misfortune that may befall a person. The nobles of centuries past were terrified of touching or experiencing any form of Kegare. If they came in contact with it, they would immediately pray at a shrine or receive a psychic exorcism. Since the exorcists working at the Imperial Court had the power to exorcise Kegare, it was only natural for common people to revere them. In this manga, Kegare are the embodiment of those aforementioned misfortunes, a manifestation of evil spirits.

#5 Your Courage, My Courage

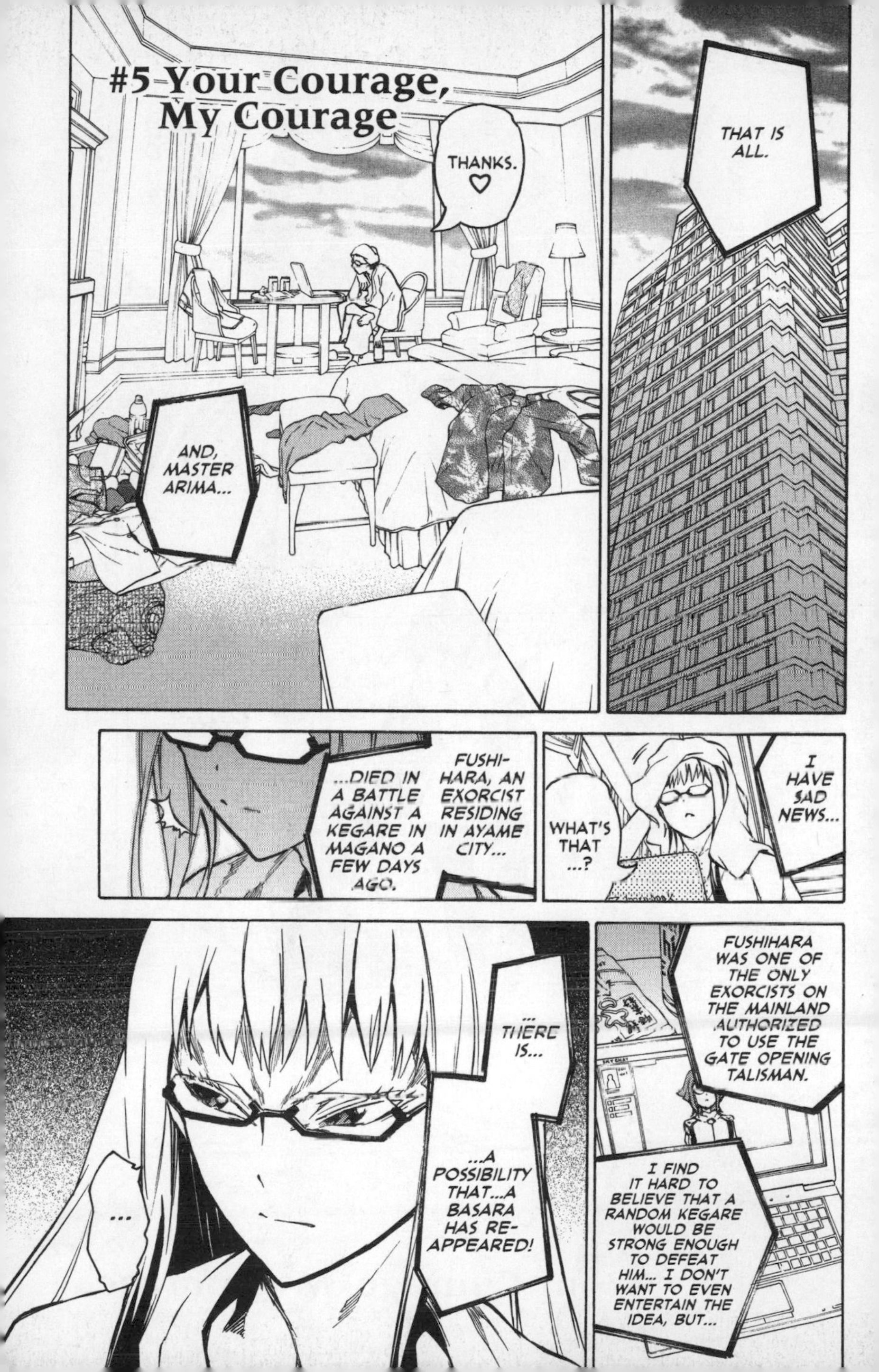
THAT IS ALL.
THANKS. ♡
AND, MASTER ARIMA...
I HAVE SAD NEWS...
WHAT'S THAT ...?
FUSHIHARA, AN EXORCIST RESIDING IN AYAME CITY...
...DIED IN A BATTLE AGAINST A KEGARE IN MAGANO A FEW DAYS AGO.
FUSHIHARA WAS ONE OF THE ONLY EXORCISTS ON THE MAINLAND AUTHORIZED TO USE THE GATE OPENING TALISMAN.
I FIND IT HARD TO BELIEVE THAT A RANDOM KEGARE WOULD BE STRONG ENOUGH TO DEFEAT HIM... I DON'T WANT TO EVEN ENTERTAIN THE IDEA, BUT...
...THERE IS...
...A POSSIBILITY THAT...A BASARA HAS RE-APPEARED!
...

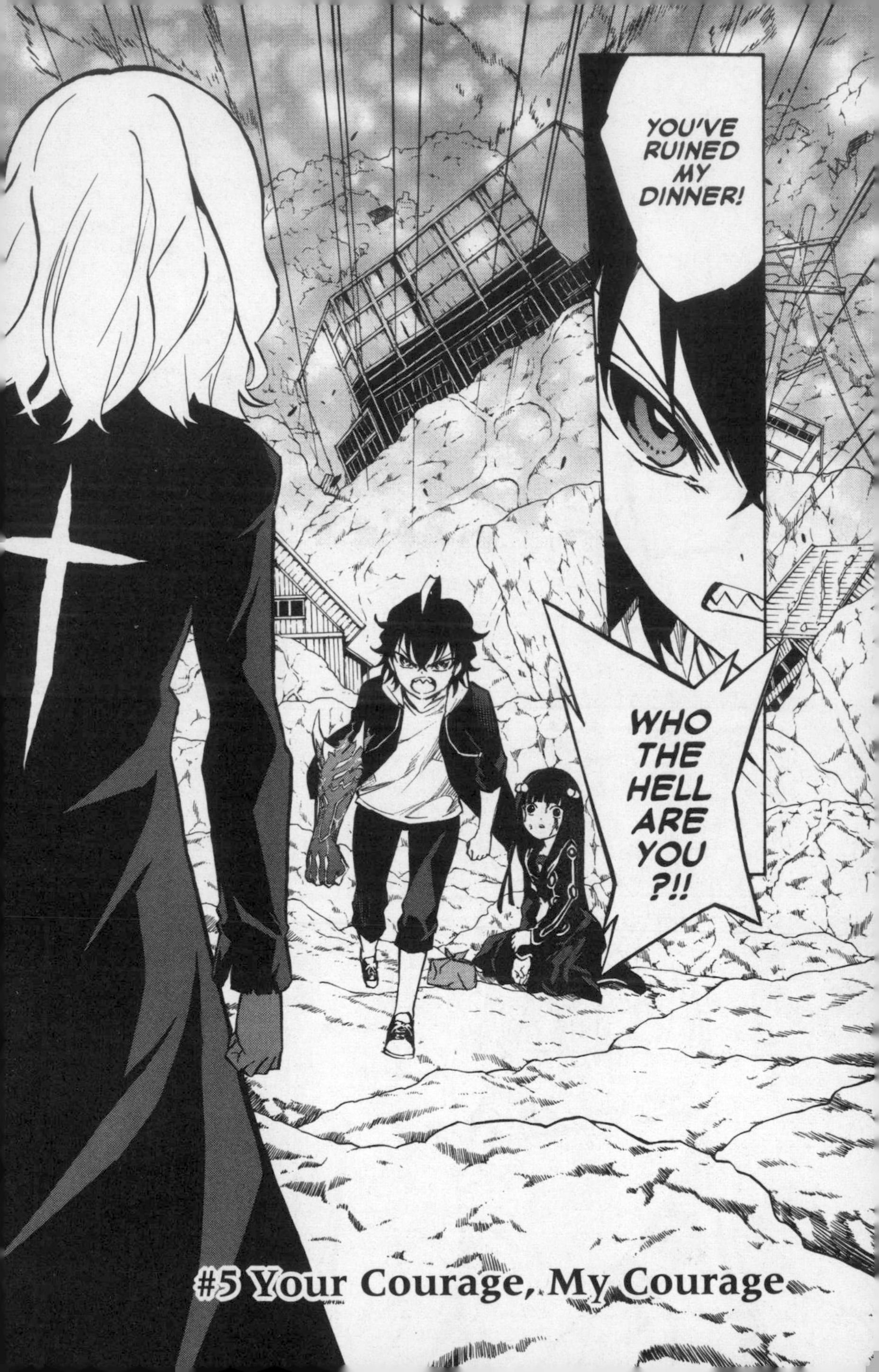
YOU'VE RUINED MY DINNER!
WHO THE HELL ARE YOU ?!!
#5 Your Courage, My Courage

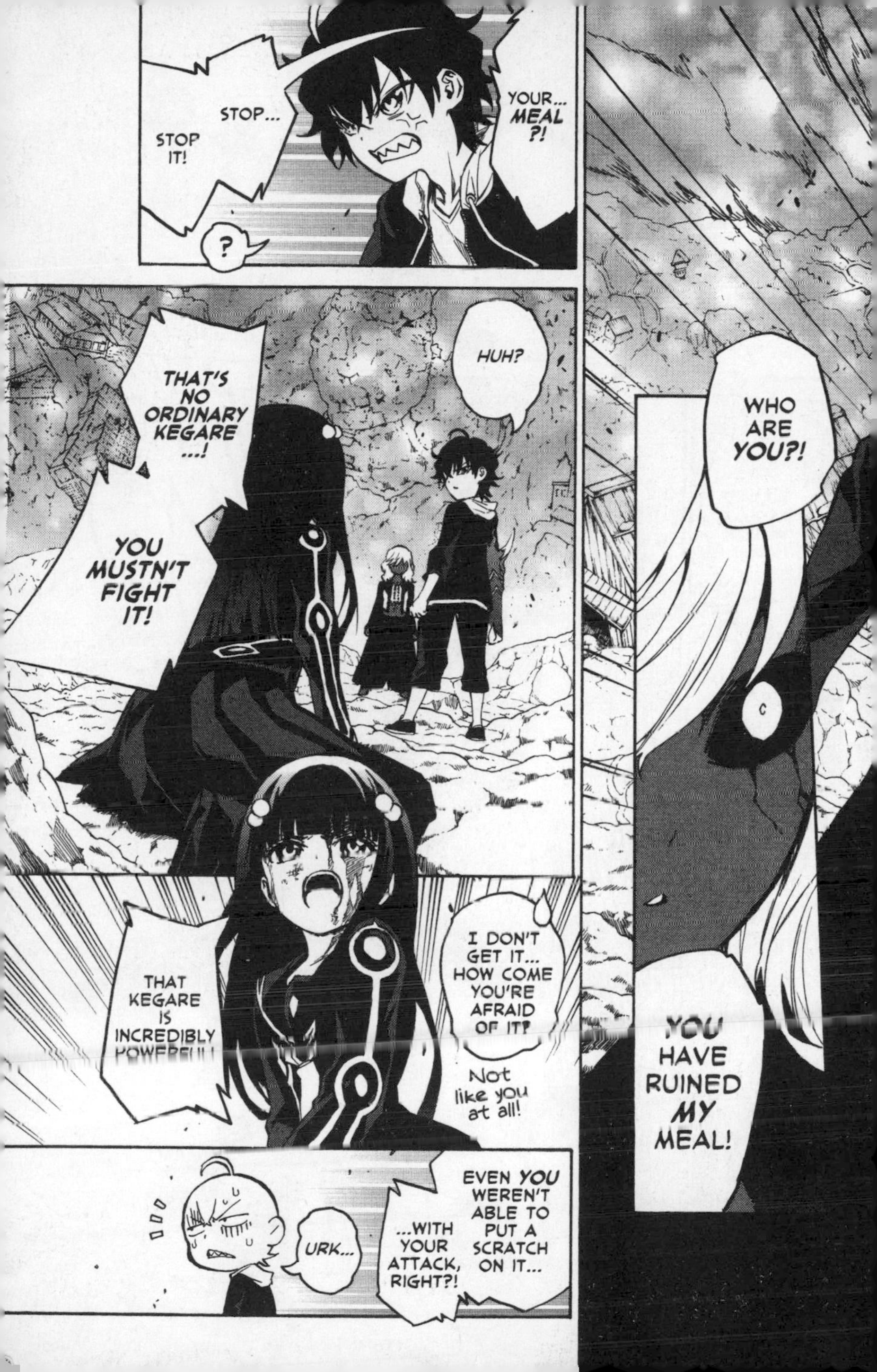
WHO ARE YOU?!
YOU HAVE RUINED MY MEAL!
YOUR... MEAL?!
STOP...
STOP IT!
?
HUH?
THAT'S NO ORDINARY KEGARE...!
YOU MUSTN'T FIGHT IT!
I DON'T GET IT... HOW COME YOU'RE AFRAID OF IT?
Not like you at all!
THAT KEGARE IS INCREDIBLY POWERFUL!
EVEN YOU WEREN'T ABLE TO PUT A SCRATCH ON IT...
...WITH YOUR ATTACK, RIGHT?!
URK...

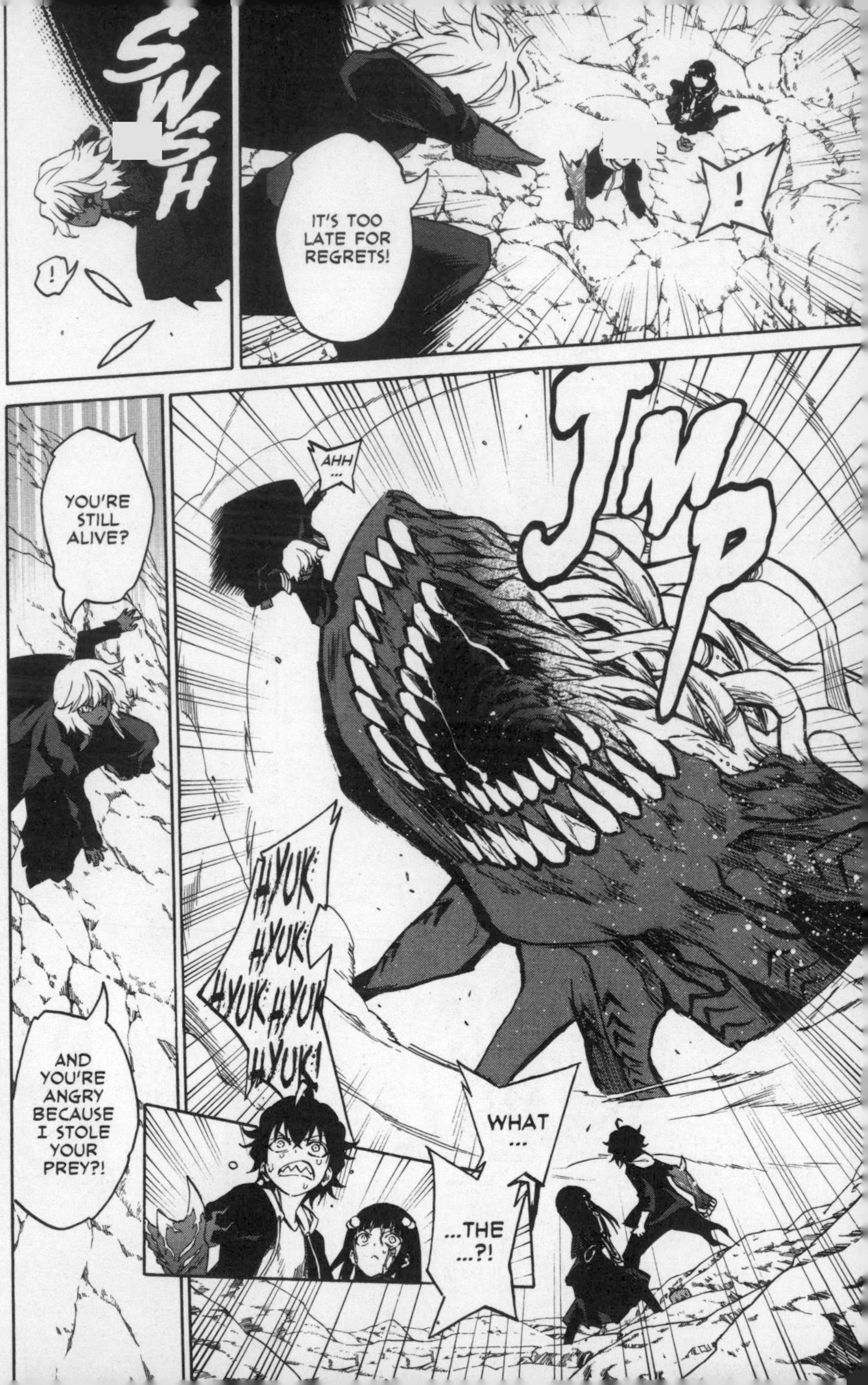
!
IT'S TOO LATE FOR REGRETS!
SWSH
!
JMP
AHH ...
HYUK HYUK HYUK HYUK HYUK HYUK!
WHAT ...
...THE ...?!
YOU'RE STILL ALIVE?
AND YOU'RE ANGRY BECAUSE I STOLE YOUR PREY?!

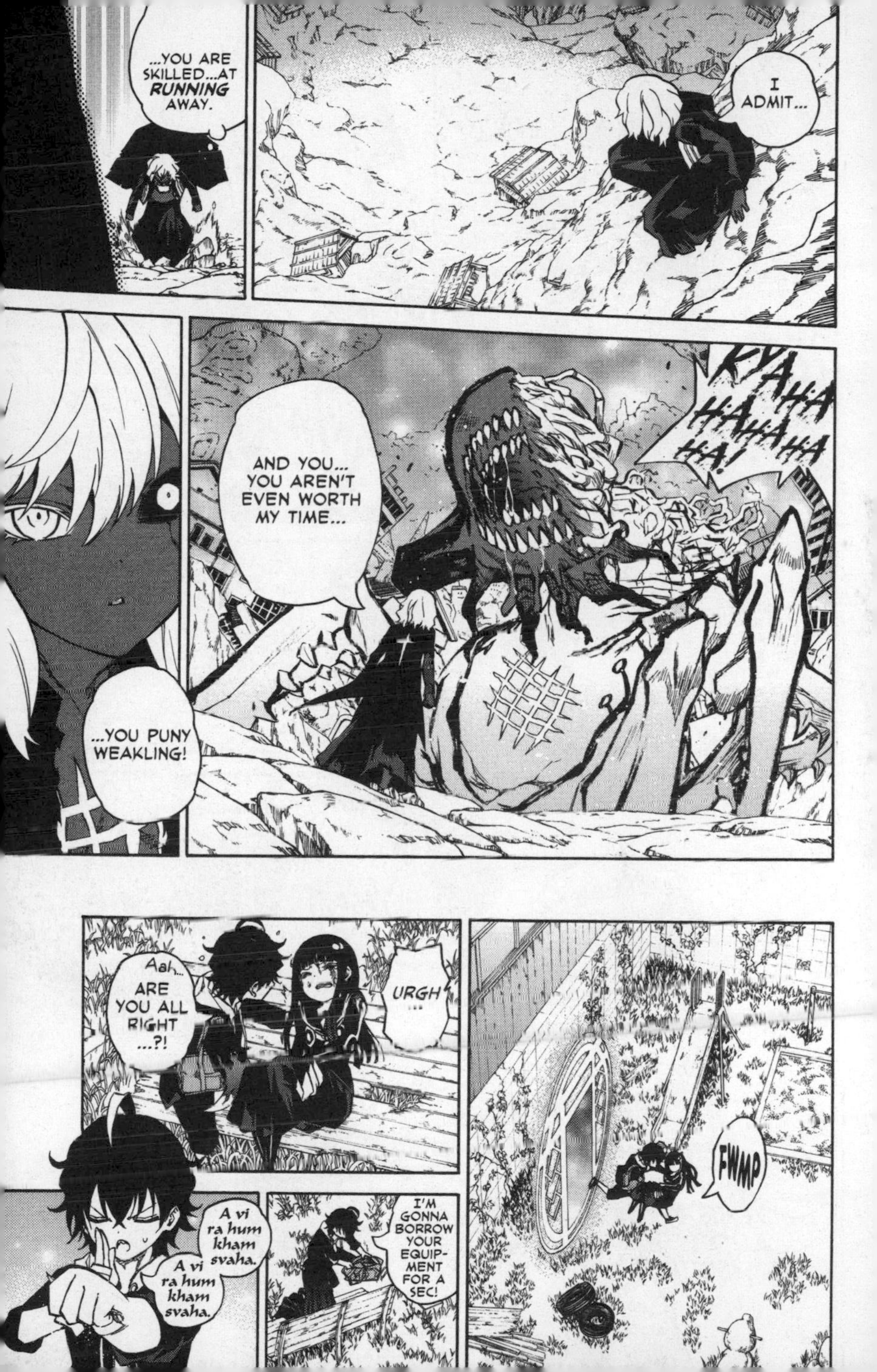
I ADMIT...
...YOU ARE SKILLED...AT RUNNING AWAY.
KYAHAHAHAHAHAHA!
AND YOU... YOU AREN'T EVEN WORTH MY TIME...
...YOU PUNY WEAKLING!
FWMP
URGH...
Aah... ARE YOU ALL RIGHT ...?!
I'M GONNA BORROW YOUR EQUIPMENT FOR A SEC!
A vi ra hum kham svaha.
A vi ra hum kham svaha.

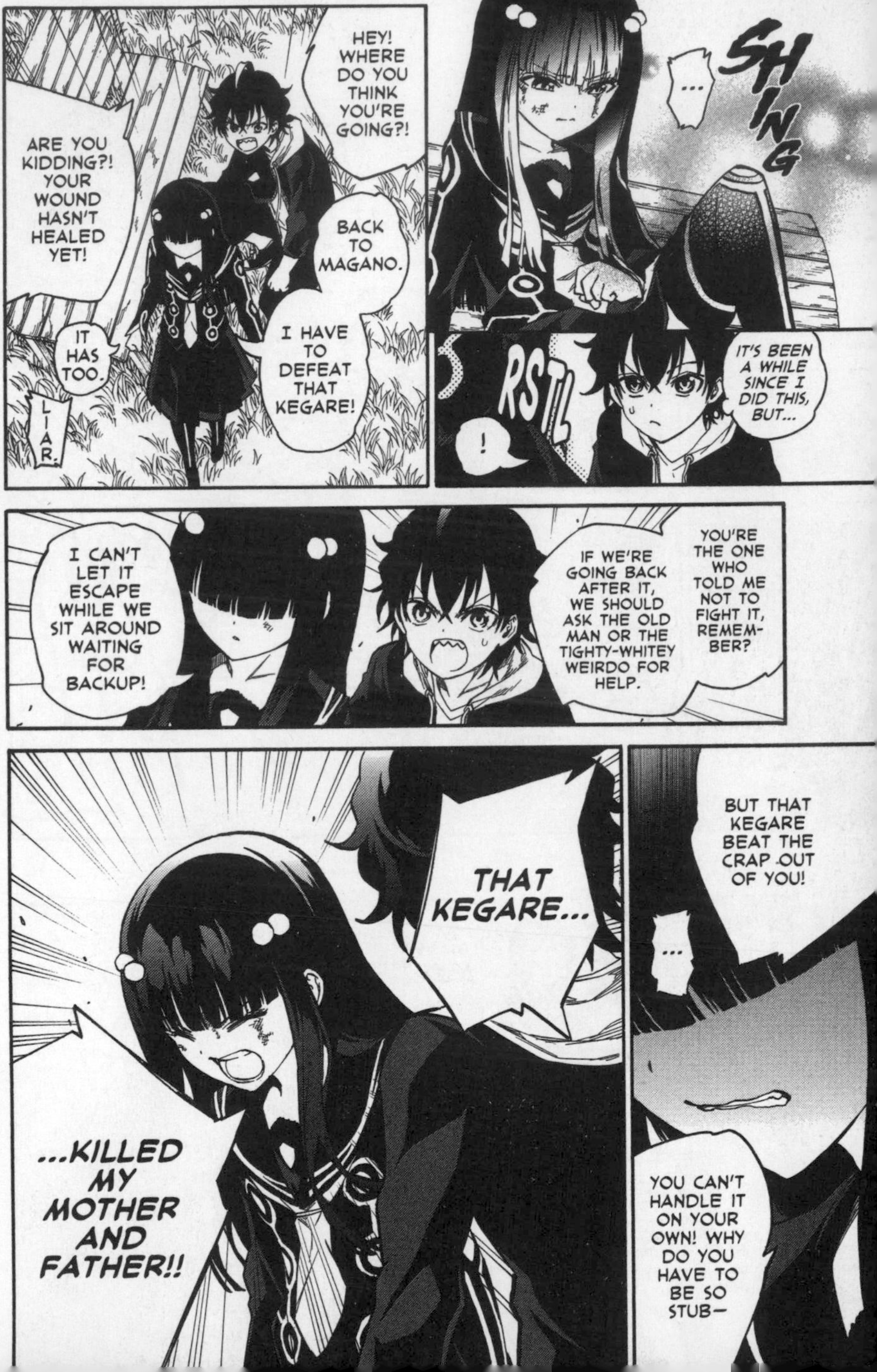
...
SHING
IT'S BEEN A WHILE SINCE I DID THIS, BUT...
RSTL
!
HEY! WHERE DO YOU THINK YOU'RE GOING?!
BACK TO MAGANO.
I HAVE TO DEFEAT THAT KEGARE!
ARE YOU KIDDING?! YOUR WOUND HASN'T HEALED YET!
IT HAS TOO.
LIAR.
YOU'RE THE ONE WHO TOLD ME NOT TO FIGHT IT, REMEMBER?
IF WE'RE GOING BACK AFTER IT, WE SHOULD ASK THE OLD MAN OR THE TIGHTY-WHITEY WEIRDO FOR HELP.
I CAN'T LET IT ESCAPE WHILE WE SIT AROUND WAITING FOR BACKUP!
BUT THAT KEGARE BEAT THE CRAP OUT OF YOU!
...
YOU CAN'T HANDLE IT ON YOUR OWN! WHY DO YOU HAVE TO BE SO STUB—
THAT KEGARE...
...KILLED MY MOTHER AND FATHER!!

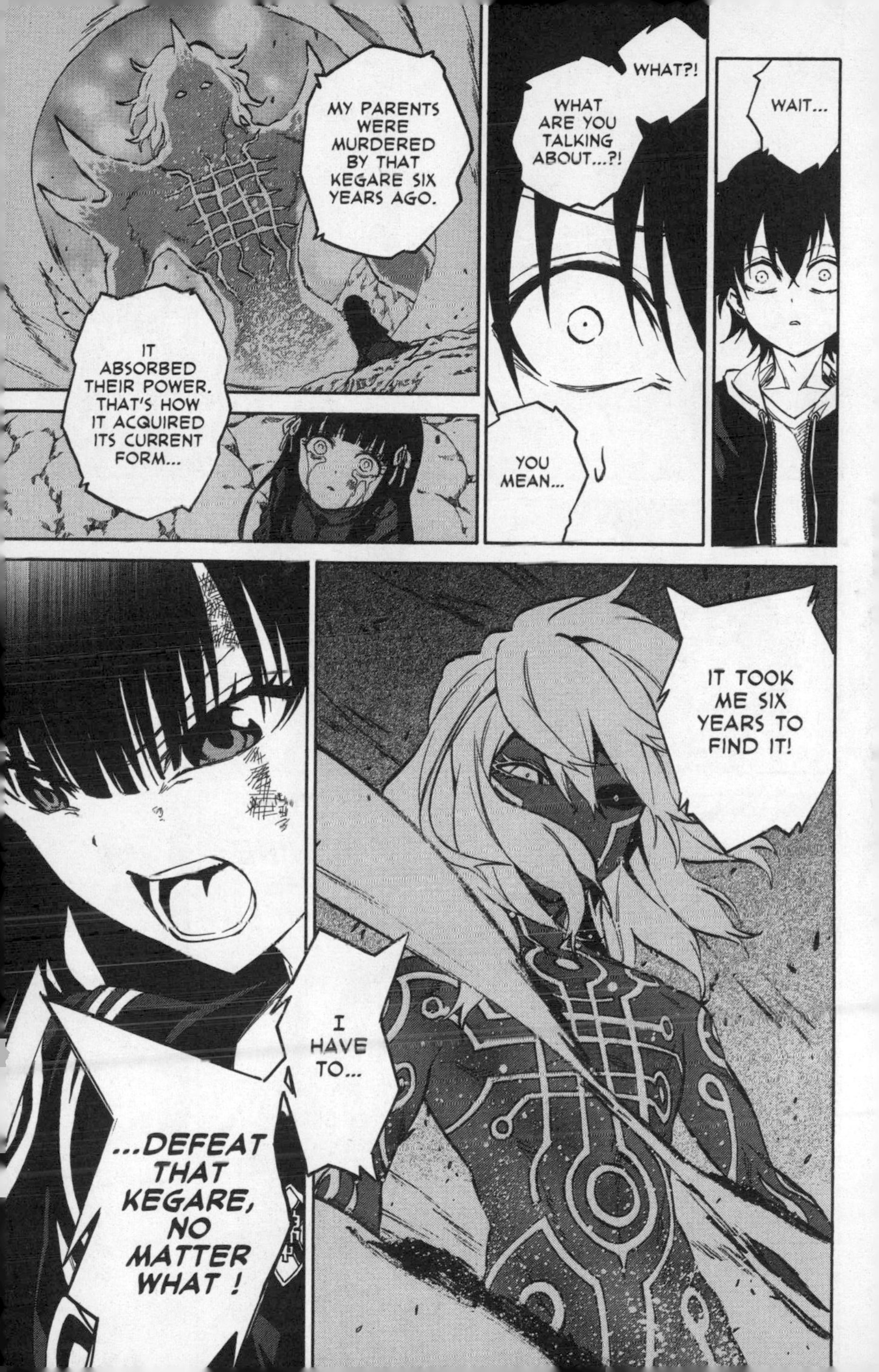
WAIT...
WHAT?!
WHAT ARE YOU TALKING ABOUT...?!
YOU MEAN...
MY PARENTS WERE MURDERED BY THAT KEGARE SIX YEARS AGO.
IT ABSORBED THEIR POWER. THAT'S HOW IT ACQUIRED ITS CURRENT FORM...
IT TOOK ME SIX YEARS TO FIND IT!
I HAVE TO...
...DEFEAT THAT KEGARE, NO MATTER WHAT!

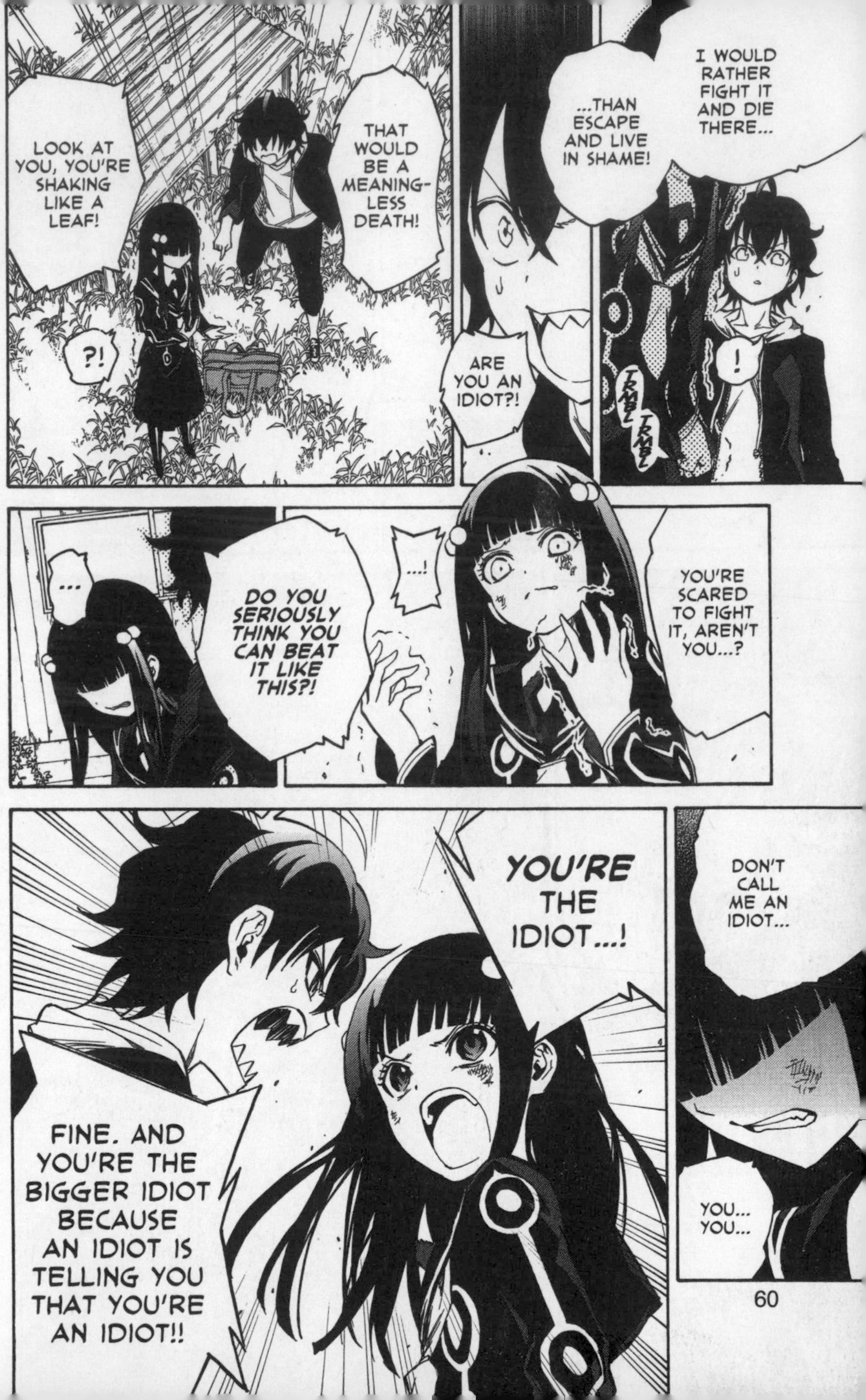

I WOULD RATHER FIGHT IT AND DIE THERE...
...THAN ESCAPE AND LIVE IN SHAME!
!
TRMBL TRMBL
ARE YOU AN IDIOT?!
THAT WOULD BE A MEANING-LESS DEATH!
LOOK AT YOU, YOU'RE SHAKING LIKE A LEAF!
?!
YOU'RE SCARED TO FIGHT IT, AREN'T YOU...?
...!
DO YOU SERIOUSLY THINK YOU CAN BEAT IT LIKE THIS?!
...
DON'T CALL ME AN IDIOT...
YOU... YOU...
YOU'RE THE IDIOT...!
FINE. AND YOU'RE THE BIGGER IDIOT BECAUSE AN IDIOT IS TELLING YOU THAT YOU'RE AN IDIOT!!

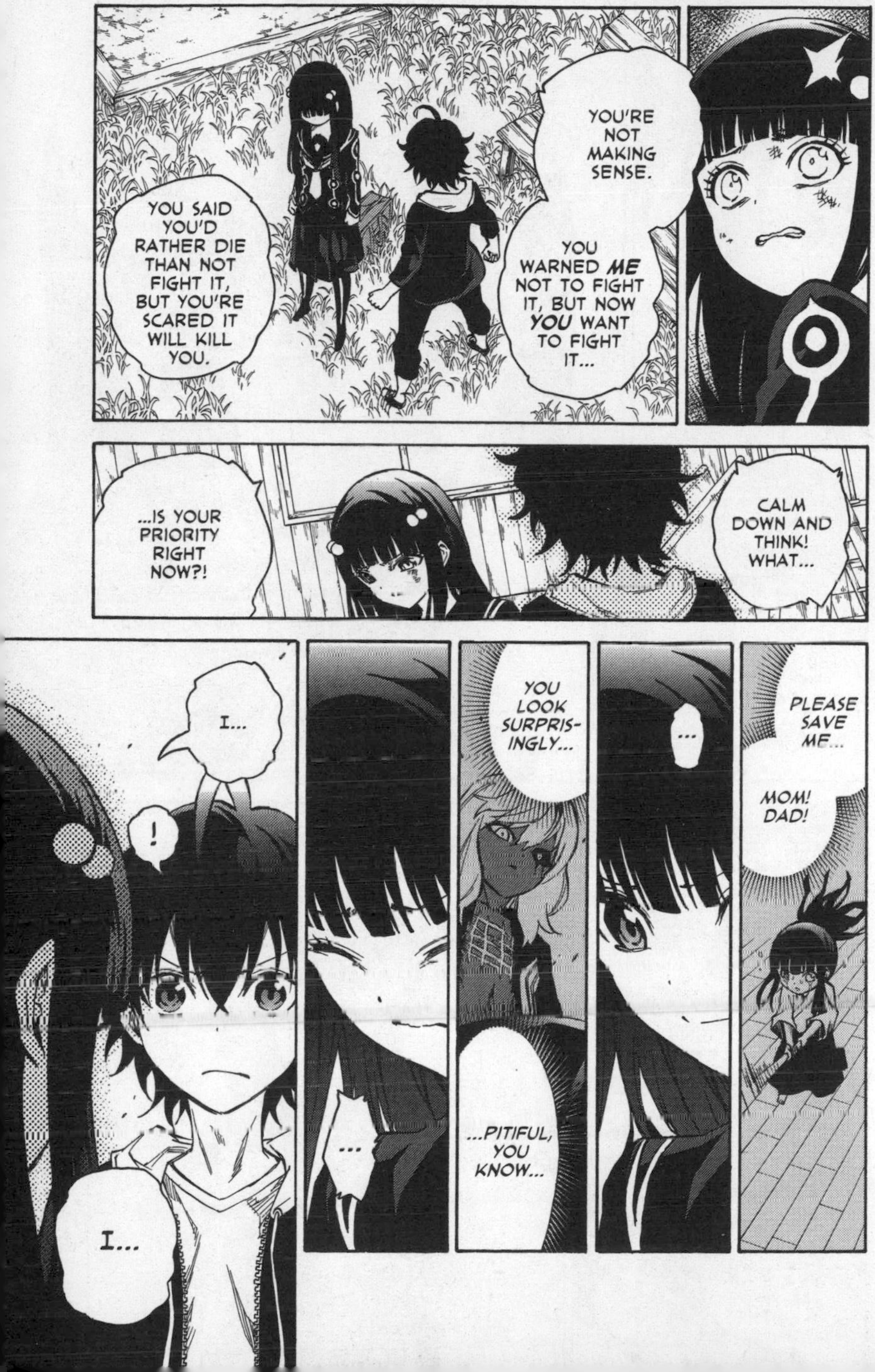

YOU'RE NOT MAKING SENSE.
YOU WARNED *ME* NOT TO FIGHT IT, BUT NOW *YOU* WANT TO FIGHT IT...
YOU SAID YOU'D RATHER DIE THAN NOT FIGHT IT, BUT YOU'RE SCARED IT WILL KILL YOU.
CALM DOWN AND THINK! WHAT...
...IS YOUR PRIORITY RIGHT NOW?!
PLEASE SAVE ME...
MOM! DAD!
...
YOU LOOK SURPRISINGLY...
...PITIFUL, YOU KNOW...
...
I...
!
I...

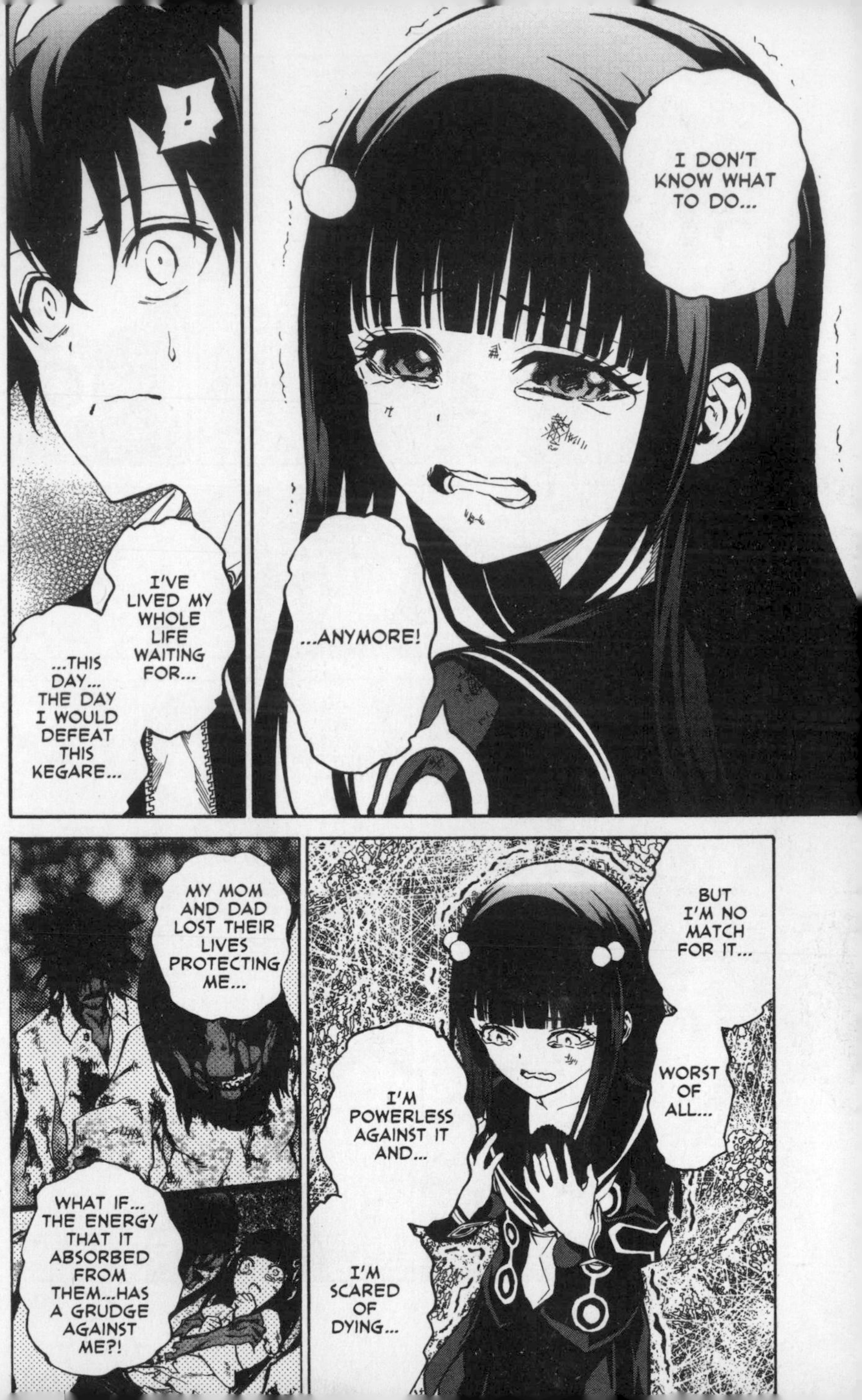
I DON'T KNOW WHAT TO DO...
...ANYMORE!
!
I'VE LIVED MY WHOLE LIFE WAITING FOR...
...THIS DAY... THE DAY I WOULD DEFEAT THIS KEGARE...
BUT I'M NO MATCH FOR IT...
WORST OF ALL...
I'M POWERLESS AGAINST IT AND...
I'M SCARED OF DYING...
MY MOM AND DAD LOST THEIR LIVES PROTECTING ME...
WHAT IF... THE ENERGY THAT IT ABSORBED FROM THEM...HAS A GRUDGE AGAINST ME?!

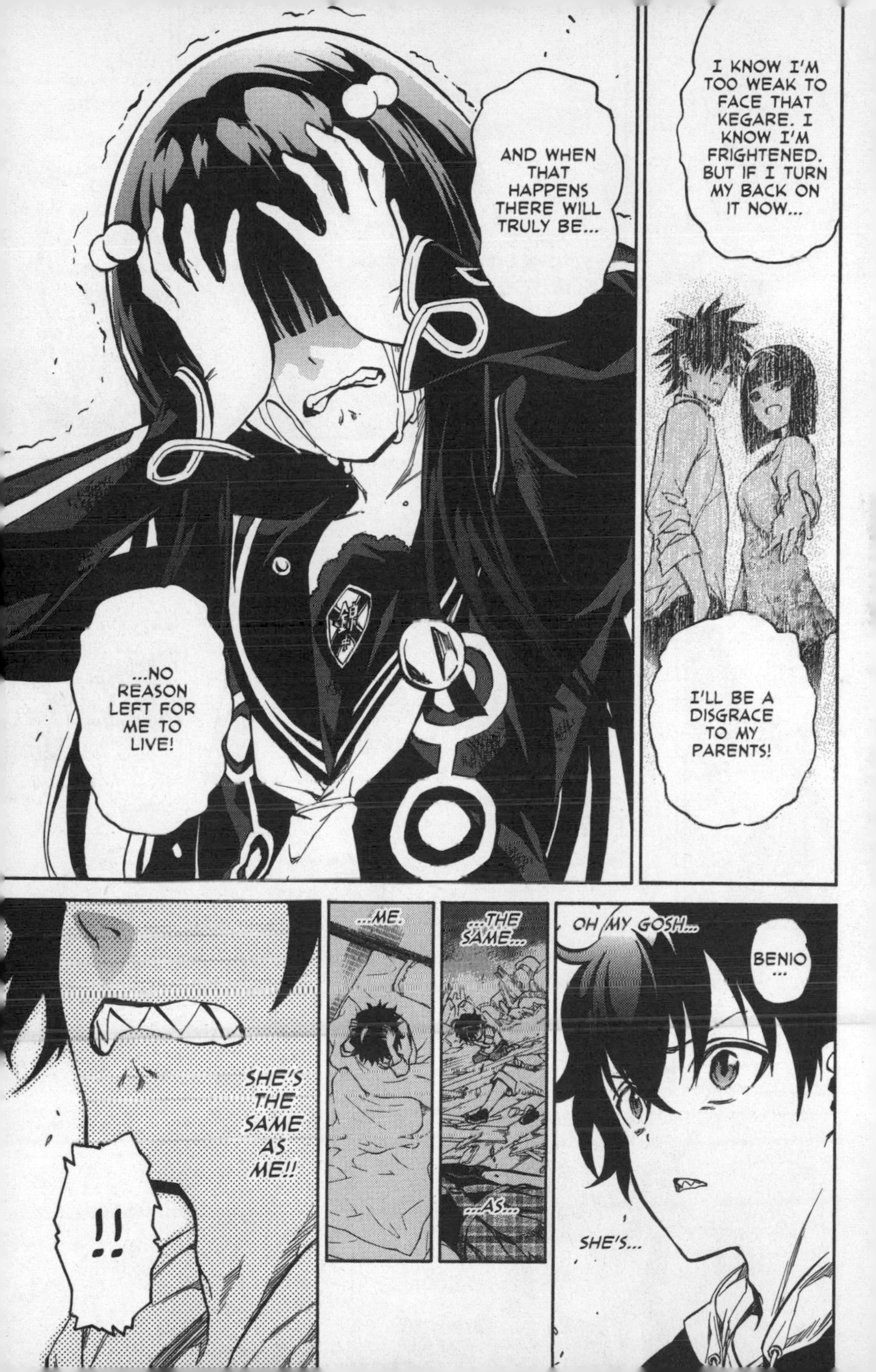
I KNOW I'M TOO WEAK TO FACE THAT KEGARE. I KNOW I'M FRIGHTENED. BUT IF I TURN MY BACK ON IT NOW...
I'LL BE A DISGRACE TO MY PARENTS!
AND WHEN THAT HAPPENS THERE WILL TRULY BE...
...NO REASON LEFT FOR ME TO LIVE!
OH MY GOSH...
BENIO ...
SHE'S...
...THE SAME...
...AS...
...ME.
SHE'S THE SAME AS ME!!
!!

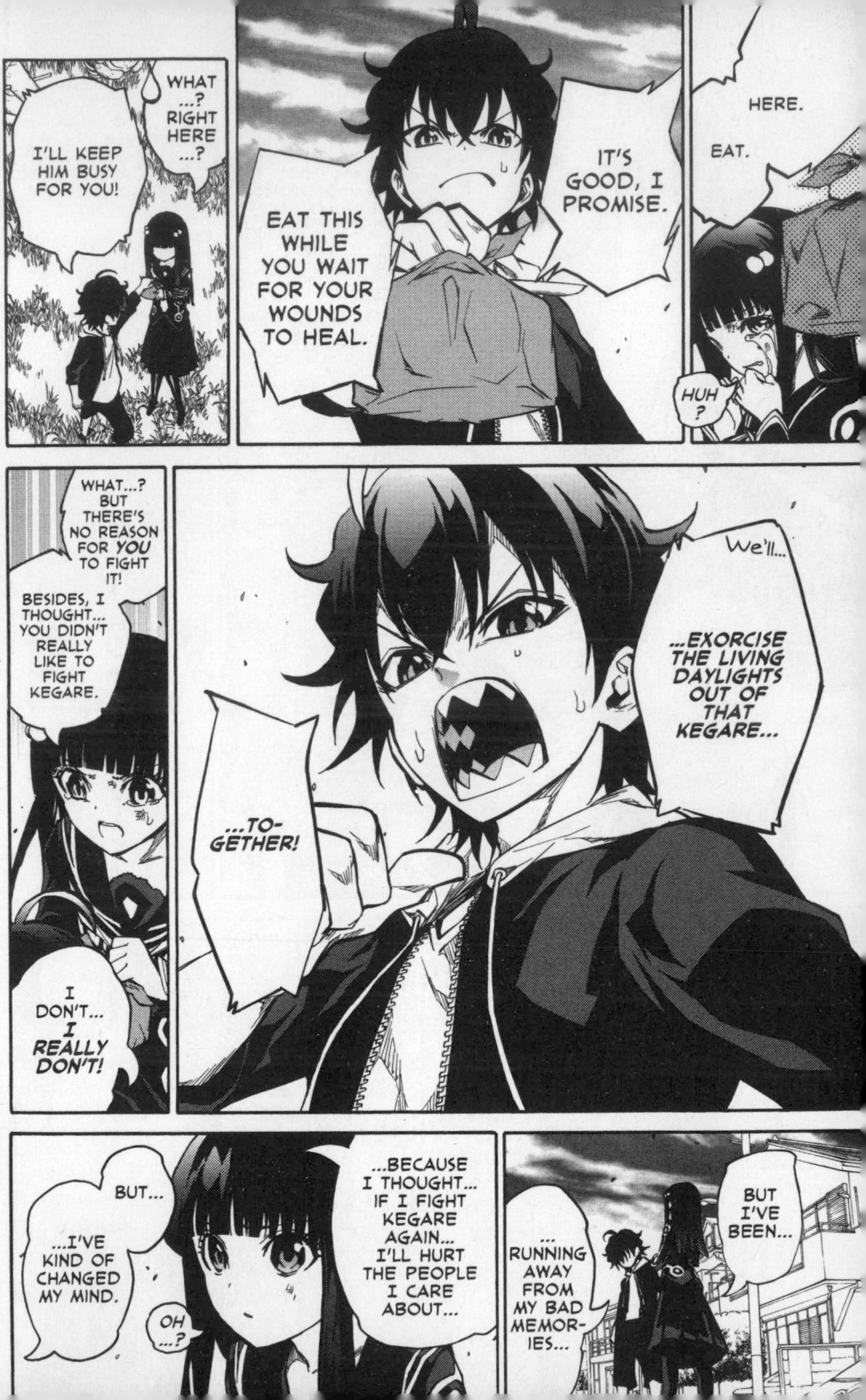
HERE.
EAT.
HUH?
IT'S GOOD, I PROMISE.
EAT THIS WHILE YOU WAIT FOR YOUR WOUNDS TO HEAL.
WHAT...? RIGHT HERE...?
I'LL KEEP HIM BUSY FOR YOU!
We'll...
...EXORCISE THE LIVING DAYLIGHTS OUT OF THAT KEGARE...
...TOGETHER!
WHAT...? BUT THERE'S NO REASON FOR YOU TO FIGHT IT!
BESIDES, I THOUGHT... YOU DIDN'T REALLY LIKE TO FIGHT KEGARE.
I DON'T... I REALLY DON'T!
BUT I'VE BEEN...
...RUNNING AWAY FROM MY BAD MEMORIES...
...BECAUSE I THOUGHT... IF I FIGHT KEGARE AGAIN... I'LL HURT THE PEOPLE I CARE ABOUT...
BUT...
...I'VE KIND OF CHANGED MY MIND.
OH...?

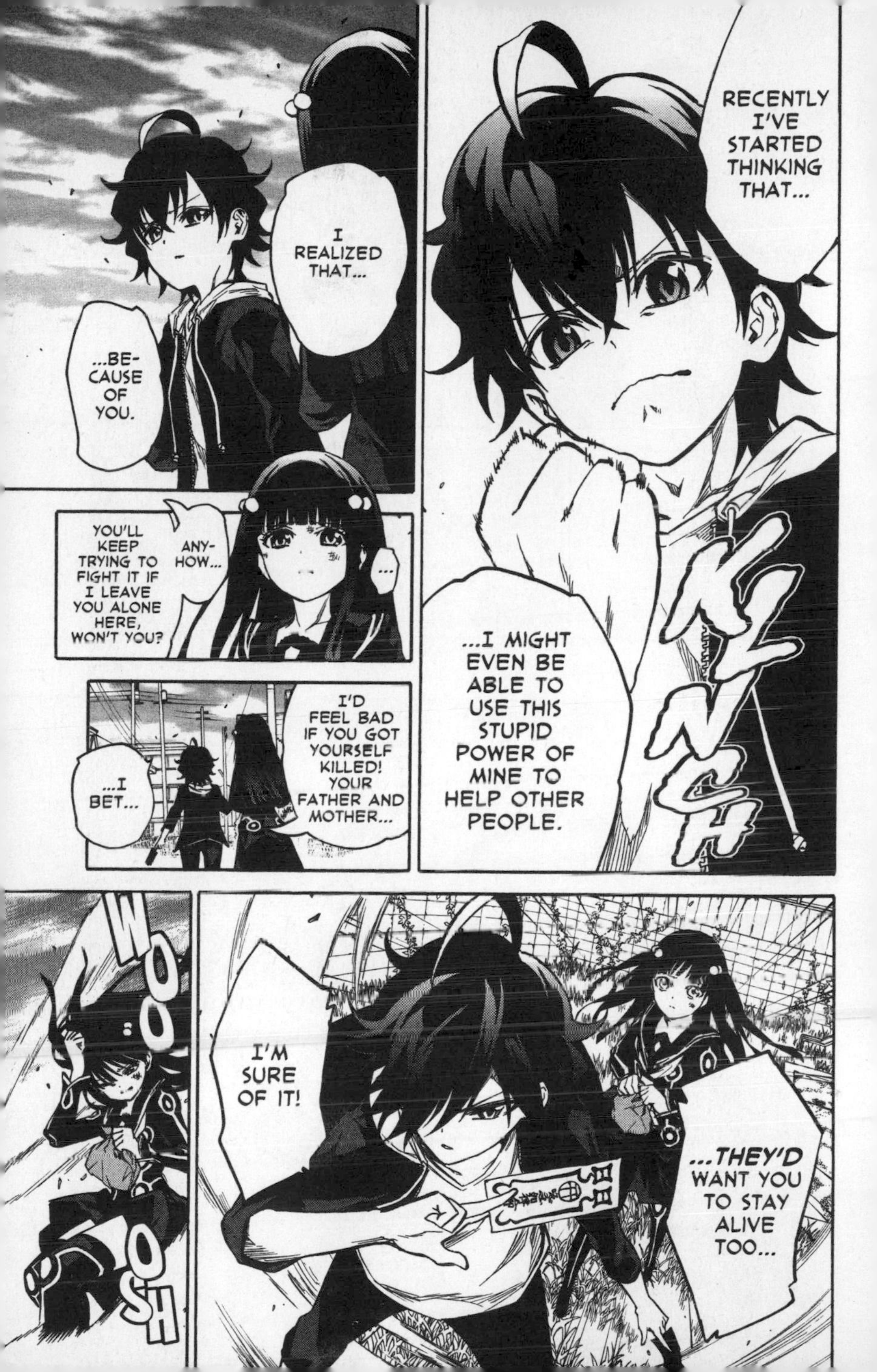
RECENTLY I'VE STARTED THINKING THAT...
...I MIGHT EVEN BE ABLE TO USE THIS STUPID POWER OF MINE TO HELP OTHER PEOPLE.
I REALIZED THAT...
...BE-CAUSE OF YOU.
...
ANY-HOW...
YOU'LL KEEP TRYING TO FIGHT IT IF I LEAVE YOU ALONE HERE, WON'T YOU?
I'D FEEL BAD IF YOU GOT YOURSELF KILLED! YOUR FATHER AND MOTHER...
...I BET...
...THEY'D WANT YOU TO STAY ALIVE TOO...
I'M SURE OF IT!
WHOOSH

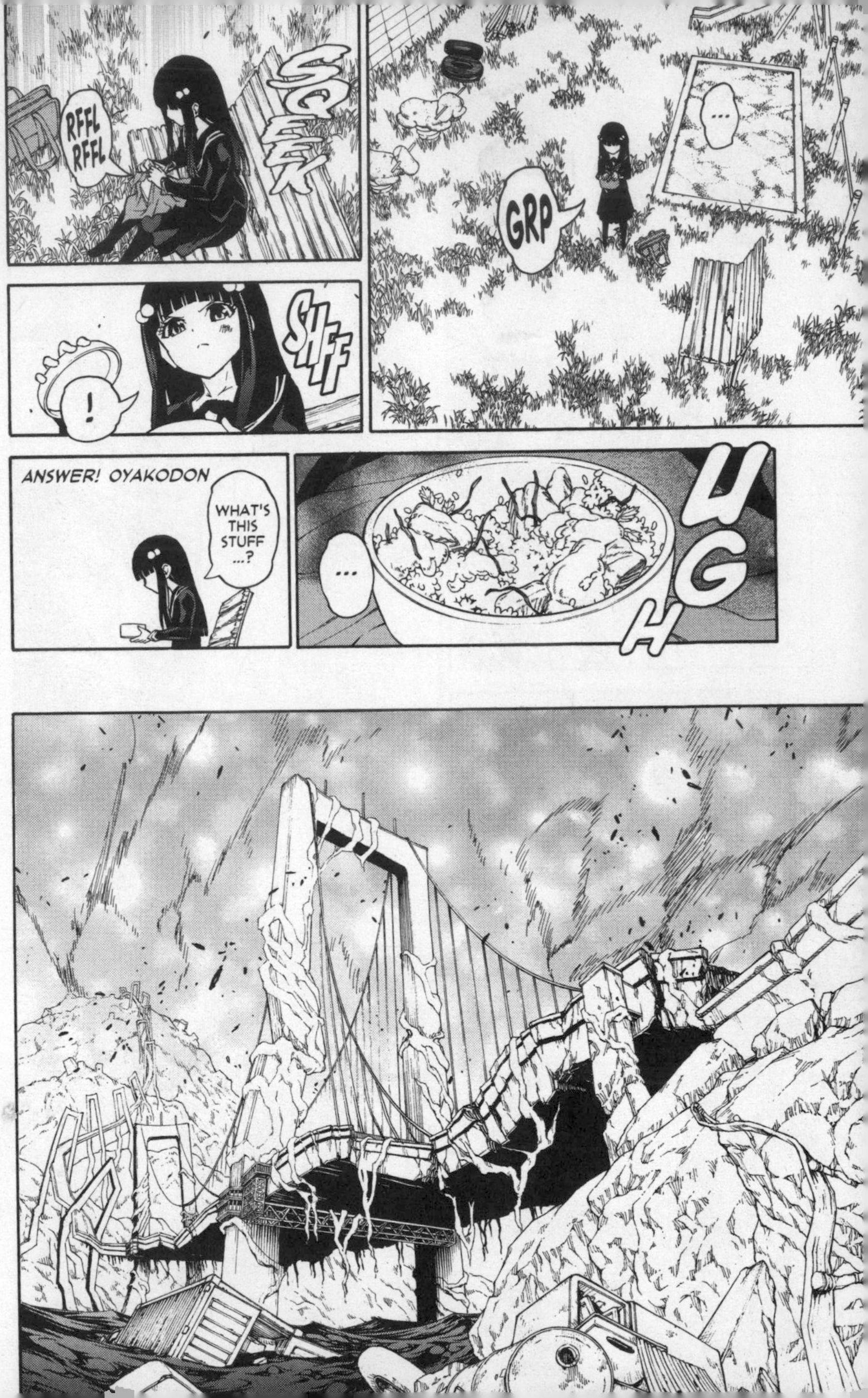
...
GRP
SQEEK
RFFL RFFL
SHFF
!
UGH
...
ANSWER! OYAKODON
WHAT'S THIS STUFF ...?

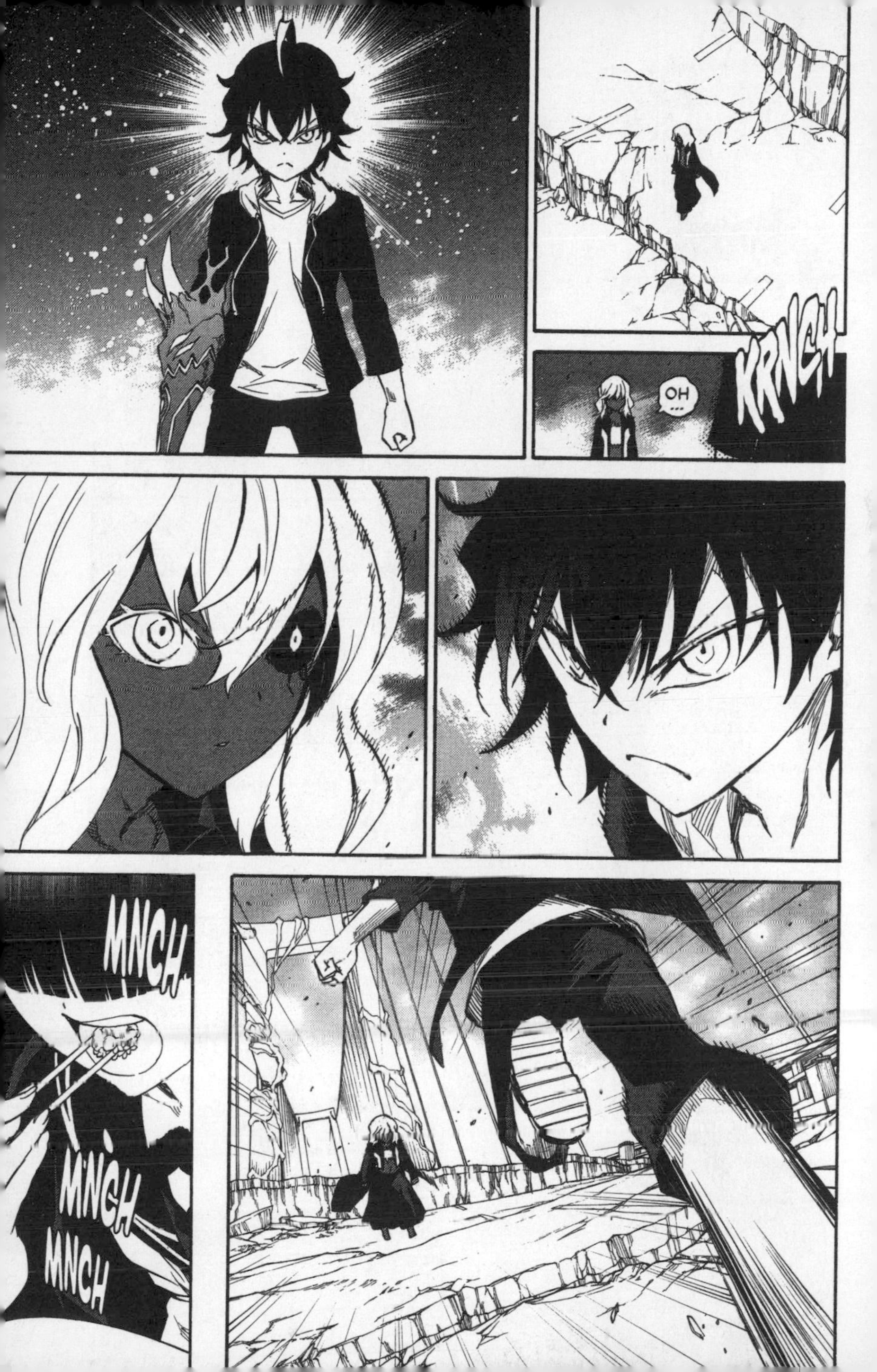
KRNCH
OH...
MNCH
MNCH
MNCH

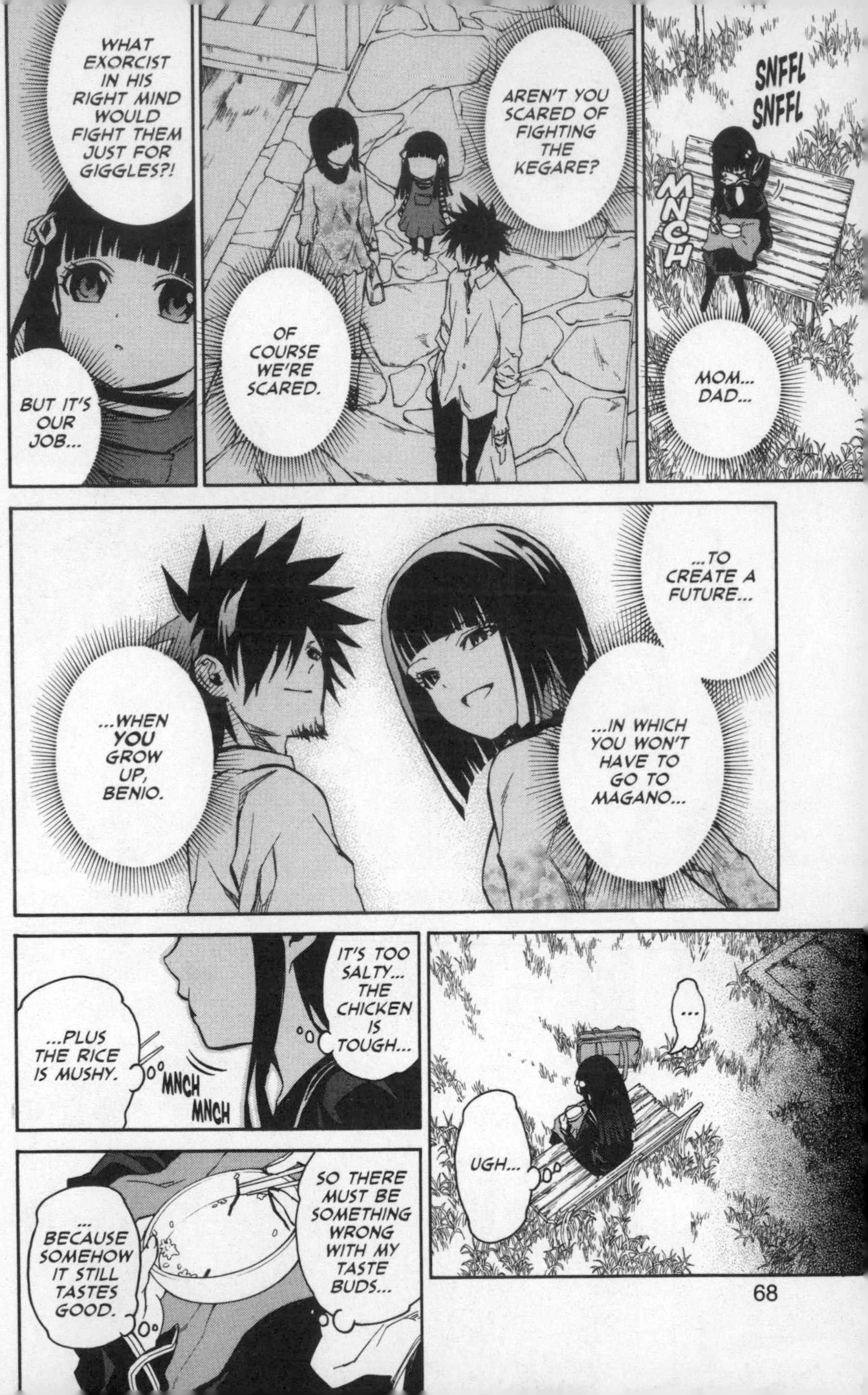
SNFFL SNFFL
MNCH
MOM... DAD...
AREN'T YOU SCARED OF FIGHTING THE KEGARE?
OF COURSE WE'RE SCARED.
WHAT EXORCIST IN HIS RIGHT MIND WOULD FIGHT THEM JUST FOR GIGGLES?!
BUT IT'S OUR JOB...
...TO CREATE A FUTURE...
...IN WHICH YOU WON'T HAVE TO GO TO MAGANO...
...WHEN YOU GROW UP, BENIO.
...
UGH...
IT'S TOO SALTY... THE CHICKEN IS TOUGH...
...PLUS THE RICE IS MUSHY.
MNCH MNCH
SO THERE MUST BE SOMETHING WRONG WITH MY TASTE BUDS...
... BECAUSE SOMEHOW IT STILL TASTES GOOD.

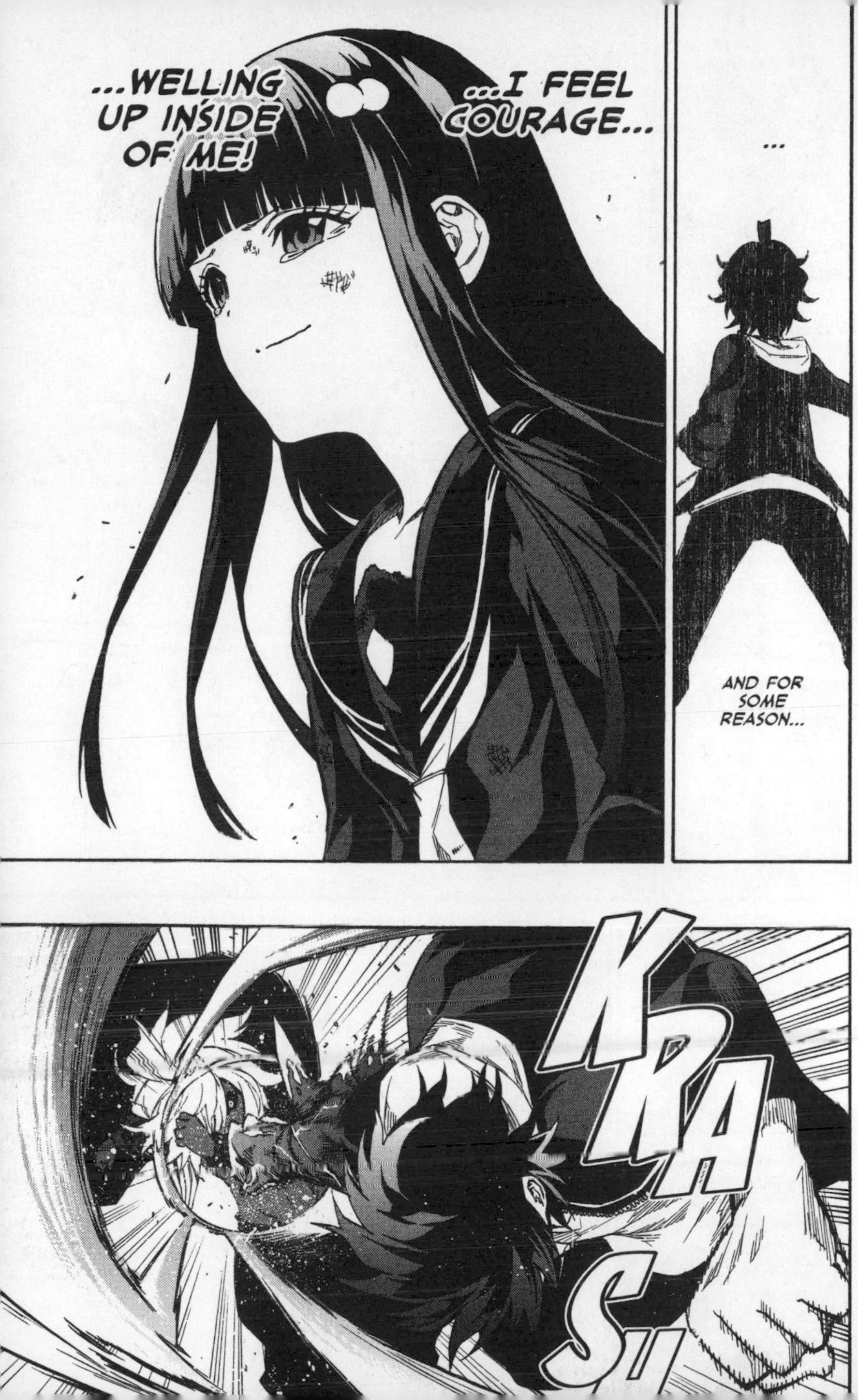
...
AND FOR SOME REASON...
...I FEEL COURAGE...
...WELLING UP INSIDE OF ME!
KRASH

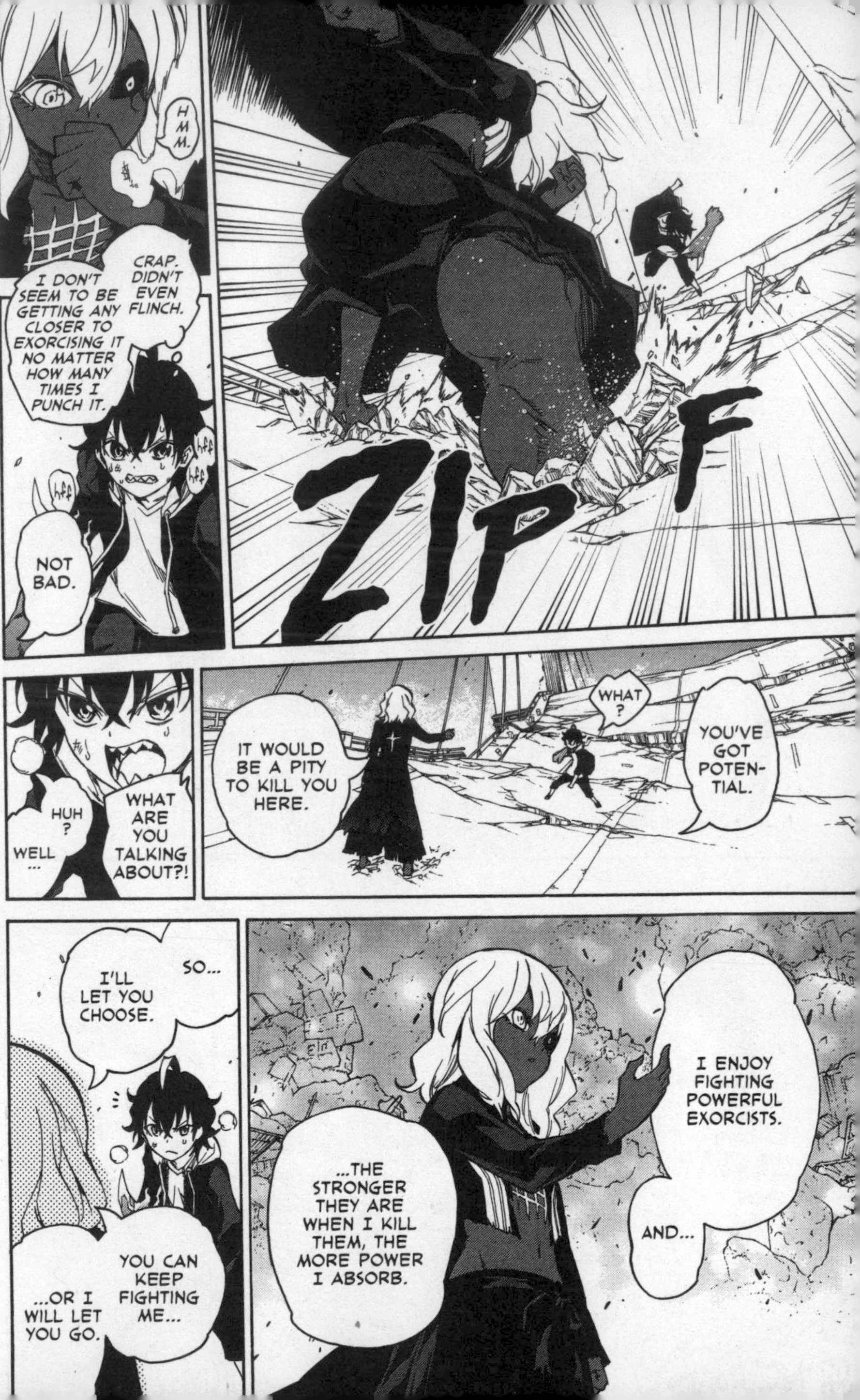
ZIP
F
HMM.
CRAP. DIDN'T EVEN FLINCH.
I DON'T SEEM TO BE GETTING ANY CLOSER TO EXORCISING IT NO MATTER HOW MANY TIMES I PUNCH IT.
hff
hff
hff
NOT BAD.
WHAT?
YOU'VE GOT POTEN-TIAL.
IT WOULD BE A PITY TO KILL YOU HERE.
WHAT ARE YOU TALKING ABOUT?!
HUH? WELL...
I ENJOY FIGHTING POWERFUL EXORCISTS.
AND...
...THE STRONGER THEY ARE WHEN I KILL THEM, THE MORE POWER I ABSORB.
SO...
I'LL LET YOU CHOOSE.
YOU CAN KEEP FIGHTING ME...
...OR I WILL LET YOU GO.

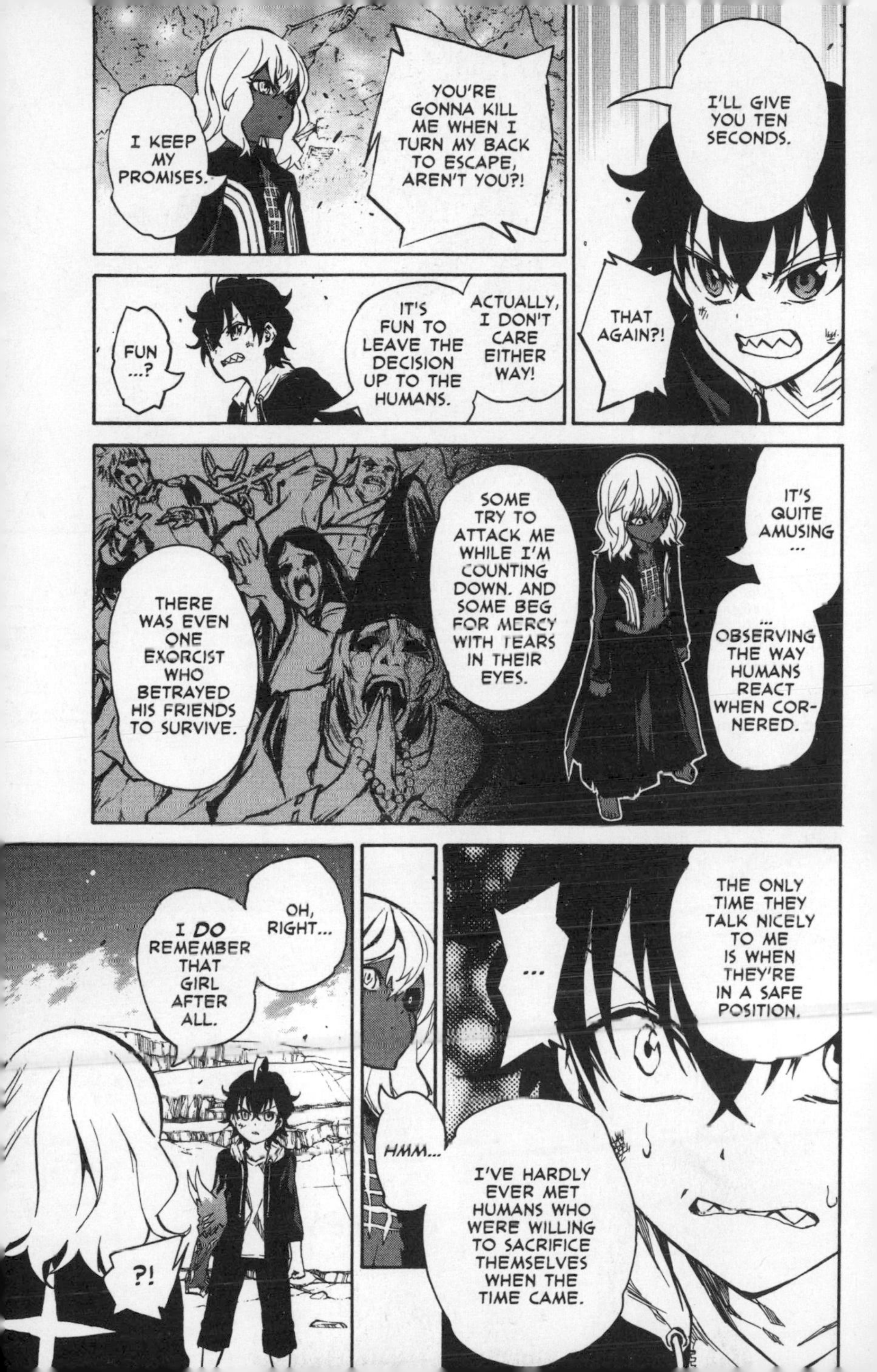
I'LL GIVE YOU TEN SECONDS.
THAT AGAIN?!
YOU'RE GONNA KILL ME WHEN I TURN MY BACK TO ESCAPE, AREN'T YOU?!
I KEEP MY PROMISES.
ACTUALLY, I DON'T CARE EITHER WAY!
IT'S FUN TO LEAVE THE DECISION UP TO THE HUMANS.
FUN ...?
IT'S QUITE AMUSING ...
... OBSERVING THE WAY HUMANS REACT WHEN CORNERED.
SOME TRY TO ATTACK ME WHILE I'M COUNTING DOWN. AND SOME BEG FOR MERCY WITH TEARS IN THEIR EYES.
THERE WAS EVEN ONE EXORCIST WHO BETRAYED HIS FRIENDS TO SURVIVE.
THE ONLY TIME THEY TALK NICELY TO ME IS WHEN THEY'RE IN A SAFE POSITION.
...
I'VE HARDLY EVER MET HUMANS WHO WERE WILLING TO SACRIFICE THEMSELVES WHEN THE TIME CAME.
HMM...
OH, RIGHT...
I *DO* REMEMBER THAT GIRL AFTER ALL.
?!

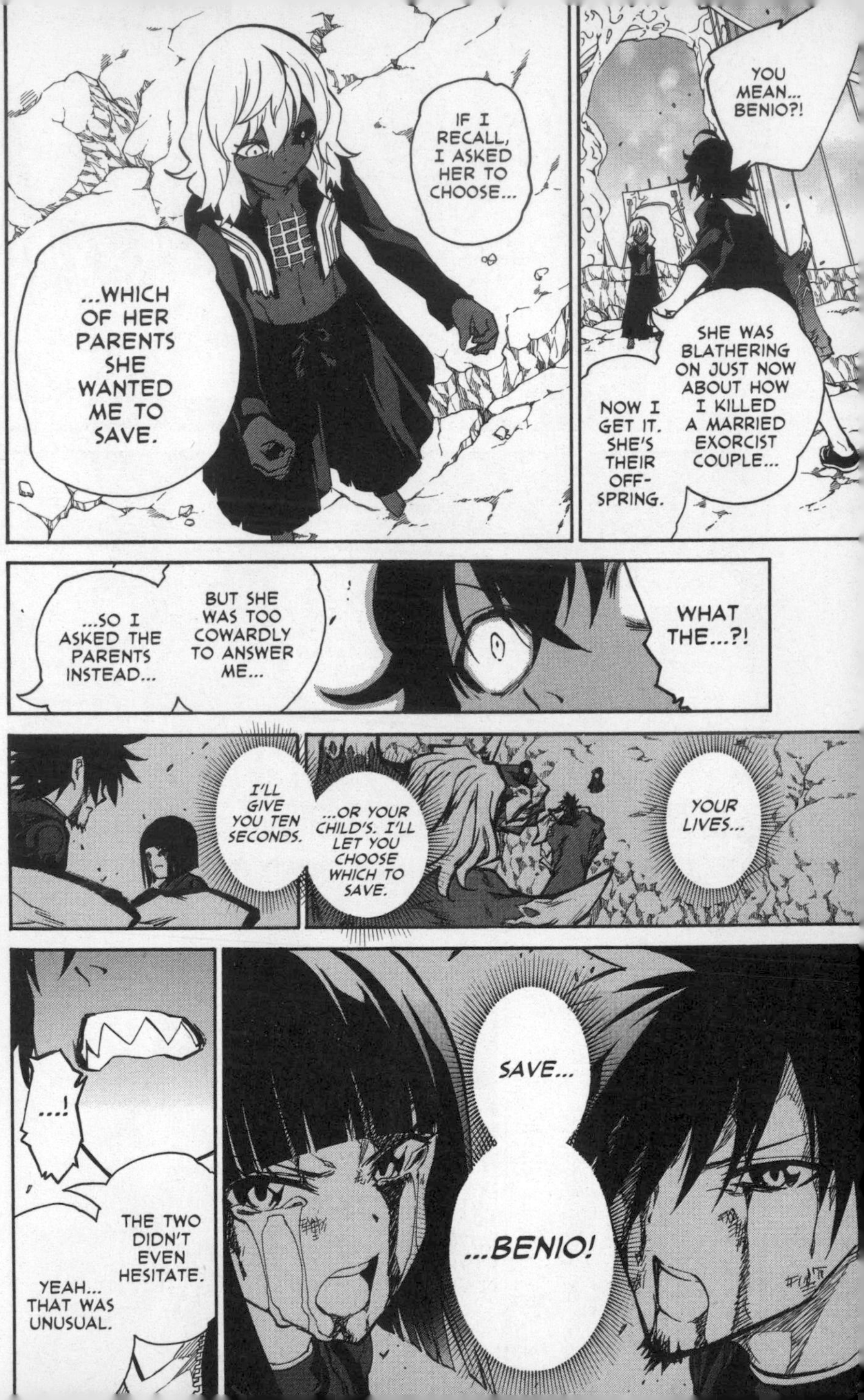
YOU MEAN... BENIO?!
SHE WAS BLATHERING ON JUST NOW ABOUT HOW I KILLED A MARRIED EXORCIST COUPLE...
NOW I GET IT. SHE'S THEIR OFF-SPRING.
IF I RECALL, I ASKED HER TO CHOOSE...
...WHICH OF HER PARENTS SHE WANTED ME TO SAVE.
WHAT THE...?!
BUT SHE WAS TOO COWARDLY TO ANSWER ME...
...SO I ASKED THE PARENTS INSTEAD...
YOUR LIVES...
...OR YOUR CHILD'S. I'LL LET YOU CHOOSE WHICH TO SAVE.
I'LL GIVE YOU TEN SECONDS.
SAVE...
...BENIO!
...!
THE TWO DIDN'T EVEN HESITATE.
YEAH... THAT WAS UNUSUAL.

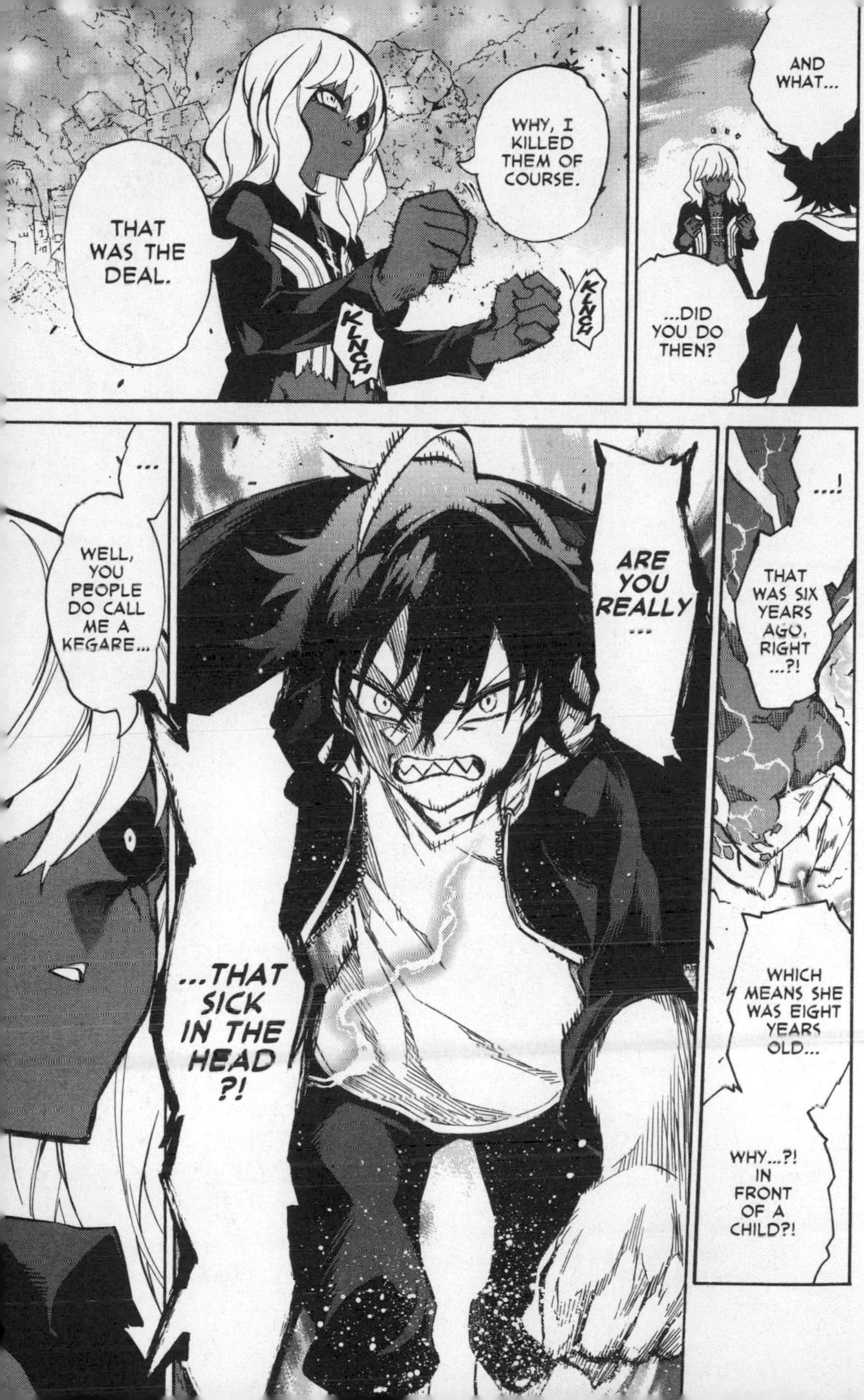
AND WHAT...
...DID YOU DO THEN?
WHY, I KILLED THEM OF COURSE.
KLNCH
KLNCH
THAT WAS THE DEAL.
...!
THAT WAS SIX YEARS AGO, RIGHT...?!
WHICH MEANS SHE WAS EIGHT YEARS OLD...
WHY...?! IN FRONT OF A CHILD?!
ARE YOU REALLY...
...THAT SICK IN THE HEAD?!
...
WELL, YOU PEOPLE DO CALL ME A KEGARE...

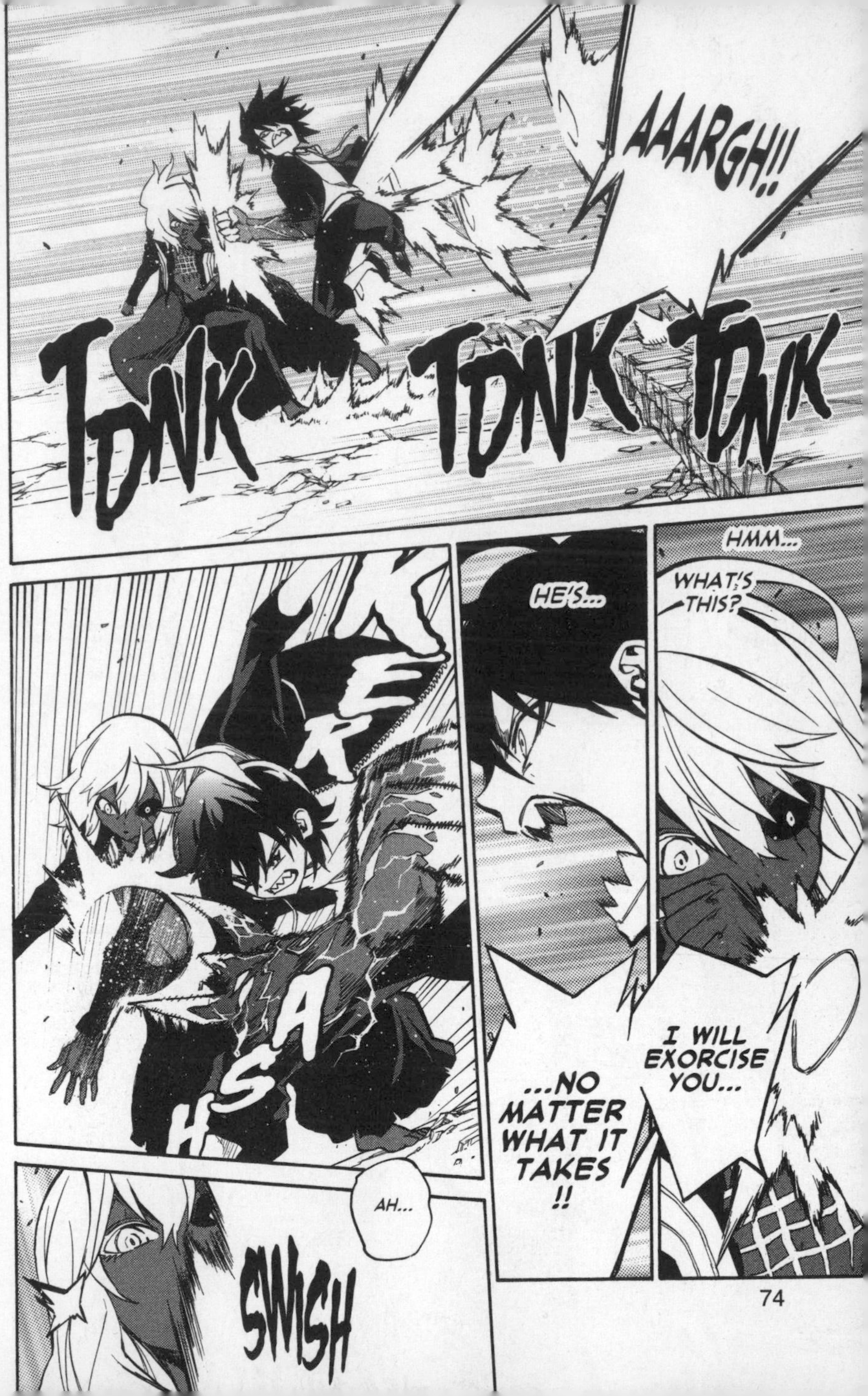
AAARGH!!
TONK
TONK
TONK
HMM...
WHAT'S THIS?
HE'S...
I WILL EXORCISE YOU...
...NO MATTER WHAT IT TAKES!!
AH...
SWISH

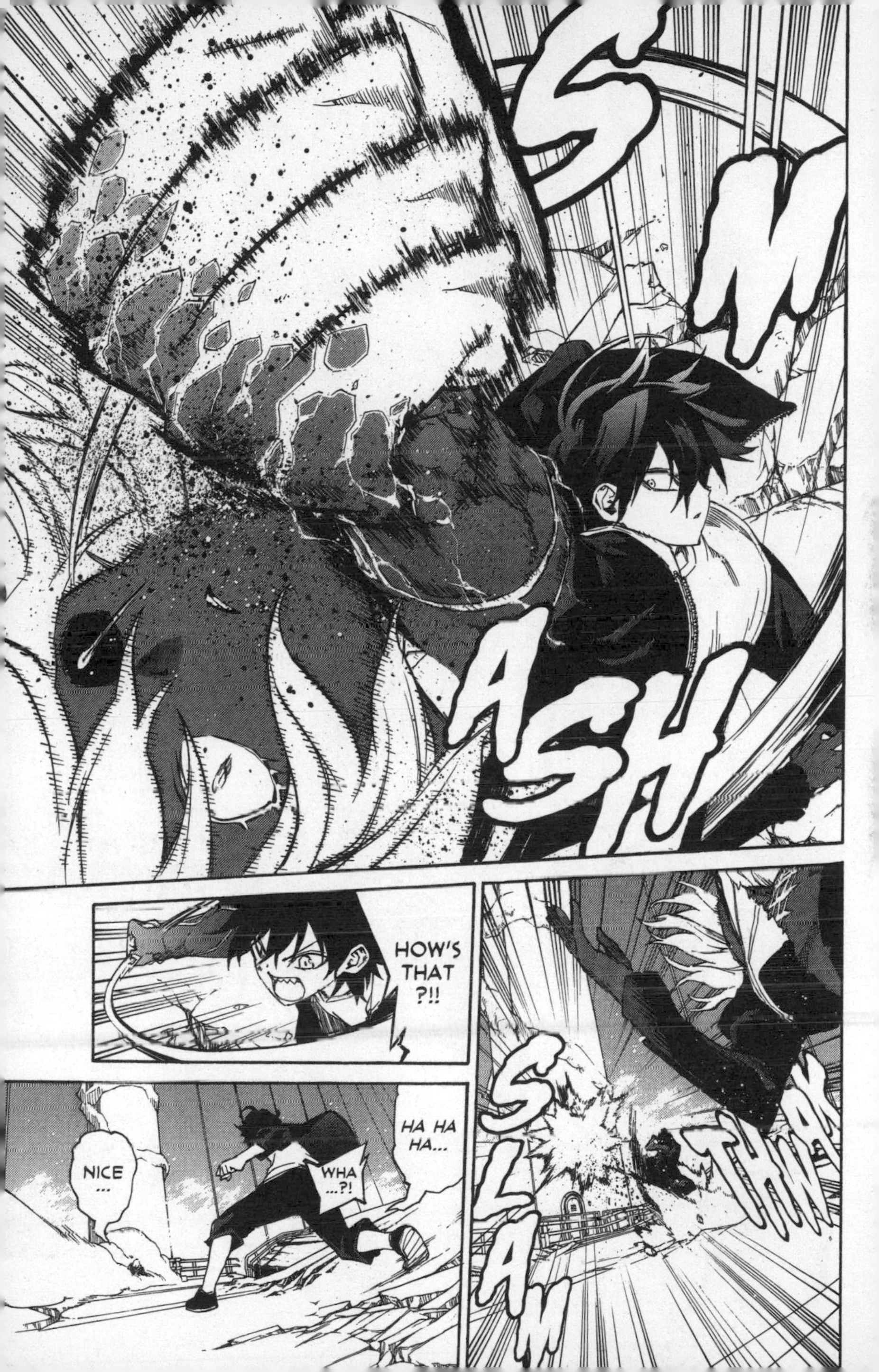
SMASH
SLAM
THWA
HOW'S THAT ?!!
HA HA HA...
WHA ...?!
NICE ...

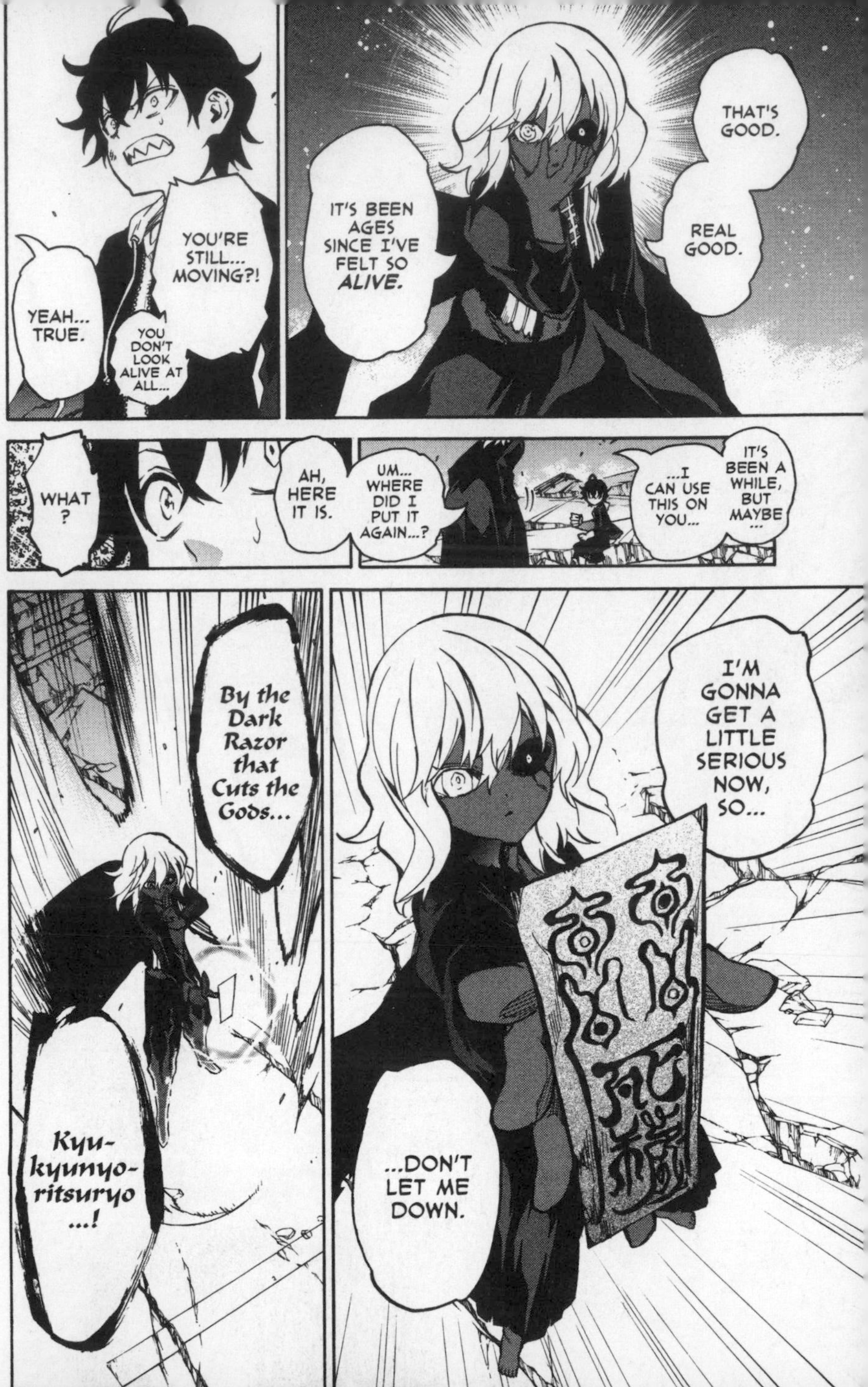
THAT'S GOOD.
REAL GOOD.
IT'S BEEN AGES SINCE I'VE FELT SO *ALIVE.*
YOU'RE STILL... MOVING?!
YOU DON'T LOOK ALIVE AT ALL...
YEAH... TRUE.
IT'S BEEN A WHILE, BUT MAYBE...
...I CAN USE THIS ON YOU...
UM... WHERE DID I PUT IT AGAIN...?
AH, HERE IT IS.
WHAT?
I'M GONNA GET A LITTLE SERIOUS NOW, SO...
...DON'T LET ME DOWN.
By the Dark Razor that Cuts the Gods...
Kyu-kyunyo-ritsuryo...!

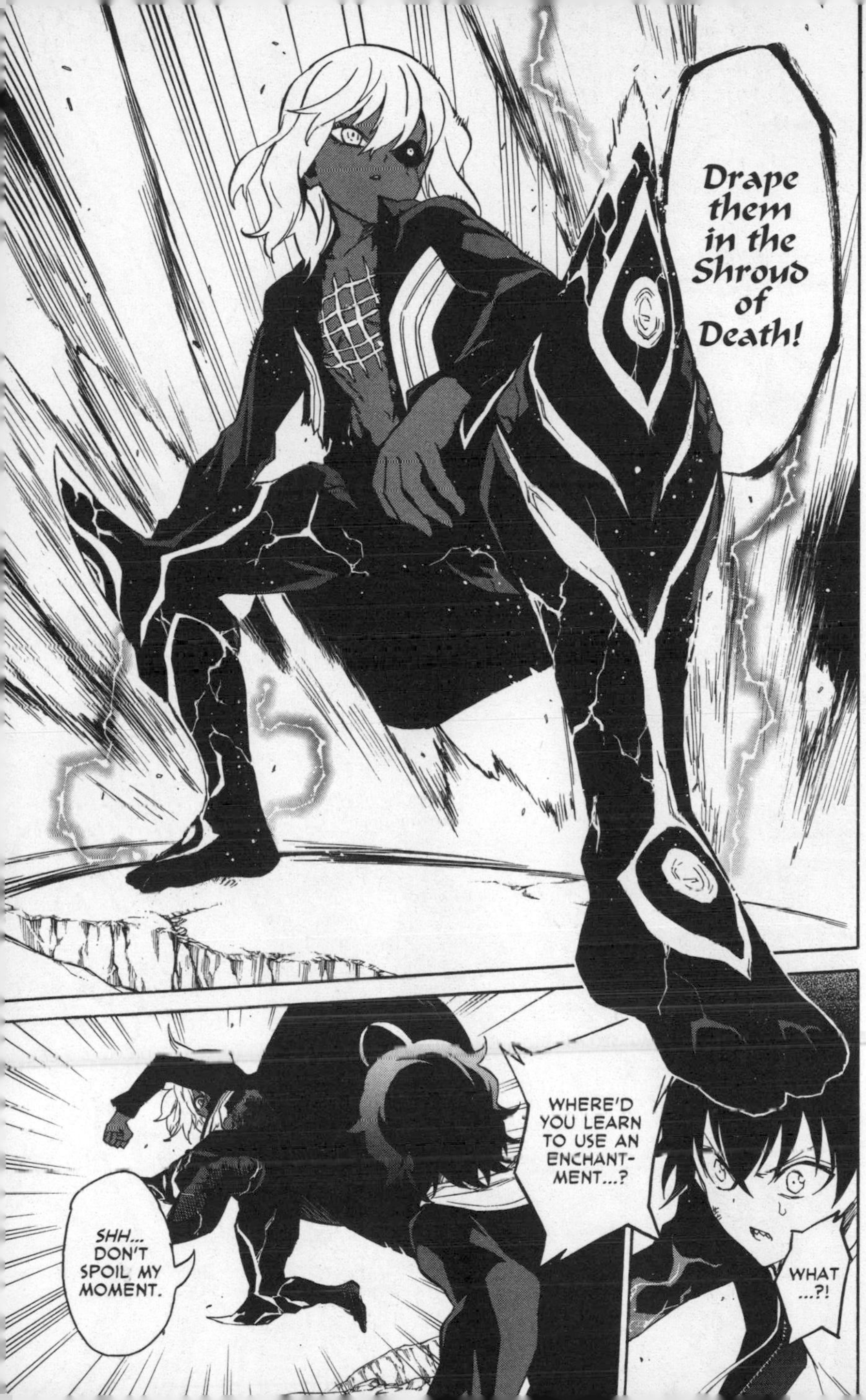
Drape them in the Shroud of Death!
WHAT ...?!
WHERE'D YOU LEARN TO USE AN ENCHANT-MENT...?
SHH... DON'T SPOIL MY MOMENT.

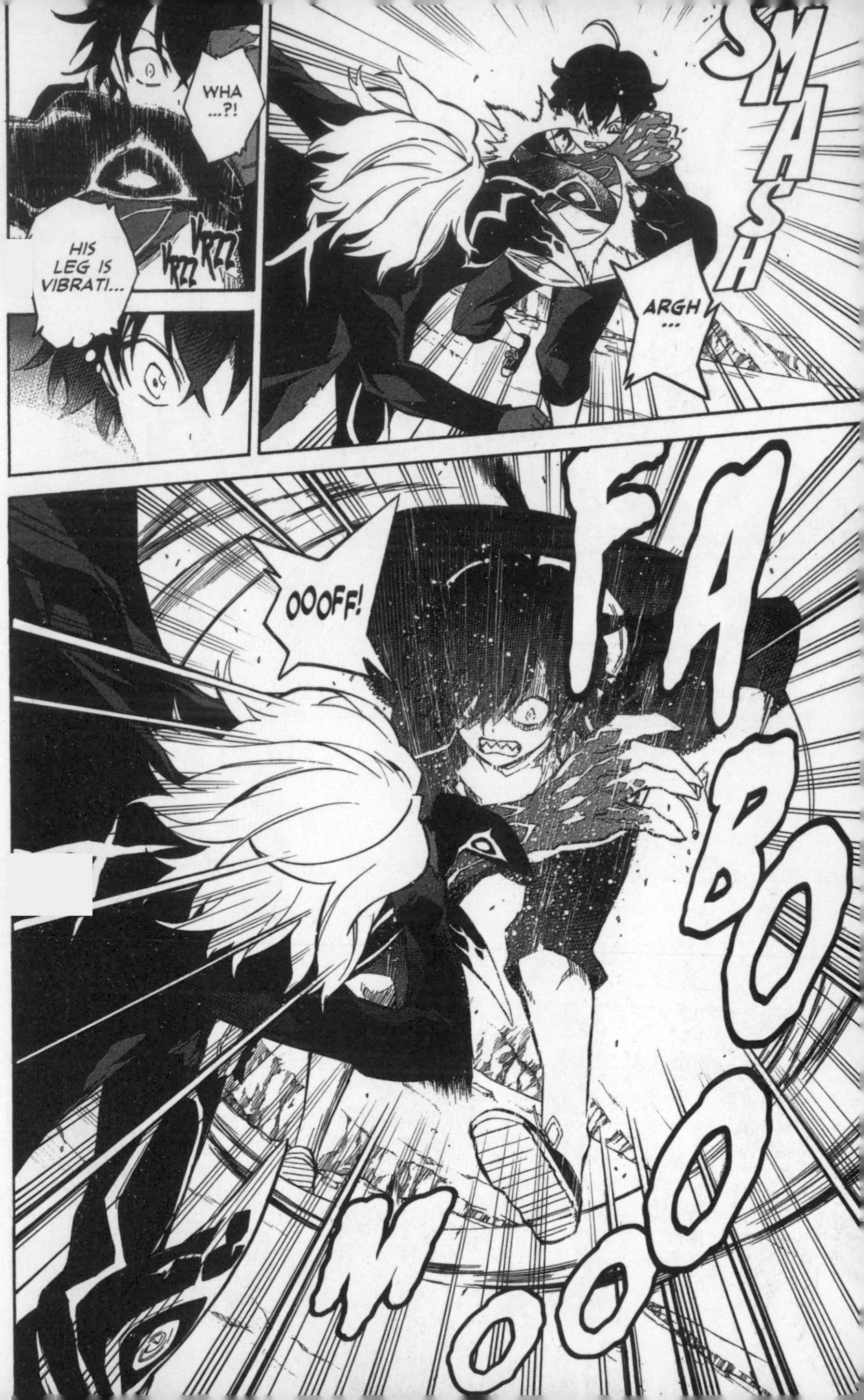
SMASH
ARGH...
WHA...?!
VRZZ VRZZ
HIS LEG IS VIBRATI...
FABOOOOM
OOOFF!

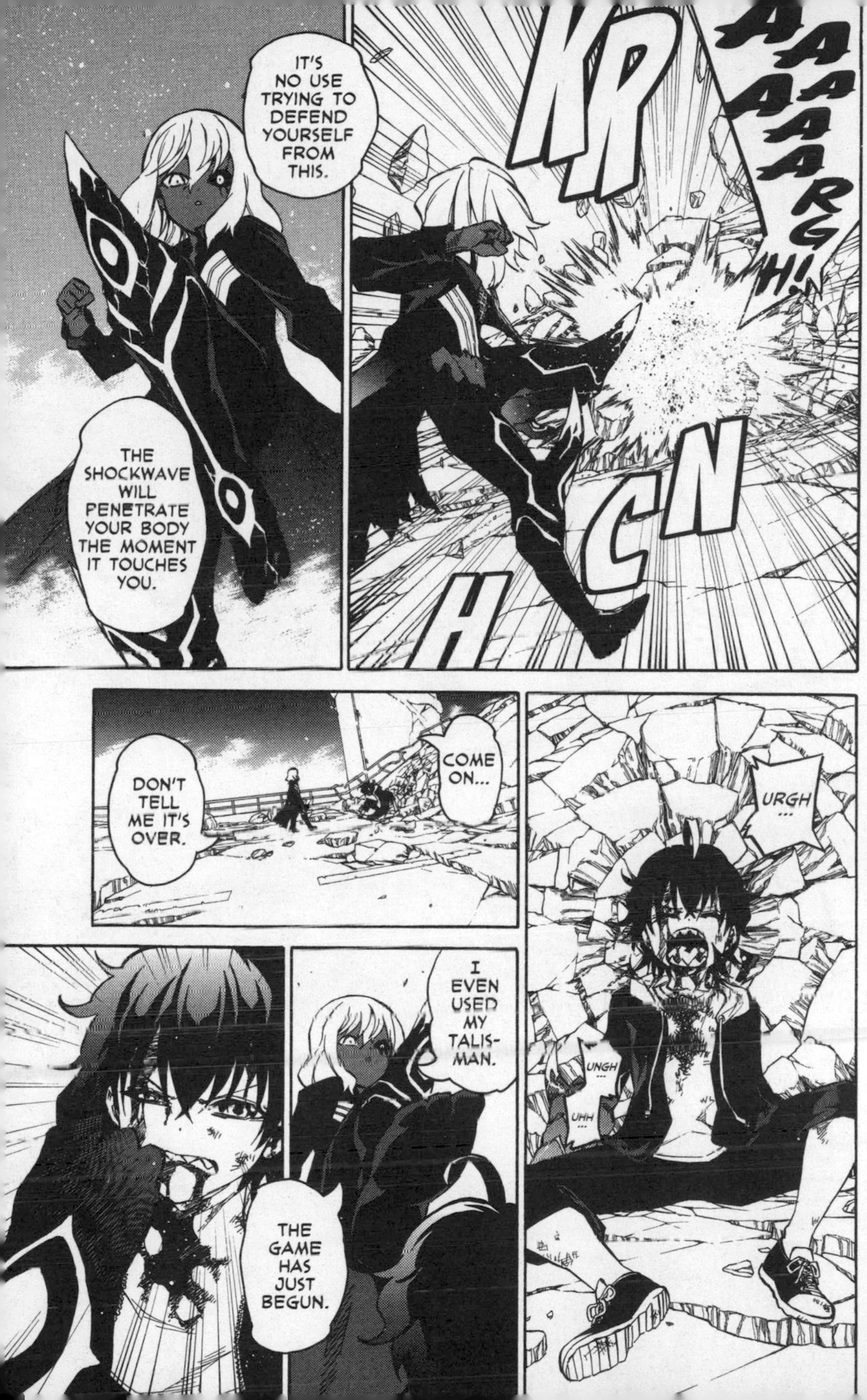

AAAAAARGH!
KR
CN
CH
IT'S NO USE TRYING TO DEFEND YOURSELF FROM THIS.
THE SHOCKWAVE WILL PENETRATE YOUR BODY THE MOMENT IT TOUCHES YOU.
URGH...
UNGH...
UHH...
COME ON...
DON'T TELL ME IT'S OVER.
I EVEN USED MY TALIS-MAN.
THE GAME HAS JUST BEGUN.

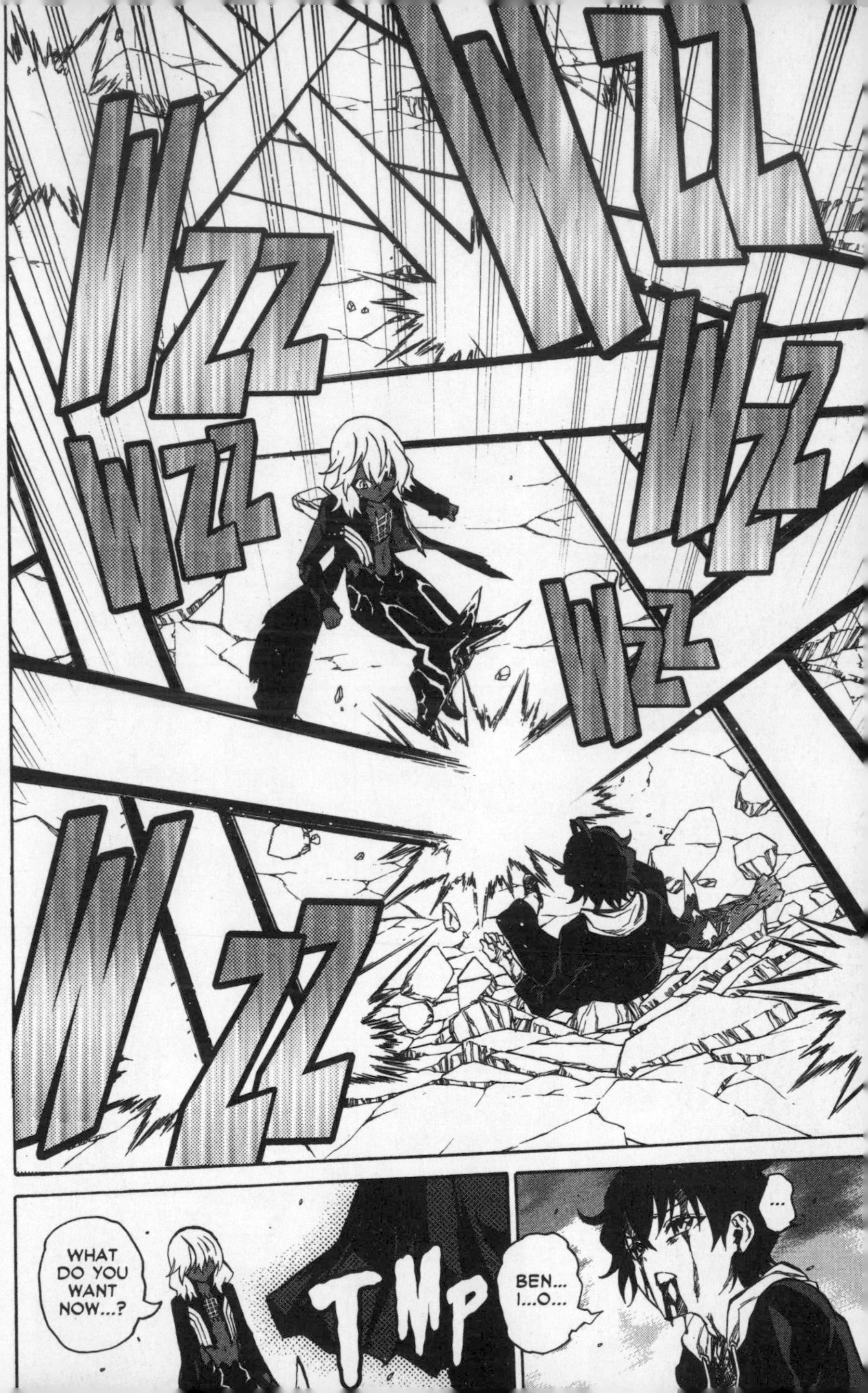
WZZ
WZZ
WZZ
WZZ
WZZ
WZZ
...
BEN... I...O...
TMP
WHAT DO YOU WANT NOW...?

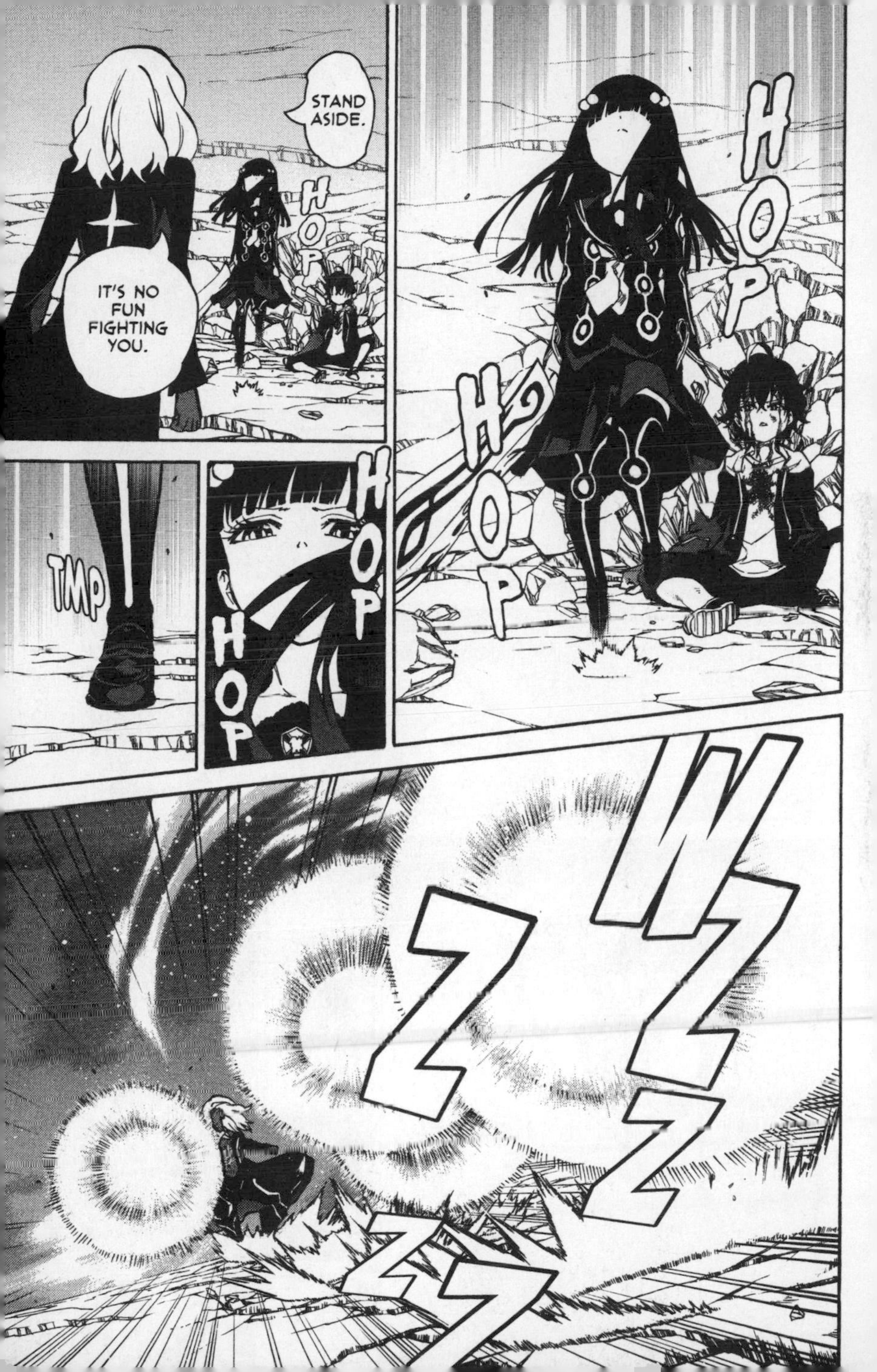
HOP
HOP
HOP
STAND ASIDE.
IT'S NO FUN FIGHTING YOU.
HOP
HOP
HOP
TMP
WZZZZ

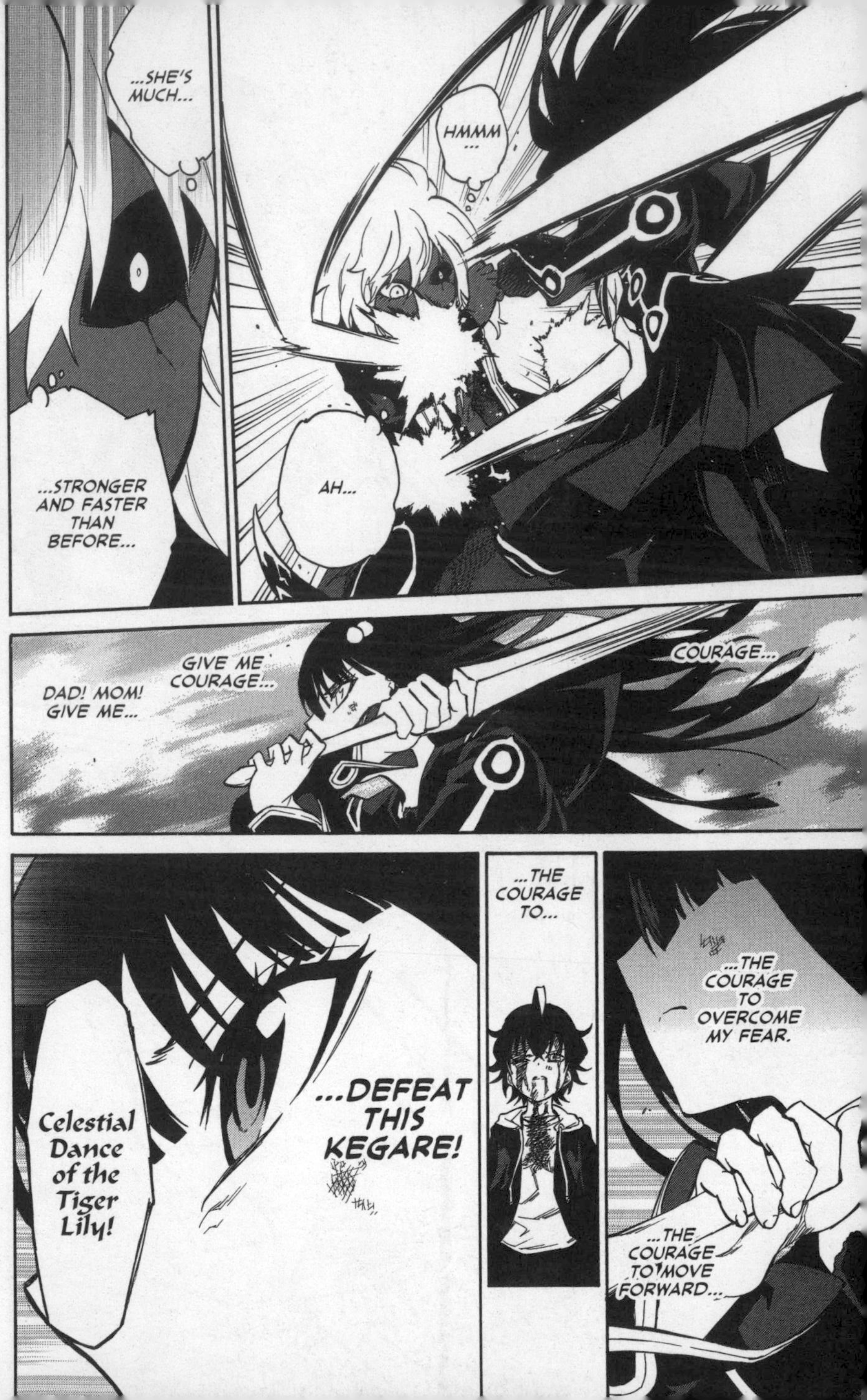
HMMM...
AH...
...SHE'S MUCH...
...STRONGER AND FASTER THAN BEFORE...
COURAGE...
GIVE ME COURAGE...
DAD! MOM! GIVE ME...
...THE COURAGE TO OVERCOME MY FEAR.
...THE COURAGE TO MOVE FORWARD...
...THE COURAGE TO...
...DEFEAT THIS KEGARE!
Celestial Dance of the Tiger Lily!

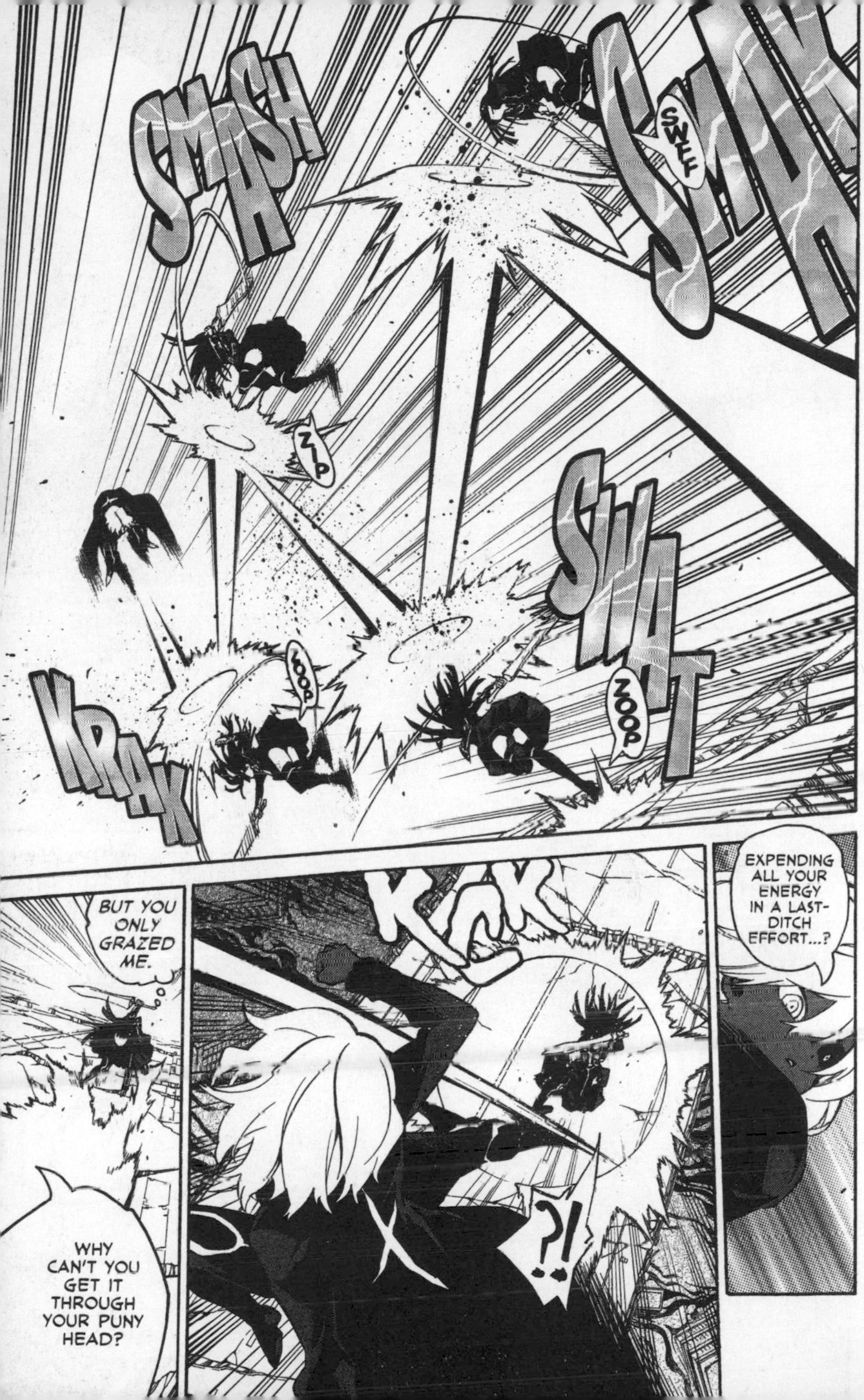
SWEFF
SMASH
ZIP
SHAT
ZOOP
ZOOP
KRAAK
EXPENDING ALL YOUR ENERGY IN A LAST-DITCH EFFORT...?
?!
BUT YOU ONLY GRAZED ME.
WHY CAN'T YOU GET IT THROUGH YOUR PUNY HEAD?

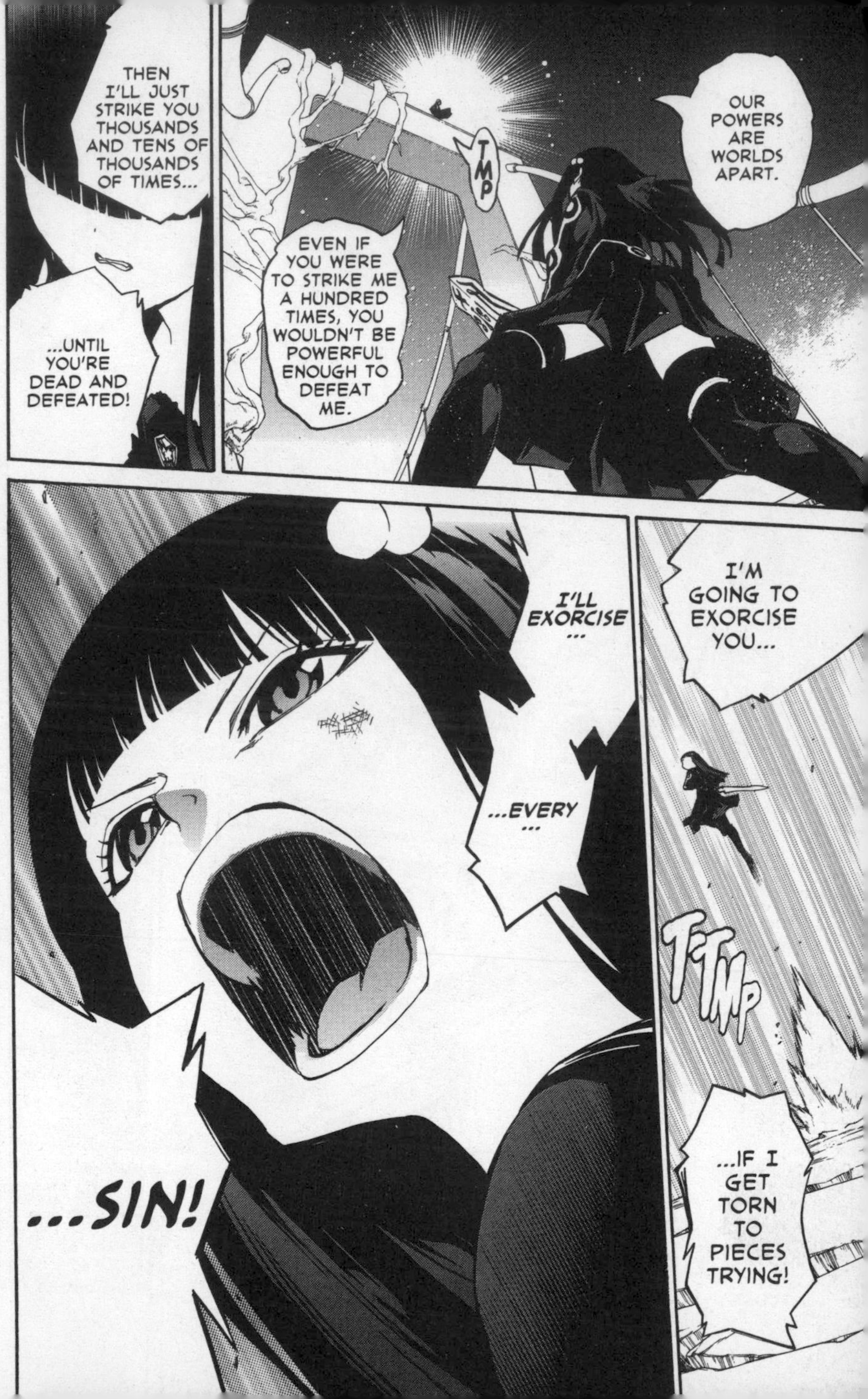
OUR POWERS ARE WORLDS APART.
TMP
EVEN IF YOU WERE TO STRIKE ME A HUNDRED TIMES, YOU WOULDN'T BE POWERFUL ENOUGH TO DEFEAT ME.
THEN I'LL JUST STRIKE YOU THOUSANDS AND TENS OF THOUSANDS OF TIMES...
...UNTIL YOU'RE DEAD AND DEFEATED!
I'M GOING TO EXORCISE YOU...
T-TMP
...IF I GET TORN TO PIECES TRYING!
I'LL EXORCISE...
...EVERY...
...SIN!

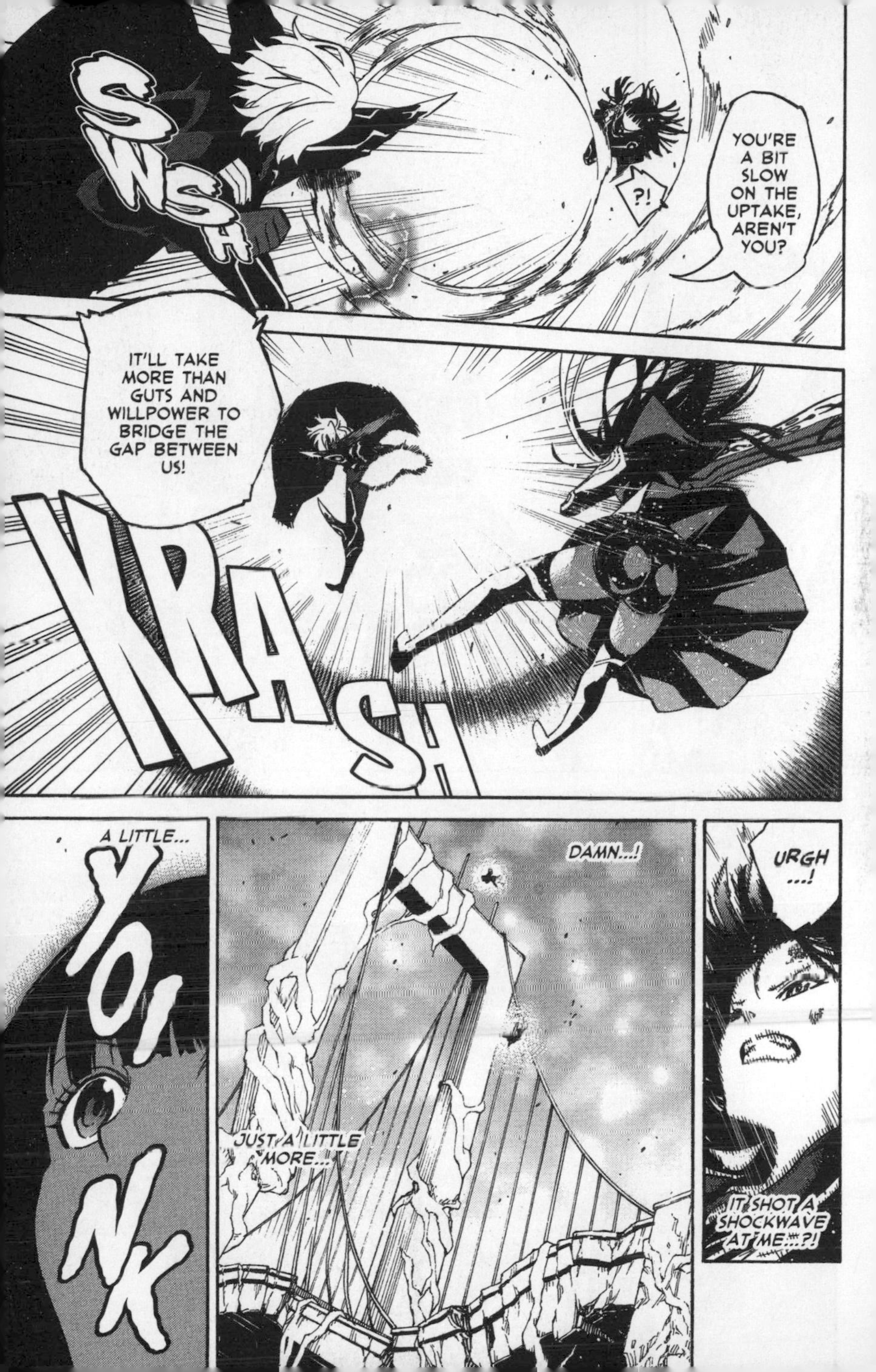
YOU'RE A BIT SLOW ON THE UPTAKE, AREN'T YOU?
?!
SWSH
IT'LL TAKE MORE THAN GUTS AND WILLPOWER TO BRIDGE THE GAP BETWEEN US!
KRASH
URGH...!
IT SHOT A SHOCKWAVE AT ME...?!
DAMN...!
JUST A LITTLE MORE...
A LITTLE...
YOINK

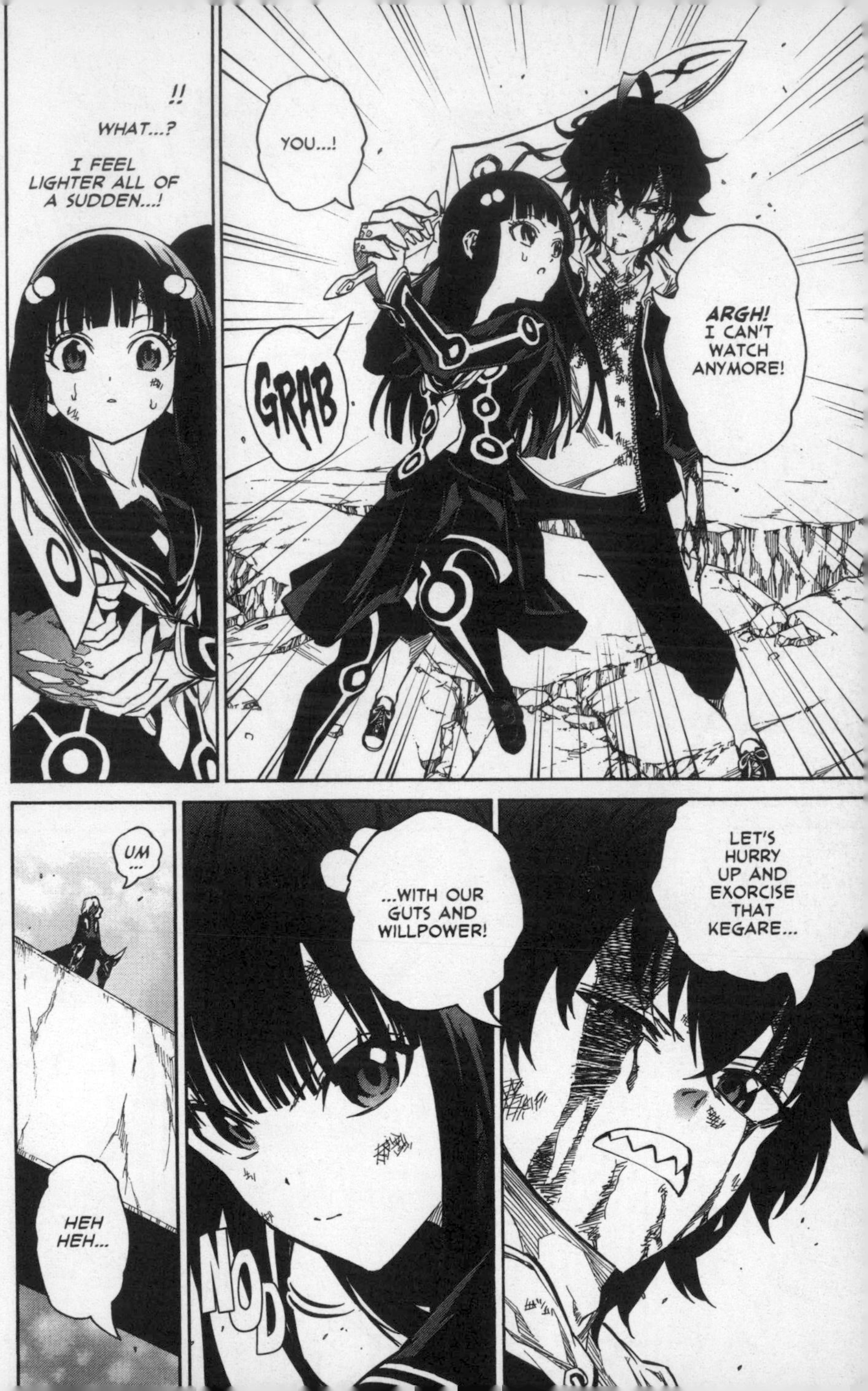
ARGH! I CAN'T WATCH ANYMORE!
GRAB
YOU...!
!!
WHAT...?
I FEEL LIGHTER ALL OF A SUDDEN...!
LET'S HURRY UP AND EXORCISE THAT KEGARE...
...WITH OUR GUTS AND WILLPOWER!
NOD
UM...
HEH HEH...

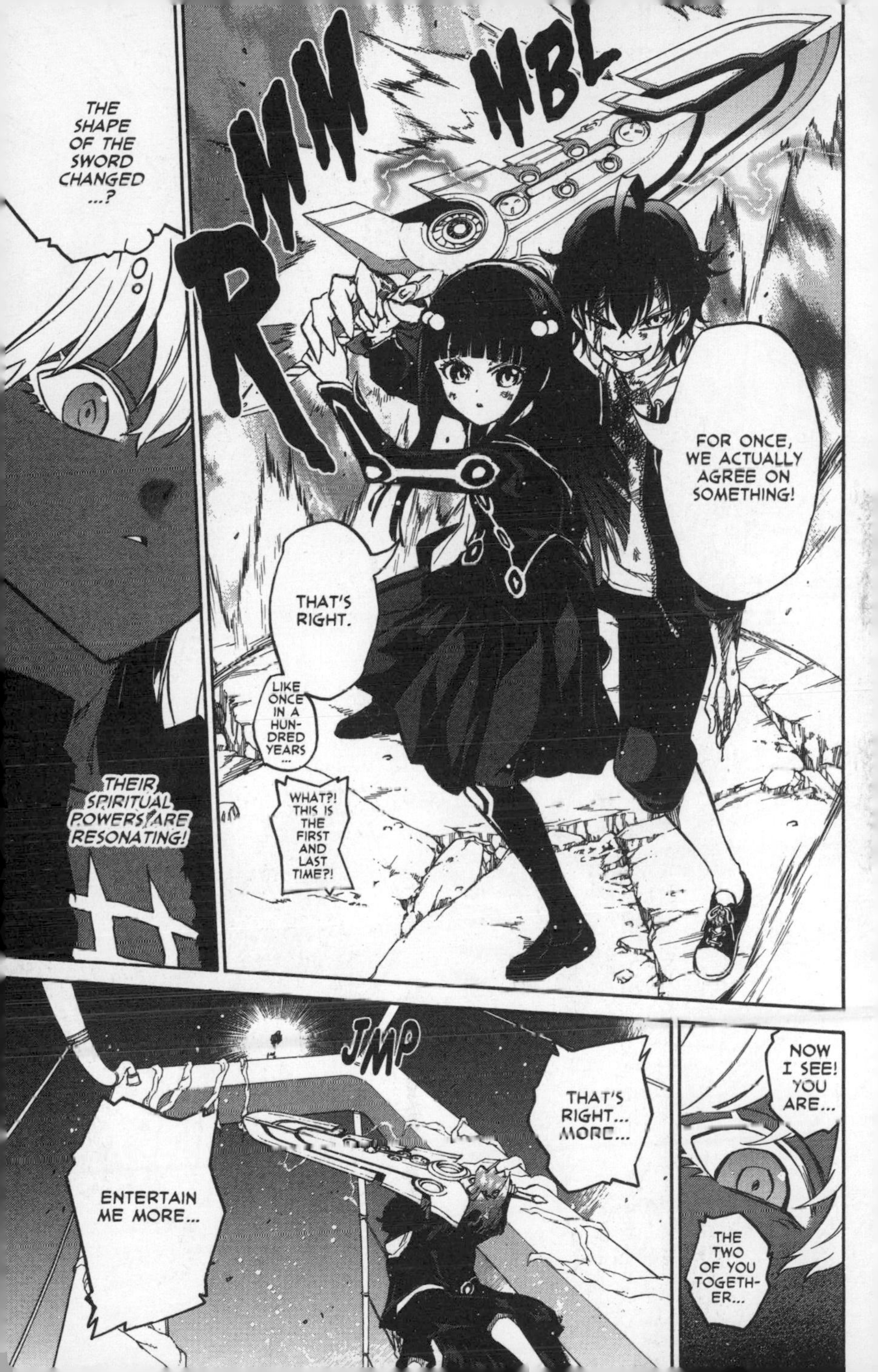
RMMMBL
FOR ONCE, WE ACTUALLY AGREE ON SOMETHING!
THAT'S RIGHT.
LIKE ONCE IN A HUNDRED YEARS...
WHAT?! THIS IS THE FIRST AND LAST TIME?!
THE SHAPE OF THE SWORD CHANGED...?
THEIR SPIRITUAL POWERS ARE RESONATING!
NOW I SEE! YOU ARE...
THE TWO OF YOU TOGETHER...
JMP
THAT'S RIGHT... MORE...
ENTERTAIN ME MORE...

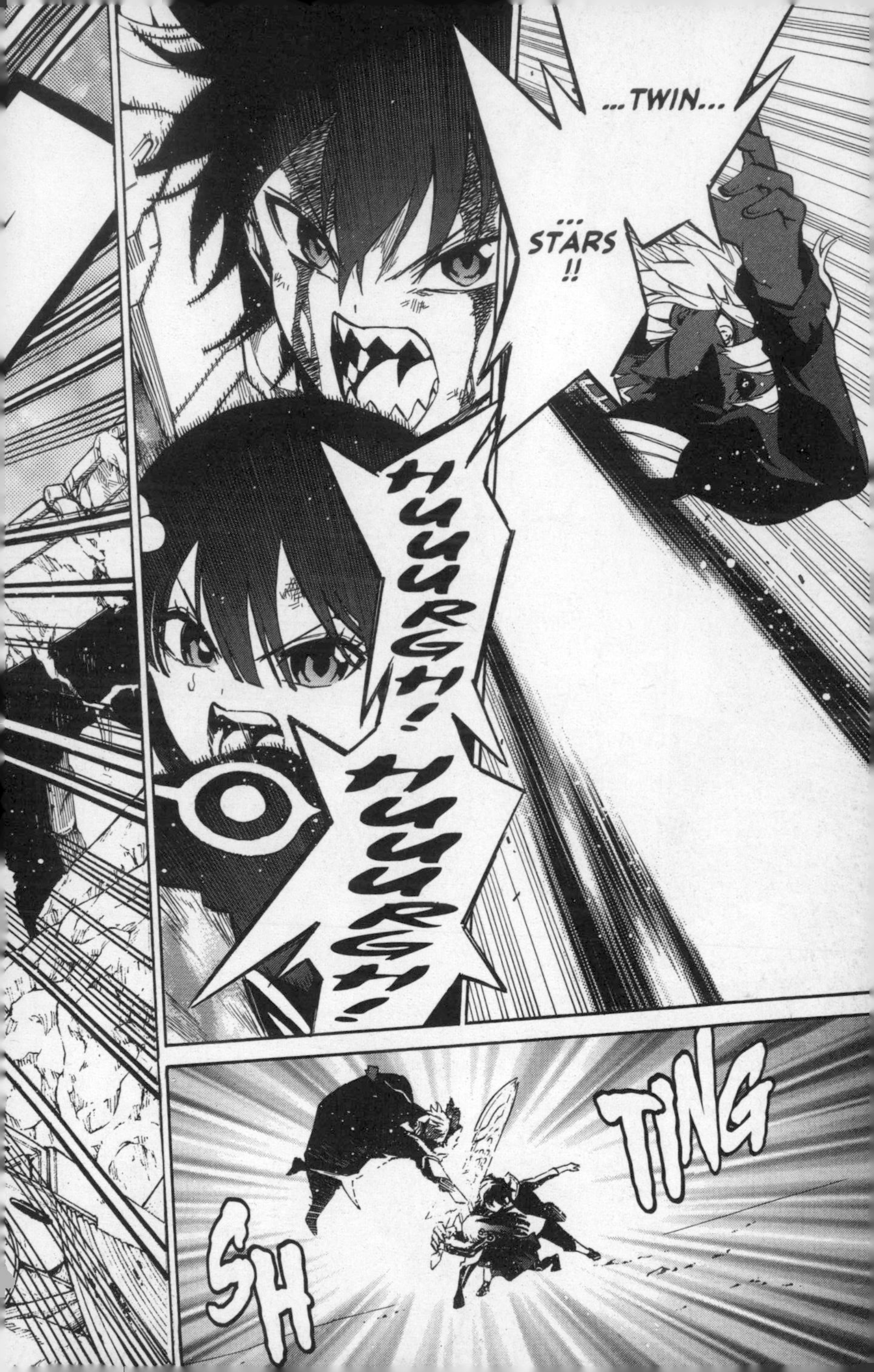
...TWIN...
... STARS !!
HUUURGH! HUUURGH!
TING
SH

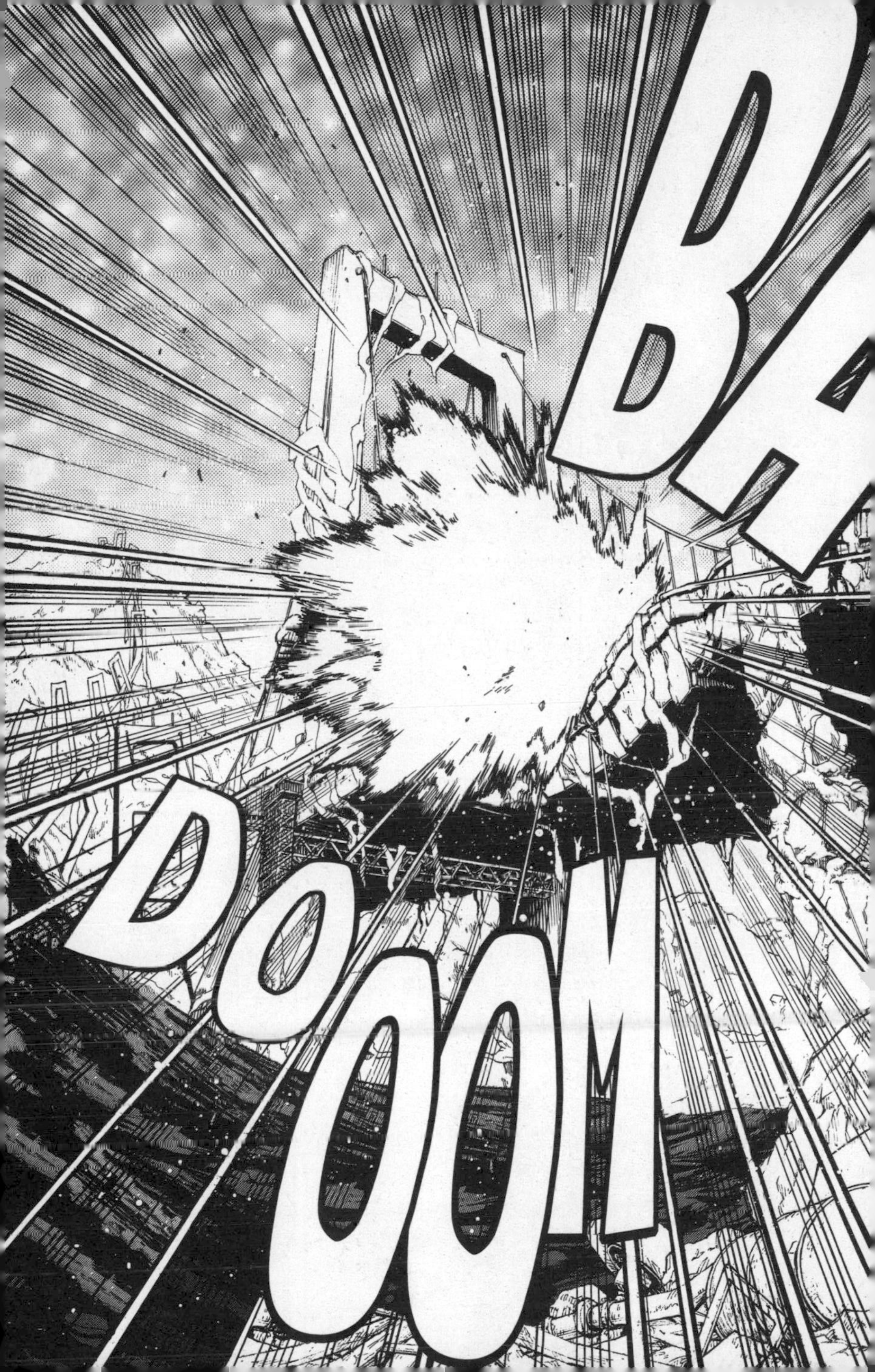
BA
DOOOM

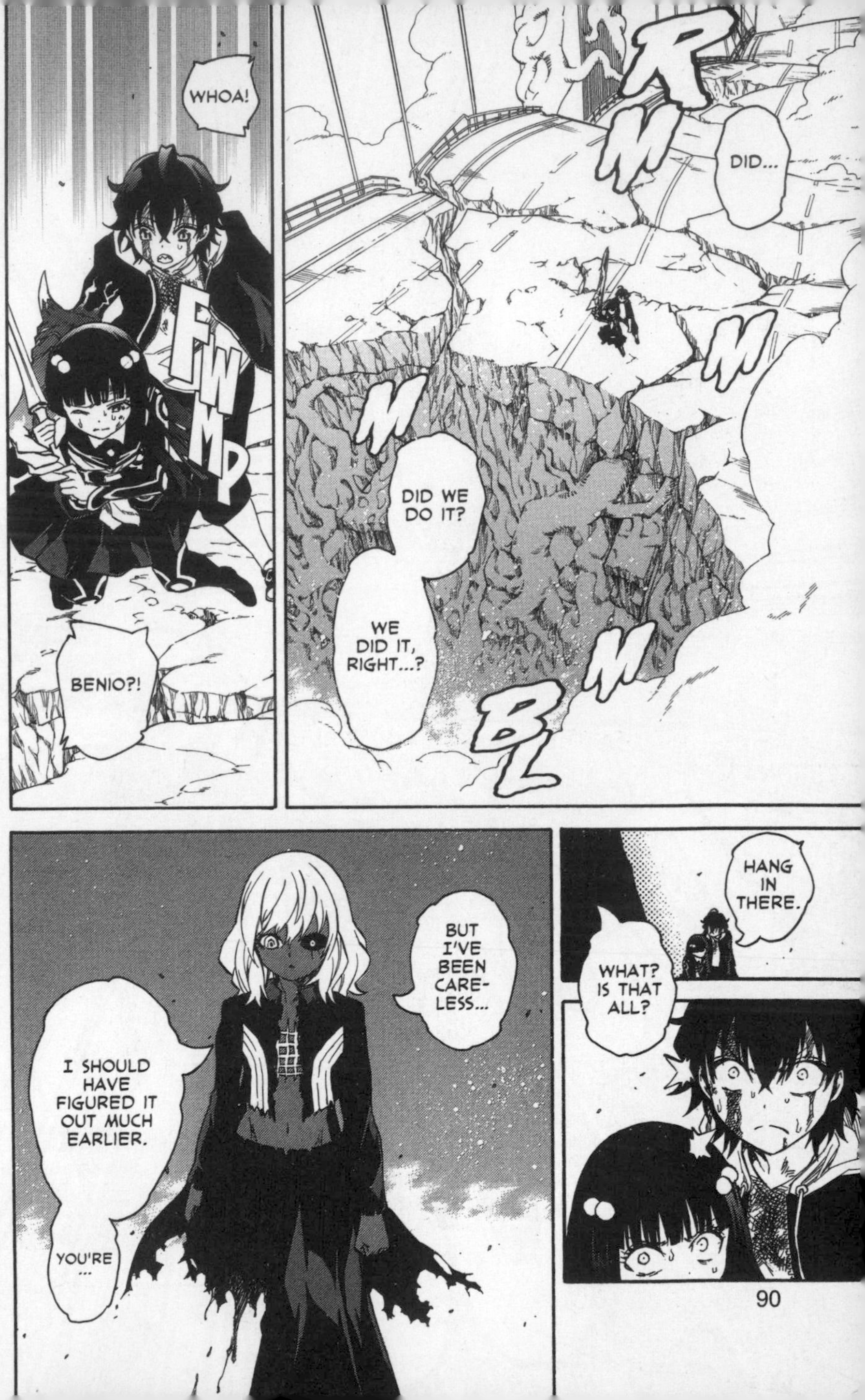
RMMMMBL
DID...
DID WE DO IT?
WE DID IT, RIGHT...?
WHOA!
FWMP
BENIO?!
HANG IN THERE.
WHAT? IS THAT ALL?
BUT I'VE BEEN CARE-LESS...
I SHOULD HAVE FIGURED IT OUT MUCH EARLIER.
YOU'RE...

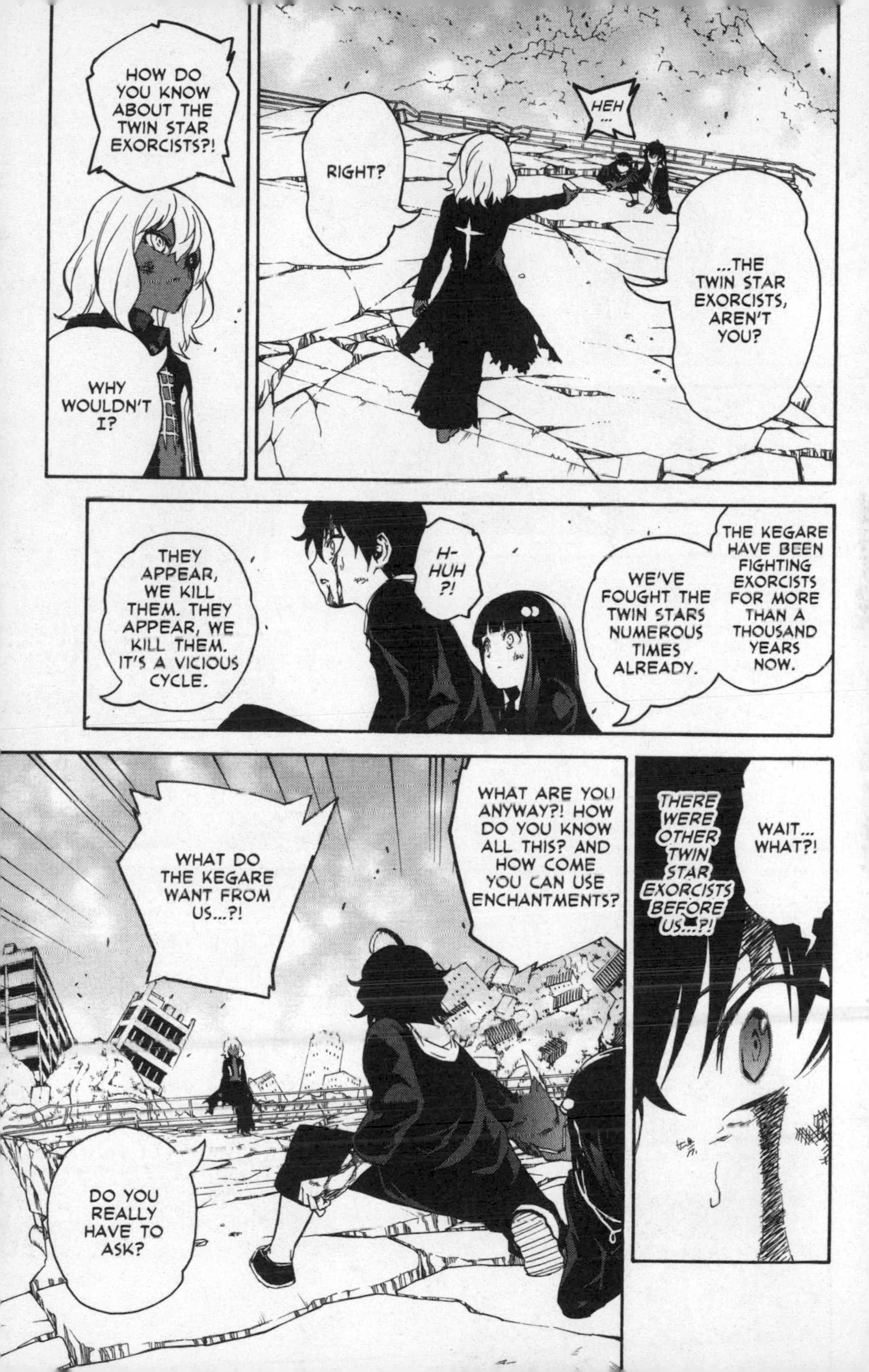
HEH...
...THE TWIN STAR EXORCISTS, AREN'T YOU?
RIGHT?
HOW DO YOU KNOW ABOUT THE TWIN STAR EXORCISTS?!
WHY WOULDN'T I?
THE KEGARE HAVE BEEN FIGHTING EXORCISTS FOR MORE THAN A THOUSAND YEARS NOW.
WE'VE FOUGHT THE TWIN STARS NUMEROUS TIMES ALREADY.
H-HUH?!
THEY APPEAR, WE KILL THEM. THEY APPEAR, WE KILL THEM. IT'S A VICIOUS CYCLE.
WAIT... WHAT?!
THERE WERE OTHER TWIN STAR EXORCISTS BEFORE US...?!
WHAT ARE YOU ANYWAY?! HOW DO YOU KNOW ALL THIS? AND HOW COME YOU CAN USE ENCHANTMENTS?
WHAT DO THE KEGARE WANT FROM US...?!
DO YOU REALLY HAVE TO ASK?

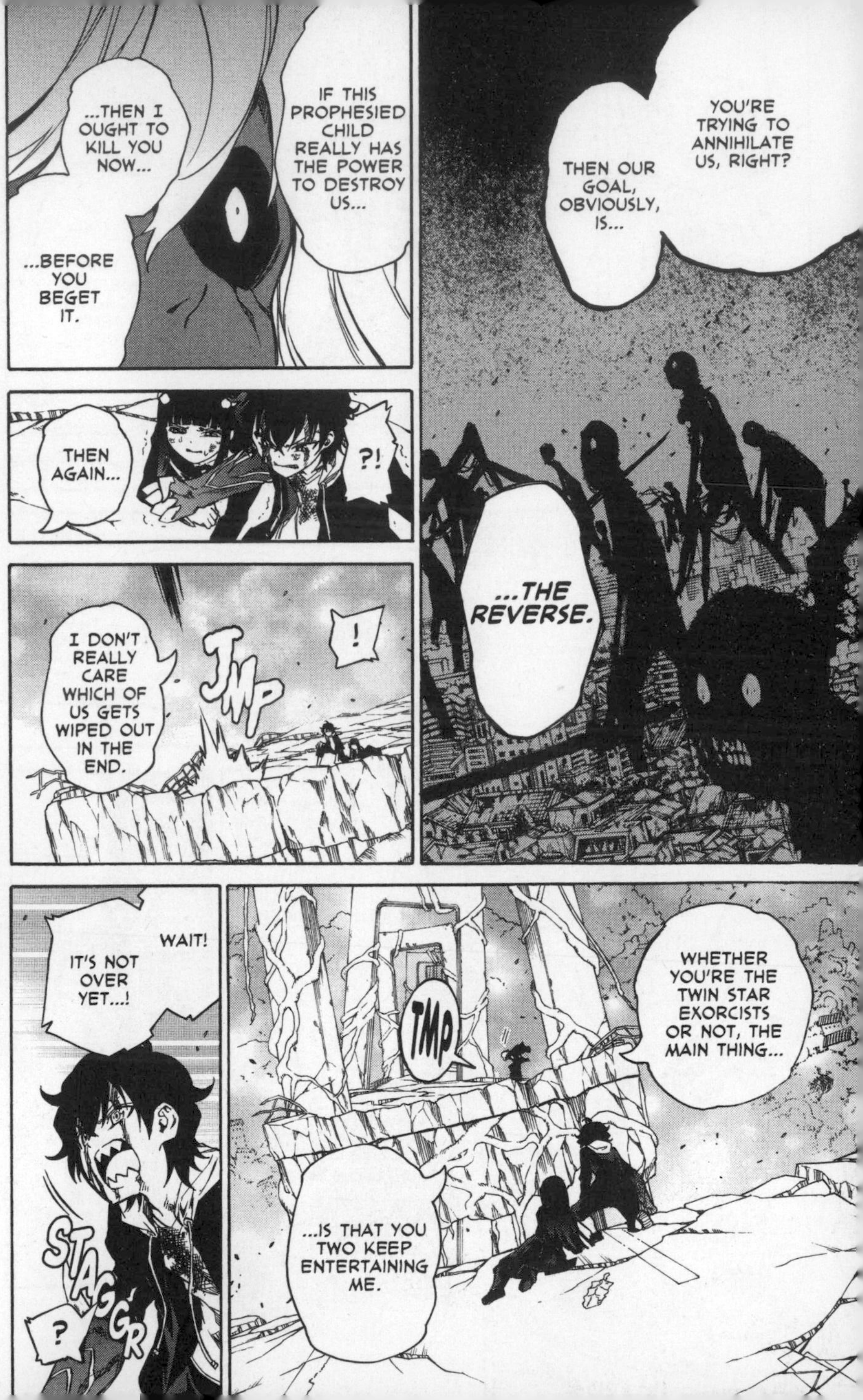
YOU'RE TRYING TO ANNIHILATE US, RIGHT?
THEN OUR GOAL, OBVIOUSLY, IS...
...THE REVERSE.
IF THIS PROPHESIED CHILD REALLY HAS THE POWER TO DESTROY US...
...THEN I OUGHT TO KILL YOU NOW...
...BEFORE YOU BEGET IT.
?!
THEN AGAIN...
!
JMP
I DON'T REALLY CARE WHICH OF US GETS WIPED OUT IN THE END.
WHETHER YOU'RE THE TWIN STAR EXORCISTS OR NOT, THE MAIN THING...
TMP
...IS THAT YOU TWO KEEP ENTERTAINING ME.
WAIT!
IT'S NOT OVER YET...!
STAGGR
?

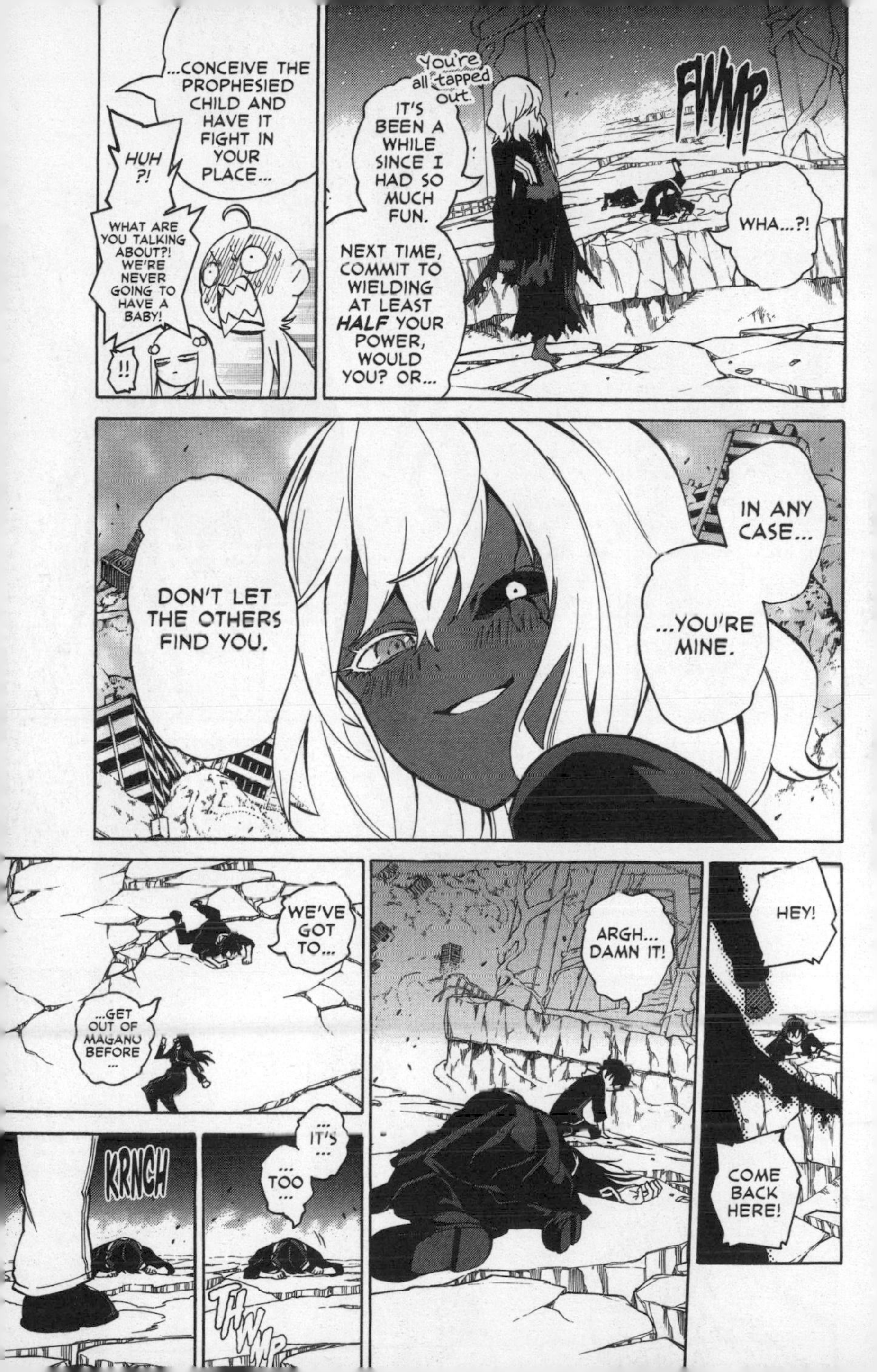
FWMP
WHA...?!
You're all tapped out.
IT'S BEEN A WHILE SINCE I HAD SO MUCH FUN.
NEXT TIME, COMMIT TO WIELDING AT LEAST *HALF* YOUR POWER, WOULD YOU? OR...
...CONCEIVE THE PROPHESIED CHILD AND HAVE IT FIGHT IN YOUR PLACE...
HUH ?!
WHAT ARE YOU TALKING ABOUT?! WE'RE NEVER GOING TO HAVE A BABY!
!!
IN ANY CASE...
...YOU'RE MINE.
DON'T LET THE OTHERS FIND YOU.
HEY!
COME BACK HERE!
ARGH... DAMN IT!
WE'VE GOT TO...
...GET OUT OF MAGANO BEFORE ...
... IT'S ...
... TOO ...
THWMP
KRNCH

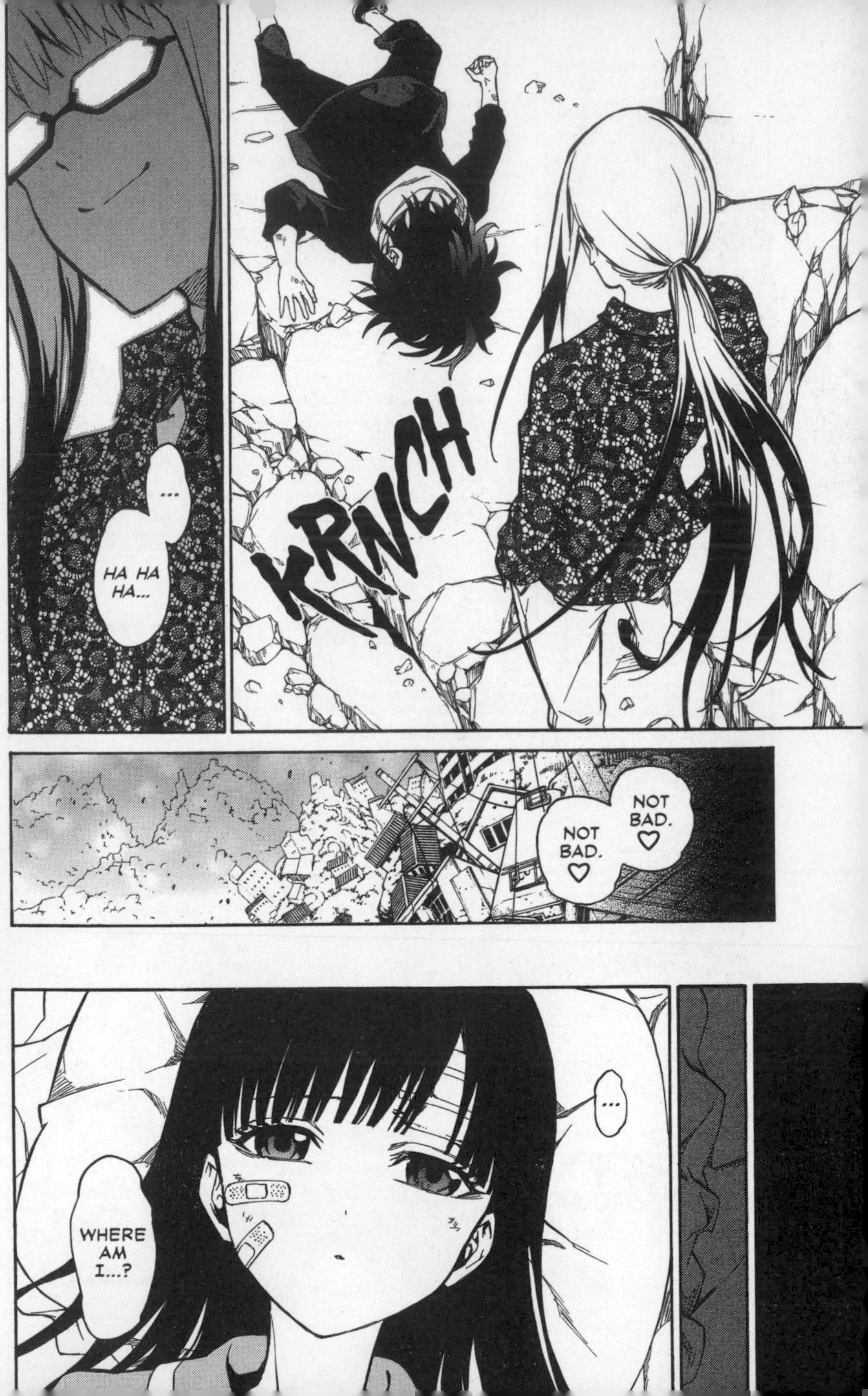
KRNCH
...
HA HA HA...
NOT BAD. ♡
NOT BAD. ♡
...
WHERE AM I...?

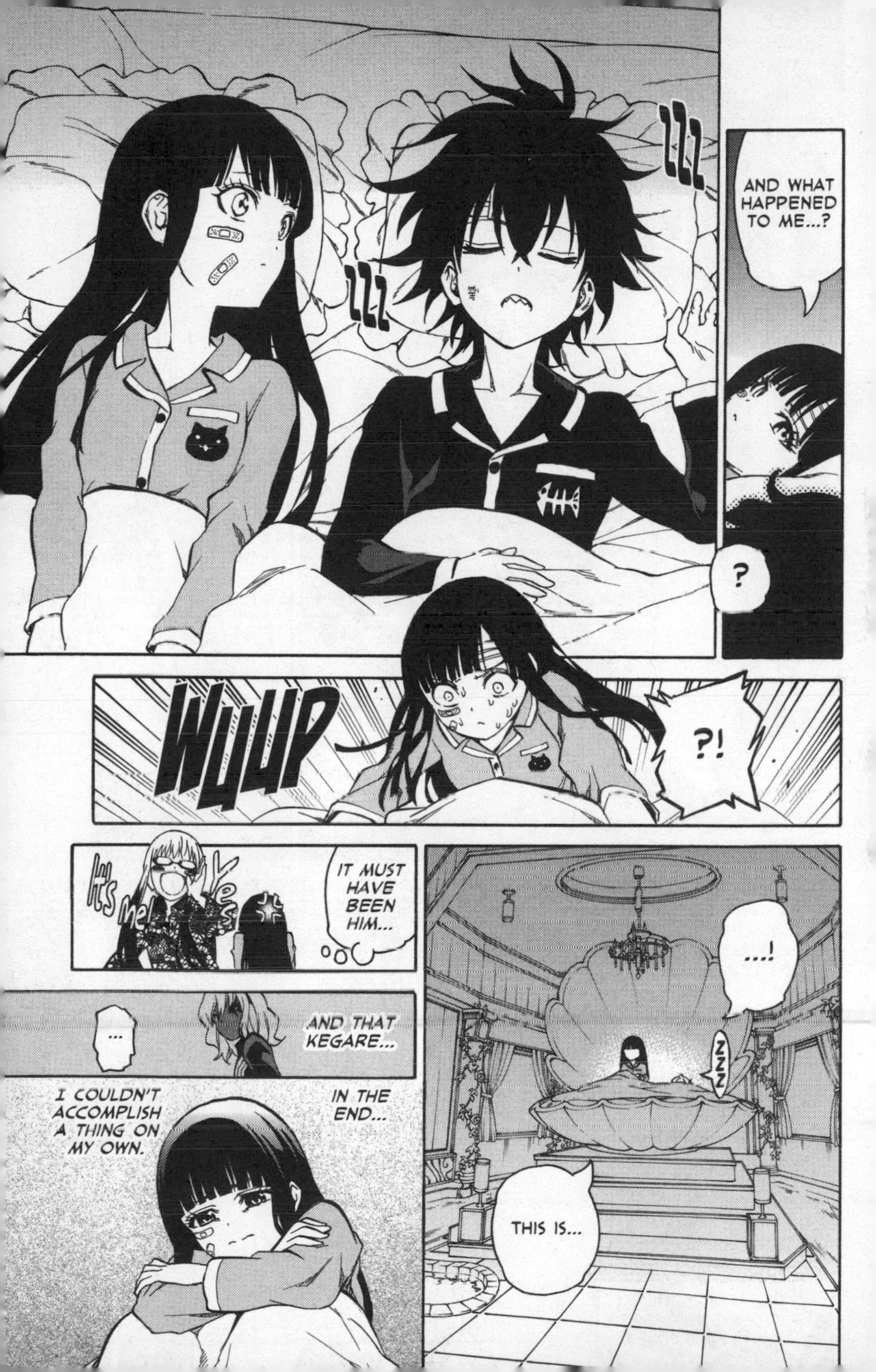
AND WHAT HAPPENED TO ME...?
?
ZZZ
ZZZ
?!
WUUP
...!
ZZZ
THIS IS...
IT MUST HAVE BEEN HIM...
It's me! Yes
AND THAT KEGARE...
...
IN THE END...
I COULDN'T ACCOMPLISH A THING ON MY OWN.

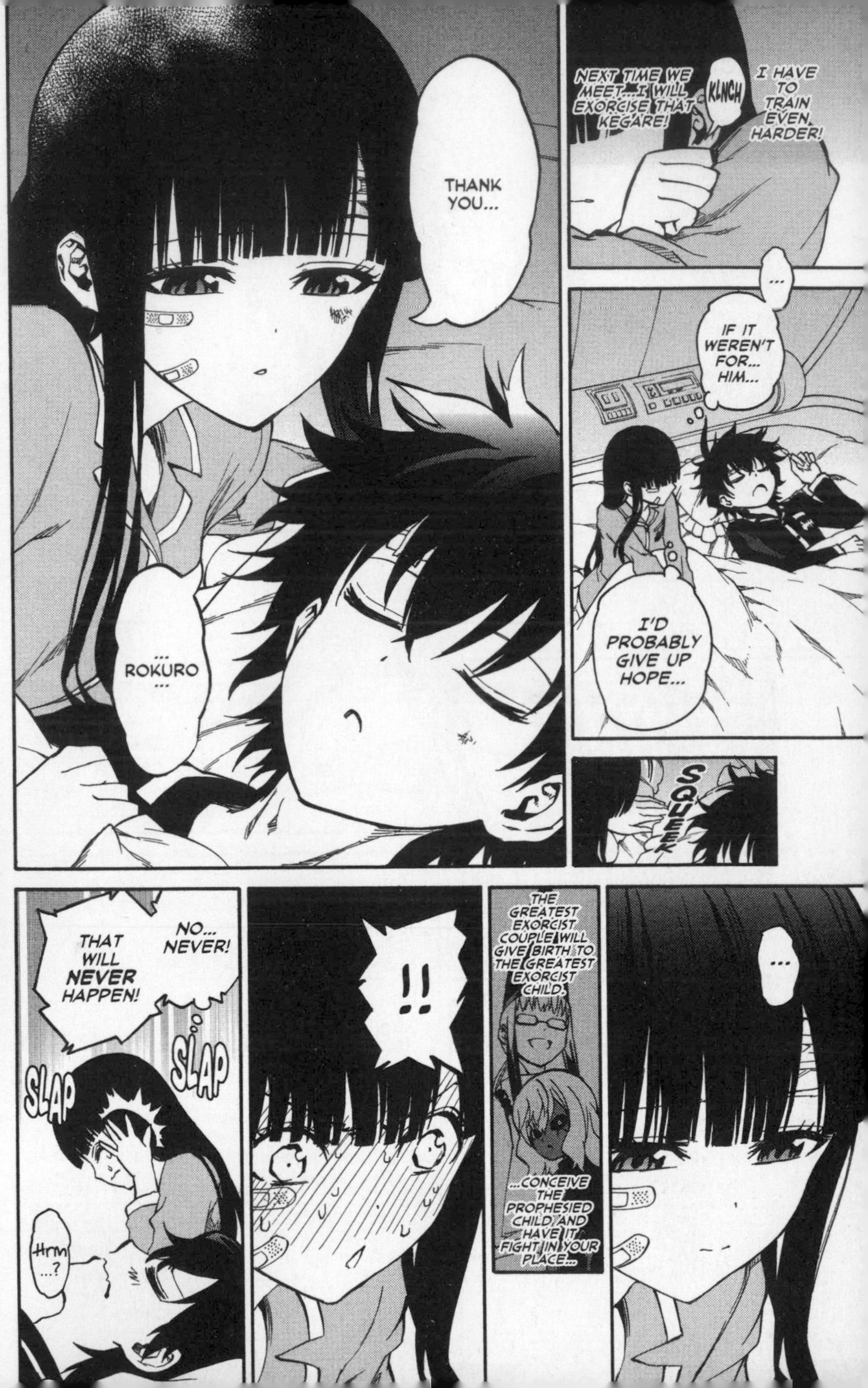
I HAVE TO TRAIN EVEN HARDER!
KLNCH
NEXT TIME WE MEET... I WILL EXORCISE THAT KEGARE!
...
IF IT WEREN'T FOR... HIM...
I'D PROBABLY GIVE UP HOPE...
SQUEEEK
THANK YOU...
... ROKURO ...
...
THE GREATEST EXORCIST COUPLE WILL GIVE BIRTH TO THE GREATEST EXORCIST CHILD.
...CONCEIVE THE PROPHESIED CHILD AND HAVE IT FIGHT IN YOUR PLACE...
!!
NO... NEVER!
THAT WILL **NEVER** HAPPEN!
SLAP
SLAP
Hrm ...?

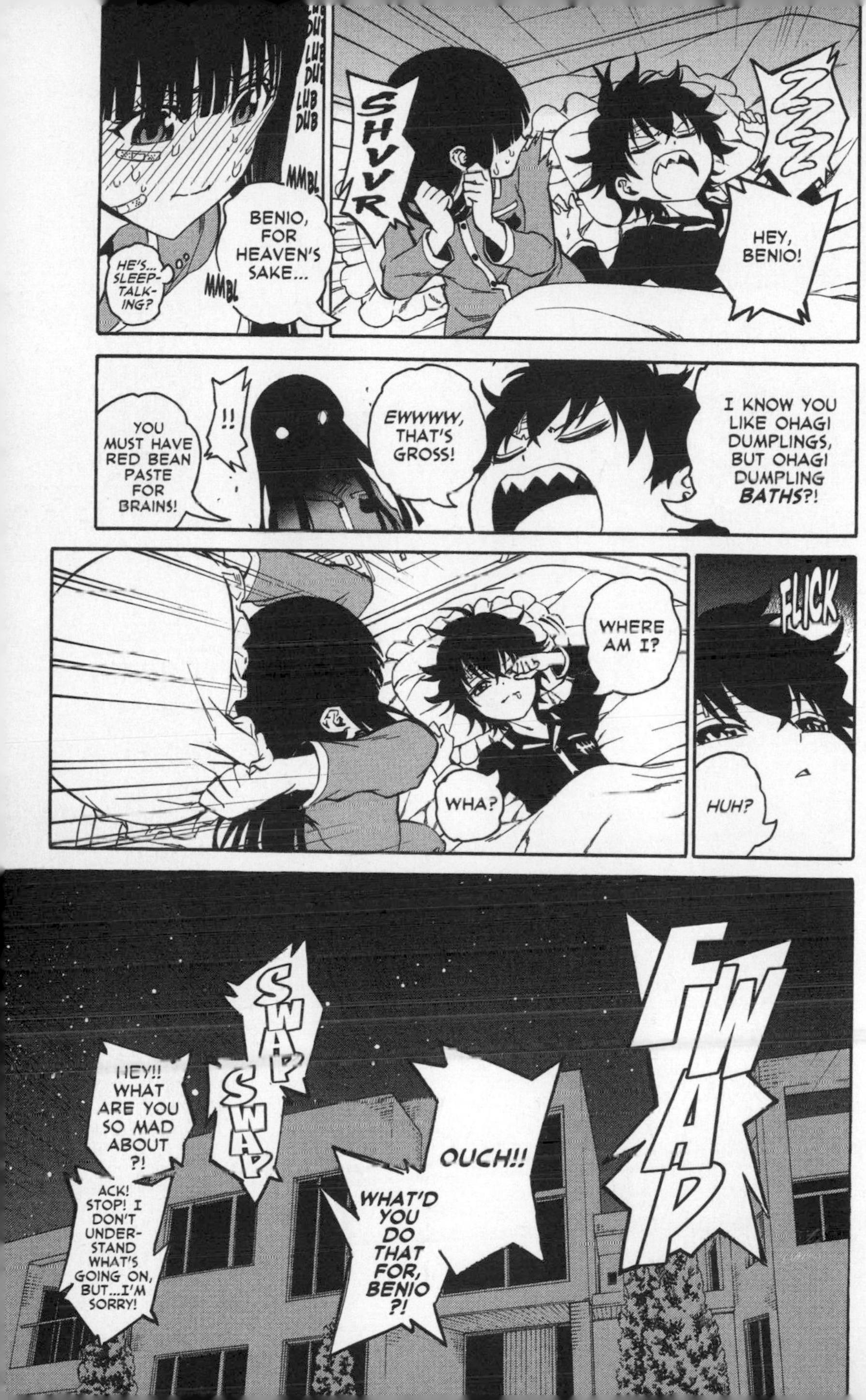
HEY, BENIO!
SHVVR
BENIO, FOR HEAVEN'S SAKE...
LUB DUB LUB DUB
MMBL
HE'S... SLEEP-TALKING?
MMBL
I KNOW YOU LIKE OHAGI DUMPLINGS, BUT OHAGI DUMPLING *BATHS*?!
EWWWW, THAT'S GROSS!
!!
YOU MUST HAVE RED BEAN PASTE FOR BRAINS!
FLICK
HUH?
WHERE AM I?
WHA?
FWAP
OUCH!!
WHAT'D YOU DO THAT FOR, BENIO?!
SWAP
SWAP
HEY!! WHAT ARE YOU SO MAD ABOUT?!
ACK! STOP! I DON'T UNDER-STAND WHAT'S GOING ON, BUT...I'M SORRY!

Wait! Who undressed me and treated my injuries...?!

Answer: Kinu, of course.

#6 Rokuro's True Feelings

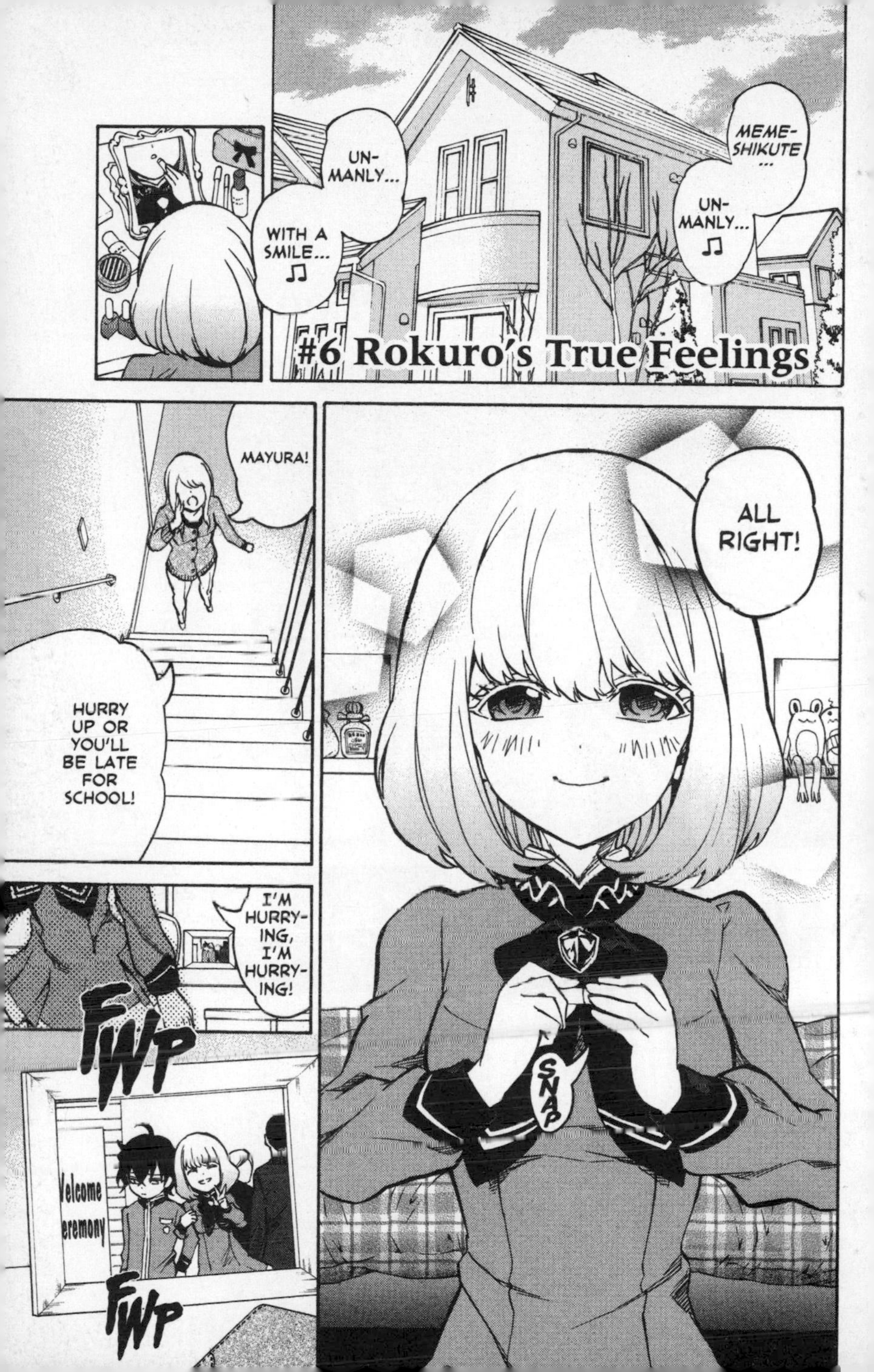
MEME-SHIKUTE...
UN-MANLY... ♫
UN-MANLY...
WITH A SMILE... ♫
ALL RIGHT!
SNAP
MAYURA!
HURRY UP OR YOU'LL BE LATE FOR SCHOOL!
I'M HURRYING, I'M HURRYING!
FWP
Velcome
eremony
FWP

#6 Rokuro's True Feelings

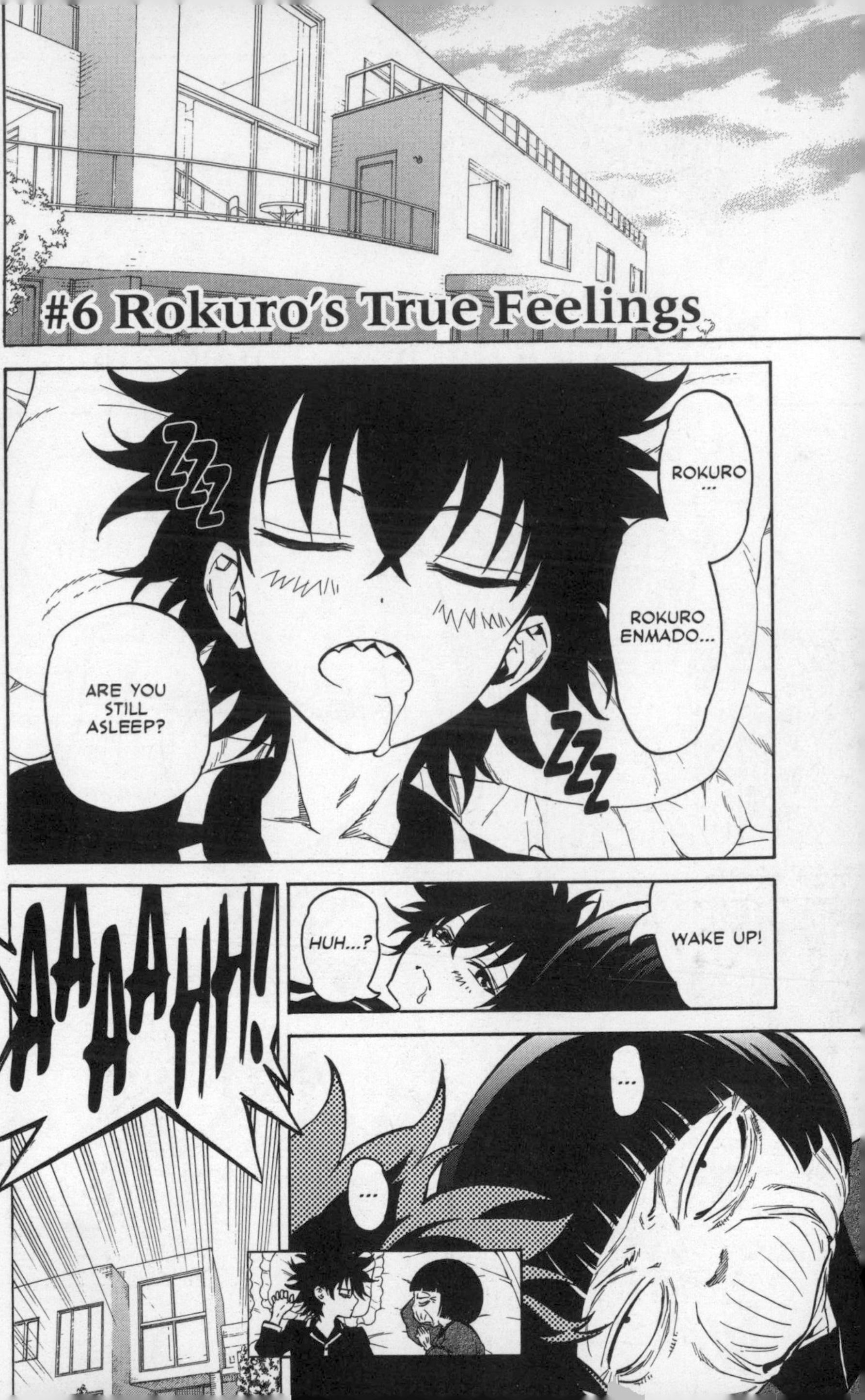
ROKURO ...
ROKURO ENMADO...
ARE YOU STILL ASLEEP?
WAKE UP!
HUH...?
...
...
AAAHH!

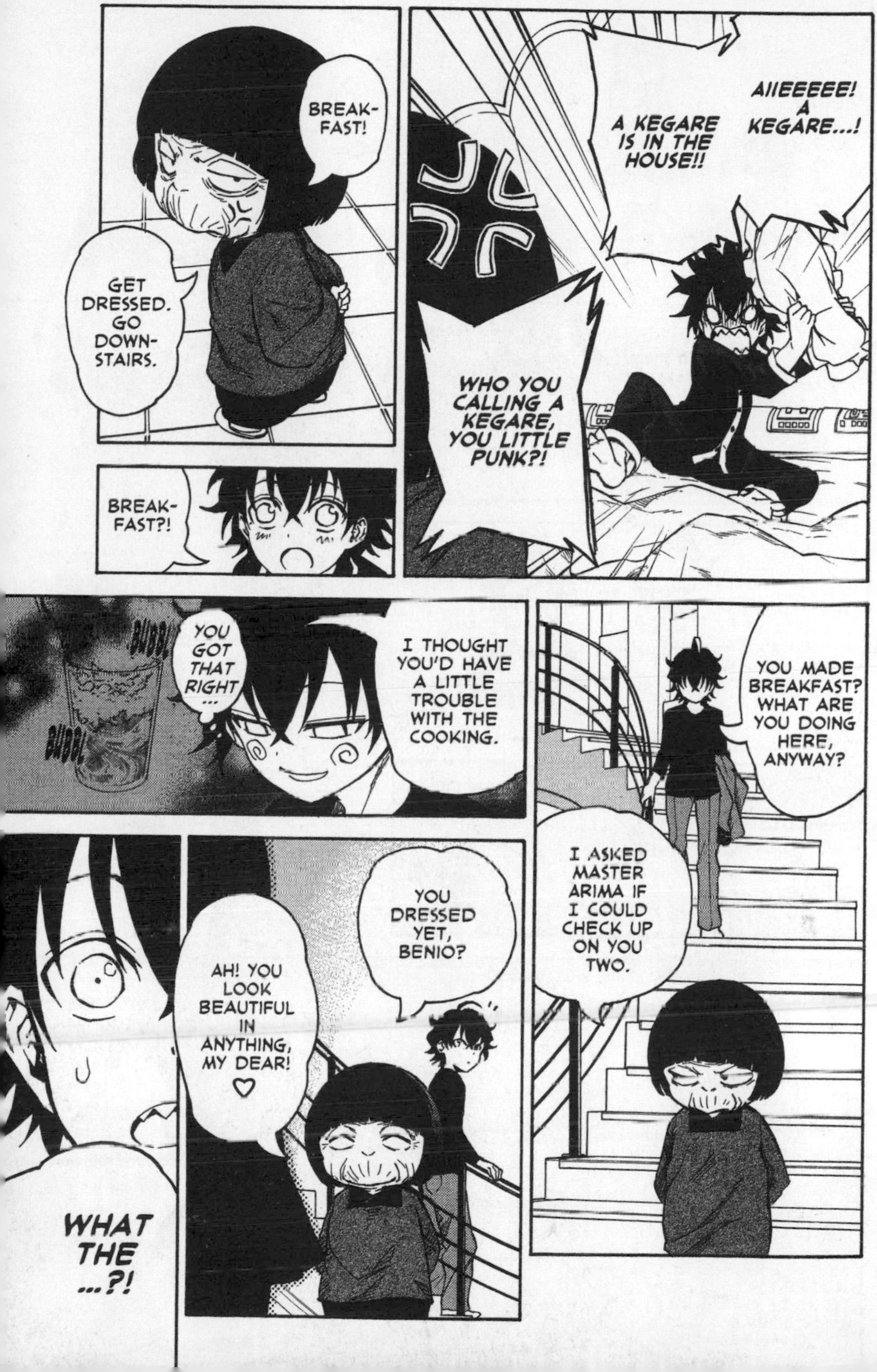
AIIEEEEE! A KEGARE...!
A KEGARE IS IN THE HOUSE!!
WHO YOU CALLING A KEGARE, YOU LITTLE PUNK?!
BREAK-FAST!
GET DRESSED. GO DOWN-STAIRS.
BREAK-FAST?!
YOU MADE BREAKFAST? WHAT ARE YOU DOING HERE, ANYWAY?
I ASKED MASTER ARIMA IF I COULD CHECK UP ON YOU TWO.
I THOUGHT YOU'D HAVE A LITTLE TROUBLE WITH THE COOKING.
YOU GOT THAT RIGHT...
BUBBL
BUBBL
YOU DRESSED YET, BENIO?
AH! YOU LOOK BEAUTIFUL IN ANYTHING, MY DEAR! ♡
WHAT THE...?!

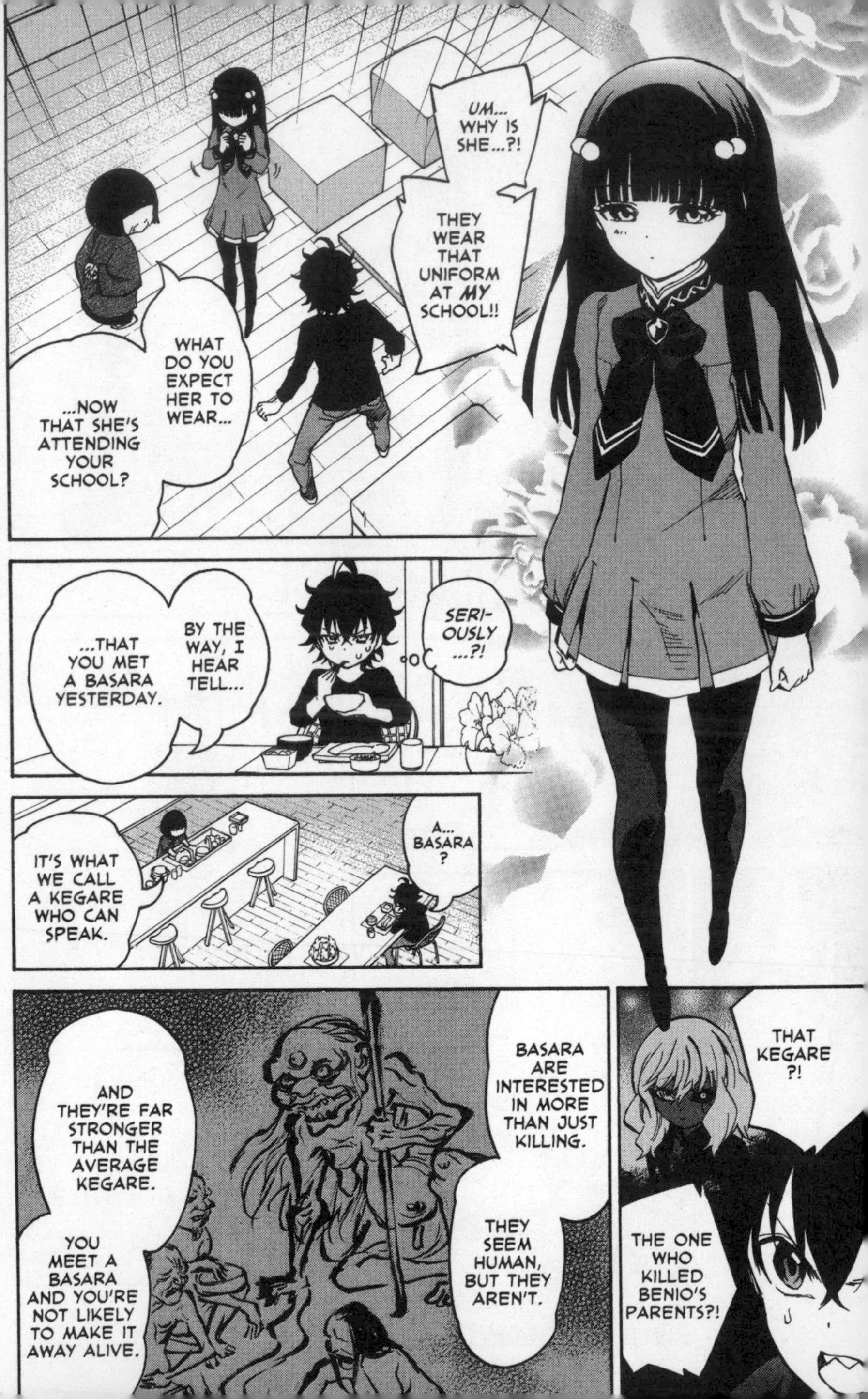
UM... WHY IS SHE...?!
THEY WEAR THAT UNIFORM AT *MY* SCHOOL!!
WHAT DO YOU EXPECT HER TO WEAR...
...NOW THAT SHE'S ATTENDING YOUR SCHOOL?
SERIOUSLY...?!
BY THE WAY, I HEAR TELL...
...THAT YOU MET A BASARA YESTERDAY.
A... BASARA?
IT'S WHAT WE CALL A KEGARE WHO CAN SPEAK.
THAT KEGARE?!
THE ONE WHO KILLED BENIO'S PARENTS?!
BASARA ARE INTERESTED IN MORE THAN JUST KILLING.
THEY SEEM HUMAN, BUT THEY AREN'T.
AND THEY'RE FAR STRONGER THAN THE AVERAGE KEGARE.
YOU MEET A BASARA AND YOU'RE NOT LIKELY TO MAKE IT AWAY ALIVE.

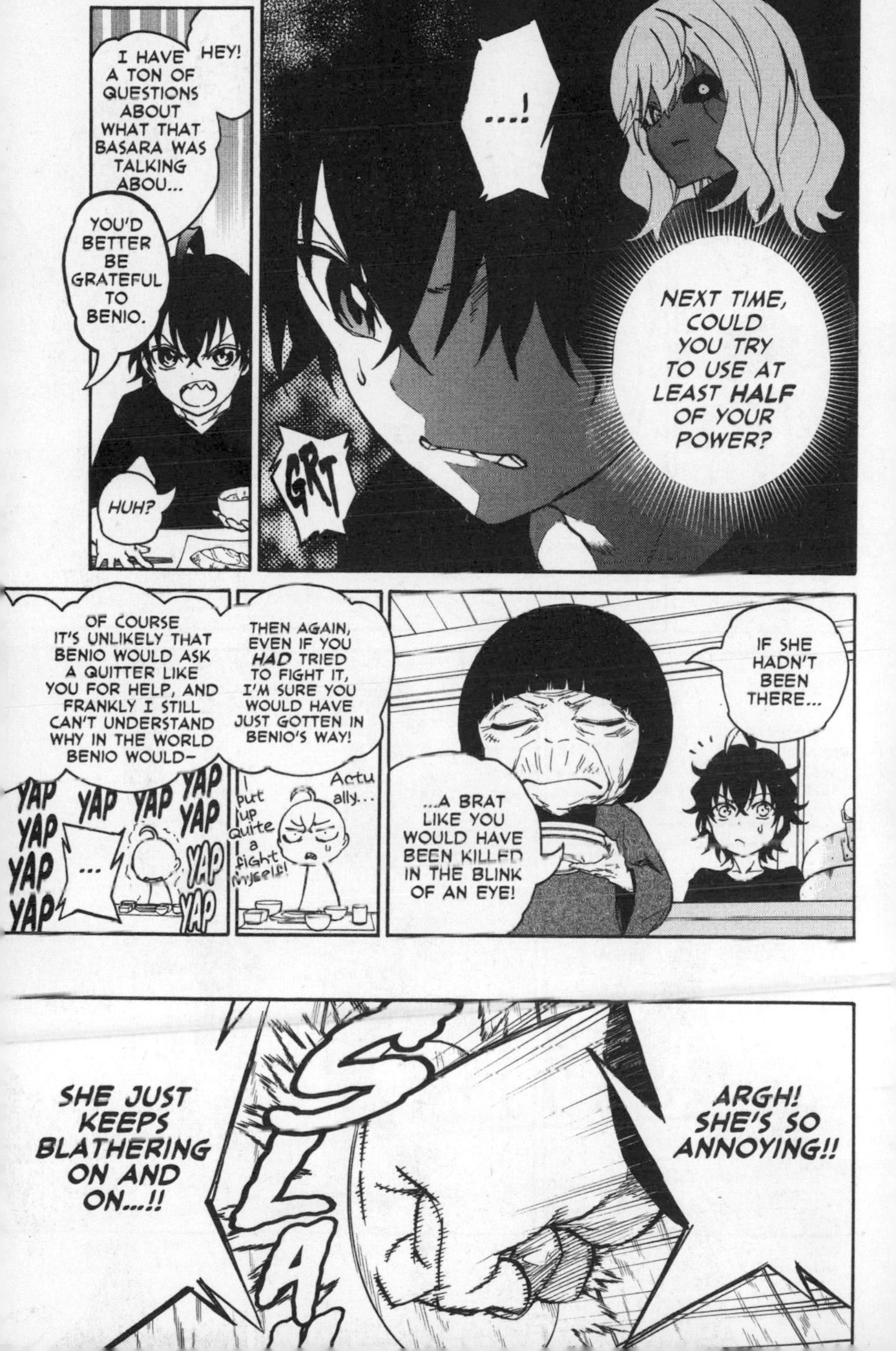
...!
NEXT TIME, COULD YOU TRY TO USE AT LEAST **HALF** OF YOUR POWER?
GRT
HEY!
I HAVE A TON OF QUESTIONS ABOUT WHAT THAT BASARA WAS TALKING ABOU...
YOU'D BETTER BE GRATEFUL TO BENIO.
HUH?
IF SHE HADN'T BEEN THERE...
...A BRAT LIKE YOU WOULD HAVE BEEN KILLED IN THE BLINK OF AN EYE!
THEN AGAIN, EVEN IF YOU *HAD* TRIED TO FIGHT IT, I'M SURE YOU WOULD HAVE JUST GOTTEN IN BENIO'S WAY!
Actually...
I put up quite a fight myself!!
OF COURSE IT'S UNLIKELY THAT BENIO WOULD ASK A QUITTER LIKE YOU FOR HELP, AND FRANKLY I STILL CAN'T UNDERSTAND WHY IN THE WORLD BENIO WOULD–
YAP YAP YAP YAP YAP YAP YAP YAP YAP YAP
...
ARGH! SHE'S SO ANNOYING!!
SHE JUST KEEPS BLATHERING ON AND ON...!!

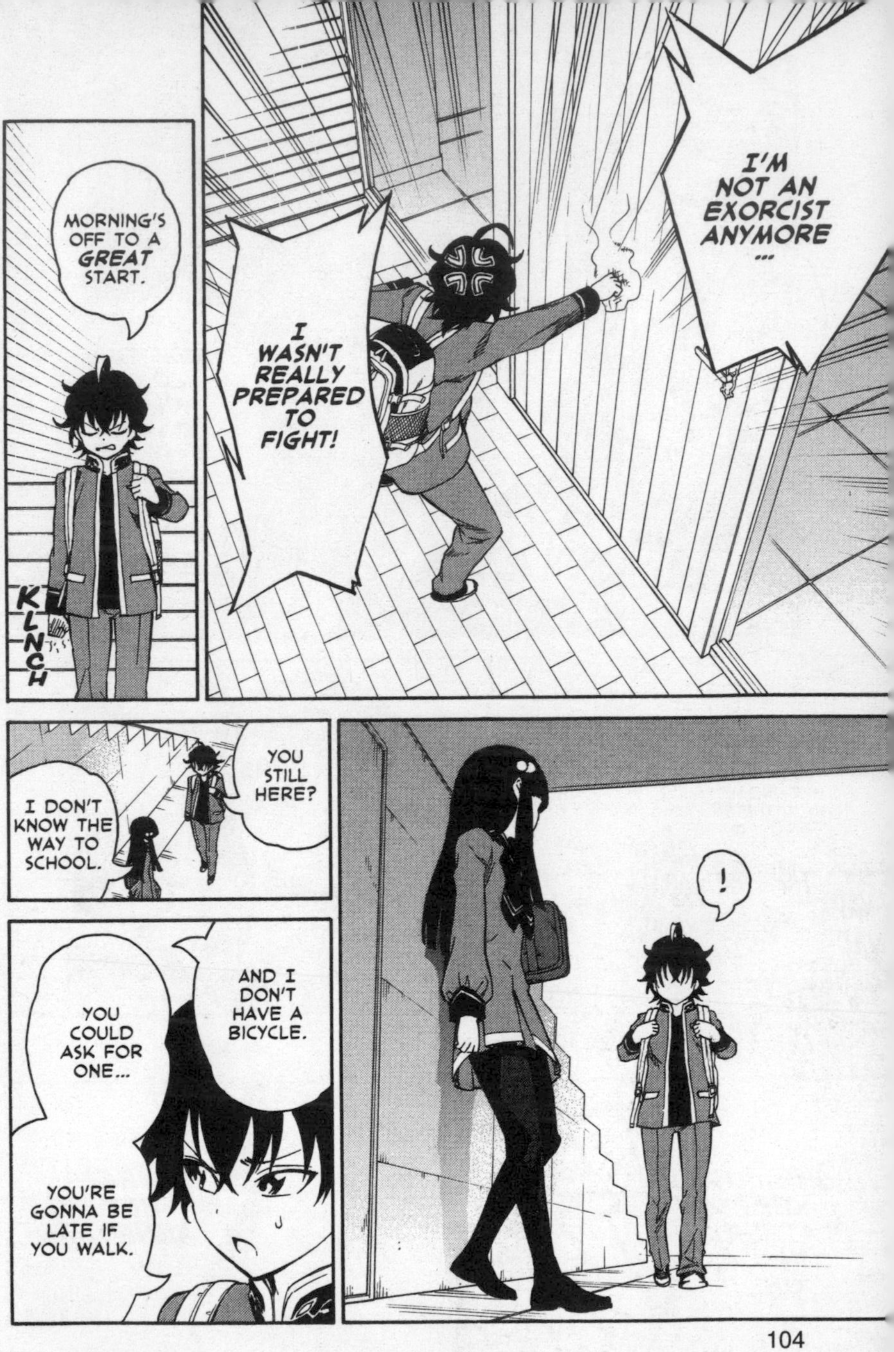
I'M NOT AN EXORCIST ANYMORE ...
I WASN'T REALLY PREPARED TO FIGHT!
MORNING'S OFF TO A GREAT START.
KLNCH
!
YOU STILL HERE?
I DON'T KNOW THE WAY TO SCHOOL.
AND I DON'T HAVE A BICYCLE.
YOU COULD ASK FOR ONE...
YOU'RE GONNA BE LATE IF YOU WALK.

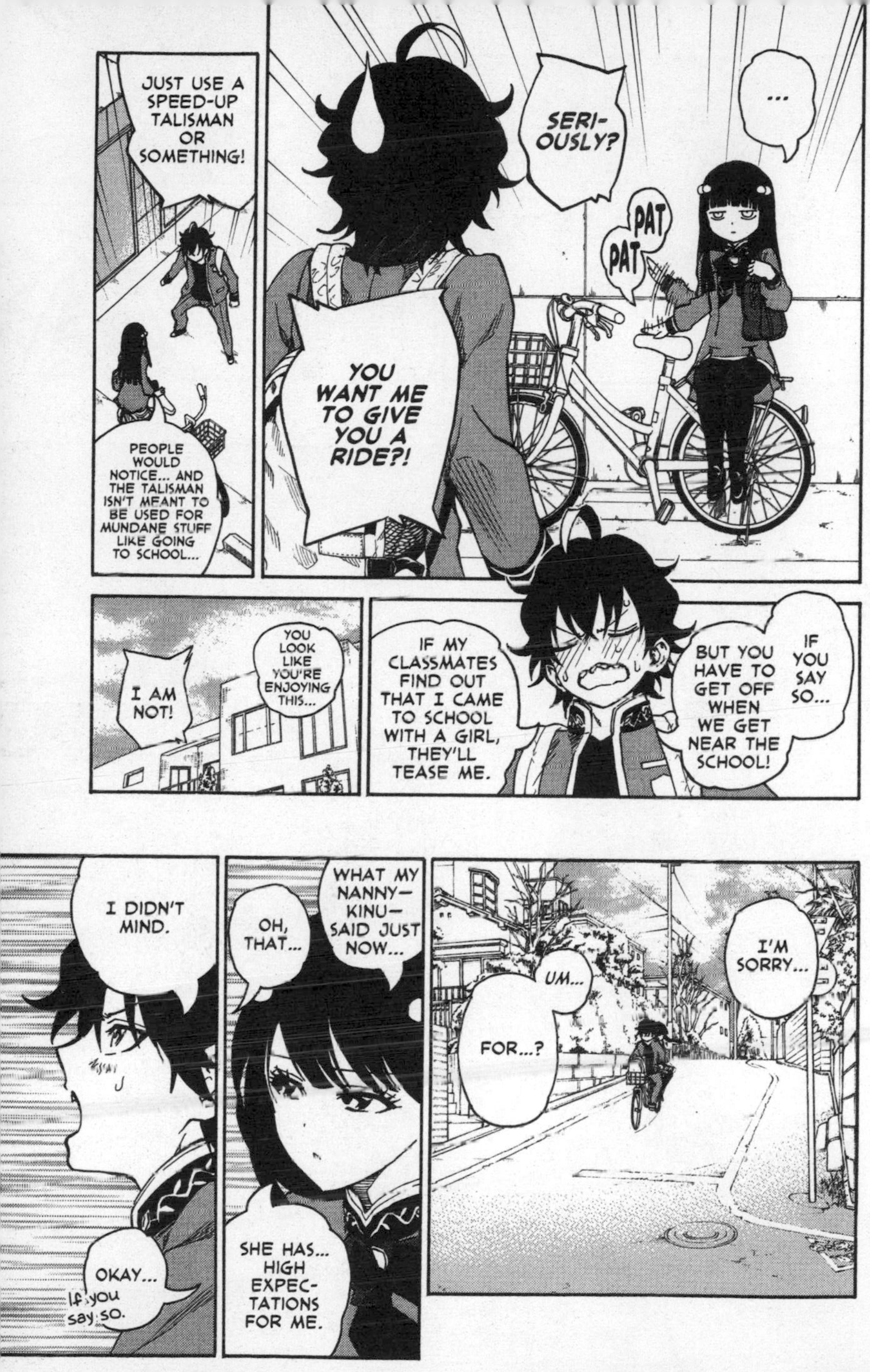
...
PAT PAT
SERI-OUSLY?
YOU WANT ME TO GIVE YOU A RIDE?!
JUST USE A SPEED-UP TALISMAN OR SOMETHING!
PEOPLE WOULD NOTICE... AND THE TALISMAN ISN'T MEANT TO BE USED FOR MUNDANE STUFF LIKE GOING TO SCHOOL...
IF YOU SAY SO...
BUT YOU HAVE TO GET OFF WHEN WE GET NEAR THE SCHOOL!
IF MY CLASSMATES FIND OUT THAT I CAME TO SCHOOL WITH A GIRL, THEY'LL TEASE ME.
YOU LOOK LIKE YOU'RE ENJOYING THIS...
I AM NOT!
I'M SORRY...
UM...
FOR...?
WHAT MY NANNY—KINU—SAID JUST NOW...
OH, THAT...
SHE HAS... HIGH EXPEC-TATIONS FOR ME.
I DIDN'T MIND.
OKAY...
If you say so.

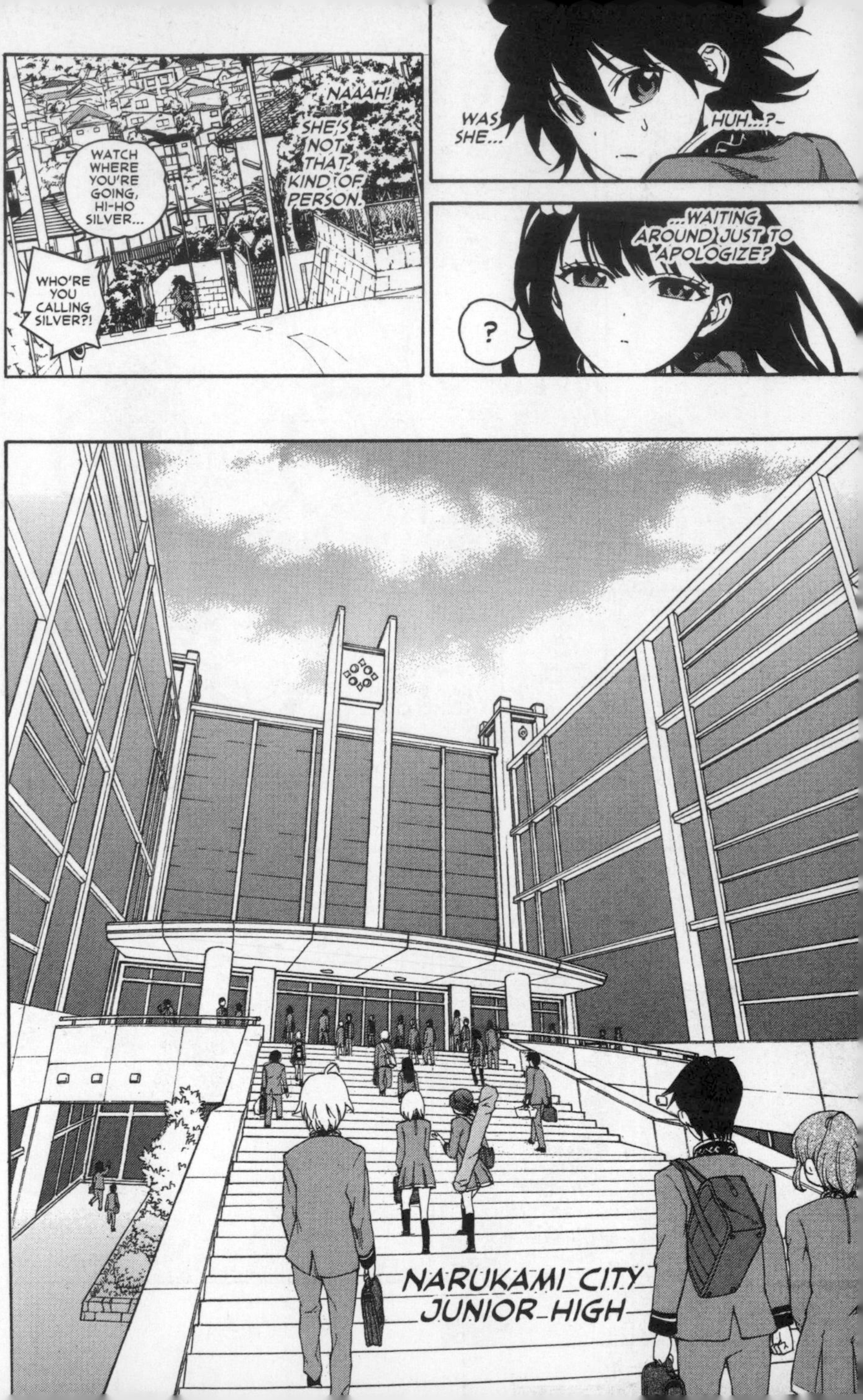
HUH...?
WAS SHE...
...WAITING AROUND JUST TO APOLOGIZE?
?
NAAAH! SHE'S NOT THAT KIND OF PERSON.
WATCH WHERE YOU'RE GOING, HI-HO SILVER...
WHO'RE YOU CALLING SILVER?!
NARUKAMI CITY JUNIOR HIGH

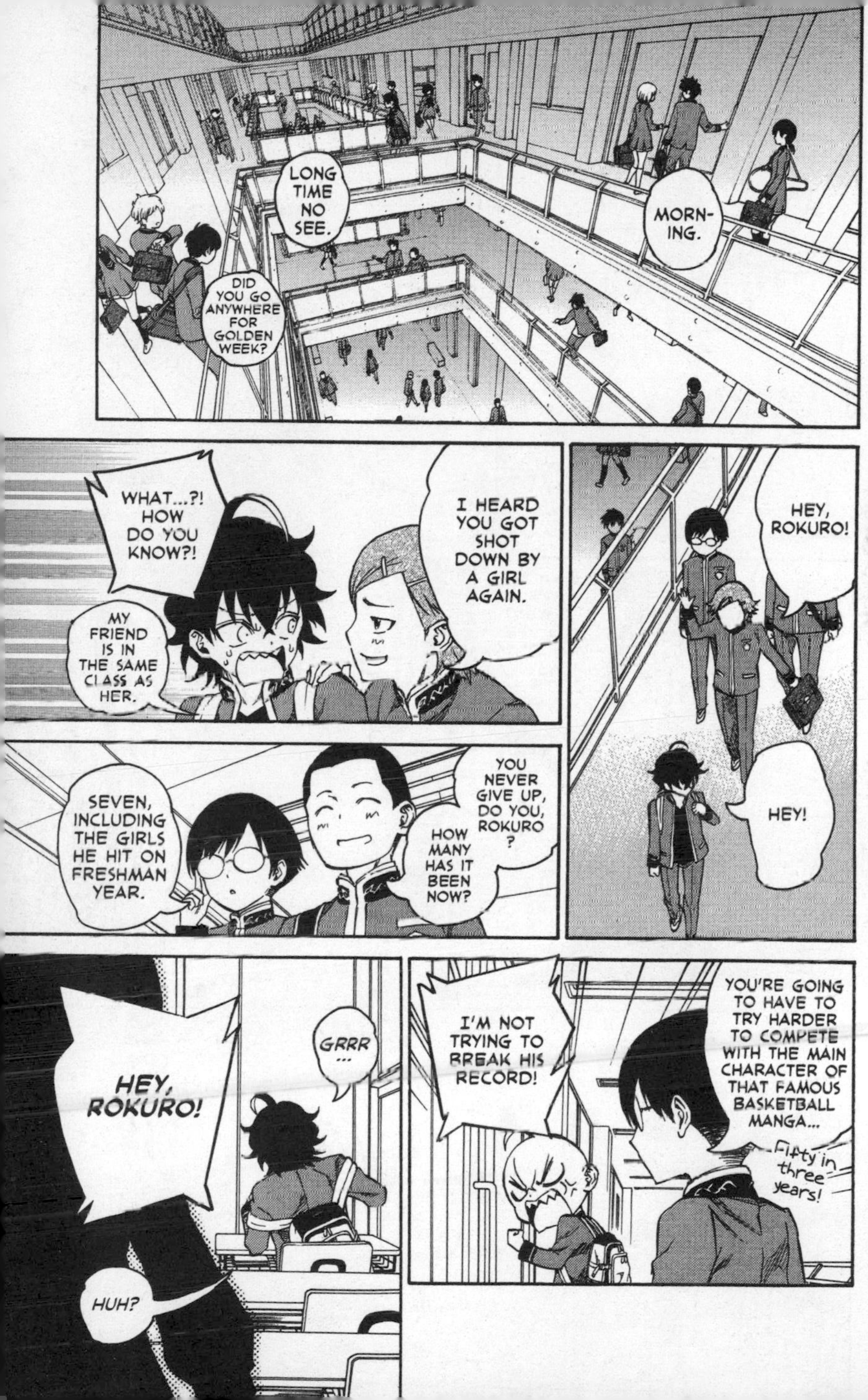
MORN-ING.
LONG TIME NO SEE.
DID YOU GO ANYWHERE FOR GOLDEN WEEK?
HEY, ROKURO!
HEY!
I HEARD YOU GOT SHOT DOWN BY A GIRL AGAIN.
WHAT...?! HOW DO YOU KNOW?!
MY FRIEND IS IN THE SAME CLASS AS HER.
YOU NEVER GIVE UP, DO YOU, ROKURO?
HOW MANY HAS IT BEEN NOW?
SEVEN, INCLUDING THE GIRLS HE HIT ON FRESHMAN YEAR.
YOU'RE GOING TO HAVE TO TRY HARDER TO COMPETE WITH THE MAIN CHARACTER OF THAT FAMOUS BASKETBALL MANGA...
Fifty in three years!
I'M NOT TRYING TO BREAK HIS RECORD!
GRRR...
HEY, ROKURO!
HUH?

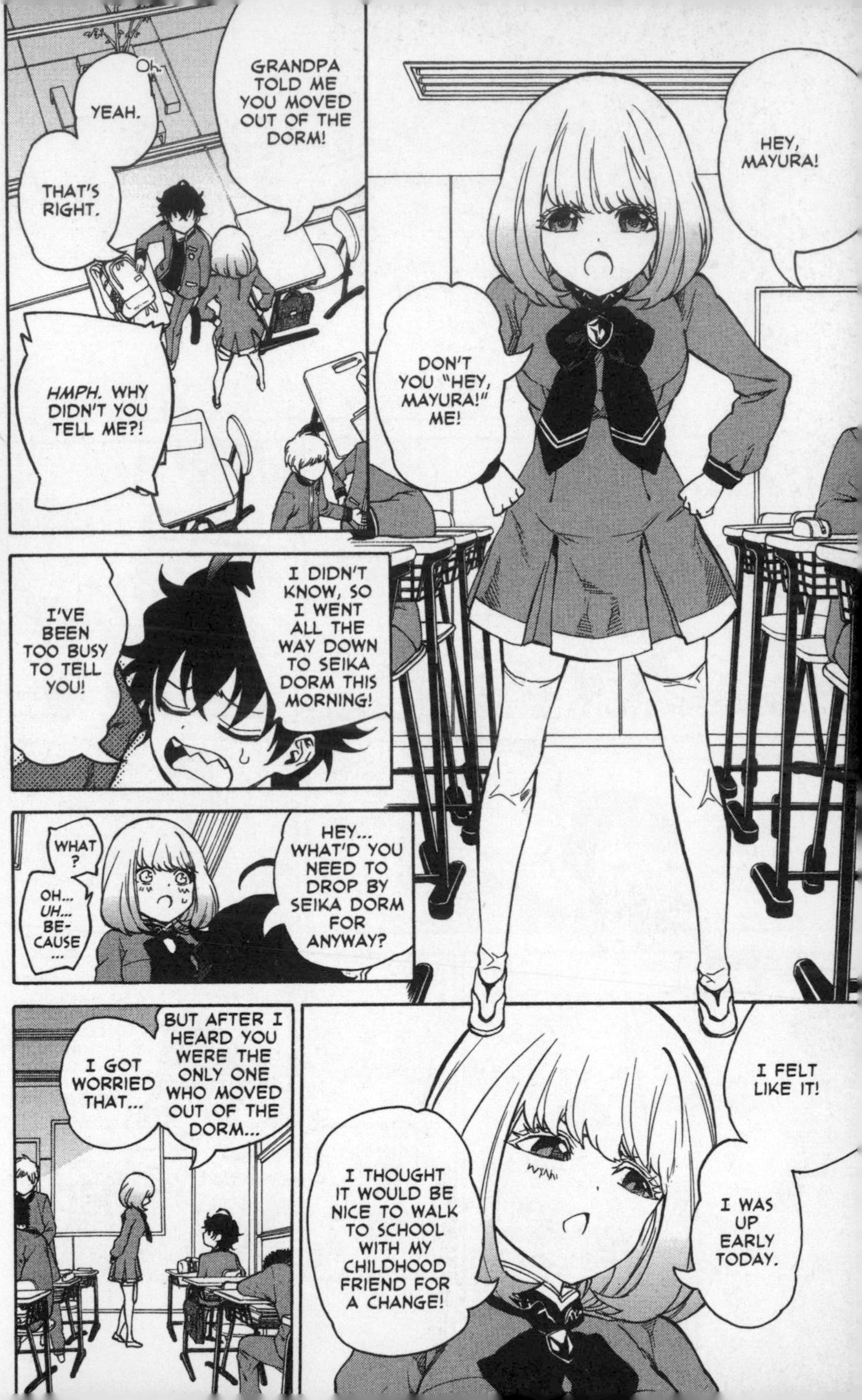
HEY, MAYURA!
DON'T YOU "HEY, MAYURA!" ME!
GRANDPA TOLD ME YOU MOVED OUT OF THE DORM!
Oh-
YEAH.
THAT'S RIGHT.
HMPH. WHY DIDN'T YOU TELL ME?!
I DIDN'T KNOW, SO I WENT ALL THE WAY DOWN TO SEIKA DORM THIS MORNING!
I'VE BEEN TOO BUSY TO TELL YOU!
HEY... WHAT'D YOU NEED TO DROP BY SEIKA DORM FOR ANYWAY?
WHAT?
OH... *UH...* BE-CAUSE...
I FELT LIKE IT!
I WAS UP EARLY TODAY.
I THOUGHT IT WOULD BE NICE TO WALK TO SCHOOL WITH MY CHILDHOOD FRIEND FOR A CHANGE!
BUT AFTER I HEARD YOU WERE THE ONLY ONE WHO MOVED OUT OF THE DORM...
I GOT WORRIED THAT...

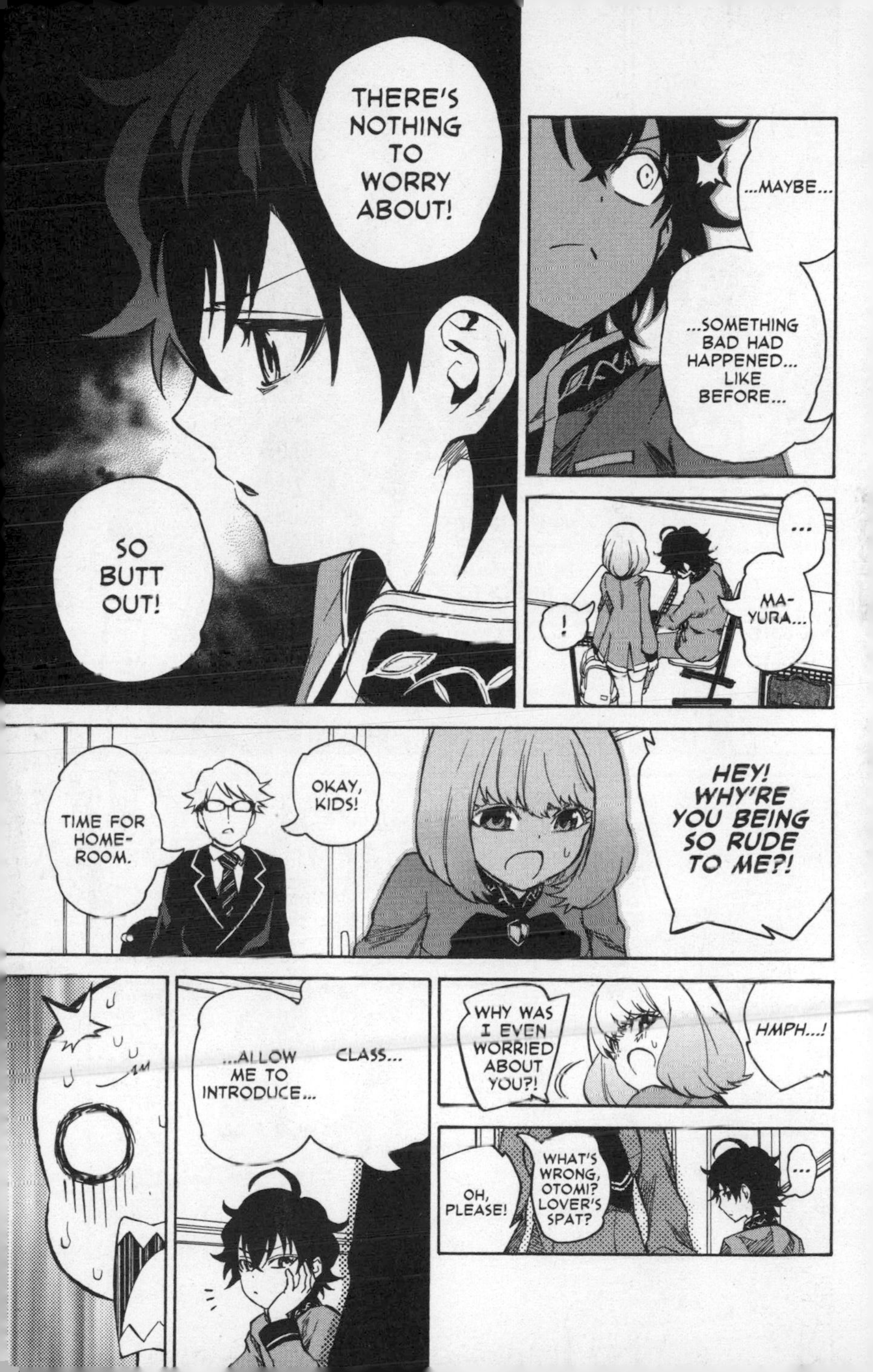
...MAYBE...
...SOMETHING BAD HAD HAPPENED... LIKE BEFORE...
...
MA-YURA...
!
THERE'S NOTHING TO WORRY ABOUT!
SO BUTT OUT!
HEY! WHY'RE YOU BEING SO RUDE TO ME?!
OKAY, KIDS!
TIME FOR HOME-ROOM.
HMPH...!
WHY WAS I EVEN WORRIED ABOUT YOU?!
...
WHAT'S WRONG, OTOMI? LOVER'S SPAT?
OH, PLEASE!
CLASS...
...ALLOW ME TO INTRODUCE...

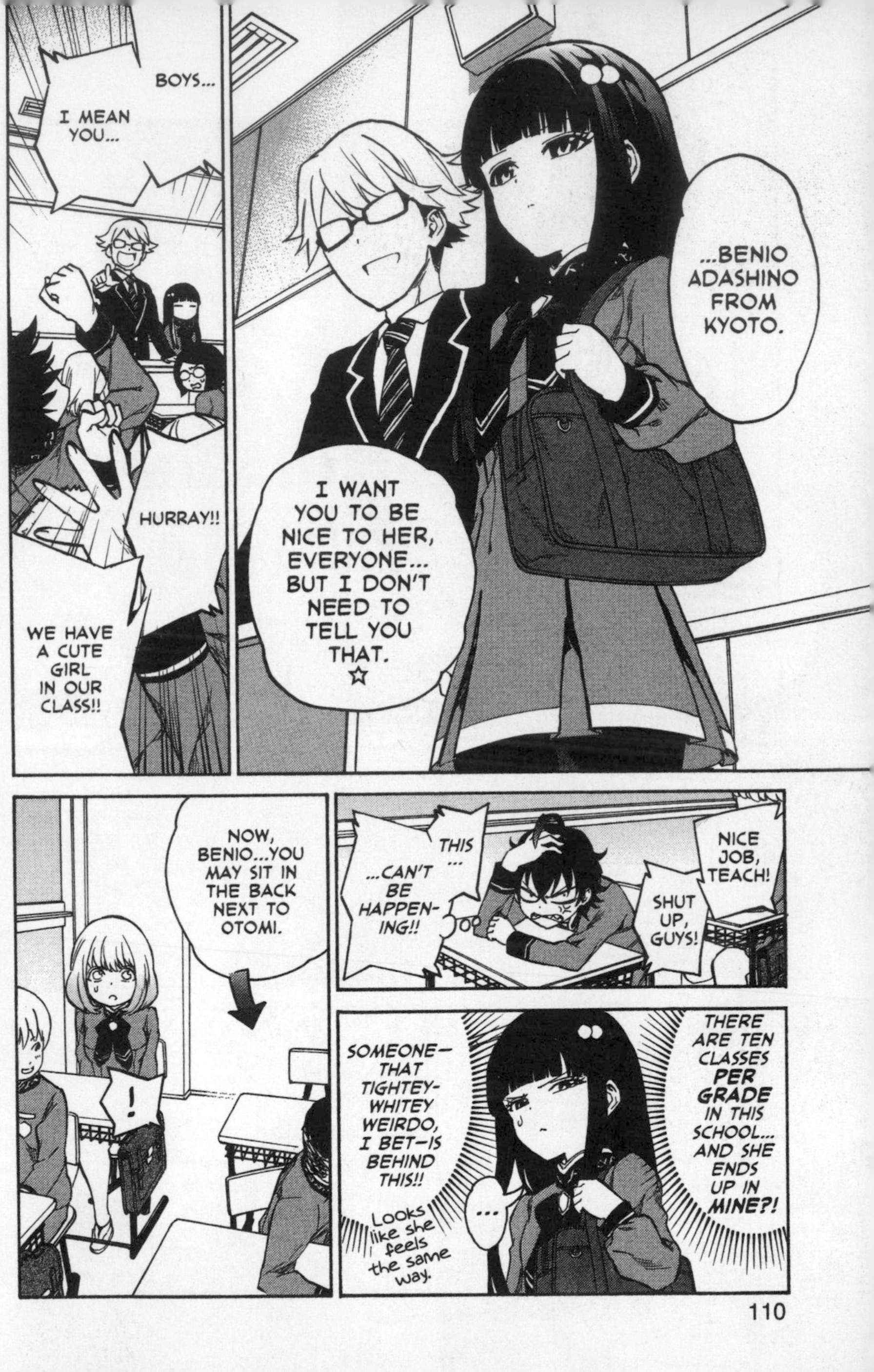
...BENIO ADASHINO FROM KYOTO.
I WANT YOU TO BE NICE TO HER, EVERYONE... BUT I DON'T NEED TO TELL YOU THAT. ☆
BOYS...
I MEAN YOU...
HURRAY!!
WE HAVE A CUTE GIRL IN OUR CLASS!!
NICE JOB, TEACH!
SHUT UP, GUYS!
THIS ...
...CAN'T BE HAPPENING!!
THERE ARE TEN CLASSES PER GRADE IN THIS SCHOOL... AND SHE ENDS UP IN MINE?!
SOMEONE—THAT TIGHTEY-WHITEY WEIRDO, I BET—IS BEHIND THIS!!
...
Looks like she feels the same way.
NOW, BENIO...YOU MAY SIT IN THE BACK NEXT TO OTOMI.
!

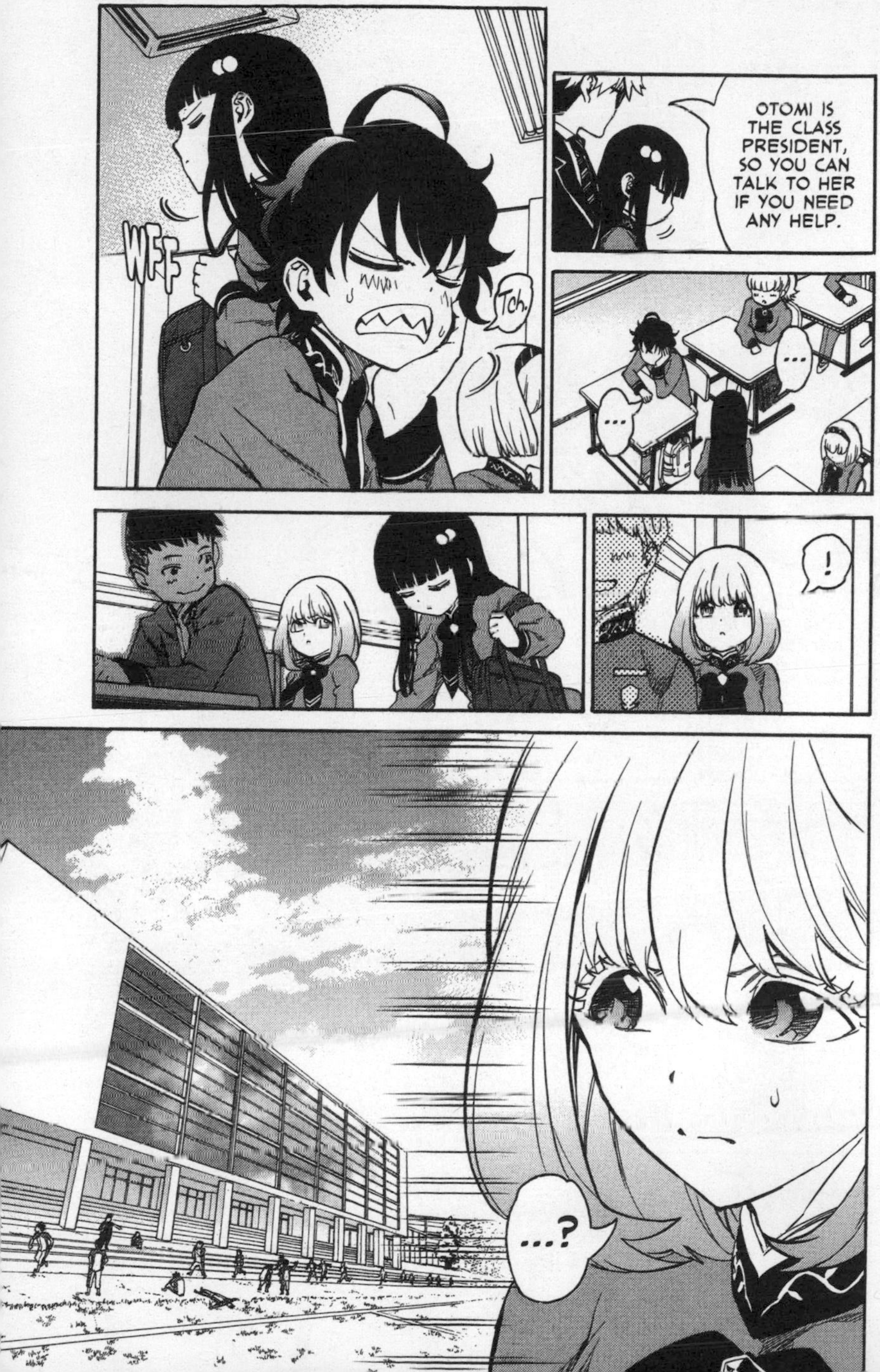
OTOMI IS THE CLASS PRESIDENT, SO YOU CAN TALK TO HER IF YOU NEED ANY HELP.
...
...
WFF
Tch.
!
...?

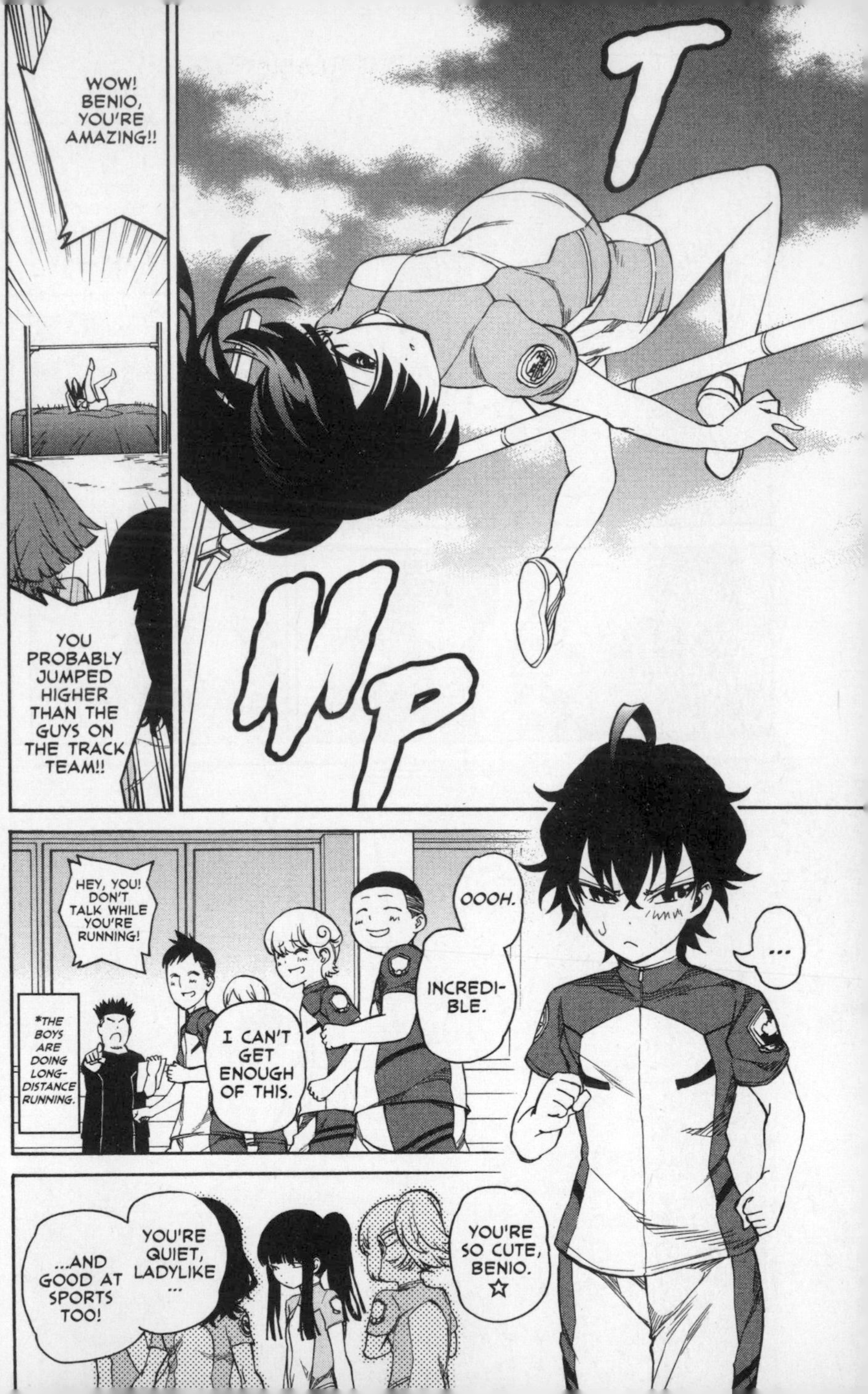
WOW! BENIO, YOU'RE AMAZING!!
YOU PROBABLY JUMPED HIGHER THAN THE GUYS ON THE TRACK TEAM!!
...
OOOH.
INCREDIBLE.
I CAN'T GET ENOUGH OF THIS.
HEY, YOU! DON'T TALK WHILE YOU'RE RUNNING!
*THE BOYS ARE DOING LONG-DISTANCE RUNNING.
YOU'RE SO CUTE, BENIO. ☆
YOU'RE QUIET, LADYLIKE ...
...AND GOOD AT SPORTS TOO!

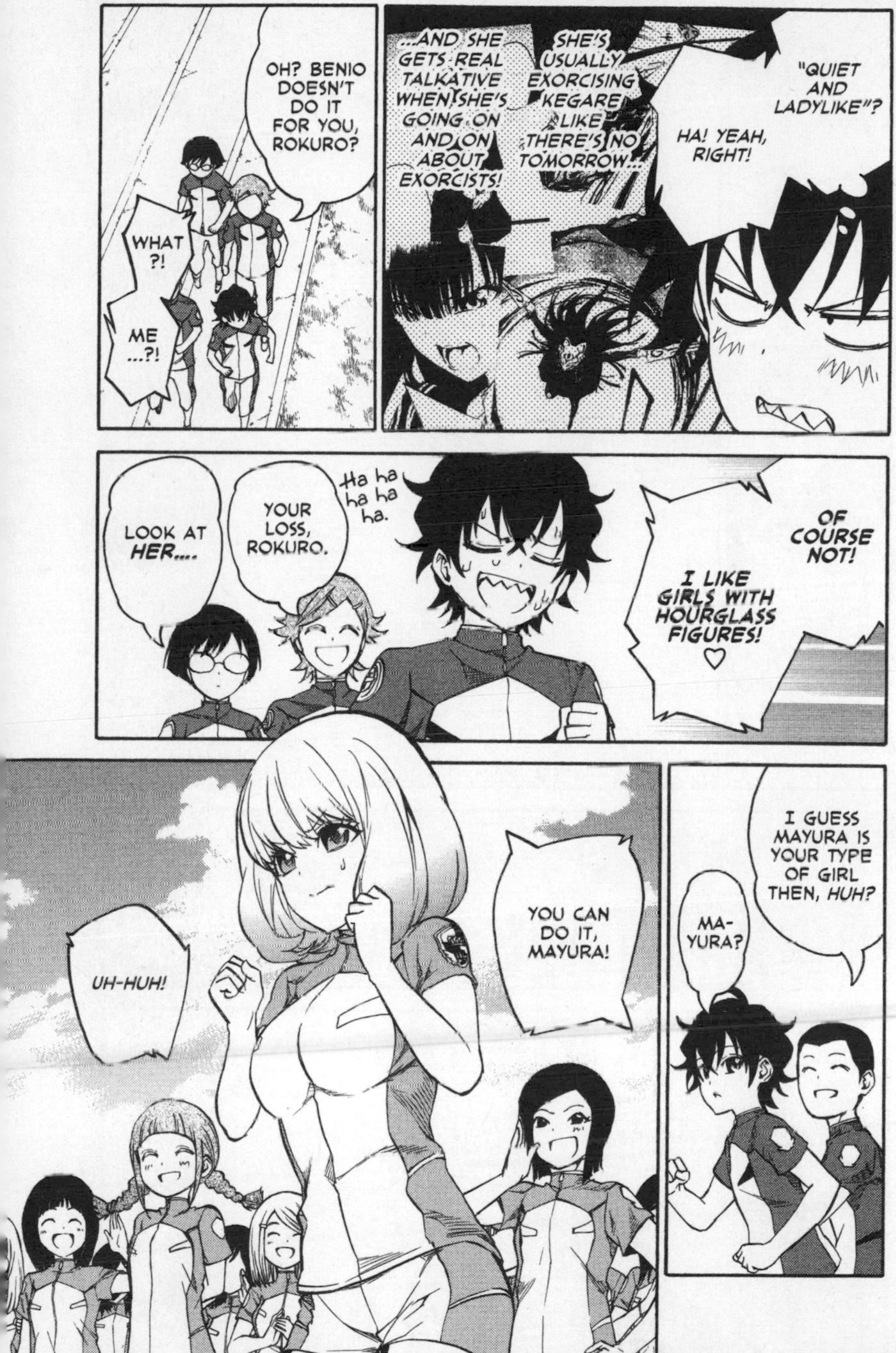
"QUIET AND LADYLIKE"?
HA! YEAH, RIGHT!
SHE'S USUALLY EXORCISING KEGARE LIKE THERE'S NO TOMORROW...
...AND SHE GETS REAL TALKATIVE WHEN SHE'S GOING ON AND ON ABOUT EXORCISTS!
OH? BENIO DOESN'T DO IT FOR YOU, ROKURO?
WHAT?!
ME ...?!
OF COURSE NOT!
I LIKE GIRLS WITH HOURGLASS FIGURES! ♡
Ha ha ha ha ha.
YOUR LOSS, ROKURO.
LOOK AT *HER*....
I GUESS MAYURA IS YOUR TYPE OF GIRL THEN, *HUH*?
MA-YURA?
YOU CAN DO IT, MAYURA!
UH-HUH!

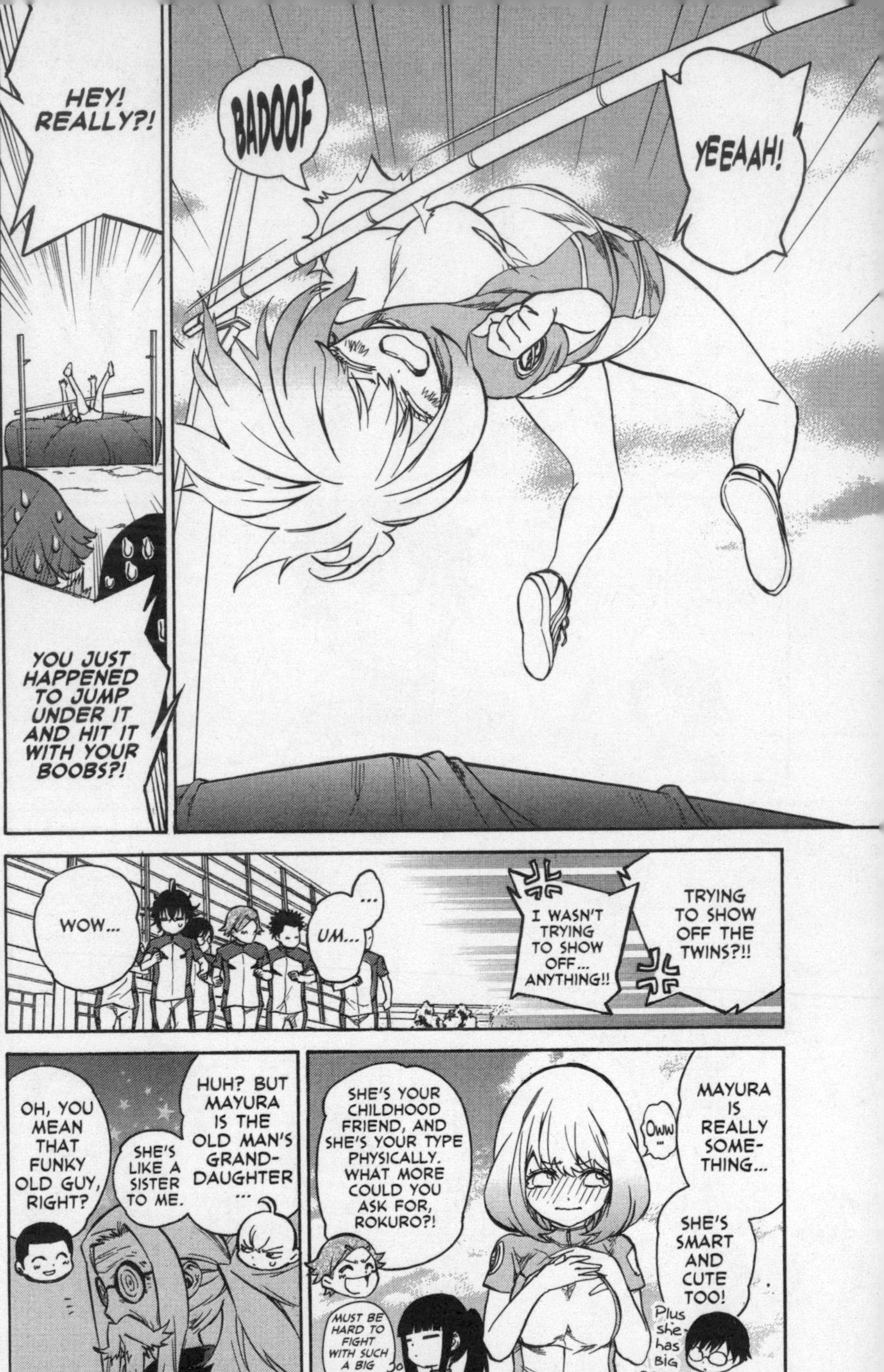
YEEAAH!
BADOOF
HEY! REALLY?!
YOU JUST HAPPENED TO JUMP UNDER IT AND HIT IT WITH YOUR BOOBS?!
TRYING TO SHOW OFF THE TWINS?!!
I WASN'T TRYING TO SHOW OFF... ANYTHING!!
...UM...
WOW...
MAYURA IS REALLY SOME-THING...
Oww...
SHE'S SMART AND CUTE TOO!
Plus she has BIG BOOBS.
SHE'S YOUR CHILDHOOD FRIEND, AND SHE'S YOUR TYPE PHYSICALLY. WHAT MORE COULD YOU ASK FOR, ROKURO?!
MUST BE HARD TO FIGHT WITH SUCH A BIG RACK...
HUH? BUT MAYURA IS THE OLD MAN'S GRAND-DAUGHTER...
SHE'S LIKE A SISTER TO ME.
OH, YOU MEAN THAT FUNKY OLD GUY, RIGHT?

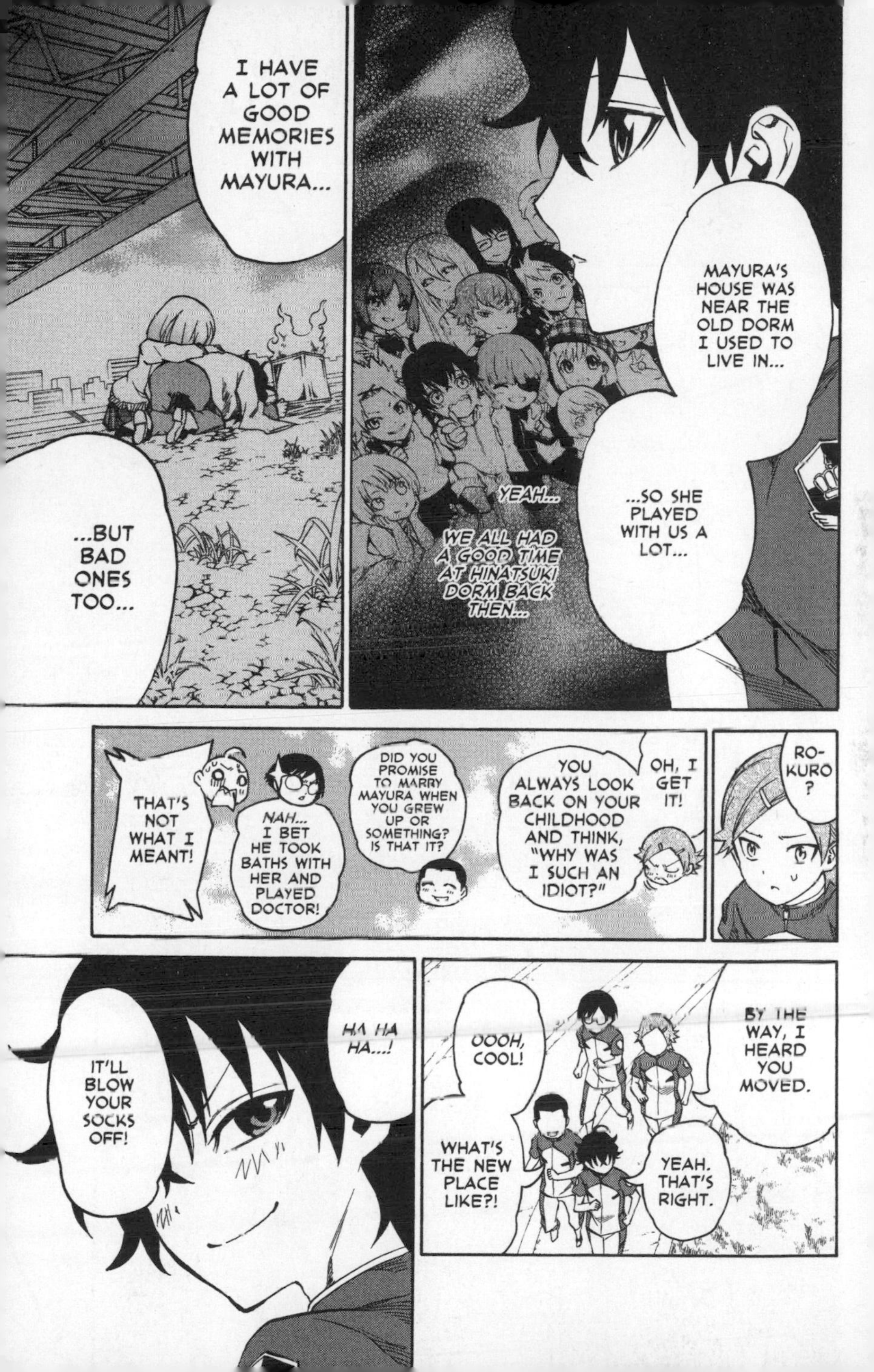
MAYURA'S HOUSE WAS NEAR THE OLD DORM I USED TO LIVE IN...
...SO SHE PLAYED WITH US A LOT...
YEAH...
WE ALL HAD A GOOD TIME AT HINATSUKI DORM BACK THEN...
I HAVE A LOT OF GOOD MEMORIES WITH MAYURA...
...BUT BAD ONES TOO...
RO-KURO?
OH, I GET IT!
YOU ALWAYS LOOK BACK ON YOUR CHILDHOOD AND THINK, "WHY WAS I SUCH AN IDIOT?"
DID YOU PROMISE TO MARRY MAYURA WHEN YOU GREW UP OR SOMETHING? IS THAT IT?
NAH... I BET HE TOOK BATHS WITH HER AND PLAYED DOCTOR!
THAT'S NOT WHAT I MEANT!
BY THE WAY, I HEARD YOU MOVED.
YEAH. THAT'S RIGHT.
OOOH, COOL!
WHAT'S THE NEW PLACE LIKE?!
HA HA HA...!
IT'LL BLOW YOUR SOCKS OFF!

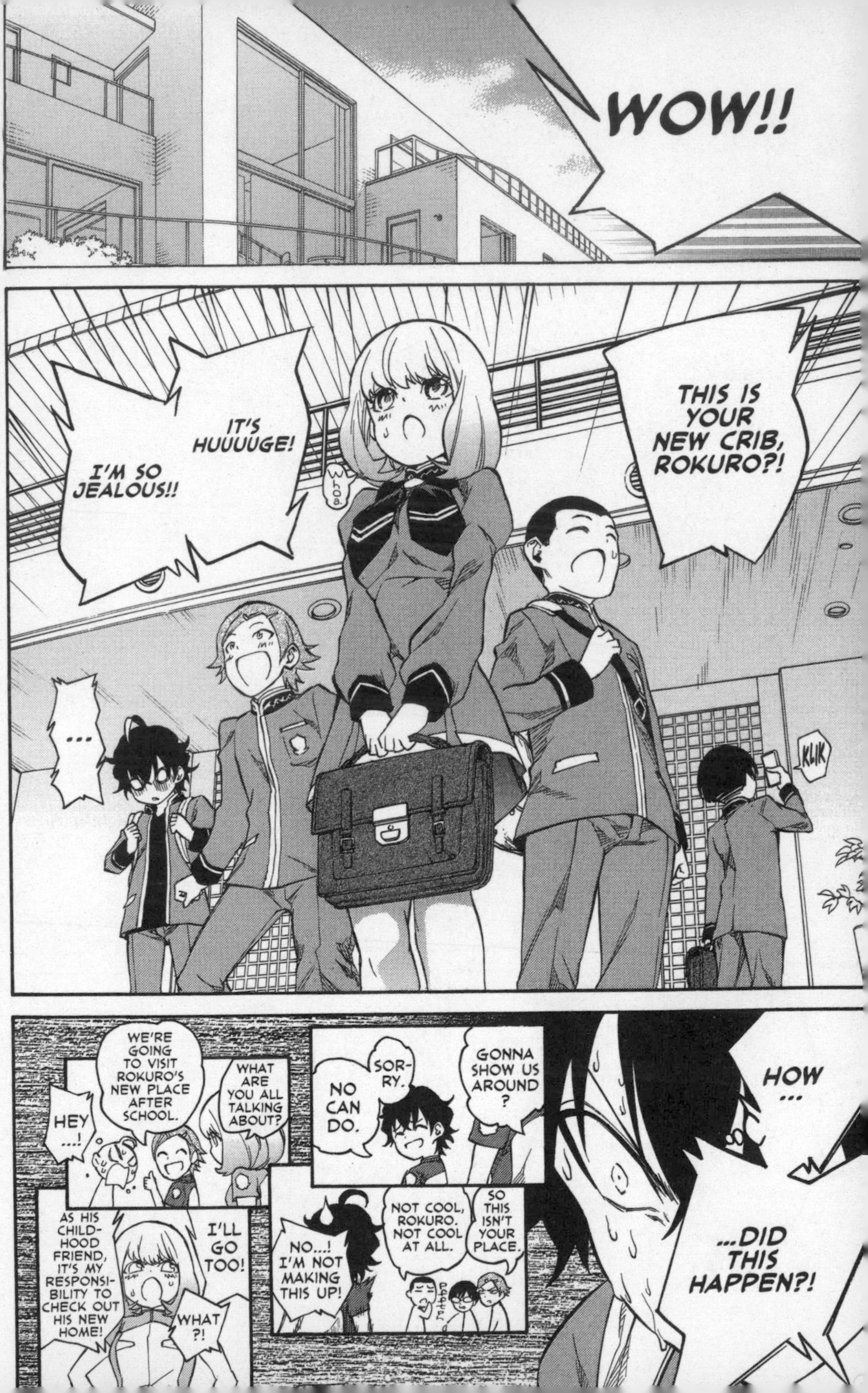
WOW!!
THIS IS YOUR NEW CRIB, ROKURO?!
Whoa.
IT'S HUUUUGE!
I'M SO JEALOUS!!
KLIK
...
HOW ...
...DID THIS HAPPEN?!
GONNA SHOW US AROUND?
SOR-RY.
NO CAN DO.
WHAT ARE YOU ALL TALKING ABOUT?
WE'RE GOING TO VISIT ROKURO'S NEW PLACE AFTER SCHOOL.
HEY ...!
SO THIS ISN'T YOUR PLACE.
NOT COOL, ROKURO. NOT COOL AT ALL.
NO...! I'M NOT MAKING THIS UP!
I'LL GO TOO!
AS HIS CHILD-HOOD FRIEND, IT'S MY RESPONSI-BILITY TO CHECK OUT HIS NEW HOME!
WHAT ?!

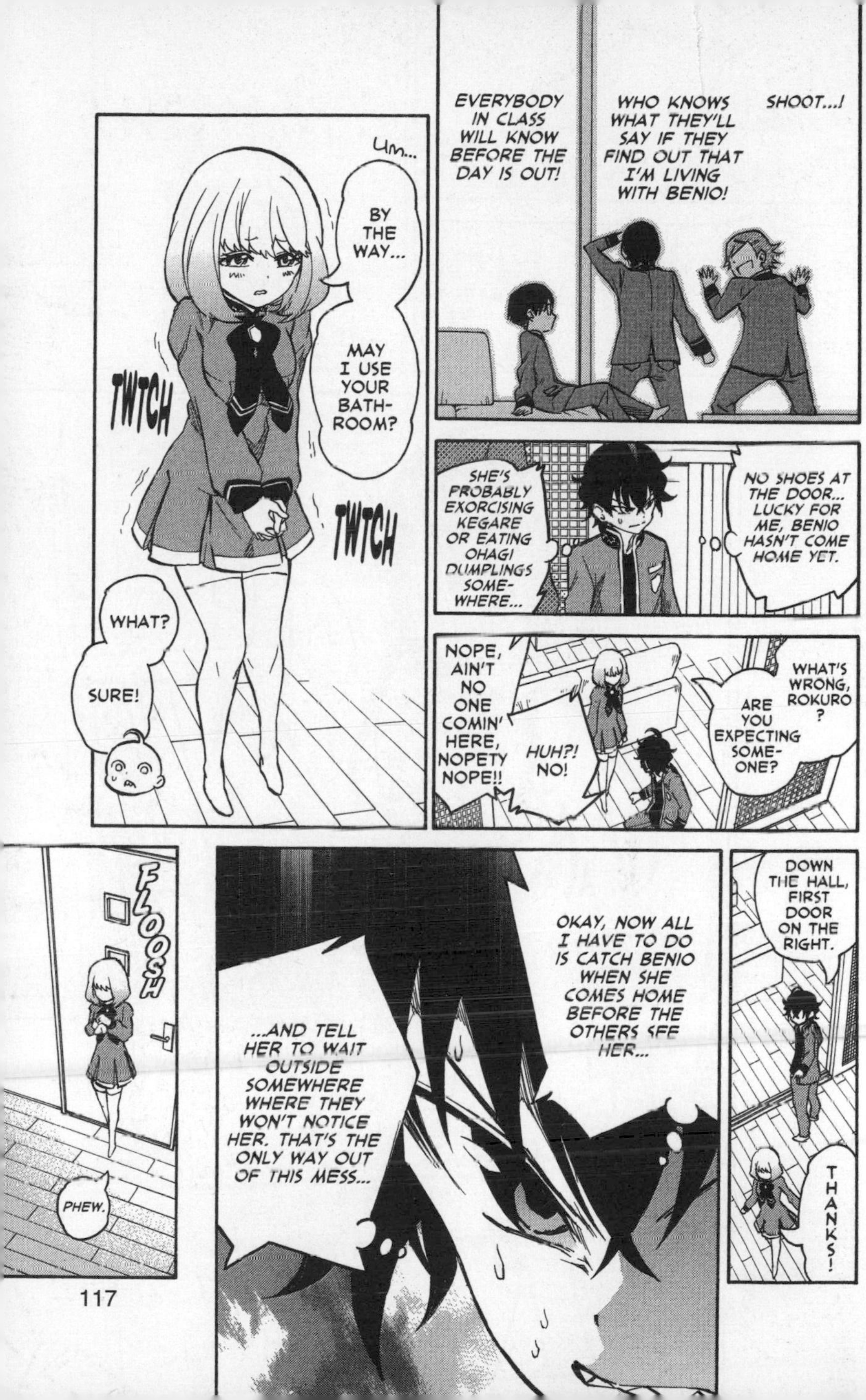
SHOOT...!
WHO KNOWS WHAT THEY'LL SAY IF THEY FIND OUT THAT I'M LIVING WITH BENIO!
EVERYBODY IN CLASS WILL KNOW BEFORE THE DAY IS OUT!
NO SHOES AT THE DOOR... LUCKY FOR ME, BENIO HASN'T COME HOME YET.
SHE'S PROBABLY EXORCISING KEGARE OR EATING OHAGI DUMPLINGS SOMEWHERE...
WHAT'S WRONG, ROKURO?
ARE YOU EXPECTING SOMEONE?
HUH?! NO!
NOPE, AIN'T NO ONE COMIN' HERE, NOPETY NOPE!!
Um...
BY THE WAY...
MAY I USE YOUR BATHROOM?
TWTCH
TWTCH
WHAT?
SURE!
DOWN THE HALL, FIRST DOOR ON THE RIGHT.
THANKS!
OKAY, NOW ALL I HAVE TO DO IS CATCH BENIO WHEN SHE COMES HOME BEFORE THE OTHERS SEE HER...
...AND TELL HER TO WAIT OUTSIDE SOMEWHERE WHERE THEY WON'T NOTICE HER. THAT'S THE ONLY WAY OUT OF THIS MESS...
FLOOSH
PHEW.

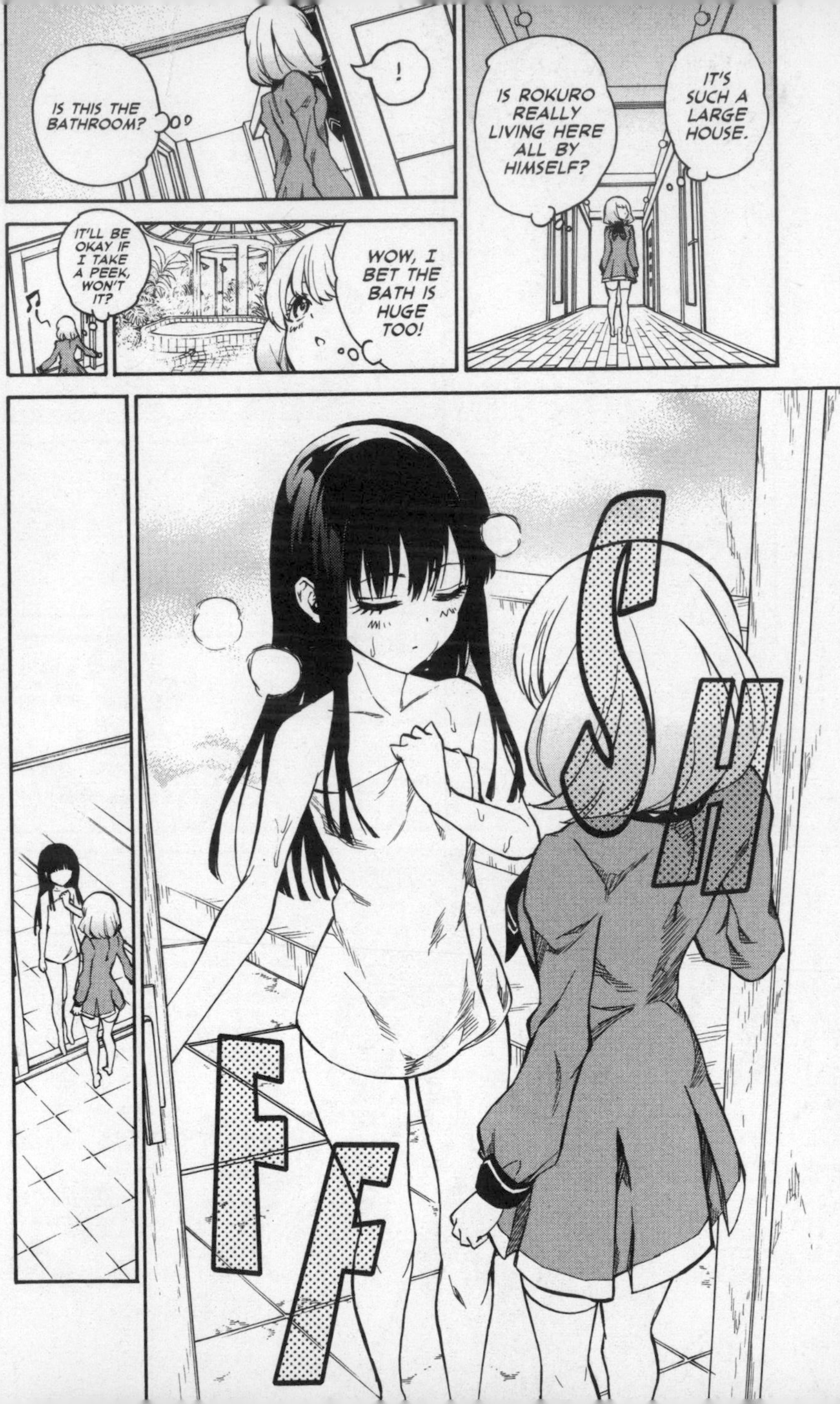
IT'S SUCH A LARGE HOUSE.
IS ROKURO REALLY LIVING HERE ALL BY HIMSELF?
!
IS THIS THE BATHROOM?
WOW, I BET THE BATH IS HUGE TOO!
IT'LL BE OKAY IF I TAKE A PEEK, WON'T IT?
SHFF

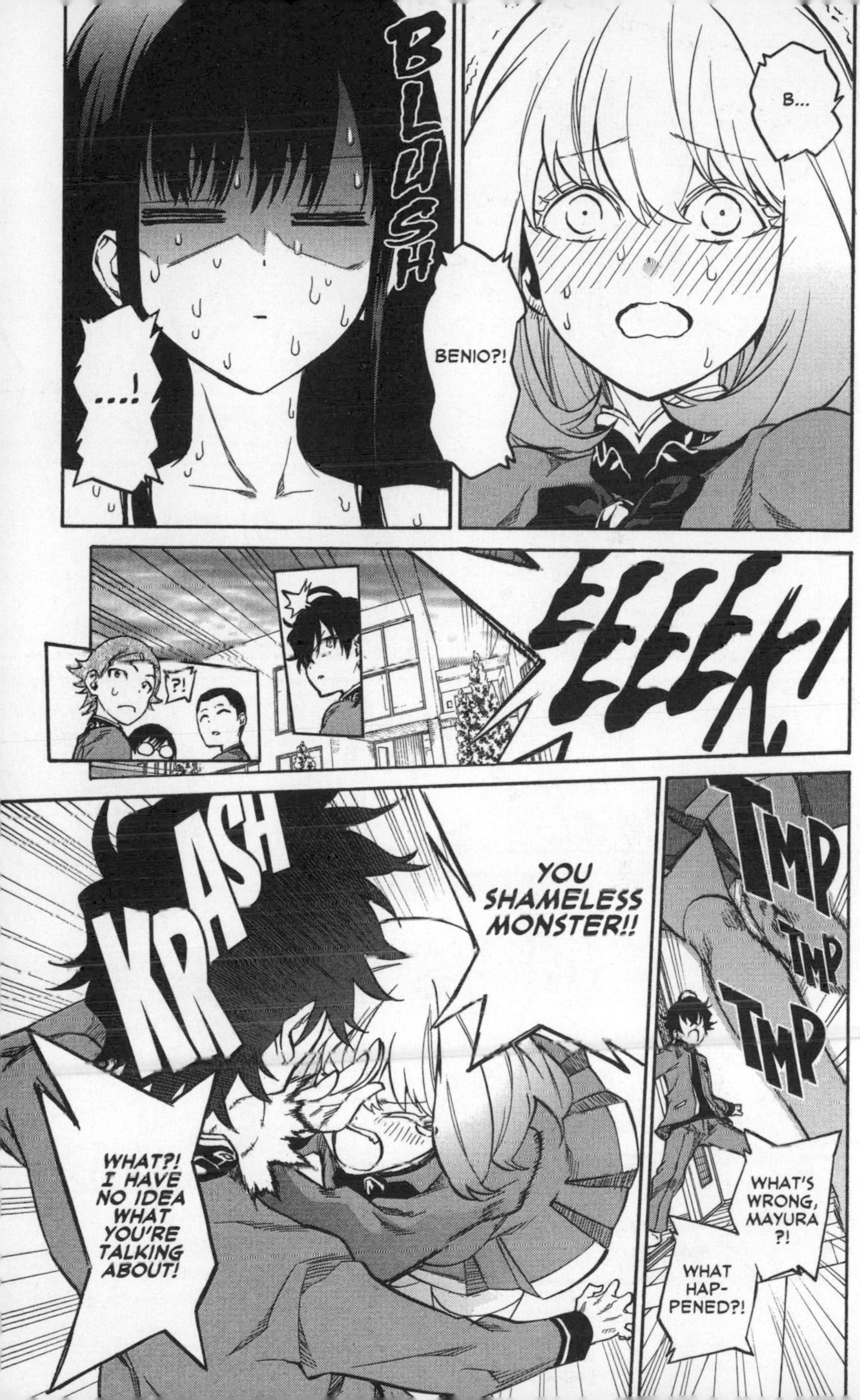
B...
BENIO?!
BLUSH
...!
EEEEK!
?!
TMP
TMP
TMP
WHAT'S WRONG, MAYURA?!
WHAT HAP-PENED?!
YOU SHAMELESS MONSTER!!
KRASH
WHAT?! I HAVE NO IDEA WHAT YOU'RE TALKING ABOUT!

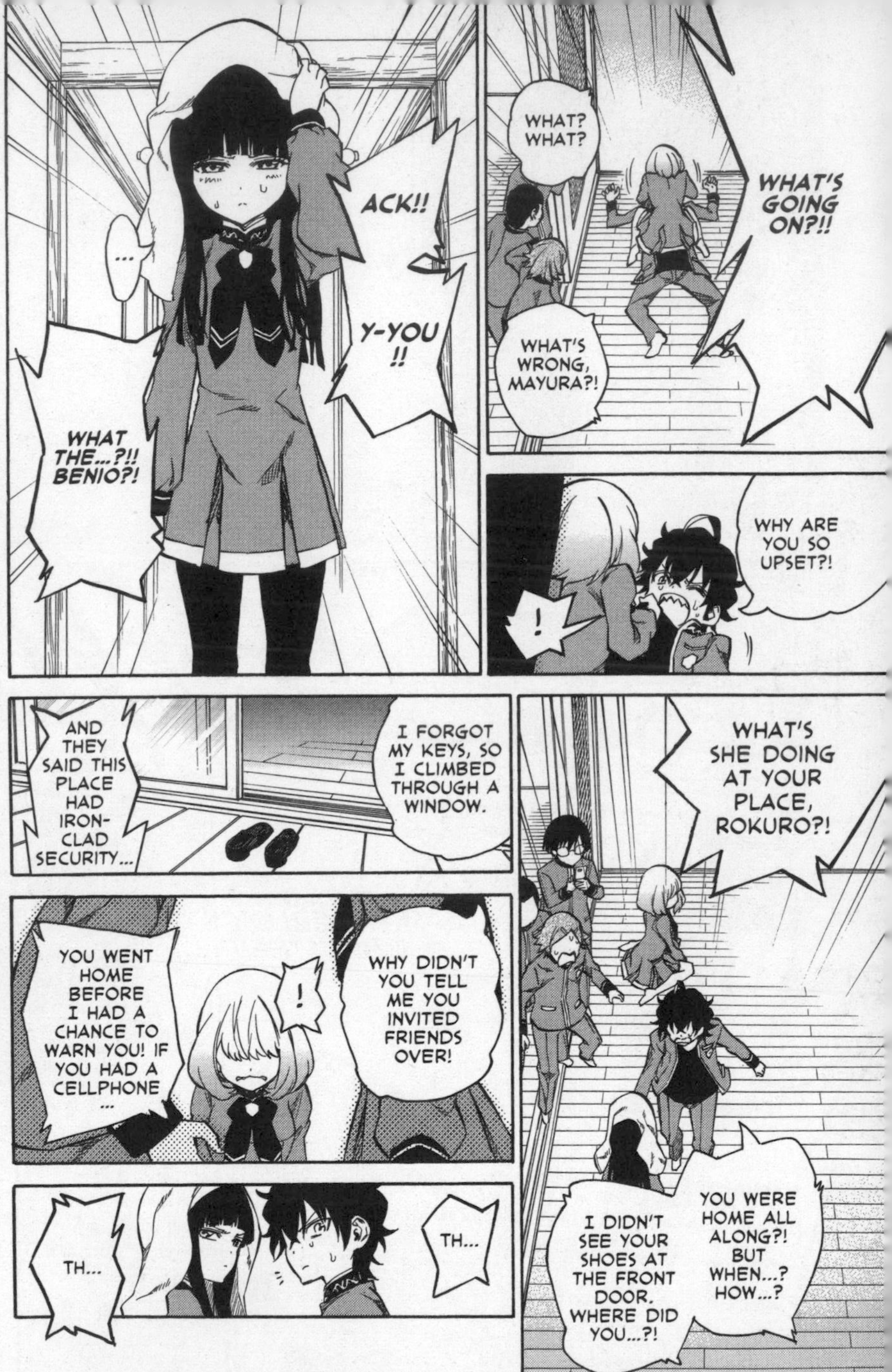
WHAT? WHAT?
WHAT'S GOING ON?!!
WHAT'S WRONG, MAYURA?!
WHY ARE YOU SO UPSET?!
!
ACK!!
Y-YOU !!
...
WHAT THE...?!! BENIO?!
WHAT'S SHE DOING AT YOUR PLACE, ROKURO?!
YOU WERE HOME ALL ALONG?! BUT WHEN...? HOW...?
I DIDN'T SEE YOUR SHOES AT THE FRONT DOOR. WHERE DID YOU...?!
I FORGOT MY KEYS, SO I CLIMBED THROUGH A WINDOW.
AND THEY SAID THIS PLACE HAD IRON-CLAD SECURITY...
WHY DIDN'T YOU TELL ME YOU INVITED FRIENDS OVER!
!
YOU WENT HOME BEFORE I HAD A CHANCE TO WARN YOU! IF YOU HAD A CELLPHONE ...
TH...
TH...

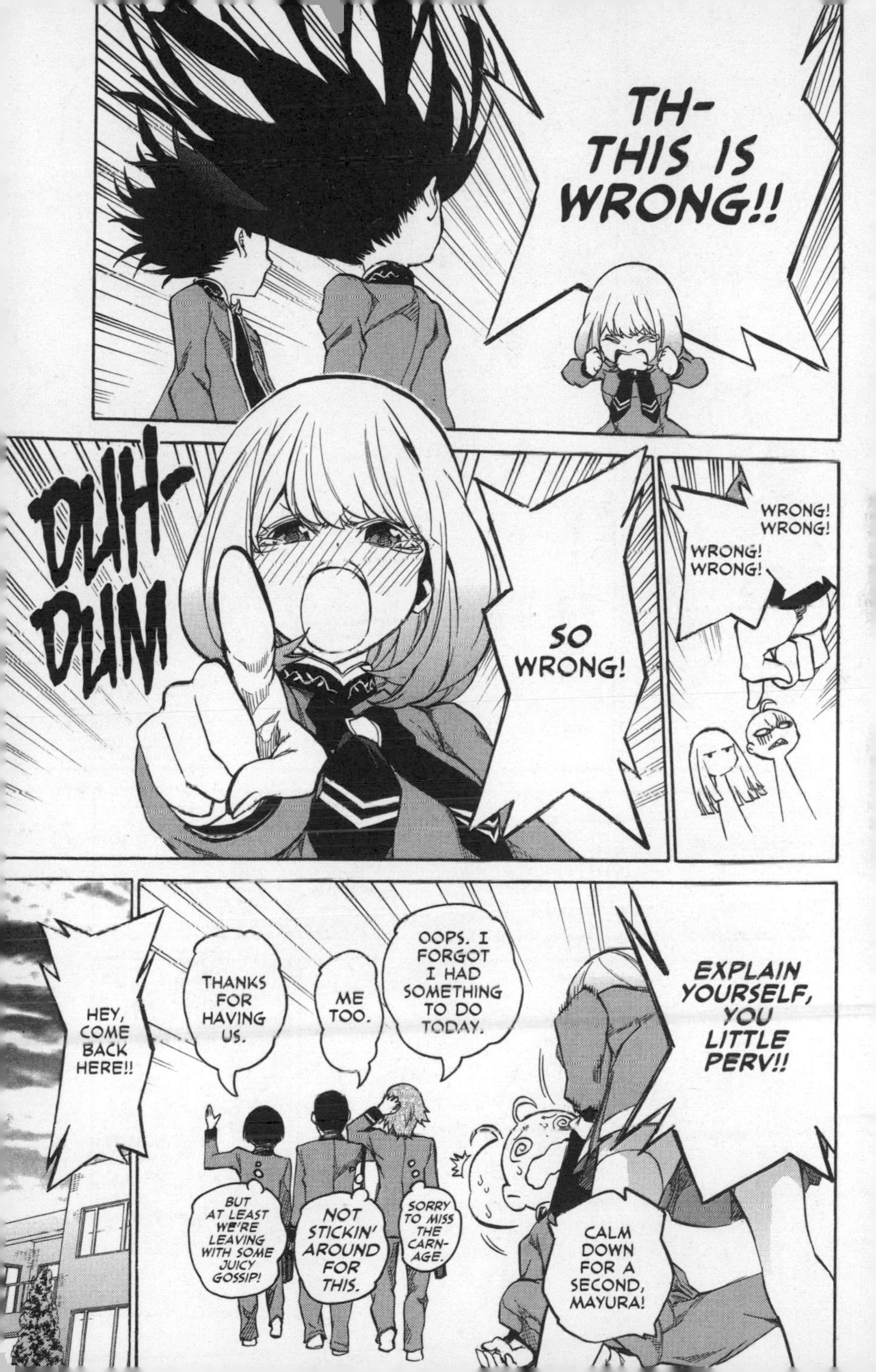
TH- THIS IS WRONG!!
WRONG! WRONG!
WRONG! WRONG!
SO WRONG!
DUH-DUM
EXPLAIN YOURSELF, YOU LITTLE PERV!!
OOPS. I FORGOT I HAD SOMETHING TO DO TODAY.
ME TOO.
THANKS FOR HAVING US.
CALM DOWN FOR A SECOND, MAYURA!
SORRY TO MISS THE CARNAGE.
NOT STICKIN' AROUND FOR THIS.
BUT AT LEAST WE'RE LEAVING WITH SOME JUICY GOSSIP!
HEY, COME BACK HERE!!

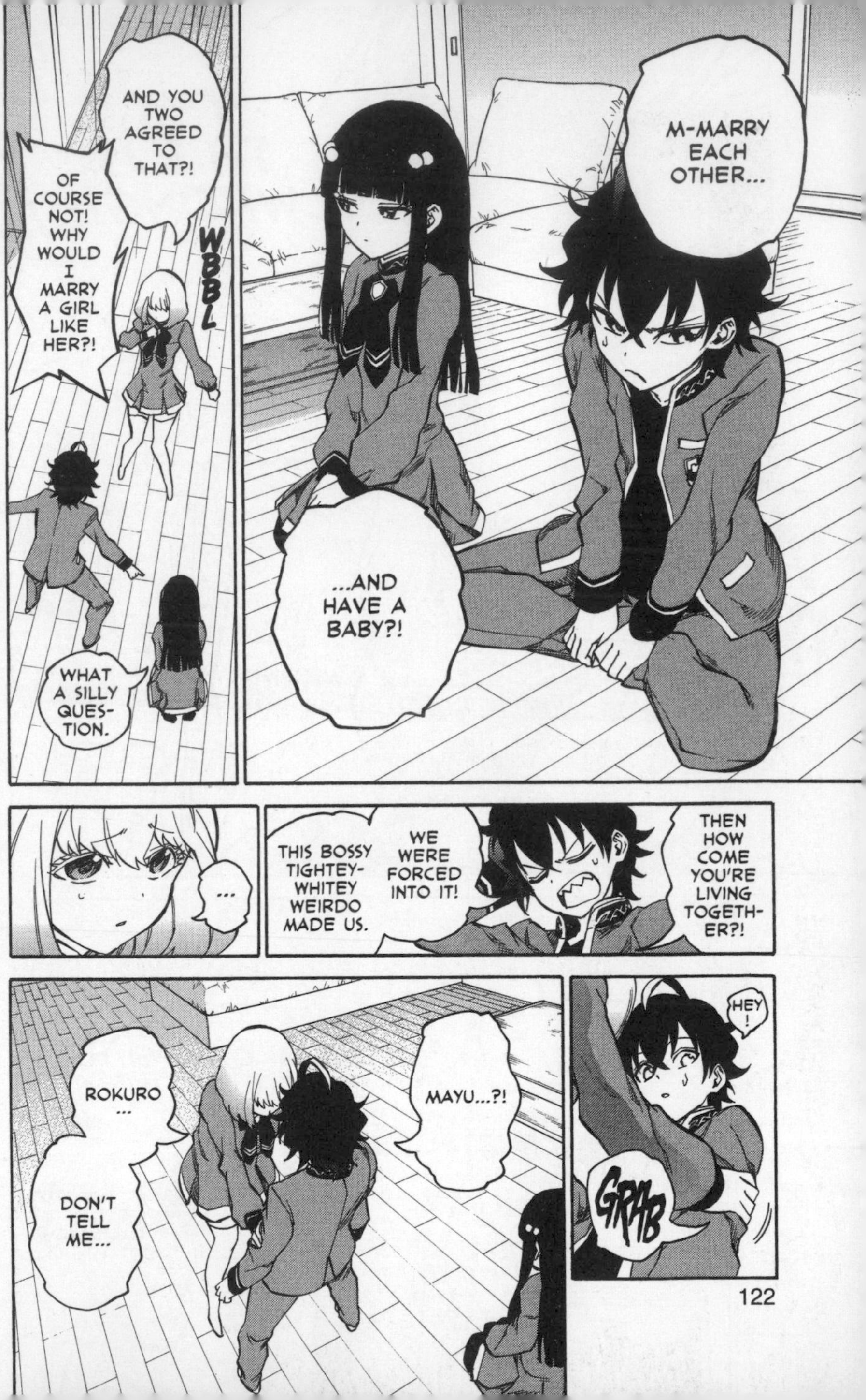
M-MARRY EACH OTHER...
...AND HAVE A BABY?!
AND YOU TWO AGREED TO THAT?!
OF COURSE NOT! WHY WOULD I MARRY A GIRL LIKE HER?!
WBBL
WHAT A SILLY QUESTION.
THEN HOW COME YOU'RE LIVING TOGETHER?!
WE WERE FORCED INTO IT!
THIS BOSSY TIGHTEY-WHITEY WEIRDO MADE US.
...
HEY!
GRAB
MAYU...?!
ROKURO...
DON'T TELL ME...

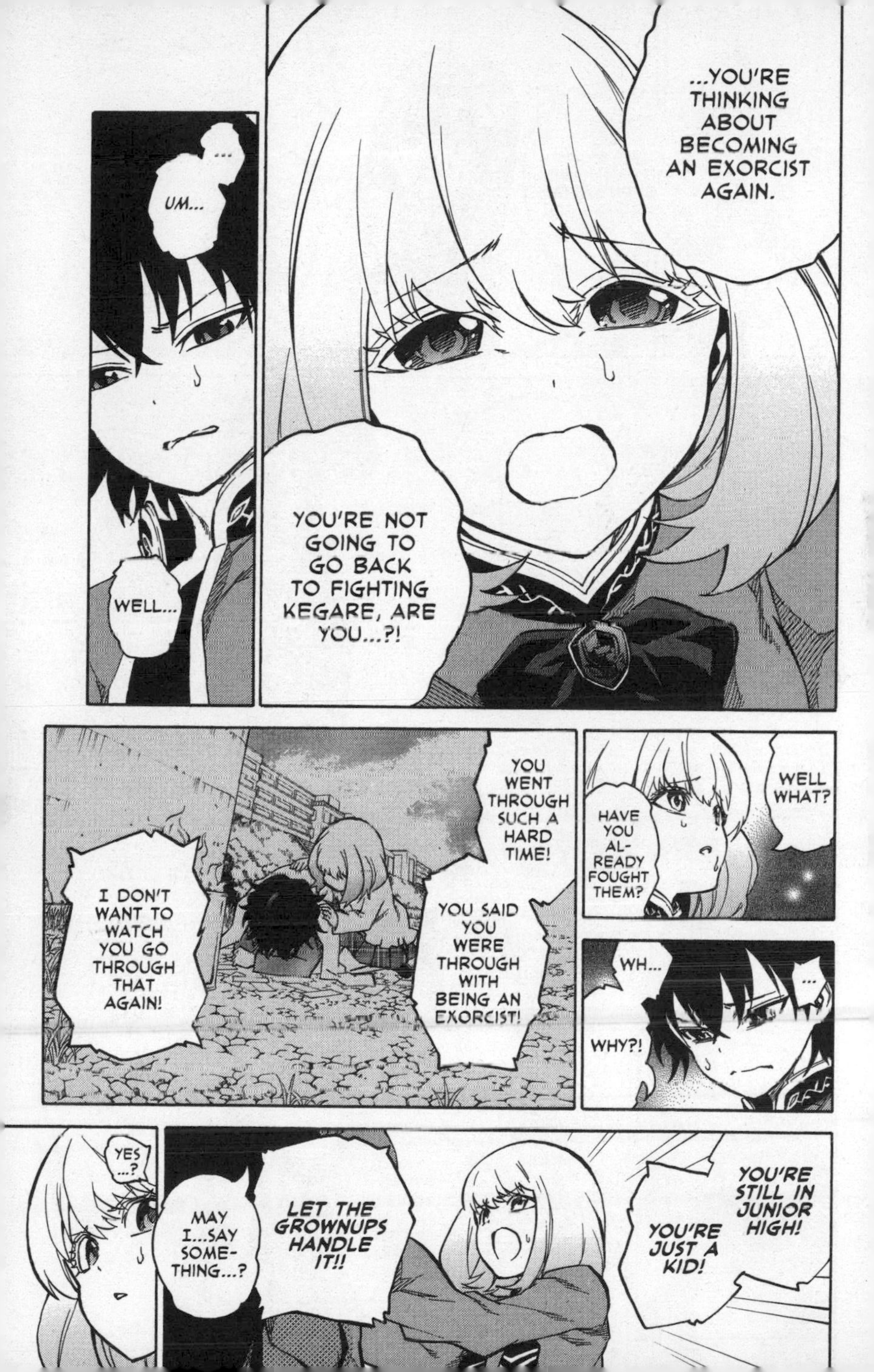
...YOU'RE THINKING ABOUT BECOMING AN EXORCIST AGAIN.
YOU'RE NOT GOING TO GO BACK TO FIGHTING KEGARE, ARE YOU...?!
...
UM...
WELL...
WELL WHAT?
HAVE YOU AL-READY FOUGHT THEM?
...
WH...
WHY?!
YOU WENT THROUGH SUCH A HARD TIME!
YOU SAID YOU WERE THROUGH WITH BEING AN EXORCIST!
I DON'T WANT TO WATCH YOU GO THROUGH THAT AGAIN!
YOU'RE STILL IN JUNIOR HIGH!
YOU'RE JUST A KID!
LET THE GROWNUPS HANDLE IT!!
MAY I...SAY SOME-THING...?
YES ...?

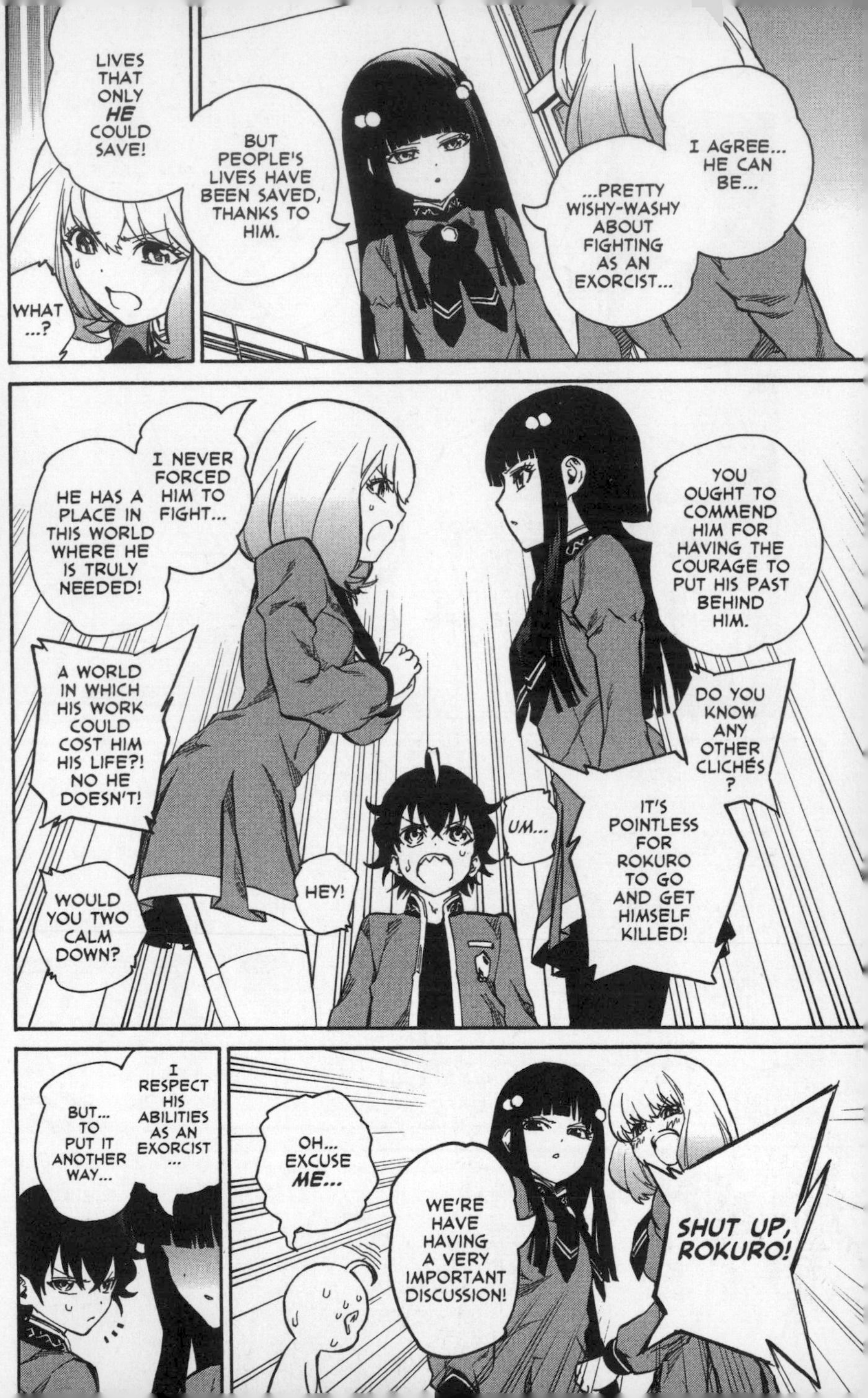
I AGREE... HE CAN BE...
...PRETTY WISHY-WASHY ABOUT FIGHTING AS AN EXORCIST...
BUT PEOPLE'S LIVES HAVE BEEN SAVED, THANKS TO HIM.
LIVES THAT ONLY *HE* COULD SAVE!
WHAT ...?
YOU OUGHT TO COMMEND HIM FOR HAVING THE COURAGE TO PUT HIS PAST BEHIND HIM.
I NEVER FORCED HIM TO FIGHT...
HE HAS A PLACE IN THIS WORLD WHERE HE IS TRULY NEEDED!
DO YOU KNOW ANY OTHER CLICHÉS?
A WORLD IN WHICH HIS WORK COULD COST HIM HIS LIFE?! NO HE DOESN'T!
IT'S POINTLESS FOR ROKURO TO GO AND GET HIMSELF KILLED!
UM...
HEY!
WOULD YOU TWO CALM DOWN?
SHUT UP, ROKURO!
WE'RE HAVE HAVING A VERY IMPORTANT DISCUSSION!
OH... EXCUSE *ME*...
I RESPECT HIS ABILITIES AS AN EXORCIST ...
BUT... TO PUT IT ANOTHER WAY...

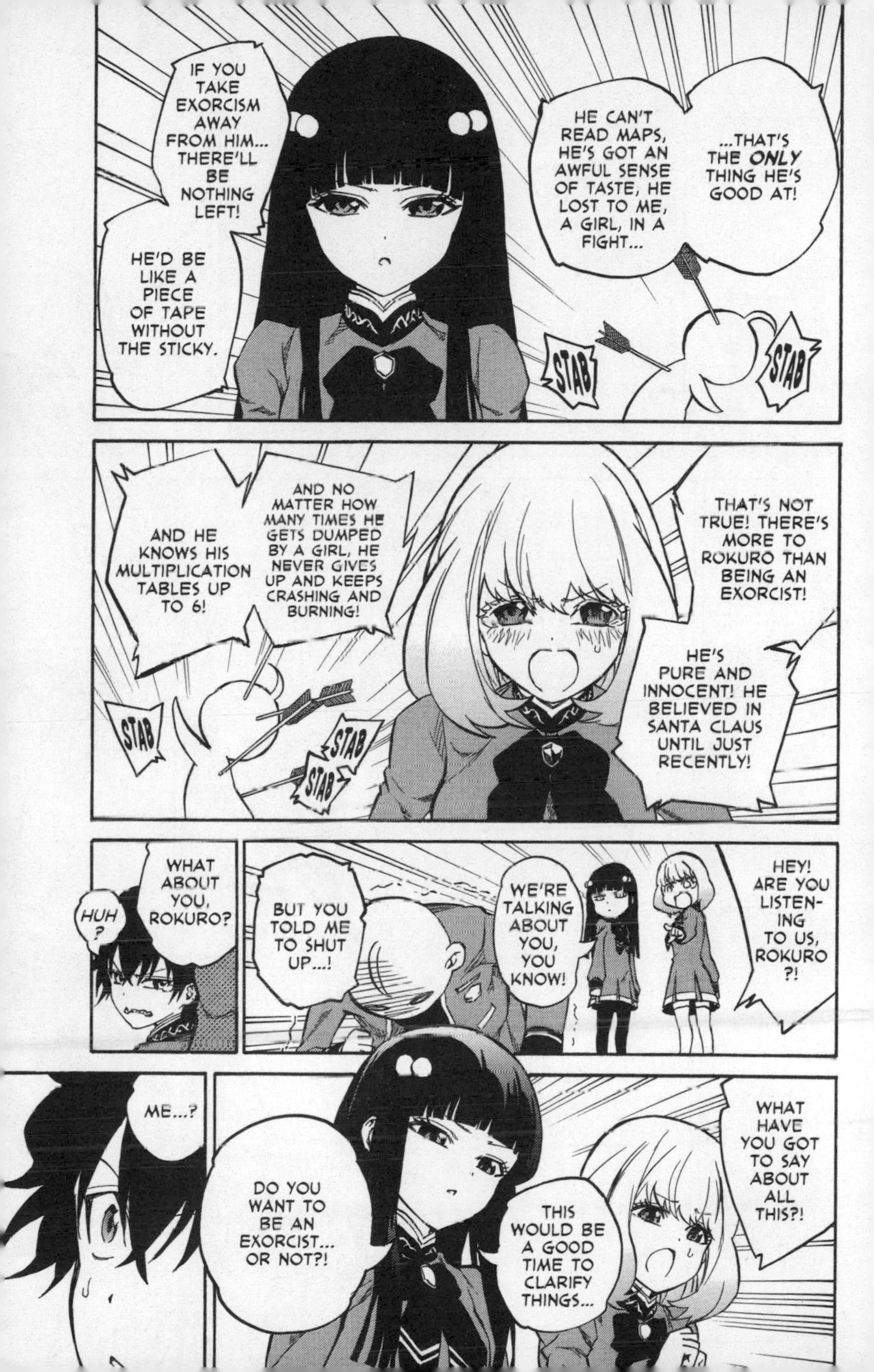
HE CAN'T READ MAPS, HE'S GOT AN AWFUL SENSE OF TASTE, HE LOST TO ME, A GIRL, IN A FIGHT...
...THAT'S THE ONLY THING HE'S GOOD AT!
STAB
STAB
IF YOU TAKE EXORCISM AWAY FROM HIM... THERE'LL BE NOTHING LEFT!
HE'D BE LIKE A PIECE OF TAPE WITHOUT THE STICKY.
THAT'S NOT TRUE! THERE'S MORE TO ROKURO THAN BEING AN EXORCIST!
HE'S PURE AND INNOCENT! HE BELIEVED IN SANTA CLAUS UNTIL JUST RECENTLY!
AND NO MATTER HOW MANY TIMES HE GETS DUMPED BY A GIRL, HE NEVER GIVES UP AND KEEPS CRASHING AND BURNING!
AND HE KNOWS HIS MULTIPLICATION TABLES UP TO 6!
STAB
STAB
STAB
HEY! ARE YOU LISTENING TO US, ROKURO?!
WE'RE TALKING ABOUT YOU, YOU KNOW!
BUT YOU TOLD ME TO SHUT UP...!
WHAT ABOUT YOU, ROKURO?
HUH?
WHAT HAVE YOU GOT TO SAY ABOUT ALL THIS?!
THIS WOULD BE A GOOD TIME TO CLARIFY THINGS...
DO YOU WANT TO BE AN EXORCIST... OR NOT?!
ME...?

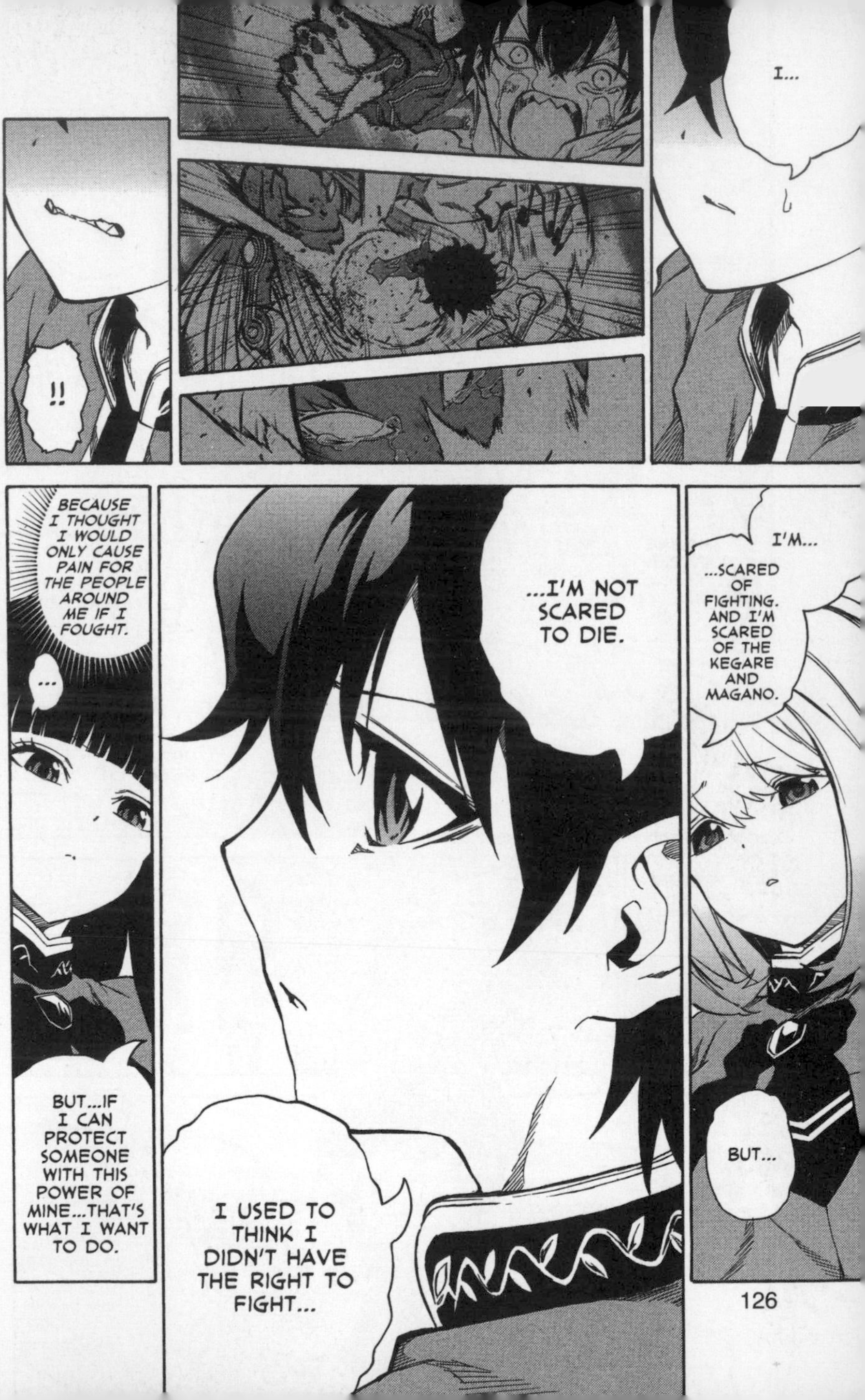
I...
!!
I'M...
...SCARED OF FIGHTING. AND I'M SCARED OF THE KEGARE AND MAGANO.
BUT...
...I'M NOT SCARED TO DIE.
I USED TO THINK I DIDN'T HAVE THE RIGHT TO FIGHT...
BECAUSE I THOUGHT I WOULD ONLY CAUSE PAIN FOR THE PEOPLE AROUND ME IF I FOUGHT.
...
BUT...IF I CAN PROTECT SOMEONE WITH THIS POWER OF MINE...THAT'S WHAT I WANT TO DO.

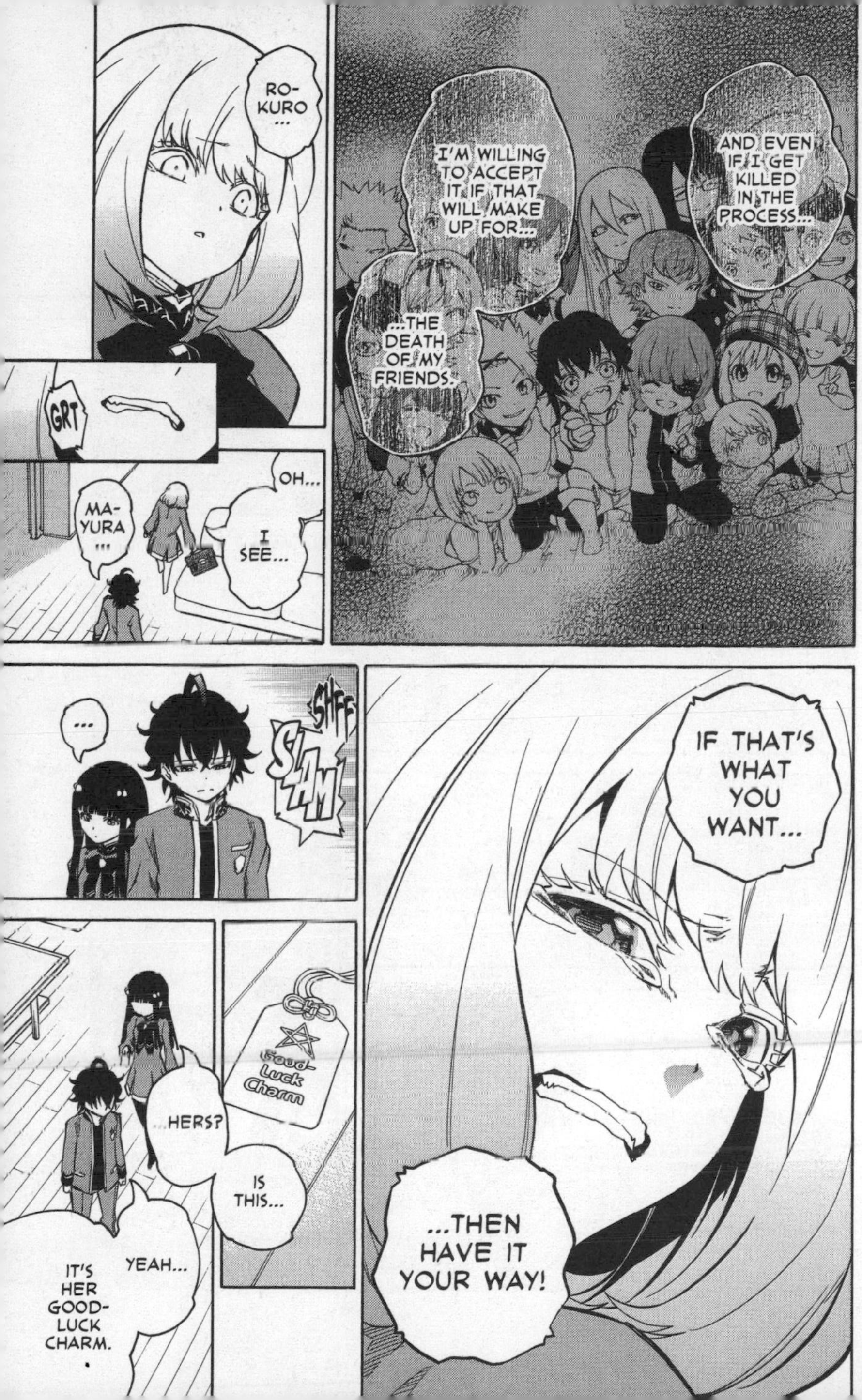
AND EVEN IF I GET KILLED IN THE PROCESS...
I'M WILLING TO ACCEPT IT IF THAT WILL MAKE UP FOR...
...THE DEATH OF MY FRIENDS.
RO-KURO...
GRT
OH... I SEE...
MA-YURA...
IF THAT'S WHAT YOU WANT...
...THEN HAVE IT YOUR WAY!
SHFF
SLAM
...
Good-Luck Charm
IS THIS...
...HERS?
YEAH...
IT'S HER GOOD-LUCK CHARM.

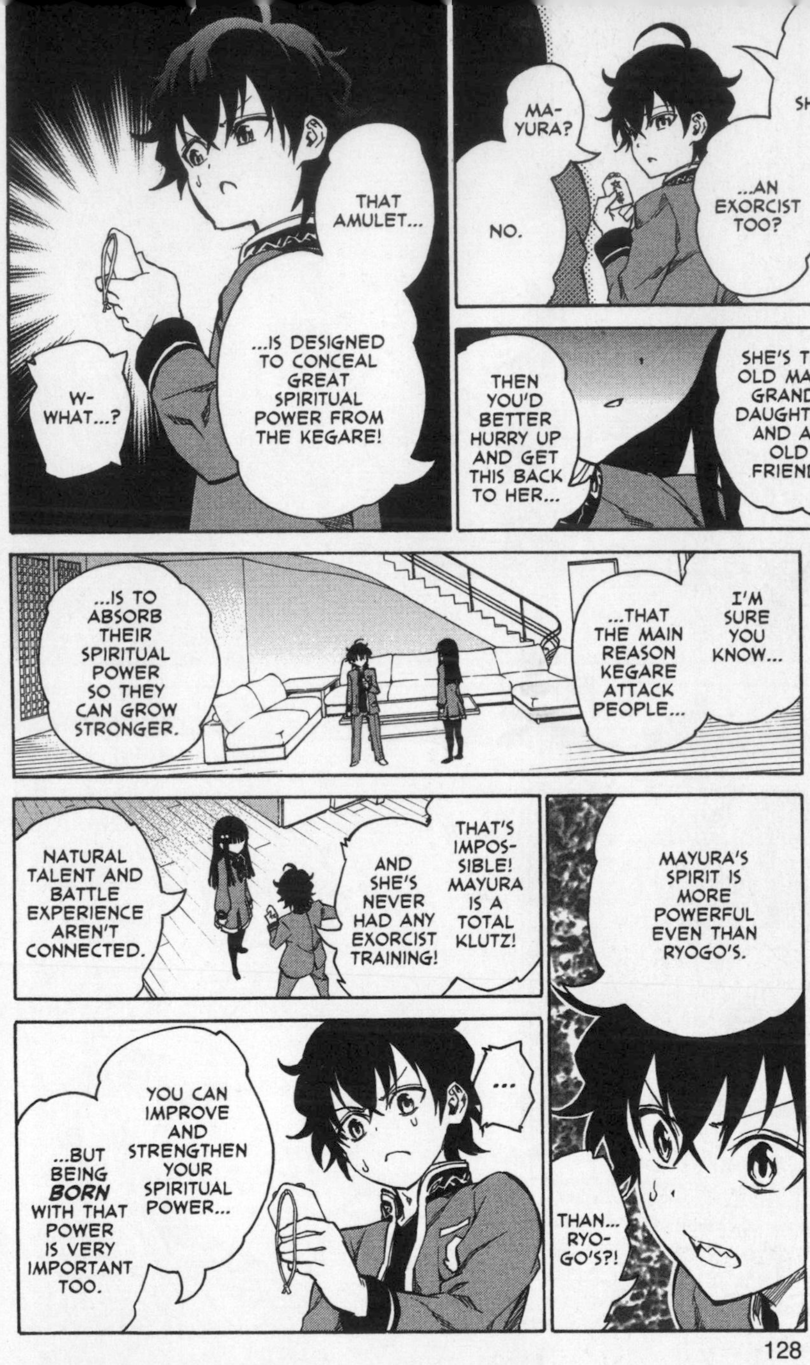
IS SHE...
...AN EXORCIST TOO?
MA-YURA?
NO.
SHE'S THE OLD MAN'S GRAND-DAUGHTER. AND AN OLD FRIEND.
THEN YOU'D BETTER HURRY UP AND GET THIS BACK TO HER...
THAT AMULET...
...IS DESIGNED TO CONCEAL GREAT SPIRITUAL POWER FROM THE KEGARE!
W-WHAT...?
I'M SURE YOU KNOW...
...THAT THE MAIN REASON KEGARE ATTACK PEOPLE...
...IS TO ABSORB THEIR SPIRITUAL POWER SO THEY CAN GROW STRONGER.
MAYURA'S SPIRIT IS MORE POWERFUL EVEN THAN RYOGO'S.
THAN... RYO-GO'S?!
THAT'S IMPOS-SIBLE! MAYURA IS A TOTAL KLUTZ!
AND SHE'S NEVER HAD ANY EXORCIST TRAINING!
NATURAL TALENT AND BATTLE EXPERIENCE AREN'T CONNECTED.
...
YOU CAN IMPROVE AND STRENGTHEN YOUR SPIRITUAL POWER...
...BUT BEING ***BORN*** WITH THAT POWER IS VERY IMPORTANT TOO.

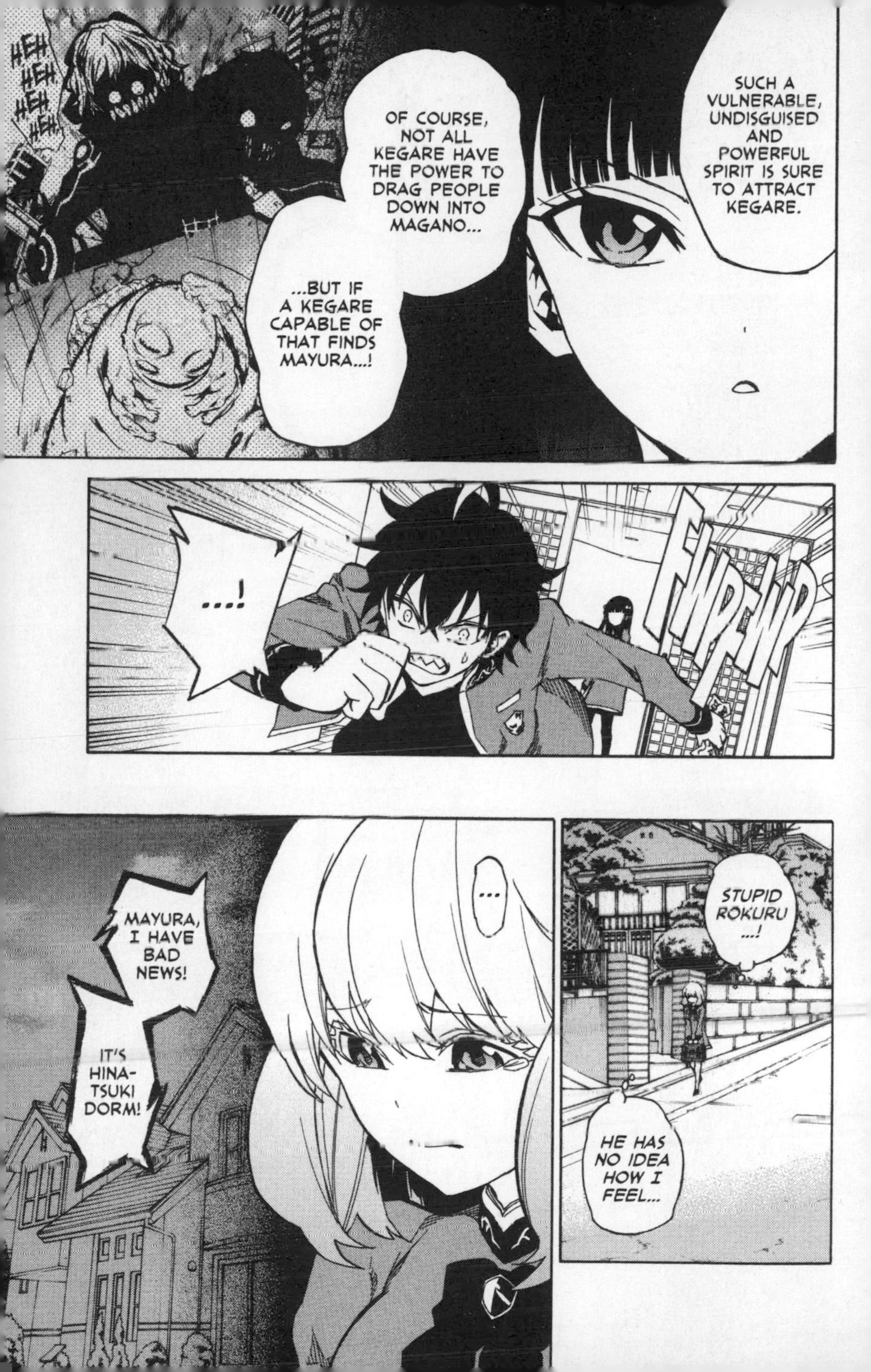
SUCH A VULNERABLE, UNDISGUISED AND POWERFUL SPIRIT IS SURE TO ATTRACT KEGARE.
OF COURSE, NOT ALL KEGARE HAVE THE POWER TO DRAG PEOPLE DOWN INTO MAGANO...
...BUT IF A KEGARE CAPABLE OF THAT FINDS MAYURA...!
HEH HEH HEH HEH
...!
STUPID ROKURU ...!
HE HAS NO IDEA HOW I FEEL...
...
MAYURA, I HAVE BAD NEWS!
IT'S HINA-TSUKI DORM!

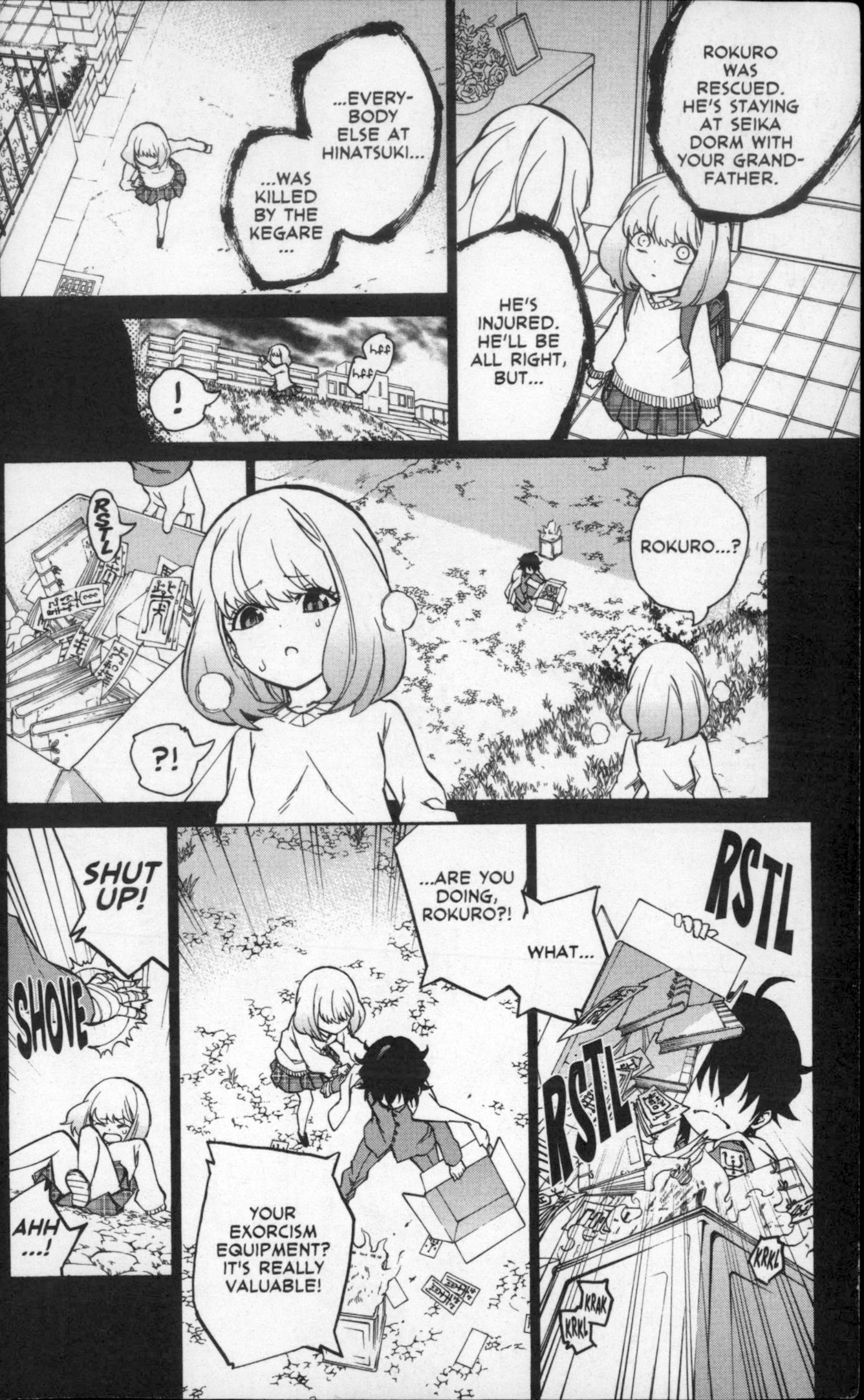
ROKURO WAS RESCUED. HE'S STAYING AT SEIKA DORM WITH YOUR GRANDFATHER.
HE'S INJURED. HE'LL BE ALL RIGHT, BUT...
...EVERYBODY ELSE AT HINATSUKI...
...WAS KILLED BY THE KEGARE...
hff
hff
!
ROKURO...?
RSTL
?!
RSTL
WHAT...
RSTL
KRKL
KRAK
KRKL
...ARE YOU DOING, ROKURO?!
YOUR EXORCISM EQUIPMENT? IT'S REALLY VALUABLE!
SHUT UP!
SHOVE
AHH...!

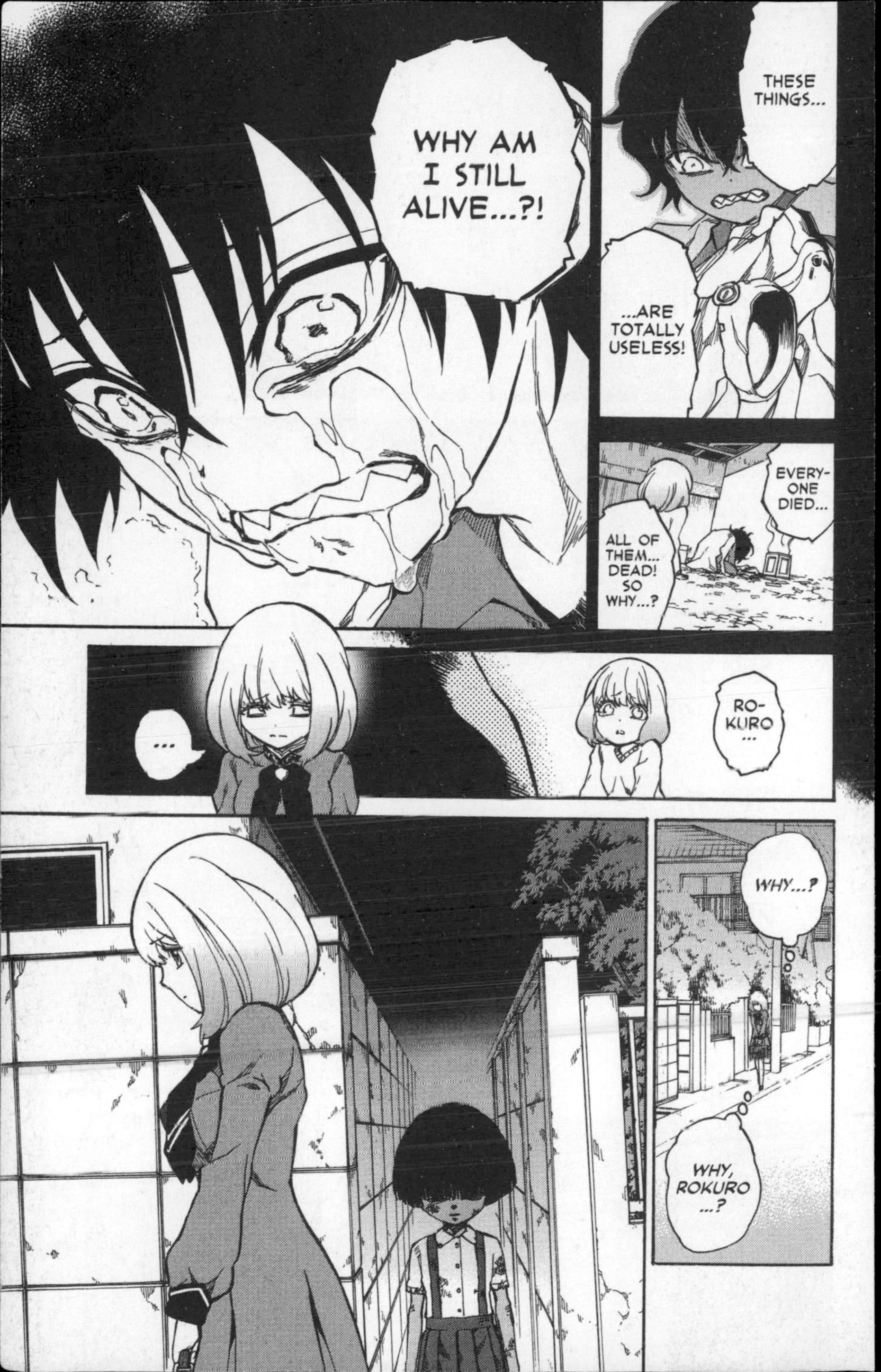
THESE THINGS...
...ARE TOTALLY USELESS!
EVERY-ONE DIED...
ALL OF THEM... DEAD! SO WHY...?
WHY AM I STILL ALIVE...?!
RO-KURO...
...
WHY...?
WHY, ROKURO...?

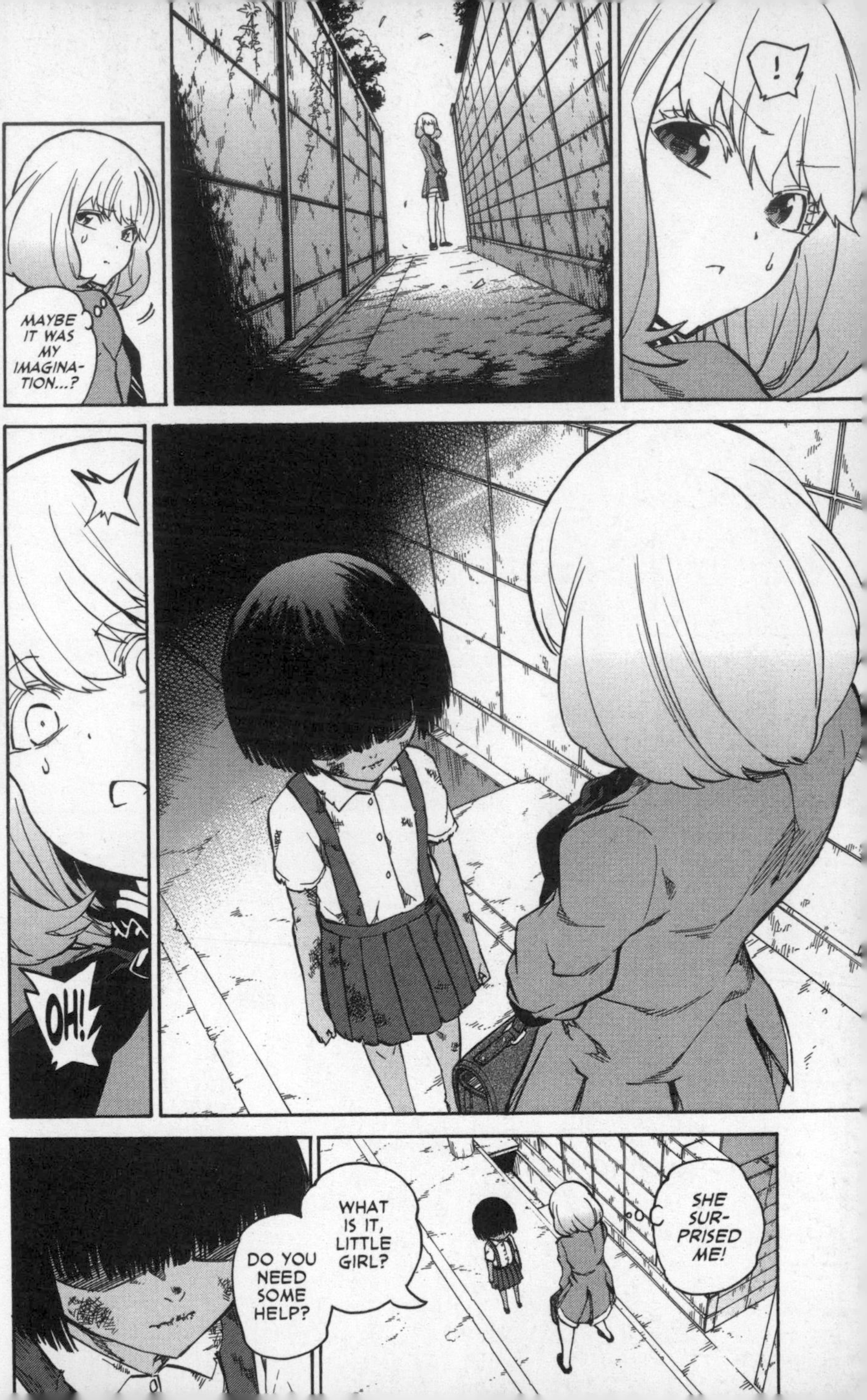
!
MAYBE IT WAS MY IMAGINATION...?
OH!
SHE SURPRISED ME!
WHAT IS IT, LITTLE GIRL?
DO YOU NEED SOME HELP?

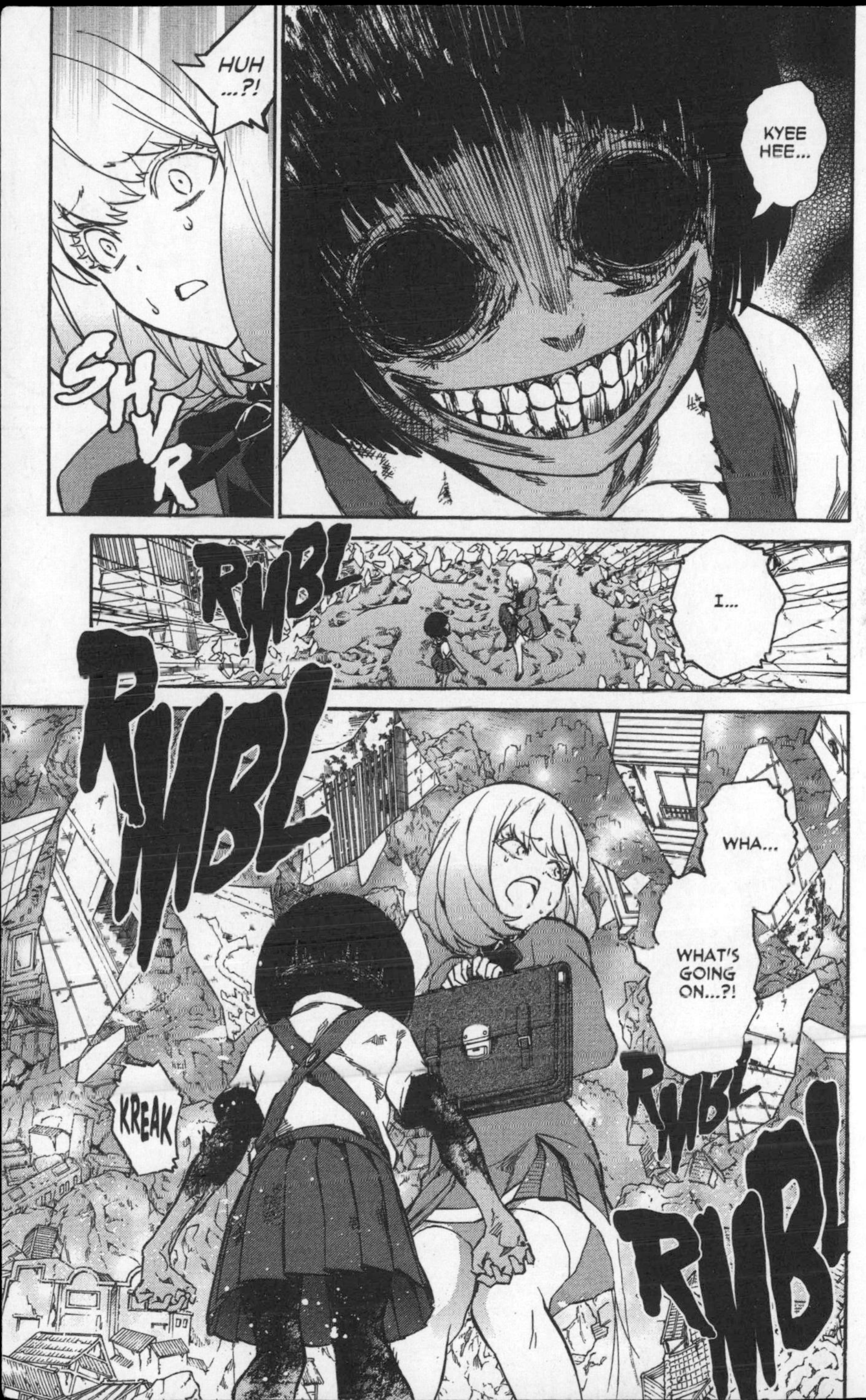
KYEE HEE...
HUH ...?!
SHVR
I...
RMBL
RMBL
WHA...
WHAT'S GOING ON...?!
RMBL
RMBL
KREAK

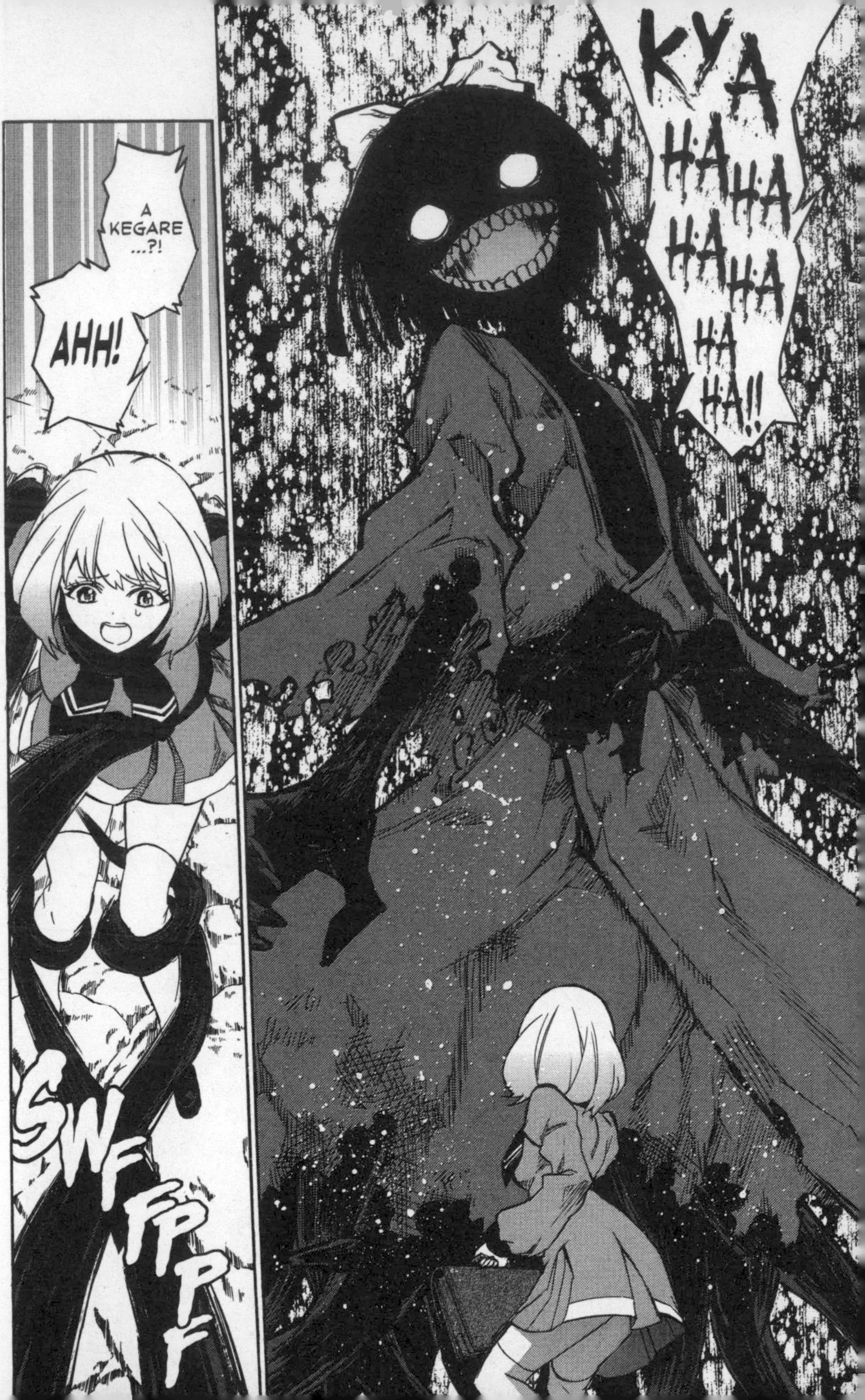
KYA HAHAHA HAHAHA HAHA HA!!
A KEGARE ...?!
AHH!
SWFFPPF

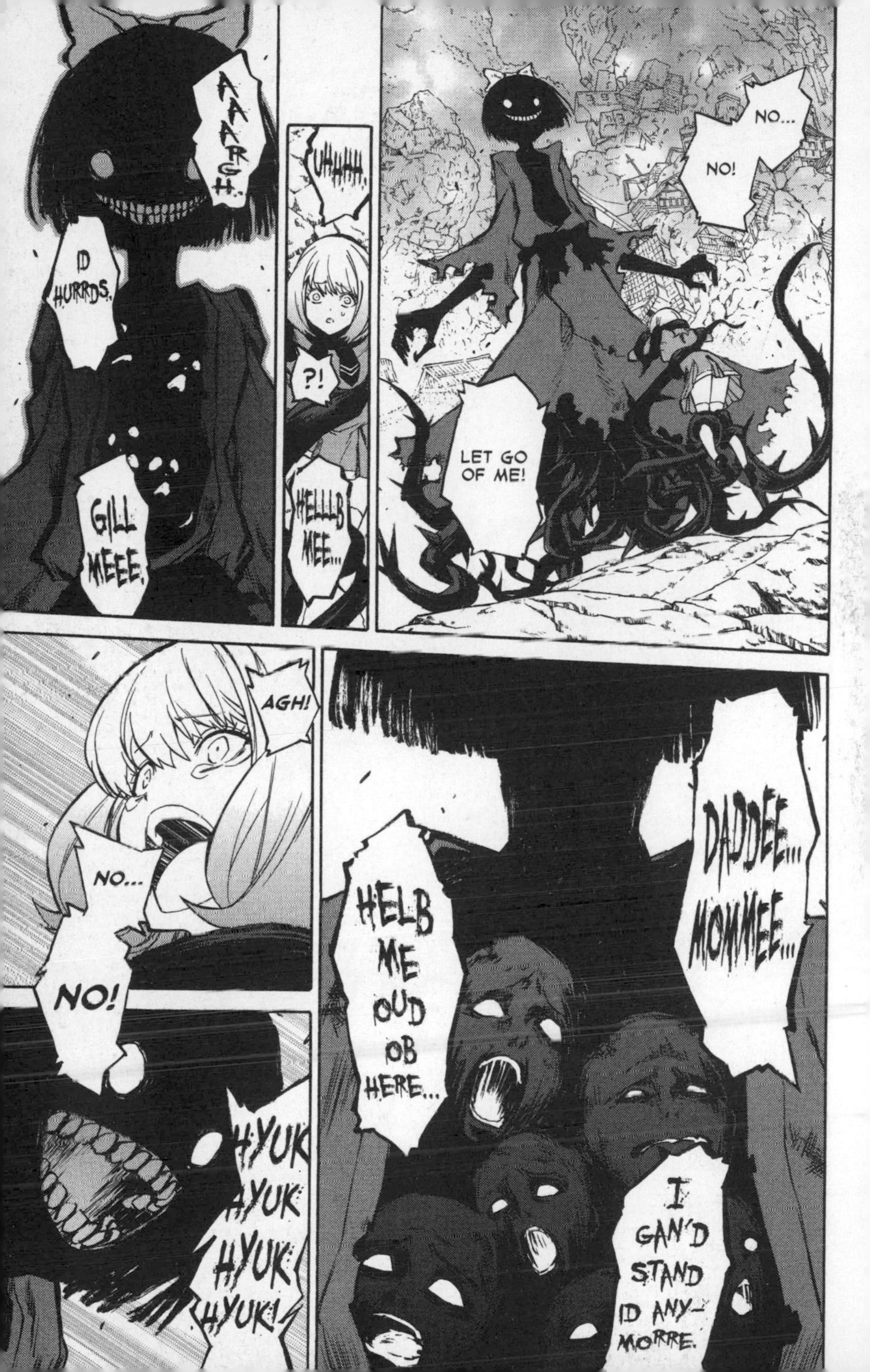
NO...
NO!
LET GO OF ME!
UHHHH,
?!
HELLLB MEE...
AAARGH..
ID HURRDS.
GILL MEEE.
DADDEE... MOMMEE...
HELB ME OUD OB HERE...
I GAN'D STAND ID ANY-MORRE.
AGH!
NO...
NO!
HYUK HYUK HYUK HYUK HYUK!

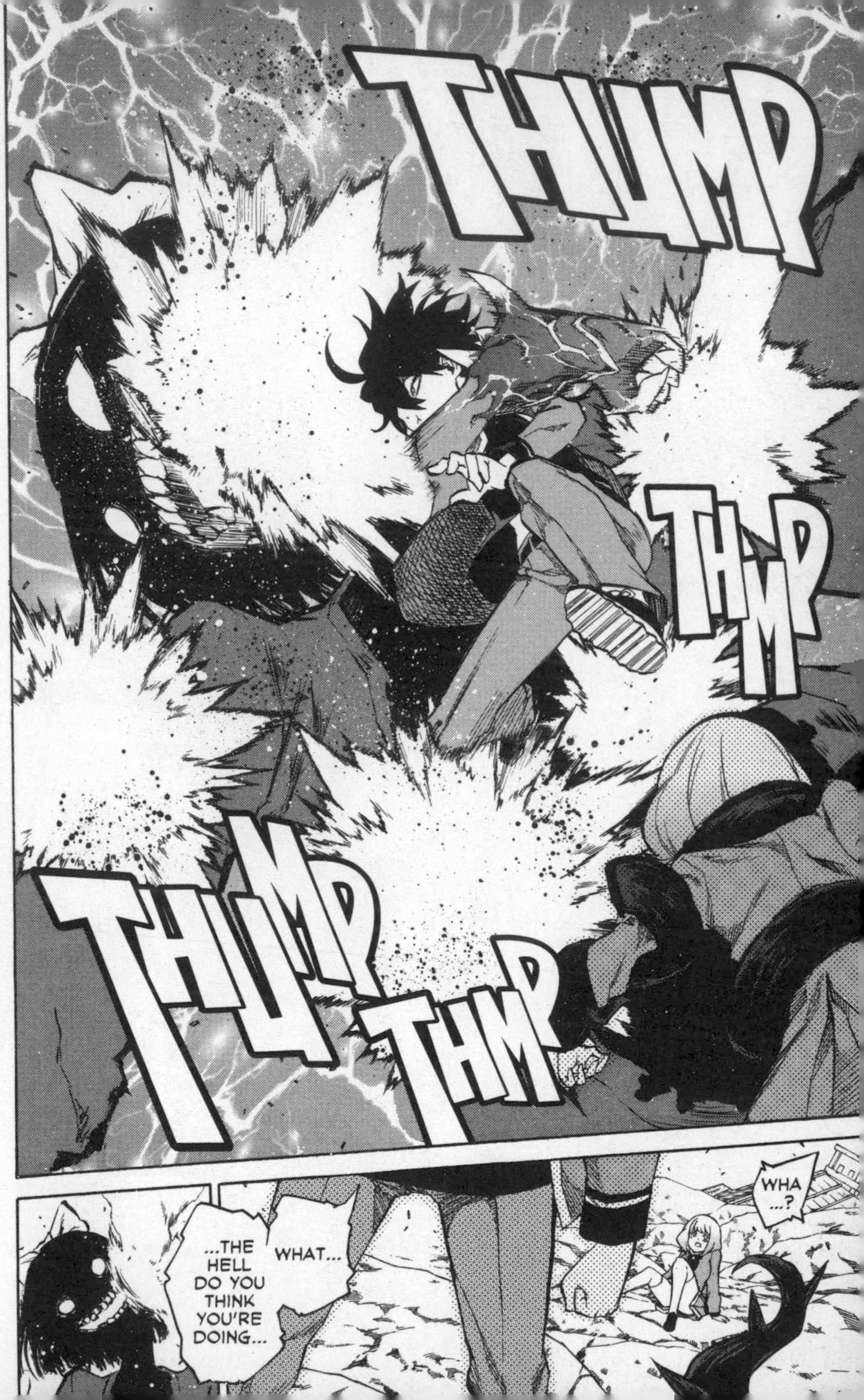
THUMP
THMP
THUMP
THMP
WHA ...?
WHAT...
...THE HELL DO YOU THINK YOU'RE DOING...

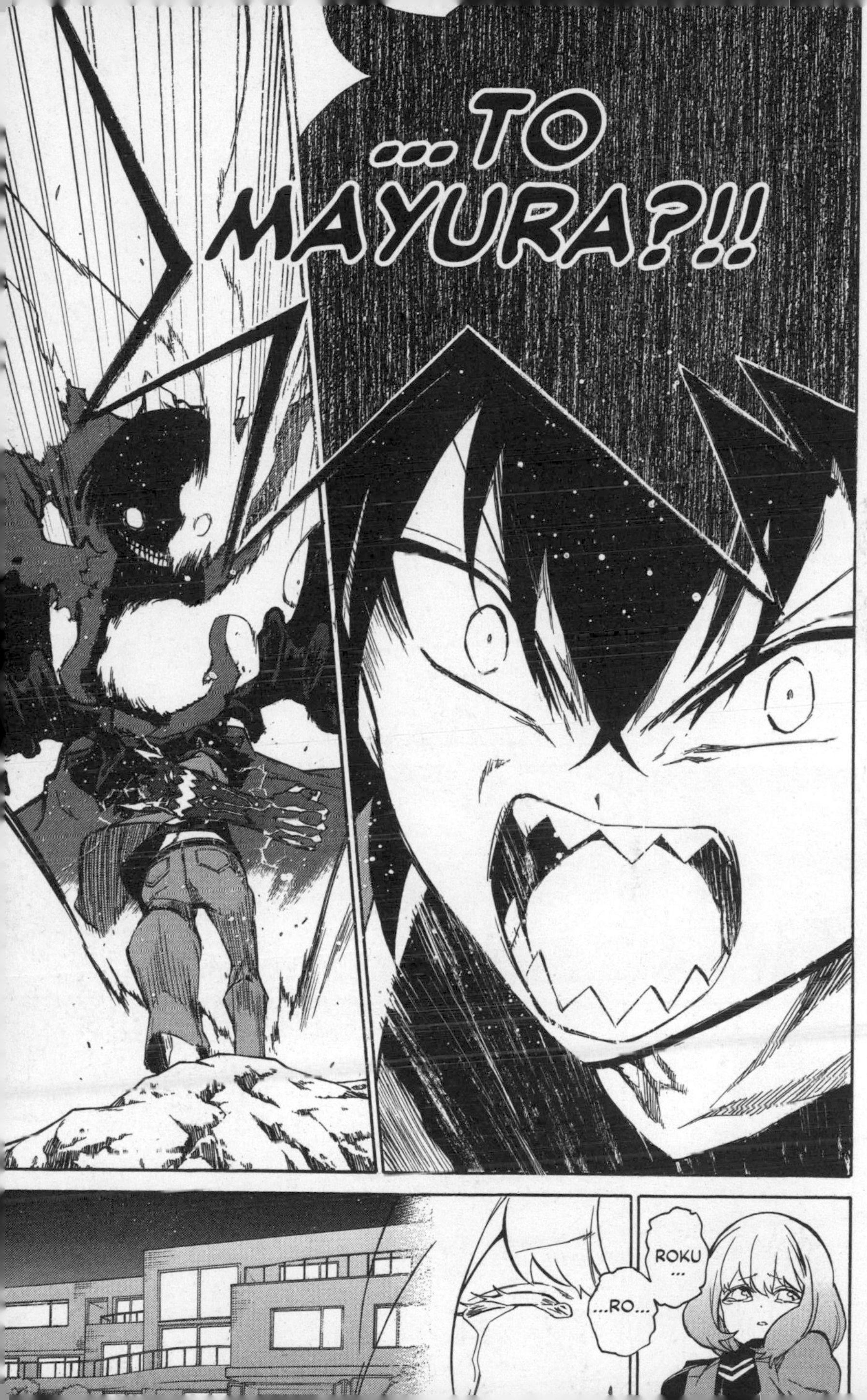
...TO MAYURA?!!
ROKU...
...RO...

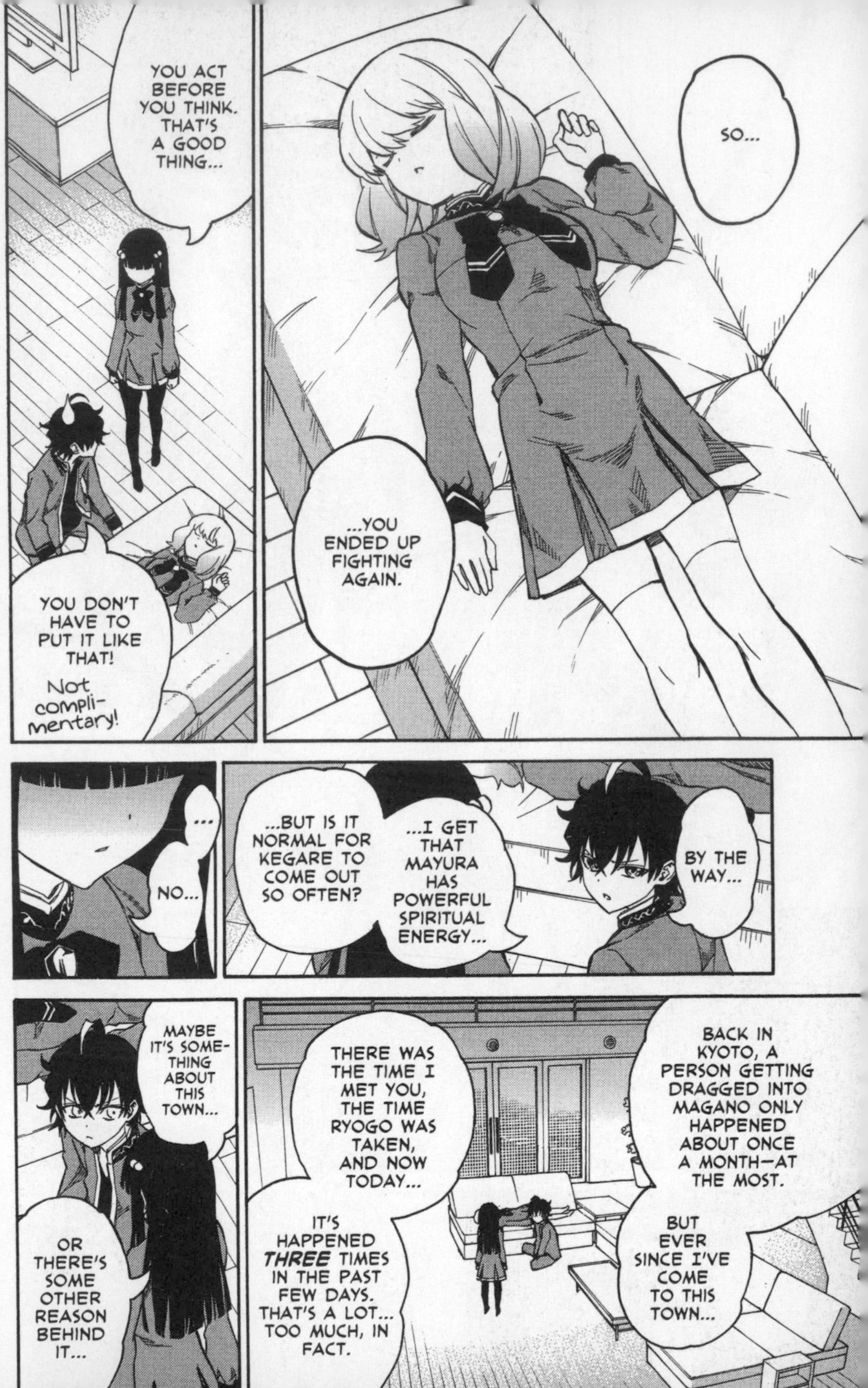

SO...
...YOU ENDED UP FIGHTING AGAIN.
YOU ACT BEFORE YOU THINK. THAT'S A GOOD THING...
YOU DON'T HAVE TO PUT IT LIKE THAT!
Not compli-mentary!
BY THE WAY...
...I GET THAT MAYURA HAS POWERFUL SPIRITUAL ENERGY...
...BUT IS IT NORMAL FOR KEGARE TO COME OUT SO OFTEN?
...
NO...
BACK IN KYOTO, A PERSON GETTING DRAGGED INTO MAGANO ONLY HAPPENED ABOUT ONCE A MONTH—AT THE MOST.
BUT EVER SINCE I'VE COME TO THIS TOWN...
THERE WAS THE TIME I MET YOU, THE TIME RYOGO WAS TAKEN, AND NOW TODAY...
IT'S HAPPENED ***THREE*** TIMES IN THE PAST FEW DAYS. THAT'S A LOT... TOO MUCH, IN FACT.
MAYBE IT'S SOME-THING ABOUT THIS TOWN...
OR THERE'S SOME OTHER REASON BEHIND IT...

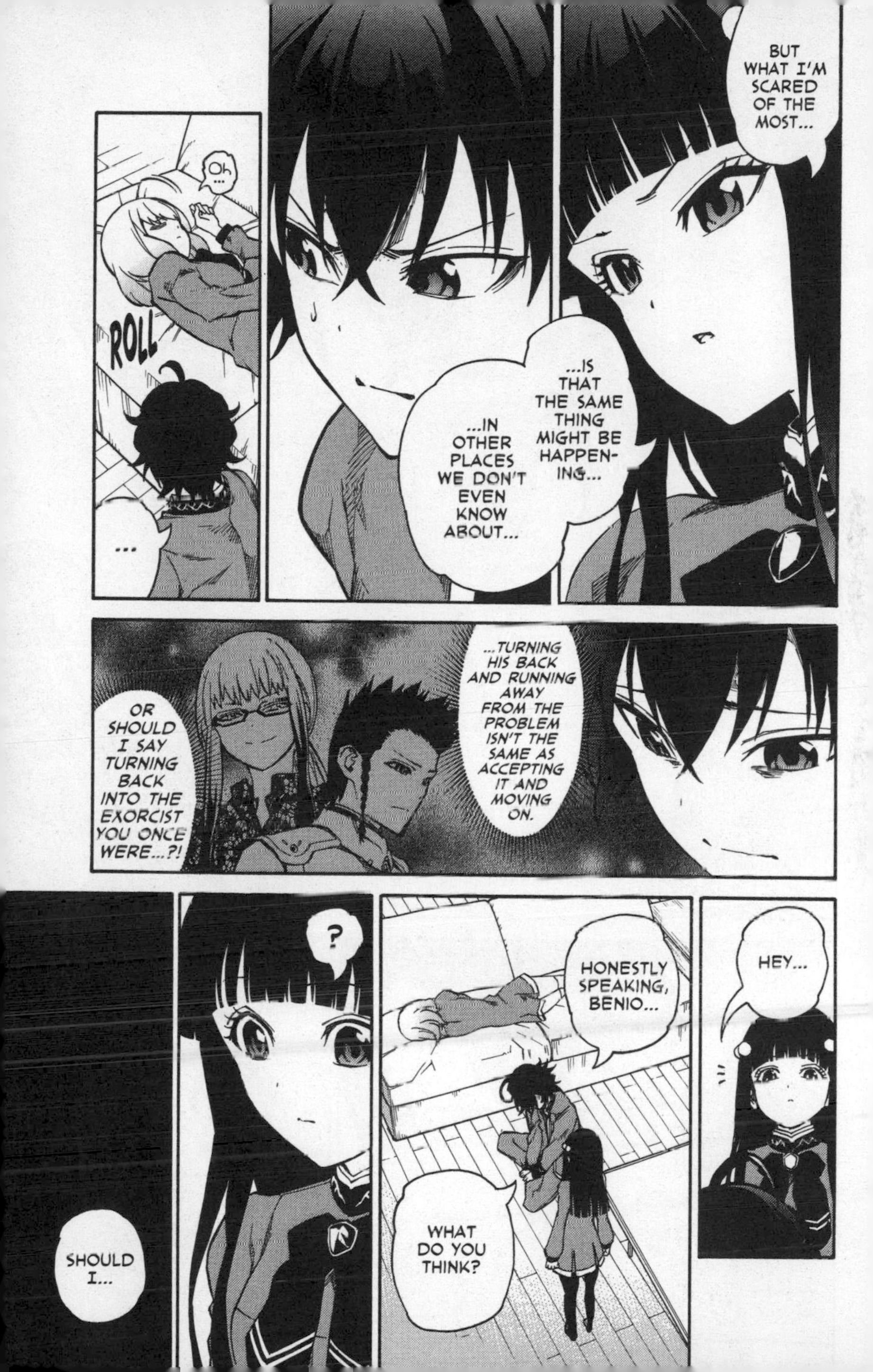
BUT WHAT I'M SCARED OF THE MOST...
...IS THAT THE SAME THING MIGHT BE HAPPENING...
...IN OTHER PLACES WE DON'T EVEN KNOW ABOUT...
Oh...
ROLL
...
...TURNING HIS BACK AND RUNNING AWAY FROM THE PROBLEM ISN'T THE SAME AS ACCEPTING IT AND MOVING ON.
OR SHOULD I SAY TURNING BACK INTO THE EXORCIST YOU ONCE WERE...?!
HEY...
HONESTLY SPEAKING, BENIO...
WHAT DO YOU THINK?
?
SHOULD I...

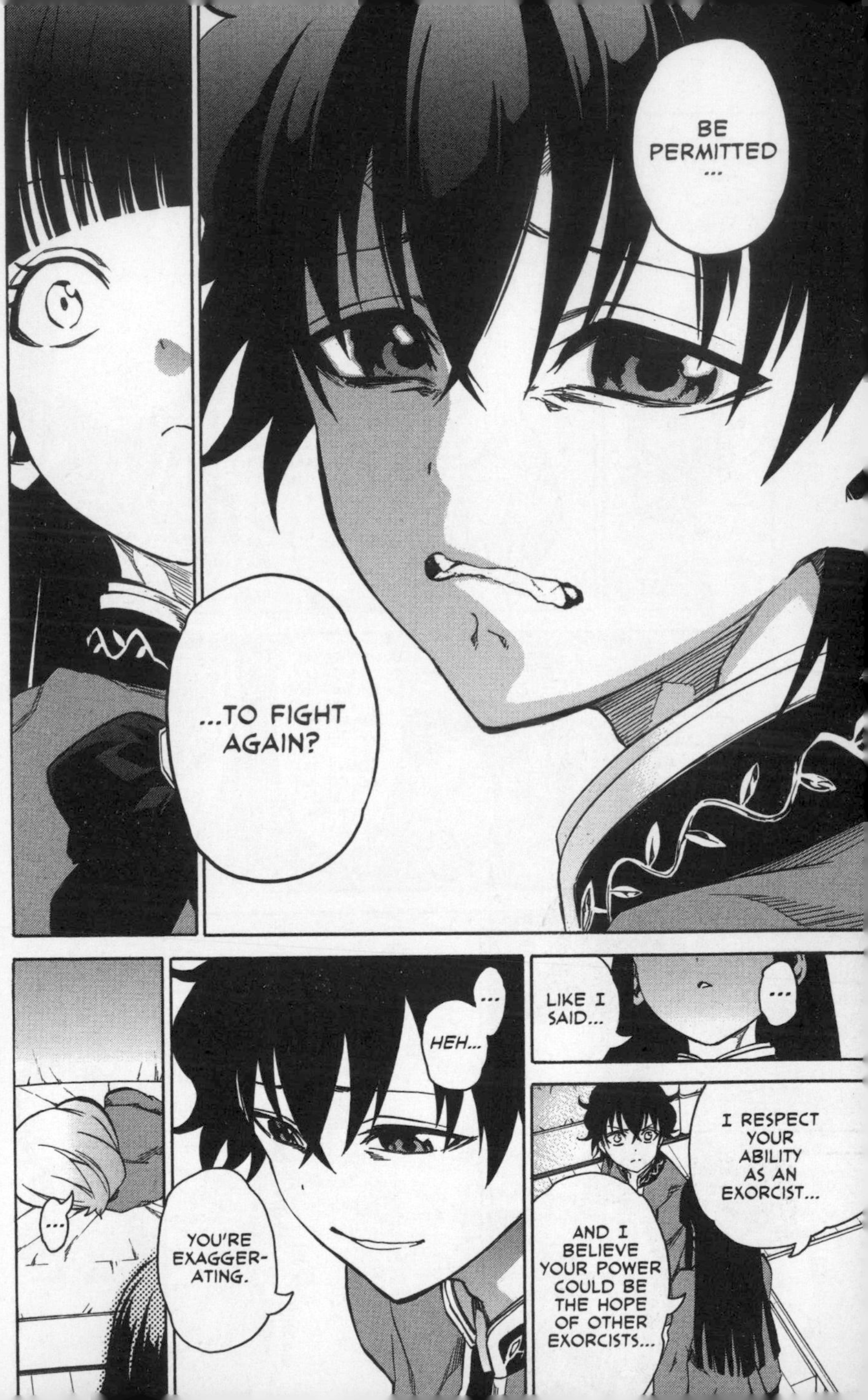
BE PERMITTED ...
...TO FIGHT AGAIN?
...
LIKE I SAID...
I RESPECT YOUR ABILITY AS AN EXORCIST...
AND I BELIEVE YOUR POWER COULD BE THE HOPE OF OTHER EXORCISTS...
...
HEH...
YOU'RE EXAGGER-ATING.
...

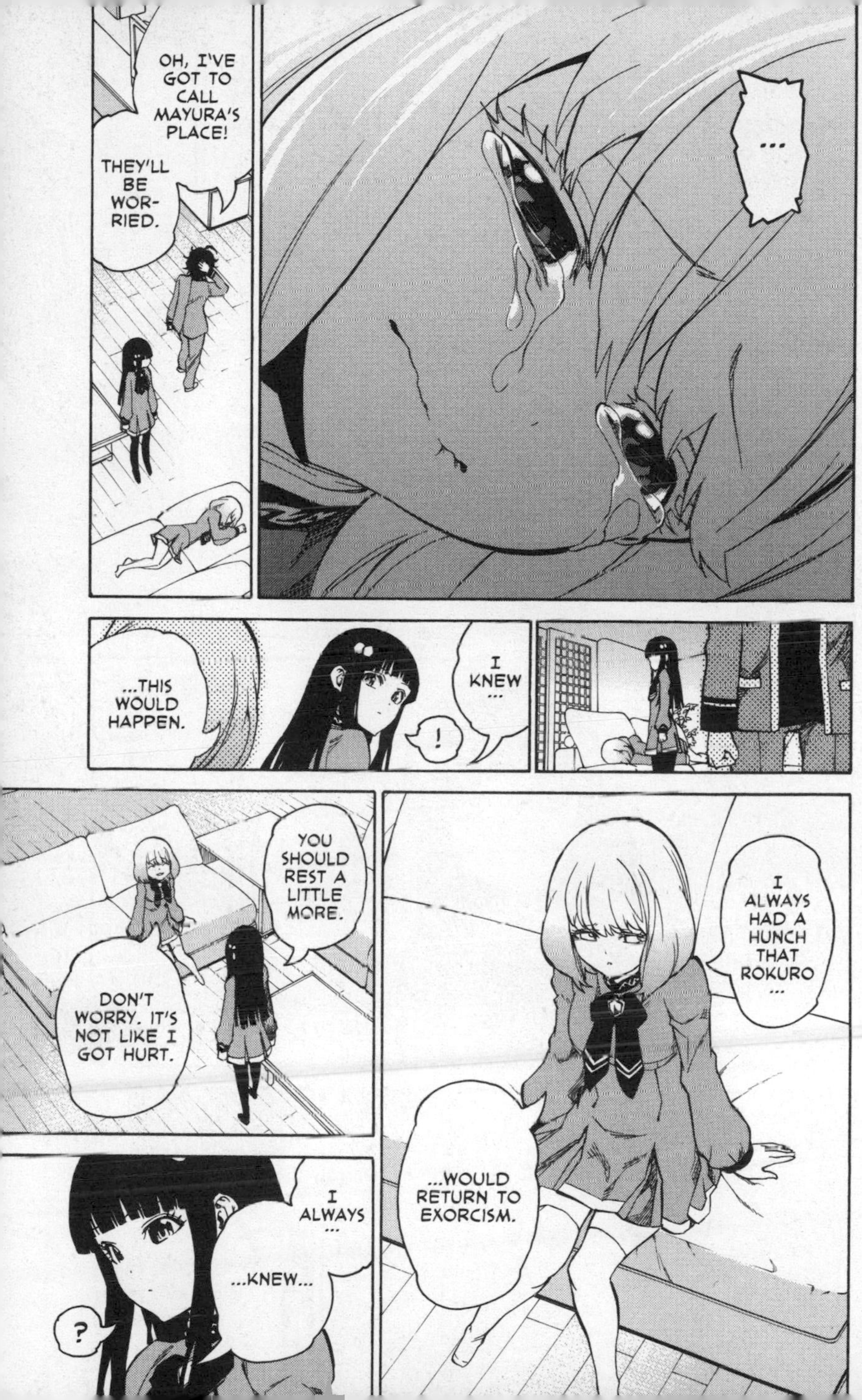
...
OH, I'VE GOT TO CALL MAYURA'S PLACE!
THEY'LL BE WOR-RIED.
I KNEW...
!
...THIS WOULD HAPPEN.
I ALWAYS HAD A HUNCH THAT ROKURO...
...WOULD RETURN TO EXORCISM.
YOU SHOULD REST A LITTLE MORE.
DON'T WORRY. IT'S NOT LIKE I GOT HURT.
I ALWAYS...
...KNEW...
?

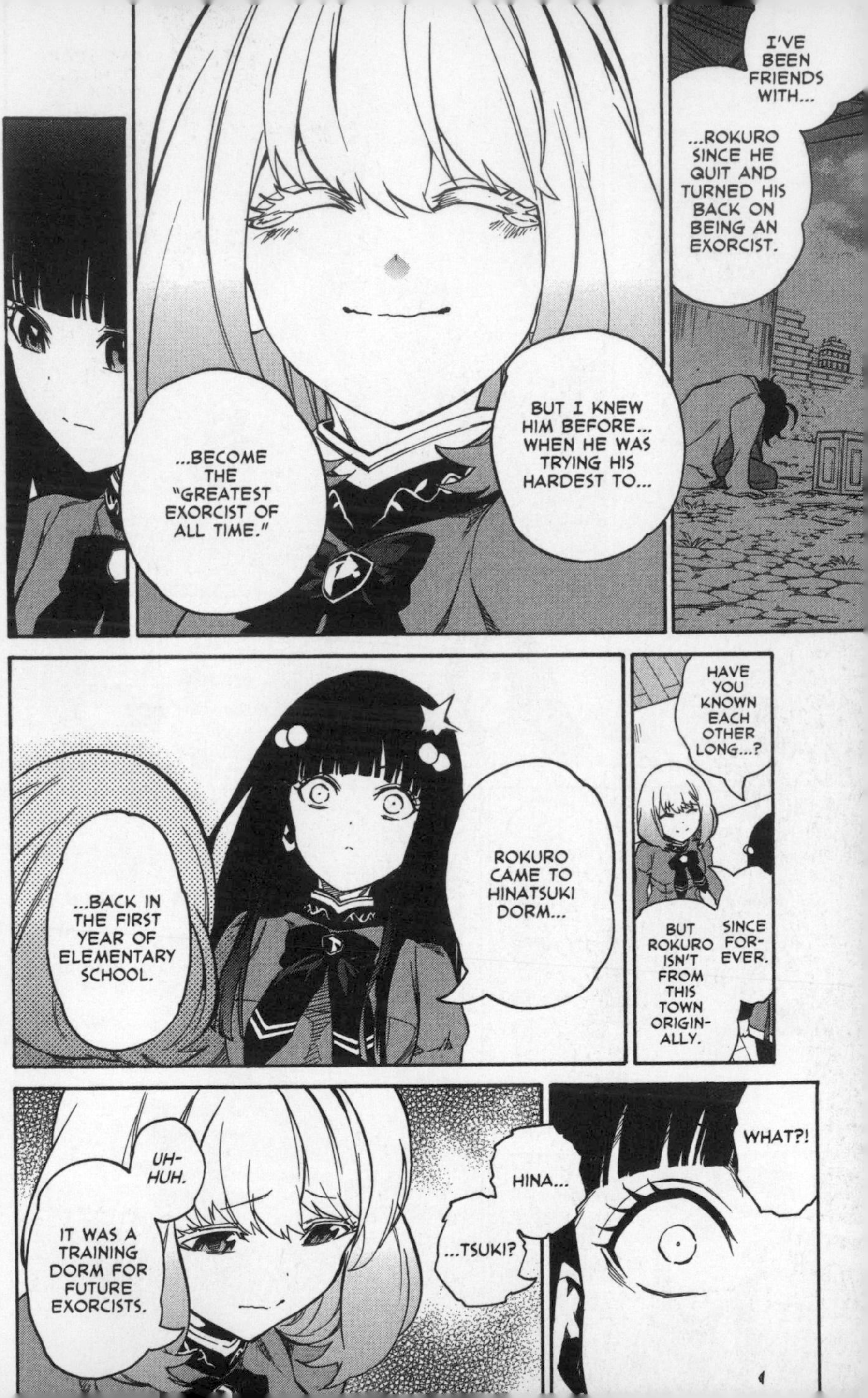
I'VE BEEN FRIENDS WITH...
...ROKURO SINCE HE QUIT AND TURNED HIS BACK ON BEING AN EXORCIST.
BUT I KNEW HIM BEFORE... WHEN HE WAS TRYING HIS HARDEST TO...
...BECOME THE "GREATEST EXORCIST OF ALL TIME."
HAVE YOU KNOWN EACH OTHER LONG...?
SINCE FOR-EVER.
BUT ROKURO ISN'T FROM THIS TOWN ORIGIN-ALLY.
ROKURO CAME TO HINATSUKI DORM...
...BACK IN THE FIRST YEAR OF ELEMENTARY SCHOOL.
WHAT?!
HINA...
...TSUKI?
UH-HUH.
IT WAS A TRAINING DORM FOR FUTURE EXORCISTS.

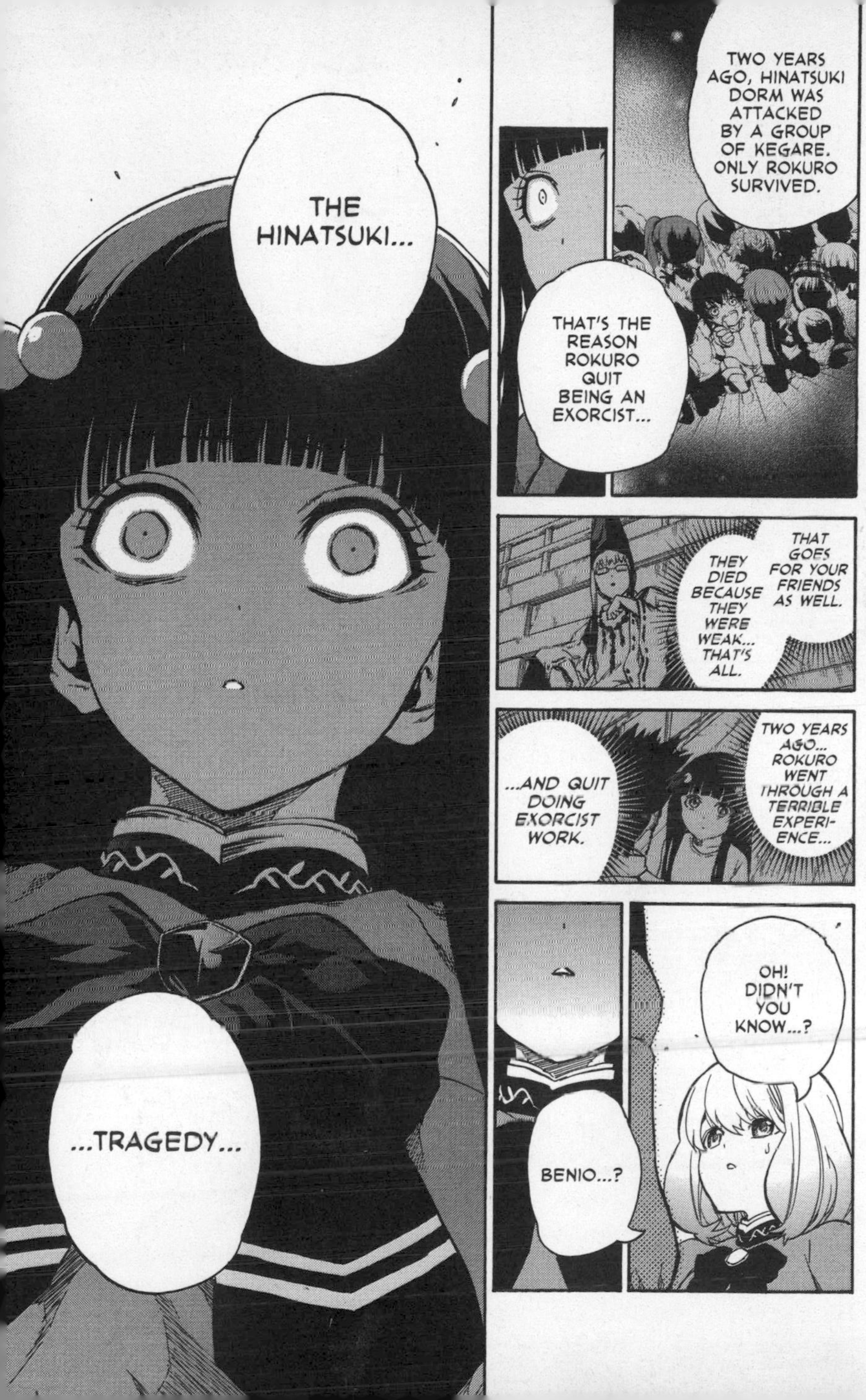
TWO YEARS AGO, HINATSUKI DORM WAS ATTACKED BY A GROUP OF KEGARE. ONLY ROKURO SURVIVED.
THAT'S THE REASON ROKURO QUIT BEING AN EXORCIST...
THAT GOES FOR YOUR FRIENDS AS WELL.
THEY DIED BECAUSE THEY WERE WEAK... THAT'S ALL.
TWO YEARS AGO... ROKURO WENT THROUGH A TERRIBLE EXPERI-ENCE...
...AND QUIT DOING EXORCIST WORK.
OH! DIDN'T YOU KNOW...?
BENIO...?
THE HINATSUKI...
...TRAGEDY...

Column 5: Shu (呪)

Although this kanji is usually read as "ju," this reading of it is not an error. "Shu" literally means "noroi," or curse, and can also denote a spell. According to the documents I researched, the shortest "shu" is your name. For example, the shu cast upon me is "I am Yoshiaki Sukeno." The enchantment spell is an original idea of this manga and this shu is basically cast upon the weapons and armor (clothes) to tell the exorcists, "You have kickass powers, you know!"

#7 Tangled Tragedy

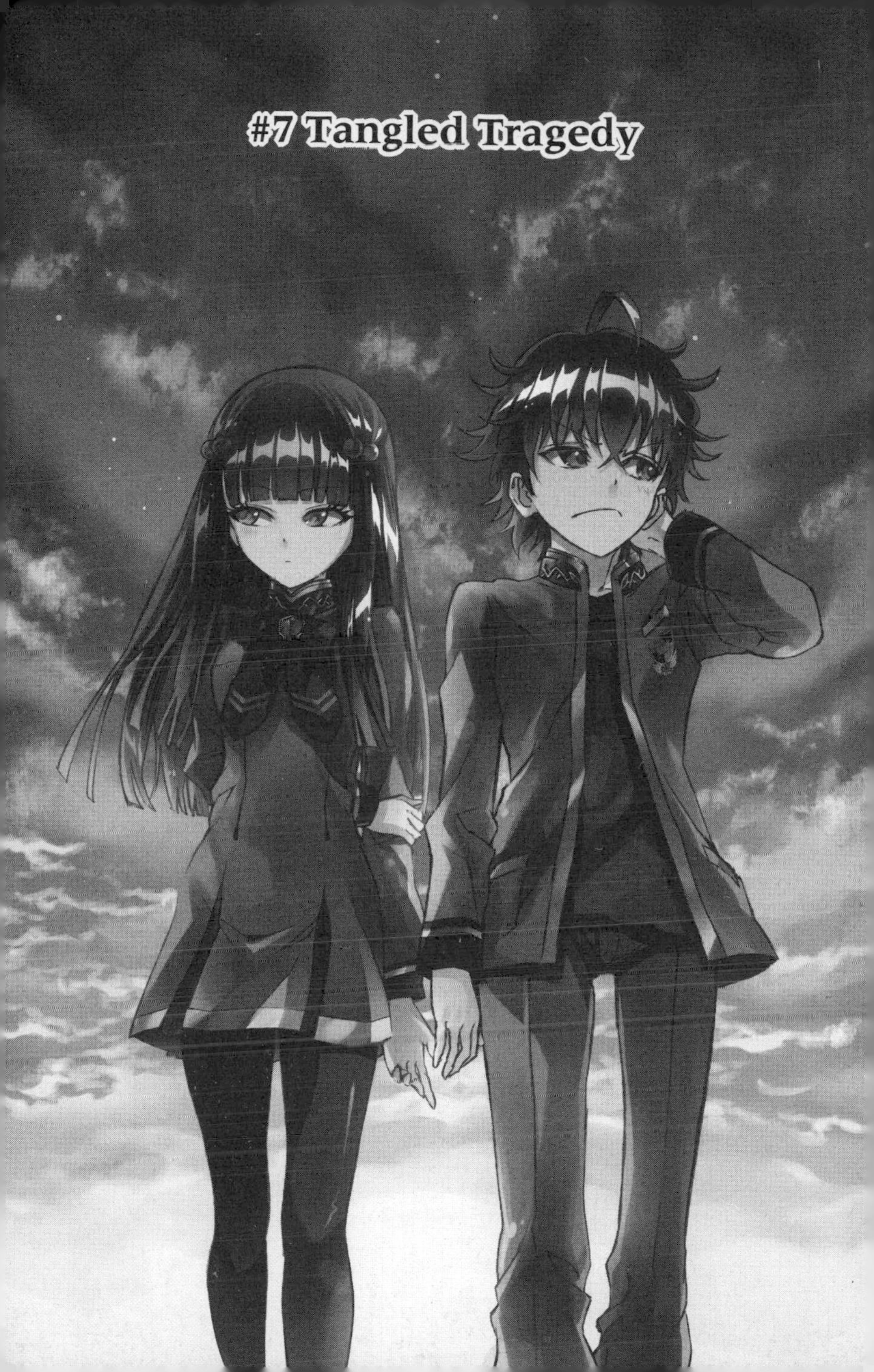

Twin Star Exorcists

ONMYOJI

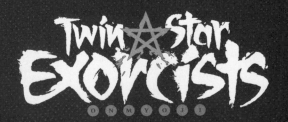

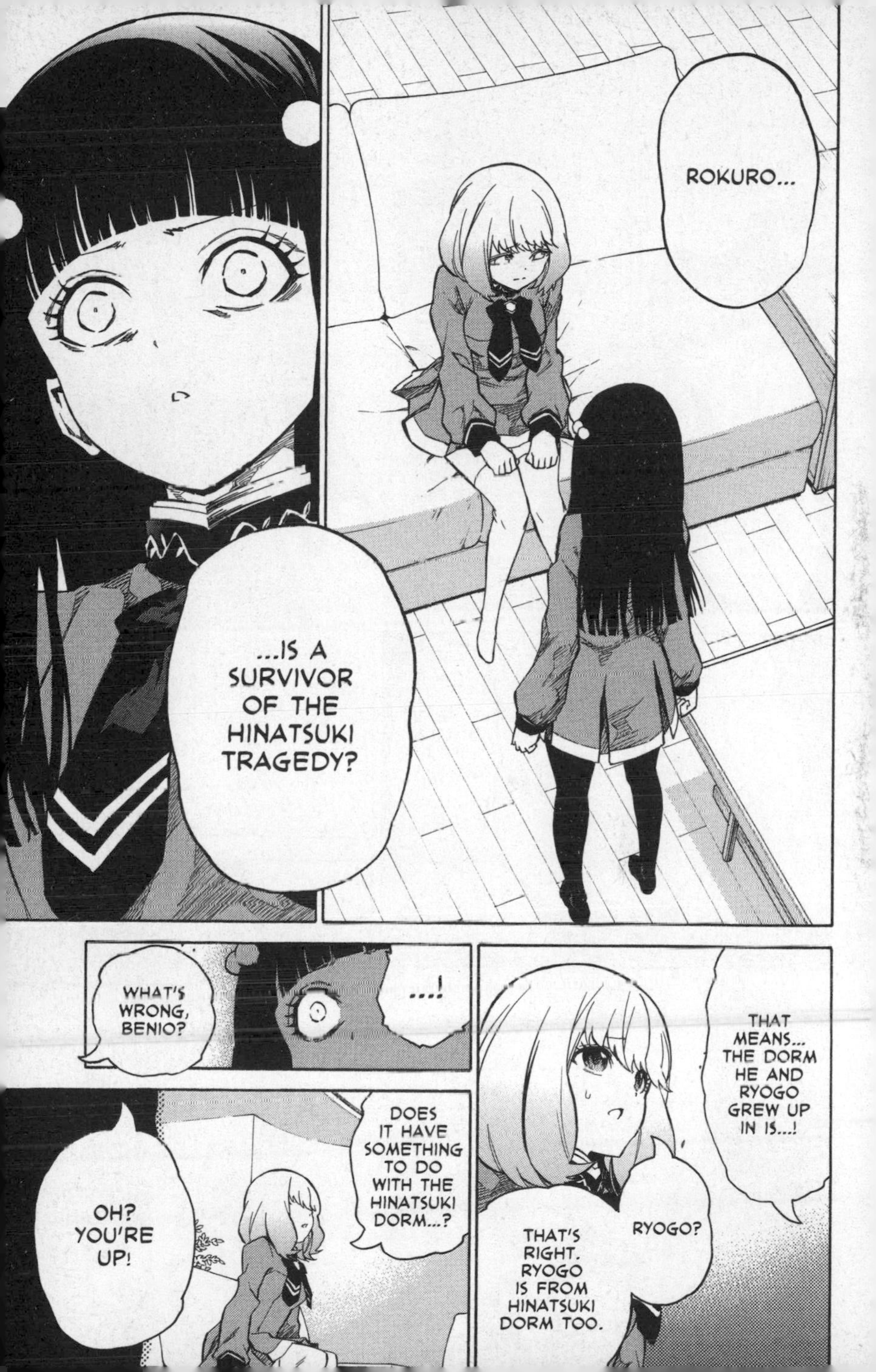
ROKURO...
...IS A SURVIVOR OF THE HINATSUKI TRAGEDY?
THAT MEANS... THE DORM HE AND RYOGO GREW UP IN IS...!
RYOGO?
THAT'S RIGHT. RYOGO IS FROM HINATSUKI DORM TOO.
...!
WHAT'S WRONG, BENIO?
DOES IT HAVE SOMETHING TO DO WITH THE HINATSUKI DORM...?
OH? YOU'RE UP!

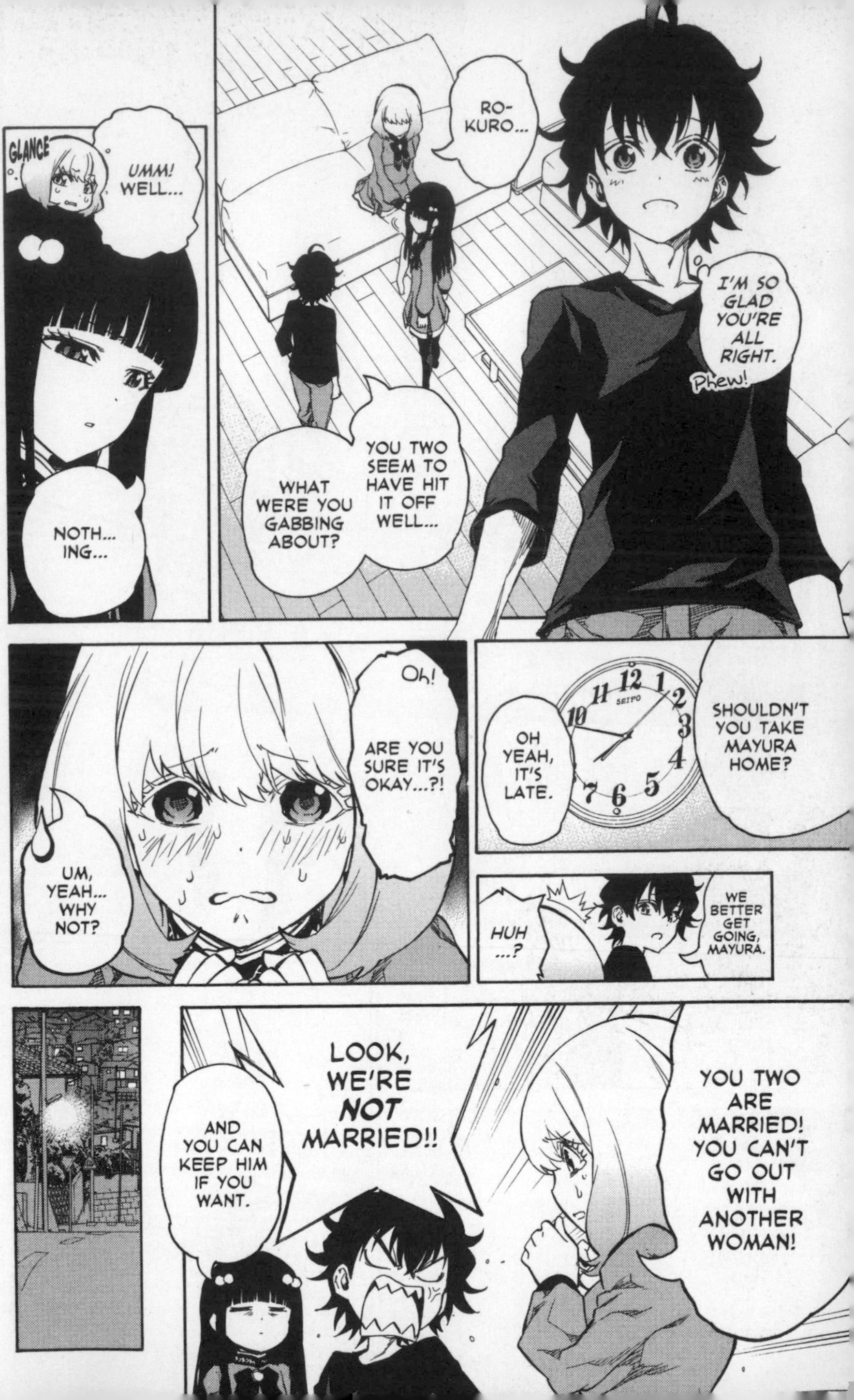
RO-KURO...
I'M SO GLAD YOU'RE ALL RIGHT.
Phew!
YOU TWO SEEM TO HAVE HIT IT OFF WELL...
WHAT WERE YOU GABBING ABOUT?
GLANCE
UMM! WELL...
NOTH... ING...
SHOULDN'T YOU TAKE MAYURA HOME?
OH YEAH, IT'S LATE.
SEIPO
WE BETTER GET GOING, MAYURA.
HUH ...?
Oh!
ARE YOU SURE IT'S OKAY...?!
UM, YEAH... WHY NOT?
YOU TWO ARE MARRIED! YOU CAN'T GO OUT WITH ANOTHER WOMAN!
LOOK, WE'RE *NOT* MARRIED!!
AND YOU CAN KEEP HIM IF YOU WANT.

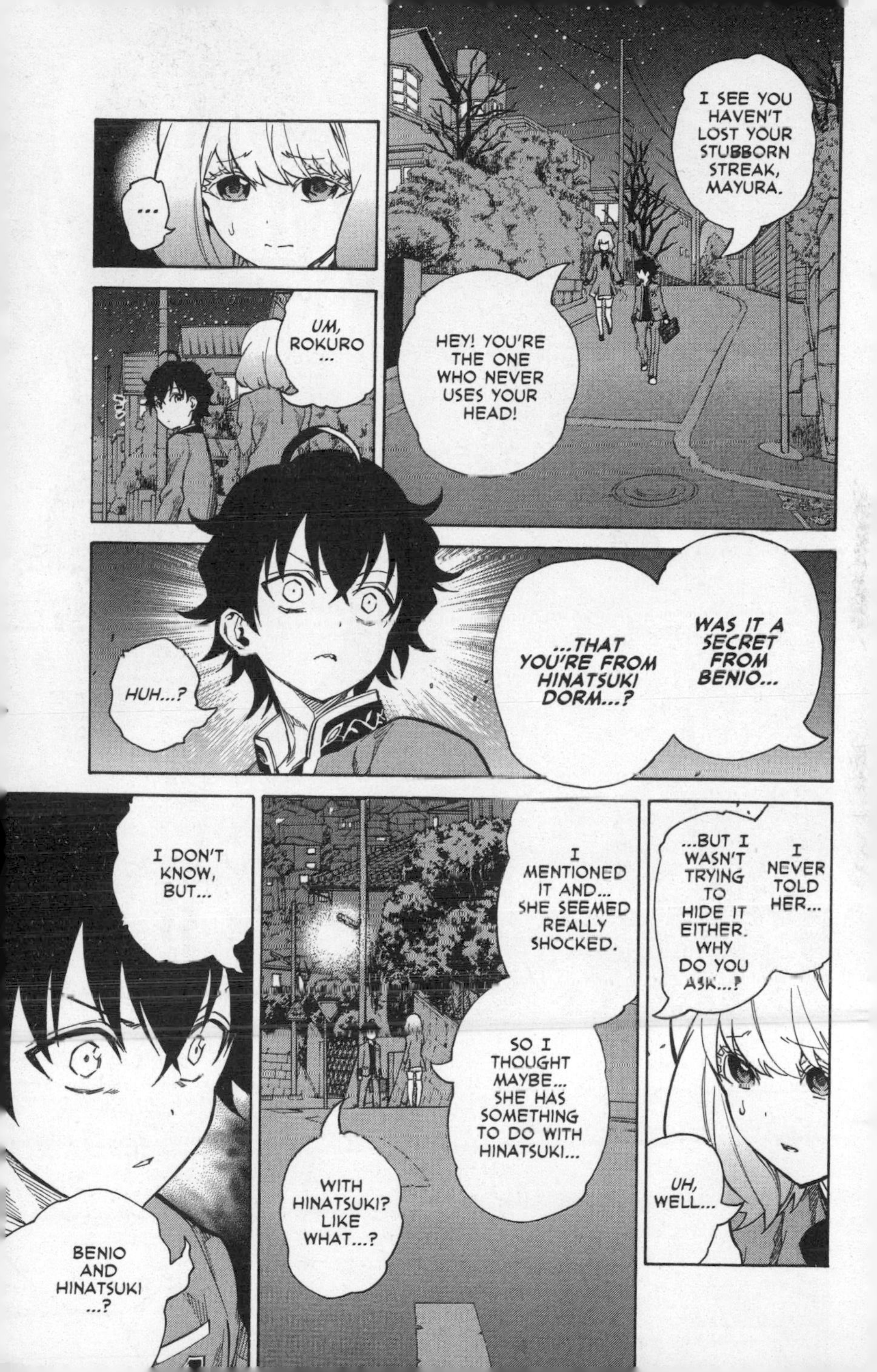
I SEE YOU HAVEN'T LOST YOUR STUBBORN STREAK, MAYURA.
HEY! YOU'RE THE ONE WHO NEVER USES YOUR HEAD!
...
UM, ROKURO...
WAS IT A SECRET FROM BENIO...
...THAT YOU'RE FROM HINATSUKI DORM...?
HUH...?
I NEVER TOLD HER...
...BUT I WASN'T TRYING TO HIDE IT EITHER. WHY DO YOU ASK...?
UH, WELL...
I MENTIONED IT AND... SHE SEEMED REALLY SHOCKED.
SO I THOUGHT MAYBE... SHE HAS SOMETHING TO DO WITH HINATSUKI...
WITH HINATSUKI? LIKE WHAT...?
I DON'T KNOW, BUT...
BENIO AND HINATSUKI...?

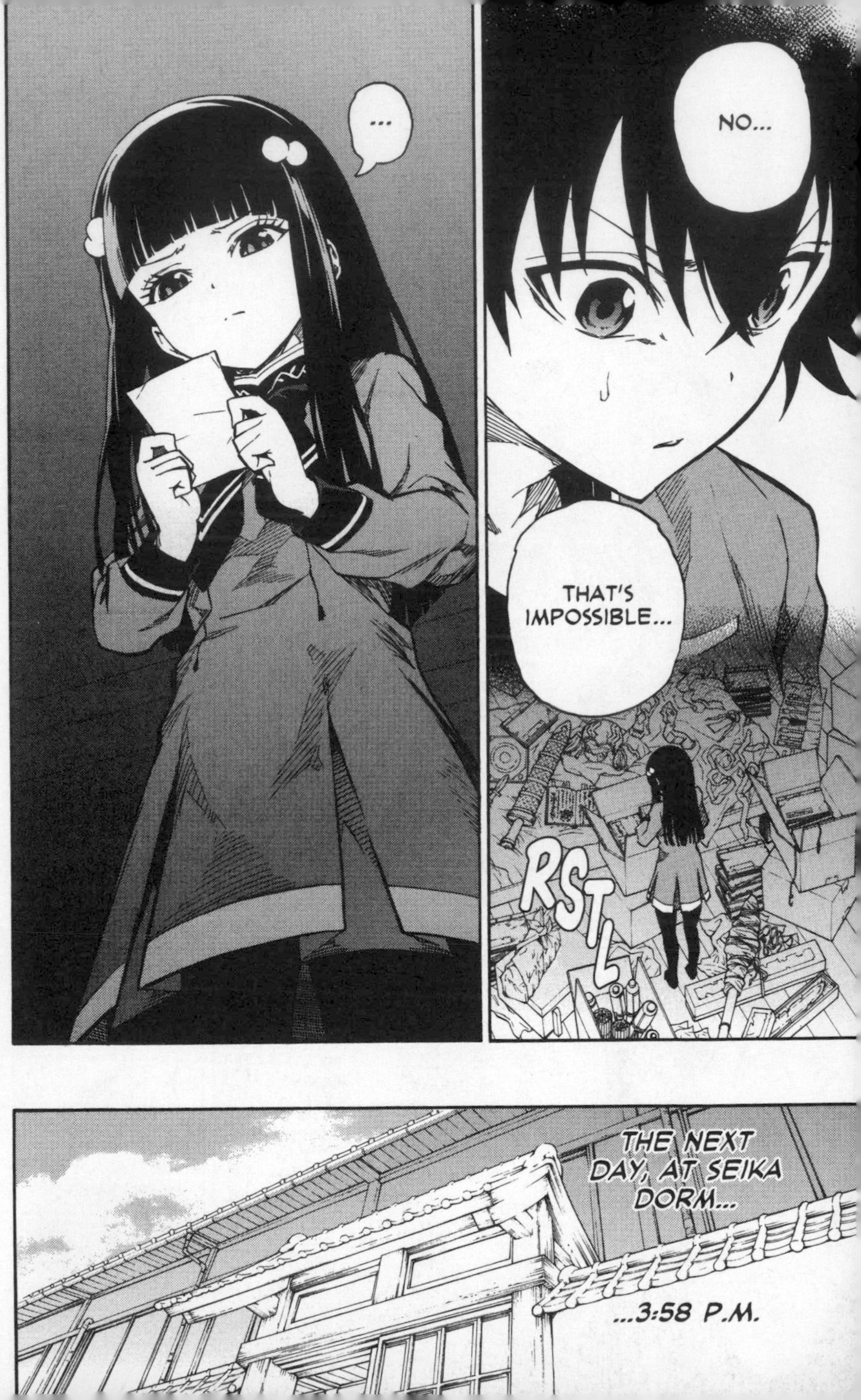
NO...
THAT'S IMPOSSIBLE...
RSTL
...
THE NEXT DAY, AT SEIKA DORM...
...3:58 P.M.

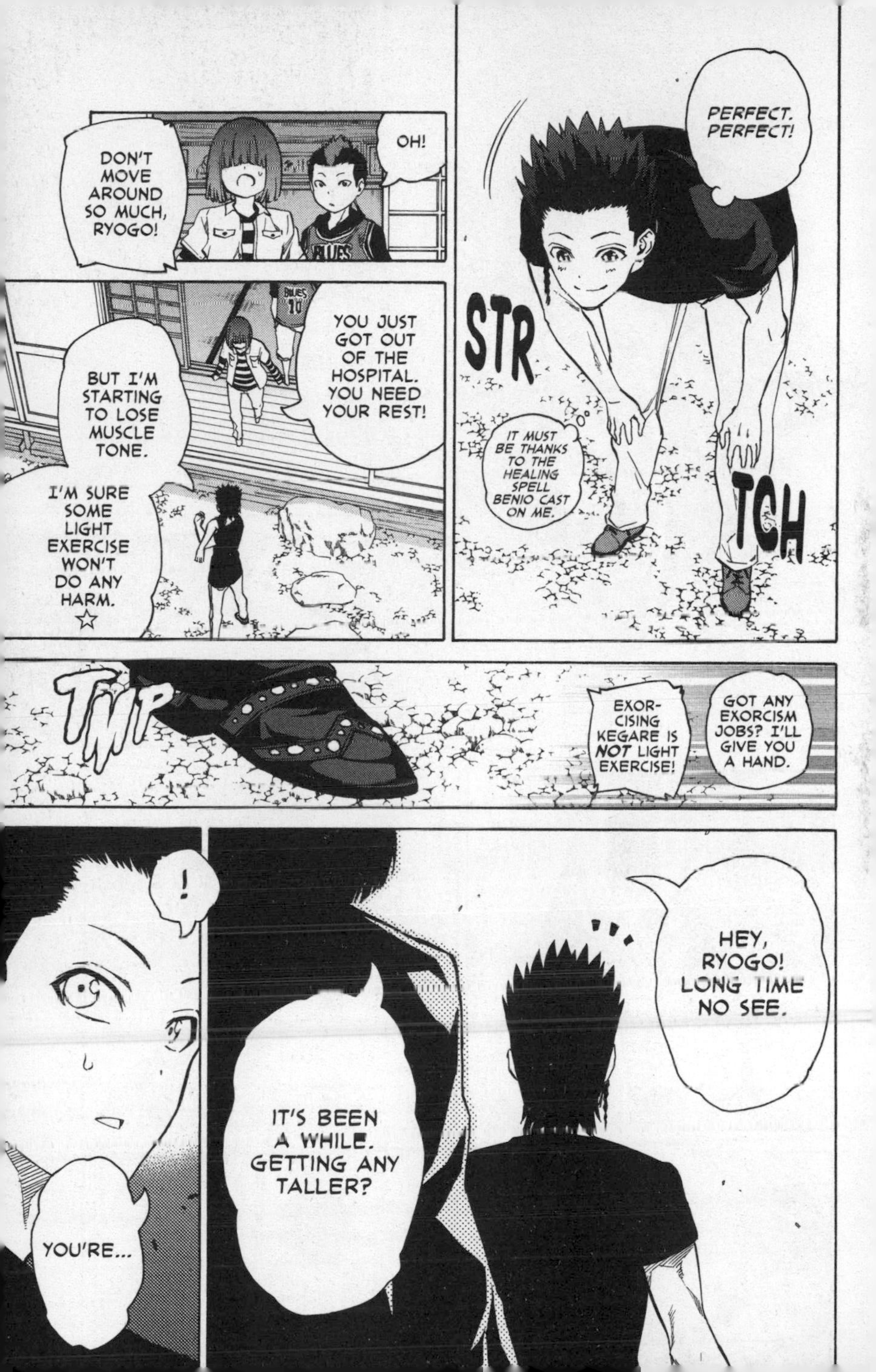
PERFECT. PERFECT!
STR
TCH
IT MUST BE THANKS TO THE HEALING SPELL BENIO CAST ON ME.
OH!
DON'T MOVE AROUND SO MUCH, RYOGO!
YOU JUST GOT OUT OF THE HOSPITAL. YOU NEED YOUR REST!
BUT I'M STARTING TO LOSE MUSCLE TONE.
I'M SURE SOME LIGHT EXERCISE WON'T DO ANY HARM. ☆
GOT ANY EXORCISM JOBS? I'LL GIVE YOU A HAND.
EXORCISING KEGARE IS NOT LIGHT EXERCISE!
TMP
HEY, RYOGO! LONG TIME NO SEE.
IT'S BEEN A WHILE. GETTING ANY TALLER?
!
YOU'RE...

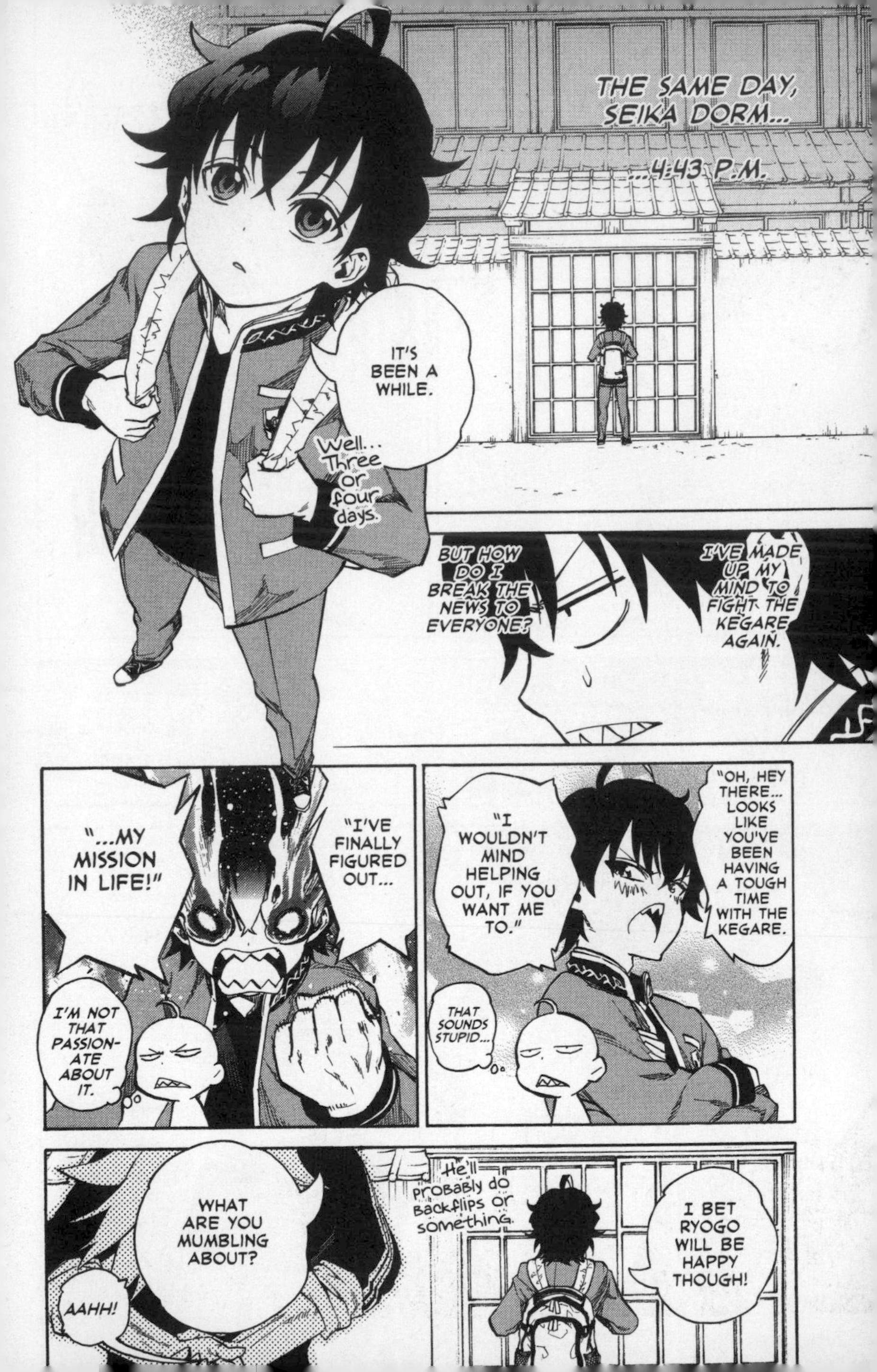
THE SAME DAY, SEIKA DORM...
...4:43 P.M.
IT'S BEEN A WHILE.
Well... Three or four days.
I'VE MADE UP MY MIND TO FIGHT THE KEGARE AGAIN.
BUT HOW DO I BREAK THE NEWS TO EVERYONE?
"OH, HEY THERE... LOOKS LIKE YOU'VE BEEN HAVING A TOUGH TIME WITH THE KEGARE.
"I WOULDN'T MIND HELPING OUT, IF YOU WANT ME TO."
THAT SOUNDS STUPID...
"I'VE FINALLY FIGURED OUT...
"...MY MISSION IN LIFE!"
I'M NOT THAT PASSION-ATE ABOUT IT.
I BET RYOGO WILL BE HAPPY THOUGH!
He'll probably do backflips or something.
WHAT ARE YOU MUMBLING ABOUT?
AAHH!

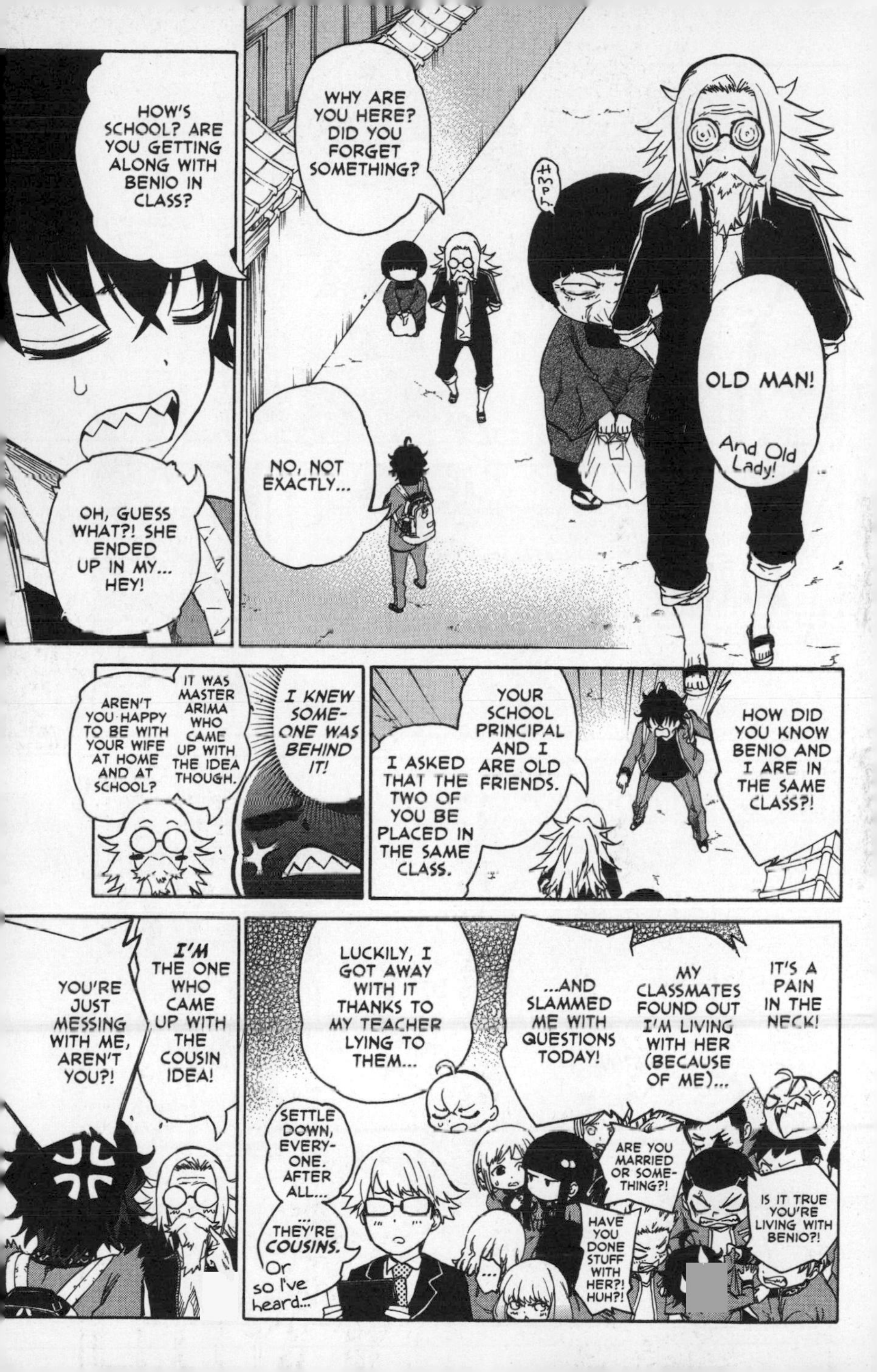
OLD MAN!
And Old Lady!
HMPH!
WHY ARE YOU HERE? DID YOU FORGET SOMETHING?
NO, NOT EXACTLY...
HOW'S SCHOOL? ARE YOU GETTING ALONG WITH BENIO IN CLASS?
OH, GUESS WHAT?! SHE ENDED UP IN MY... HEY!
HOW DID YOU KNOW BENIO AND I ARE IN THE SAME CLASS?!
YOUR SCHOOL PRINCIPAL AND I ARE OLD FRIENDS.
I ASKED THAT THE TWO OF YOU BE PLACED IN THE SAME CLASS.
I KNEW SOME-ONE WAS BEHIND IT!
IT WAS MASTER ARIMA WHO CAME UP WITH THE IDEA THOUGH.
AREN'T YOU HAPPY TO BE WITH YOUR WIFE AT HOME AND AT SCHOOL?
IT'S A PAIN IN THE NECK!
MY CLASSMATES FOUND OUT I'M LIVING WITH HER (BECAUSE OF ME)...
...AND SLAMMED ME WITH QUESTIONS TODAY!
IS IT TRUE YOU'RE LIVING WITH BENIO?!
ARE YOU MARRIED OR SOME-THING?!
HAVE YOU DONE STUFF WITH HER?! HUH?!
LUCKILY, I GOT AWAY WITH IT THANKS TO MY TEACHER LYING TO THEM...
SETTLE DOWN, EVERY-ONE. AFTER ALL...
...THEY'RE COUSINS.
Or so I've heard...
...
I'M THE ONE WHO CAME UP WITH THE COUSIN IDEA!
YOU'RE JUST MESSING WITH ME, AREN'T YOU?!

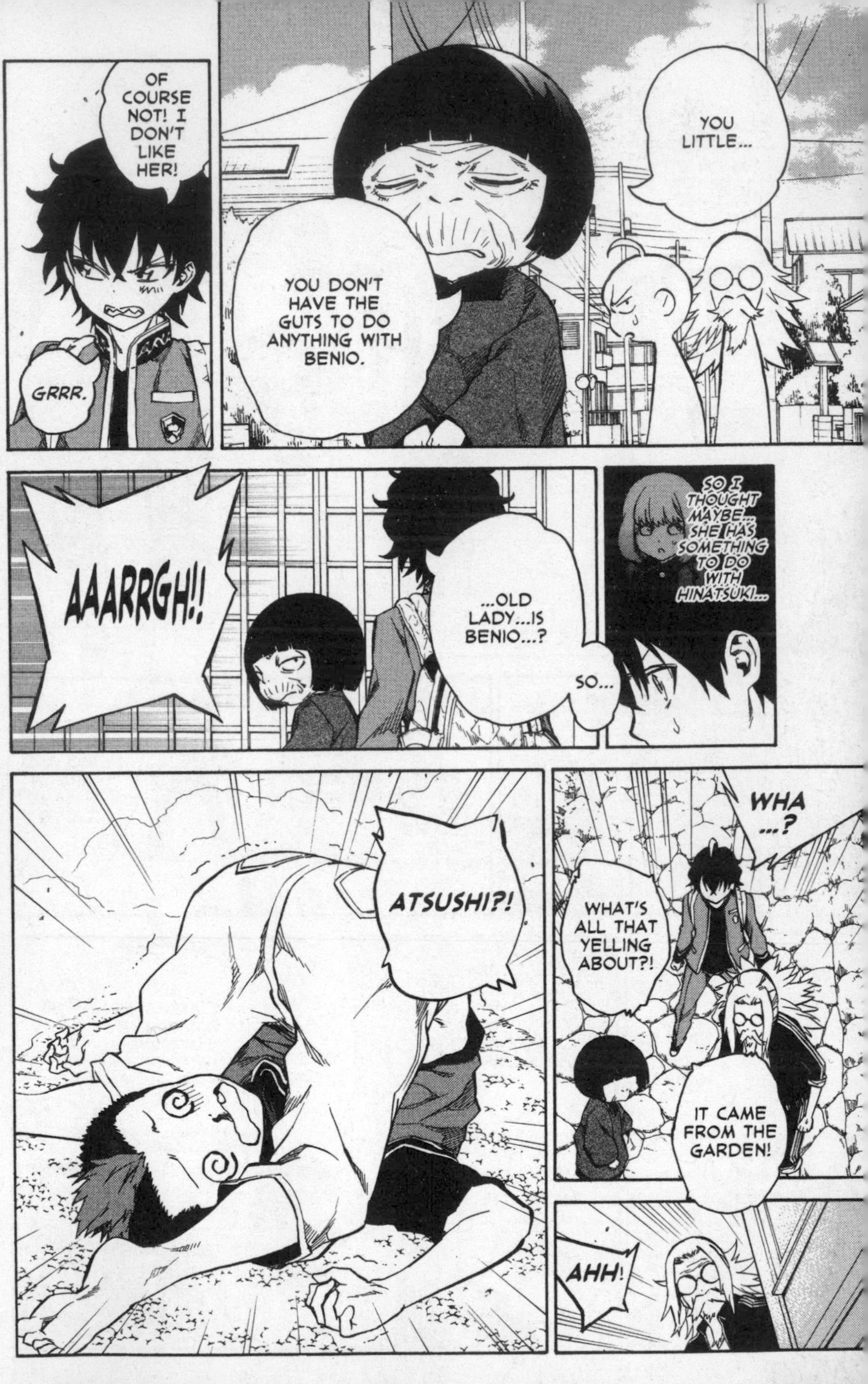
YOU LITTLE...
YOU DON'T HAVE THE GUTS TO DO ANYTHING WITH BENIO.
OF COURSE NOT! I DON'T LIKE HER!
GRRR.
SO I THOUGHT MAYBE... SHE HAS SOMETHING TO DO WITH HINATSUKI...
SO...
...OLD LADY...IS BENIO...?
AAARRGH!!
WHA ...?
WHAT'S ALL THAT YELLING ABOUT?!
IT CAME FROM THE GARDEN!
AHH!
ATSUSHI?!

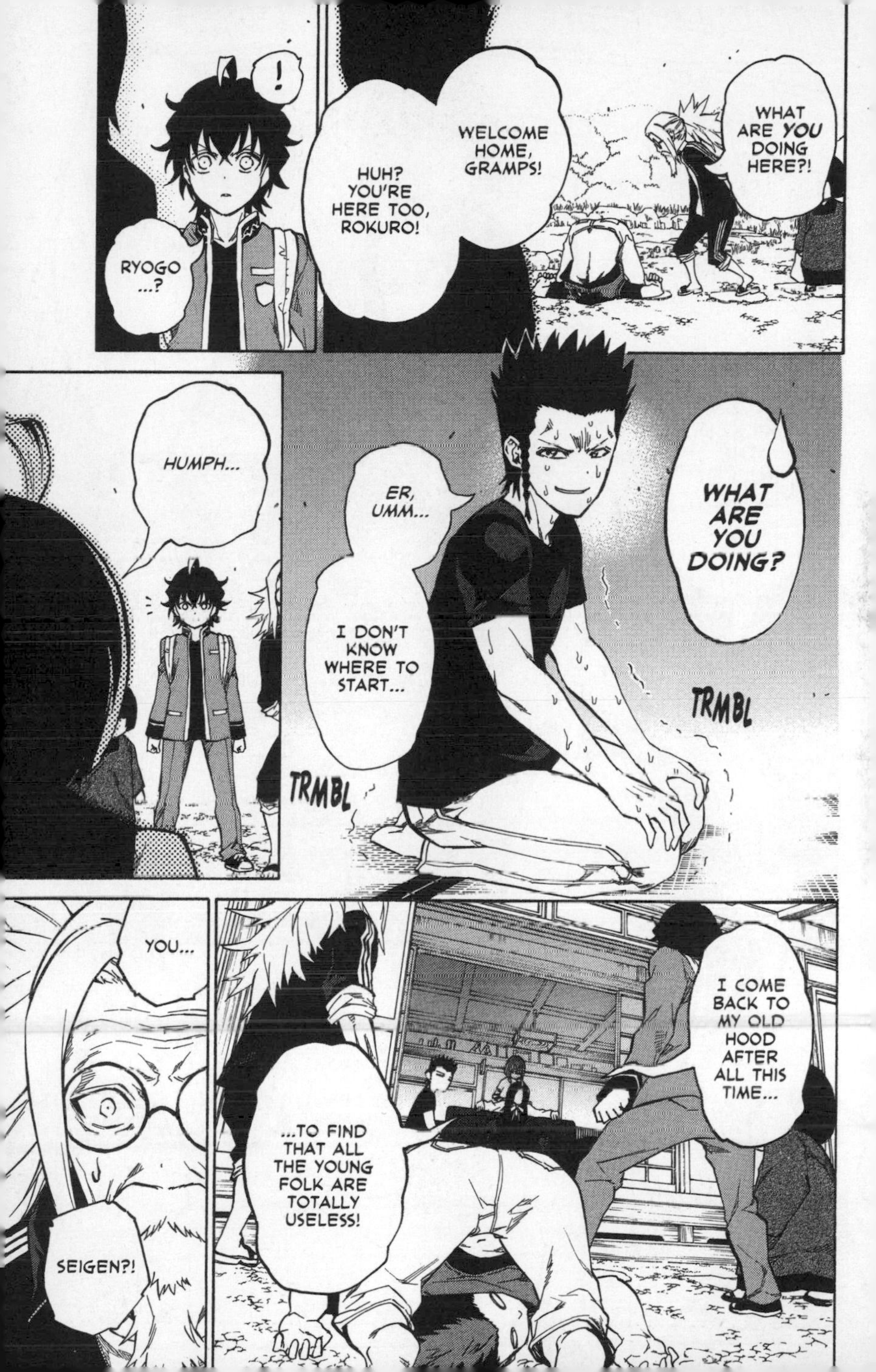
WHAT ARE YOU DOING HERE?!
WELCOME HOME, GRAMPS!
HUH? YOU'RE HERE TOO, ROKURO!
!
RYOGO ...?
WHAT ARE YOU DOING?
ER, UMM...
I DON'T KNOW WHERE TO START...
TRMBL
TRMBL
HUMPH...
I COME BACK TO MY OLD HOOD AFTER ALL THIS TIME...
...TO FIND THAT ALL THE YOUNG FOLK ARE TOTALLY USELESS!
YOU...
SEIGEN?!

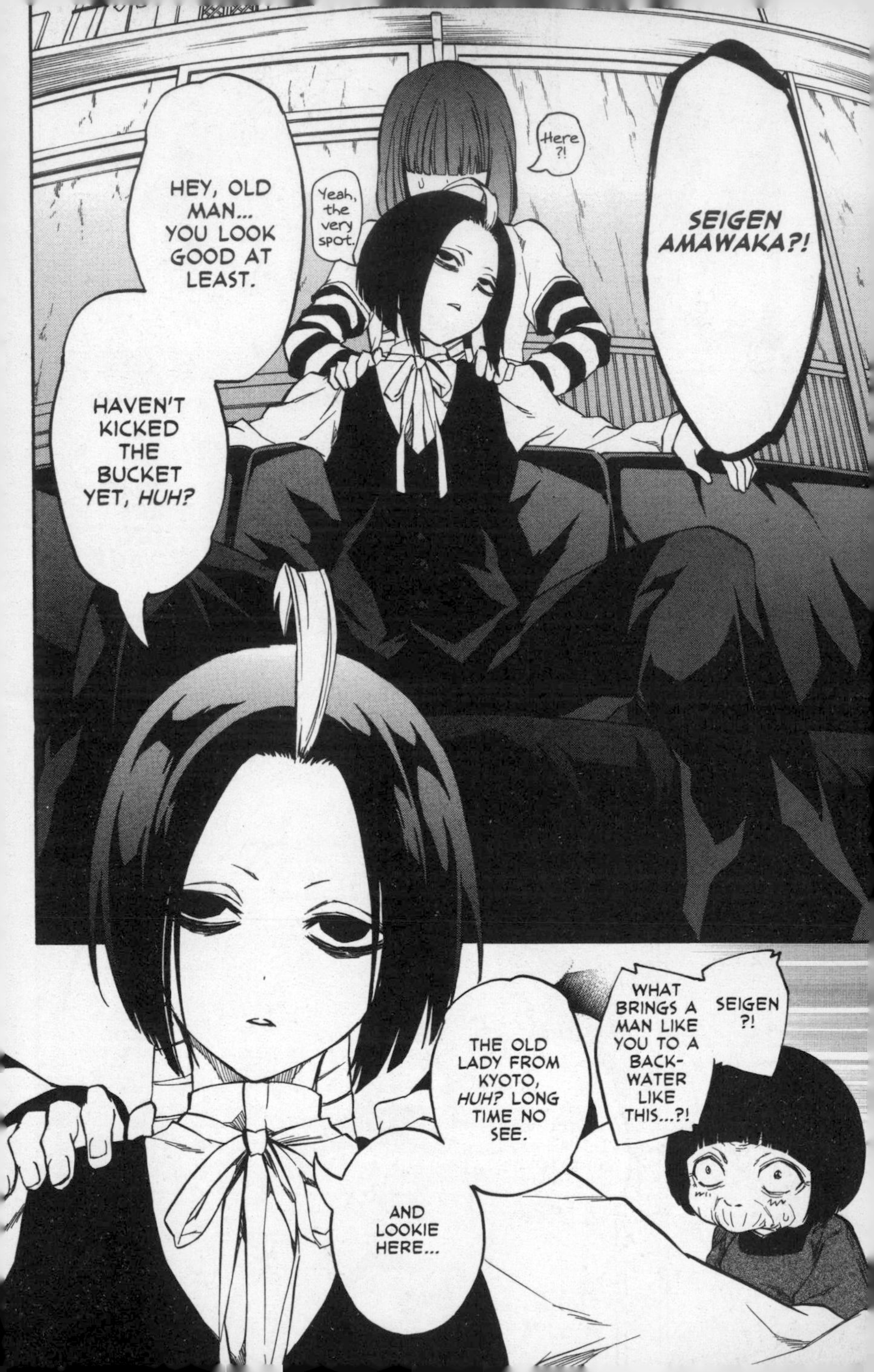
SEIGEN AMAWAKA?!
Here?!
Yeah, the very spot.
HEY, OLD MAN... YOU LOOK GOOD AT LEAST.
HAVEN'T KICKED THE BUCKET YET, *HUH?*
SEIGEN?!
WHAT BRINGS A MAN LIKE YOU TO A BACK-WATER LIKE THIS...?!
THE OLD LADY FROM KYOTO, *HUH?* LONG TIME NO SEE.
AND LOOKIE HERE...

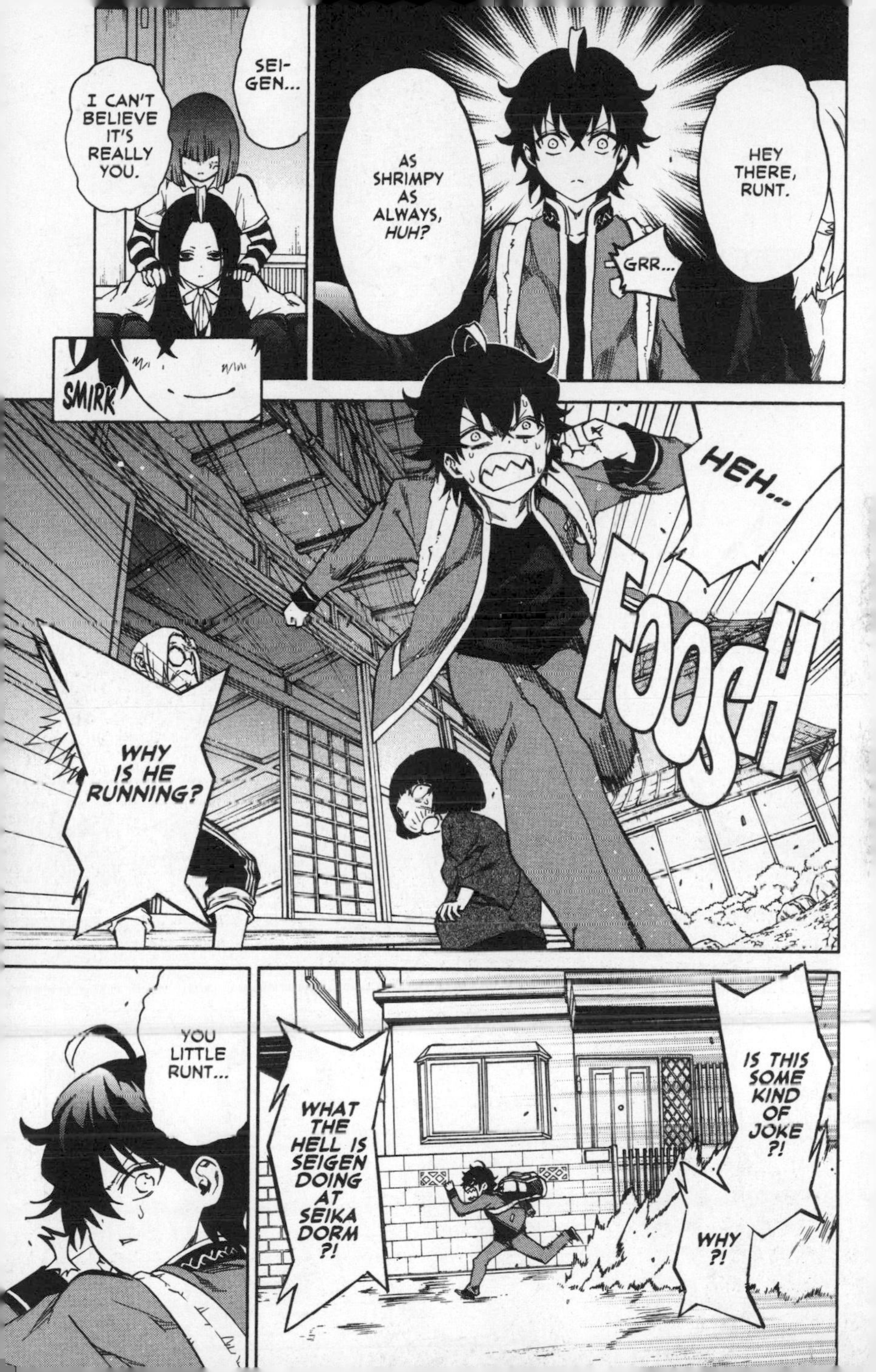
HEY THERE, RUNT.
AS SHRIMPY AS ALWAYS, HUH?
GRR...
SEI-GEN...
I CAN'T BELIEVE IT'S REALLY YOU.
SMIRK
HEH...
FOOSH
WHY IS HE RUNNING?
IS THIS SOME KIND OF JOKE?!
WHAT THE HELL IS SEIGEN DOING AT SEIKA DORM?!
WHY?!
YOU LITTLE RUNT...

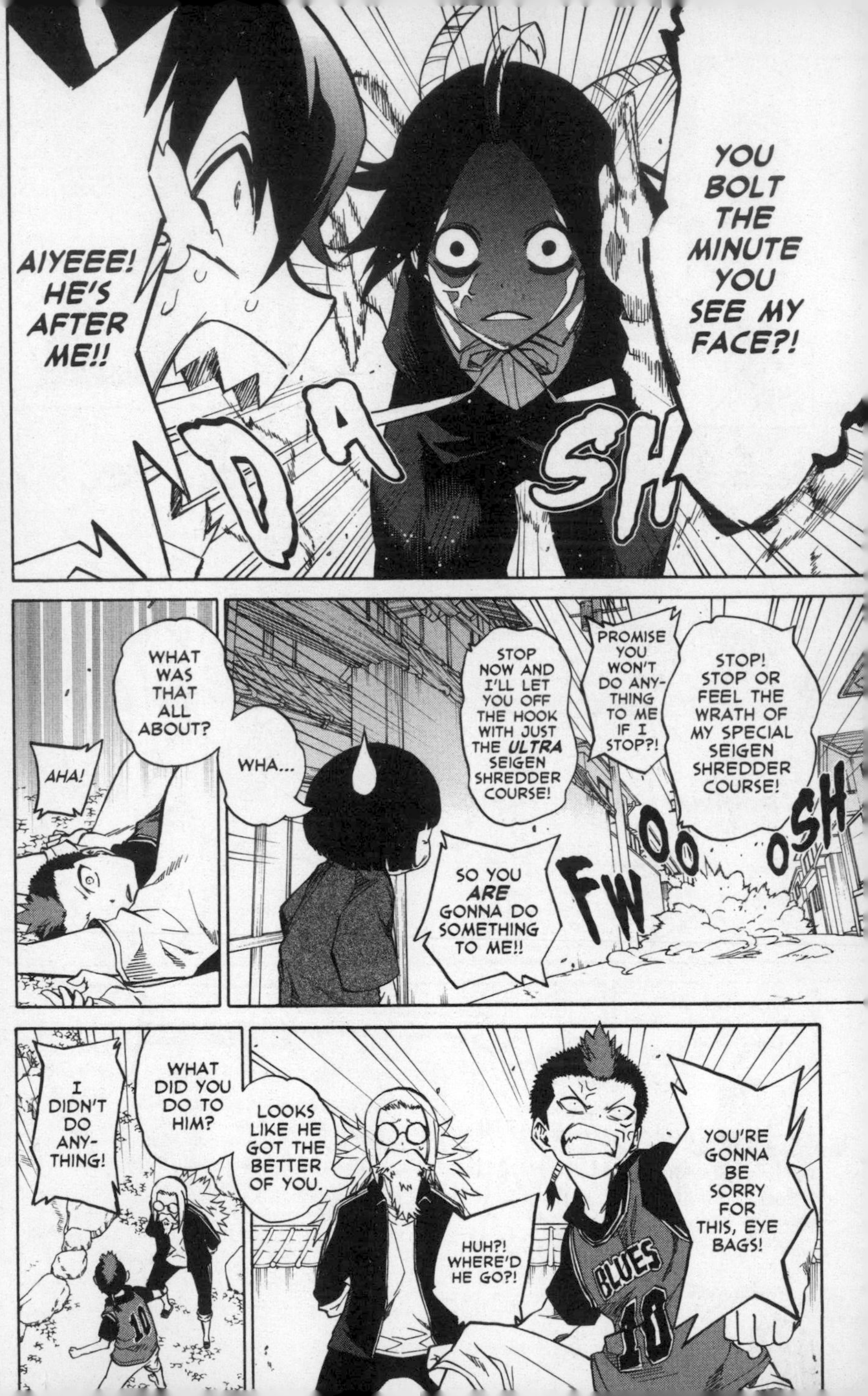
YOU BOLT THE MINUTE YOU SEE MY FACE?!
AIYEEE! HE'S AFTER ME!!
DASH
STOP! STOP OR FEEL THE WRATH OF MY SPECIAL SEIGEN SHREDDER COURSE!
PROMISE YOU WON'T DO ANY-THING TO ME IF I STOP?!
STOP NOW AND I'LL LET YOU OFF THE HOOK WITH JUST THE *ULTRA* SEIGEN SHREDDER COURSE!
FWOOOSH
SO YOU *ARE* GONNA DO SOMETHING TO ME!!
WHA...
WHAT WAS THAT ALL ABOUT?
AHA!
YOU'RE GONNA BE SORRY FOR THIS, EYE BAGS!
HUH?! WHERE'D HE GO?!
LOOKS LIKE HE GOT THE BETTER OF YOU.
WHAT DID YOU DO TO HIM?
I DIDN'T DO ANY-THING!

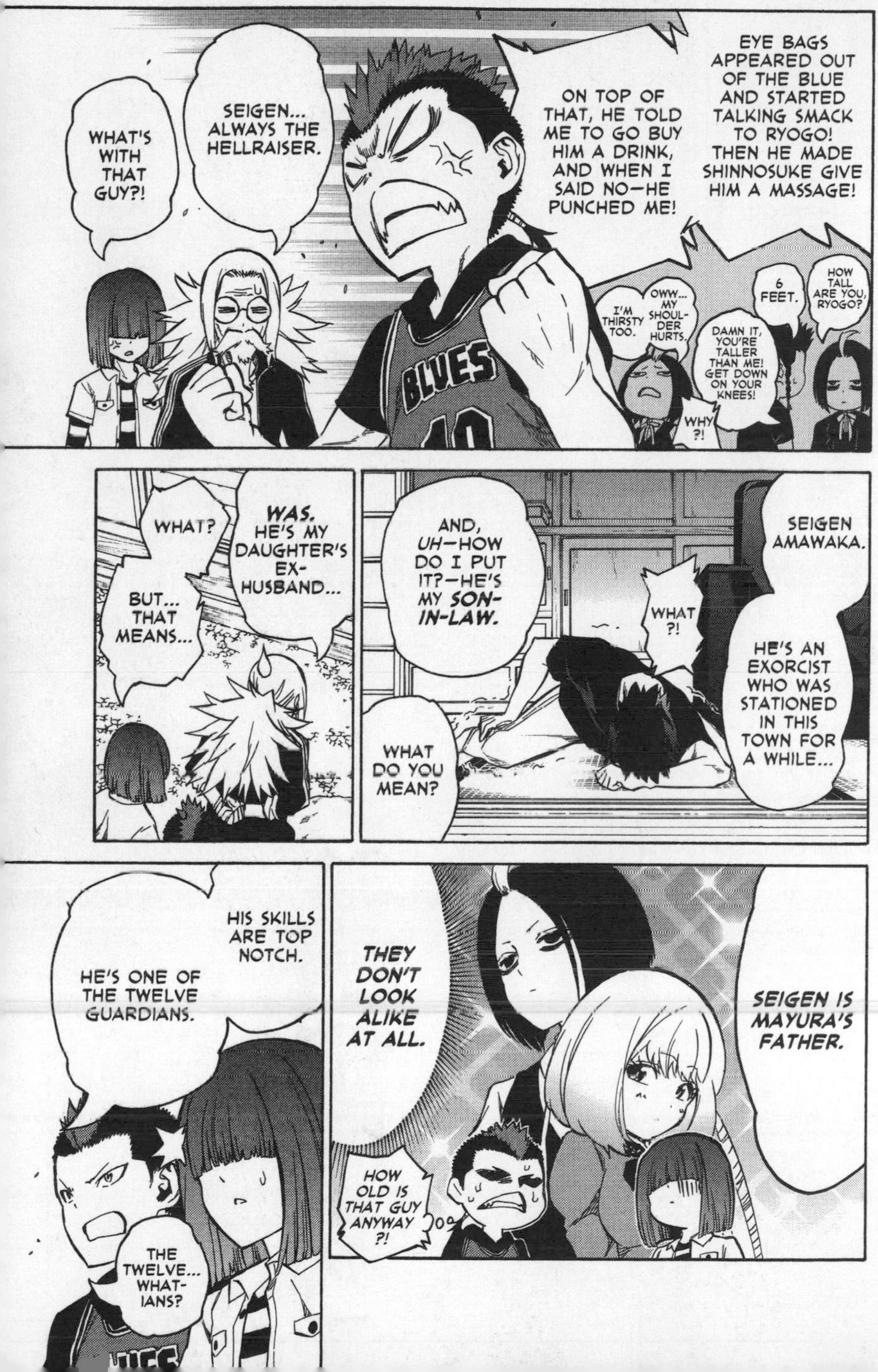
EYE BAGS APPEARED OUT OF THE BLUE AND STARTED TALKING SMACK TO RYOGO! THEN HE MADE SHINNOSUKE GIVE HIM A MASSAGE!
ON TOP OF THAT, HE TOLD ME TO GO BUY HIM A DRINK, AND WHEN I SAID NO—HE PUNCHED ME!
SEIGEN... ALWAYS THE HELLRAISER.
WHAT'S WITH THAT GUY?!
HOW TALL ARE YOU, RYOGO?
6 FEET.
DAMN IT, YOU'RE TALLER THAN ME! GET DOWN ON YOUR KNEES!
WHY?!
OWW... MY SHOULDER HURTS.
I'M THIRSTY TOO.
SEIGEN AMAWAKA.
HE'S AN EXORCIST WHO WAS STATIONED IN THIS TOWN FOR A WHILE...
WHAT?!
AND, *UH*—HOW DO I PUT IT?—HE'S MY ***SON-IN-LAW.***
WHAT DO YOU MEAN?
WAS. HE'S MY DAUGHTER'S EX-HUSBAND...
WHAT?
BUT... THAT MEANS...
SEIGEN IS MAYURA'S FATHER.
THEY DON'T LOOK ALIKE AT ALL.
HOW OLD IS THAT GUY ANYWAY?!
HIS SKILLS ARE TOP NOTCH.
HE'S ONE OF THE TWELVE GUARDIANS.
THE TWELVE... WHAT-IANS?

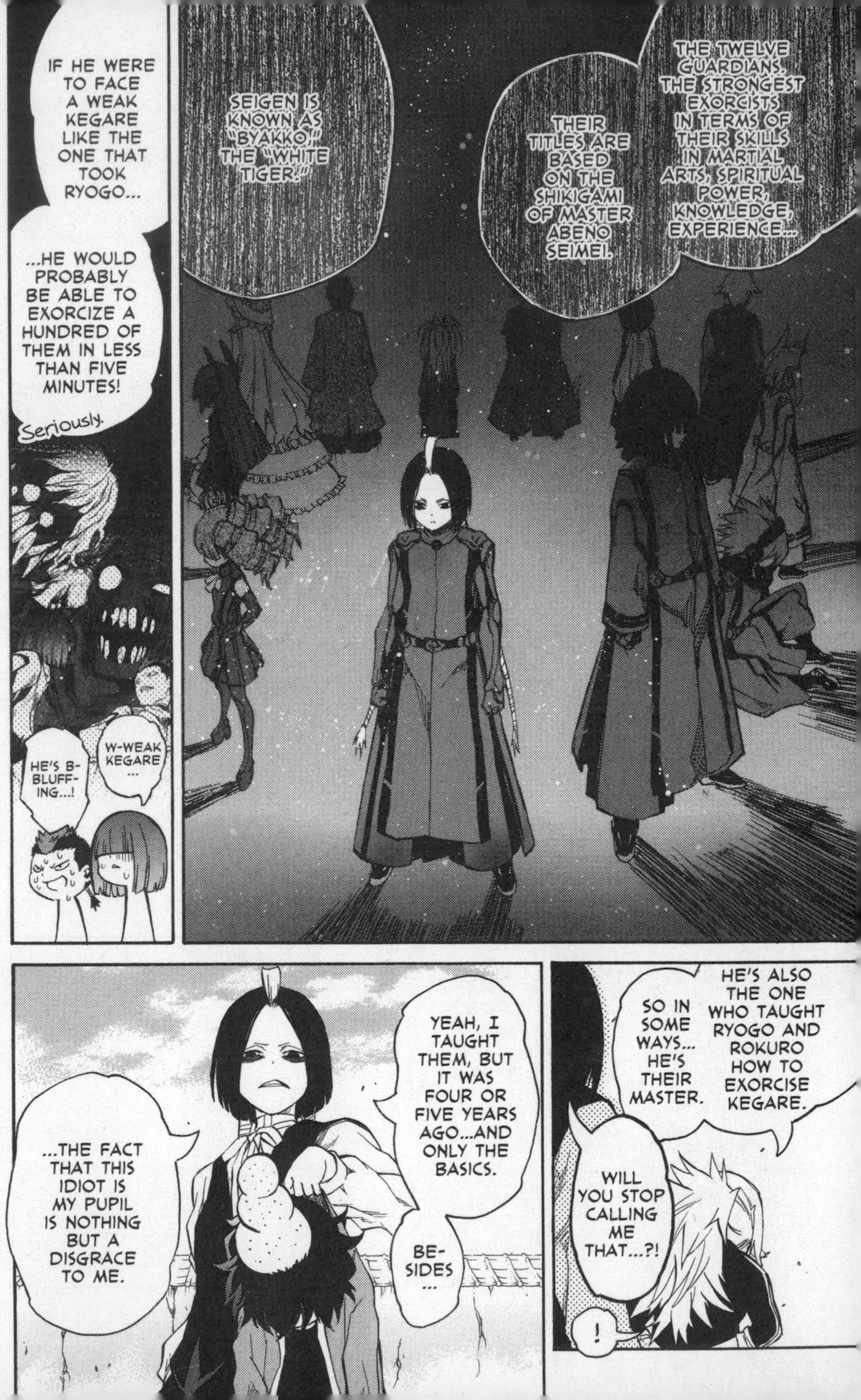
THE TWELVE GUARDIANS. THE STRONGEST EXORCISTS IN TERMS OF THEIR SKILLS IN MARTIAL ARTS, SPIRITUAL POWER, KNOWLEDGE, EXPERIENCE...
THEIR TITLES ARE BASED ON THE SHIKIGAMI OF MASTER ABENO SEIMEI.
SEIGEN IS KNOWN AS "BYAKKO," THE "WHITE TIGER."
IF HE WERE TO FACE A WEAK KEGARE LIKE THE ONE THAT TOOK RYOGO...
...HE WOULD PROBABLY BE ABLE TO EXORCIZE A HUNDRED OF THEM IN LESS THAN FIVE MINUTES!
Seriously.
W-WEAK KEGARE...
HE'S B-BLUFFING...!
HE'S ALSO THE ONE WHO TAUGHT RYOGO AND ROKURO HOW TO EXORCISE KEGARE.
SO IN SOME WAYS... HE'S THEIR MASTER.
WILL YOU STOP CALLING ME THAT...?!
!
YEAH, I TAUGHT THEM, BUT IT WAS FOUR OR FIVE YEARS AGO...AND ONLY THE BASICS.
BE-SIDES...
...THE FACT THAT THIS IDIOT IS MY PUPIL IS NOTHING BUT A DISGRACE TO ME.

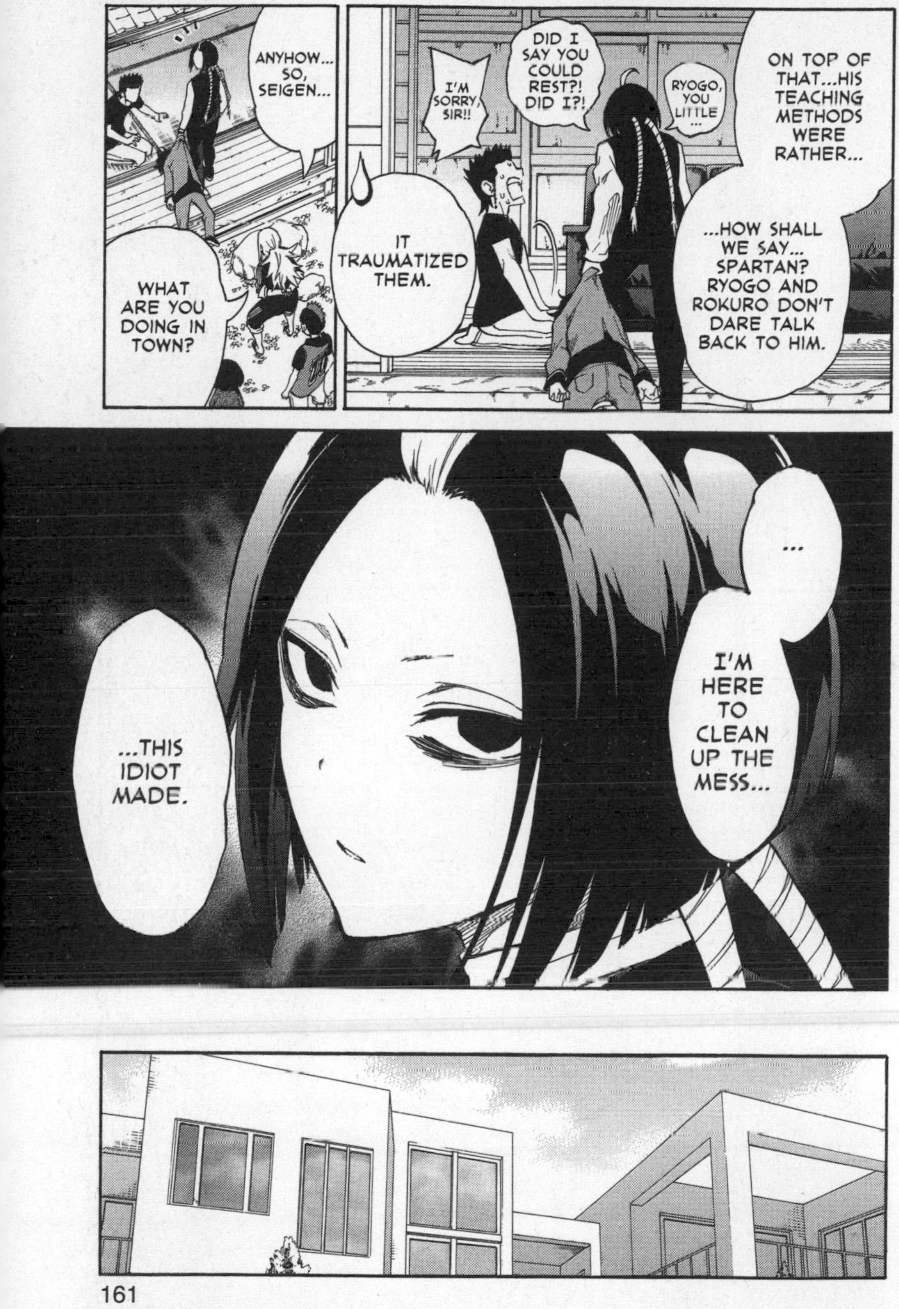
ON TOP OF THAT...HIS TEACHING METHODS WERE RATHER...
...HOW SHALL WE SAY... SPARTAN? RYOGO AND ROKURO DON'T DARE TALK BACK TO HIM.
RYOGO, YOU LITTLE ...
DID I SAY YOU COULD REST?! DID I?!
I'M SORRY, SIR!!
IT TRAUMATIZED THEM.
ANYHOW... SO, SEIGEN...
WHAT ARE YOU DOING IN TOWN?
...
I'M HERE TO CLEAN UP THE MESS...
...THIS IDIOT MADE.

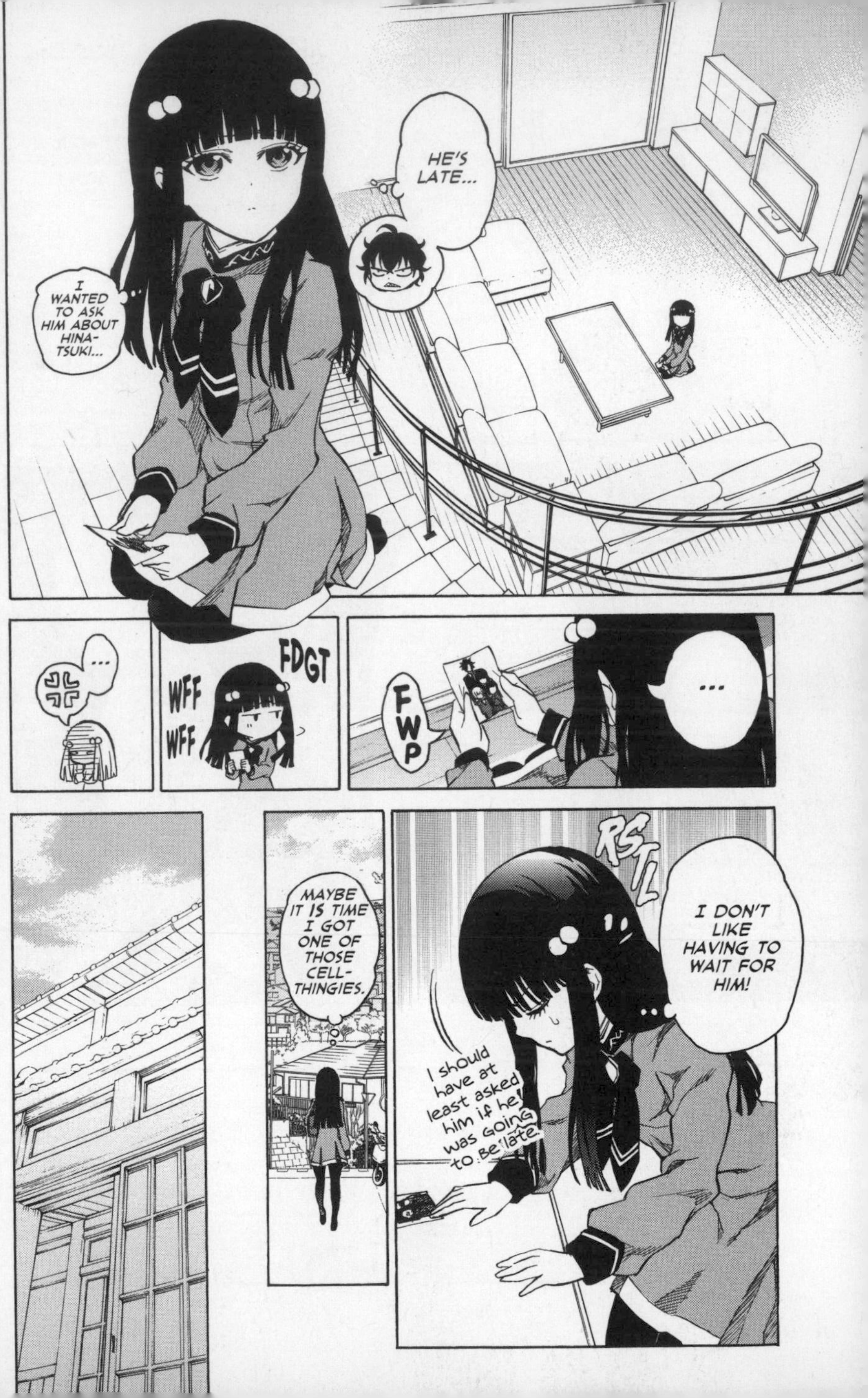
HE'S LATE...
I WANTED TO ASK HIM ABOUT HINA-TSUKI...
...
FWP
FDGT
WFF WFF
...
RSTL
I DON'T LIKE HAVING TO WAIT FOR HIM!
I should have at least asked him if he was going to be late.
MAYBE IT IS TIME I GOT ONE OF THOSE CELL-THINGIES.

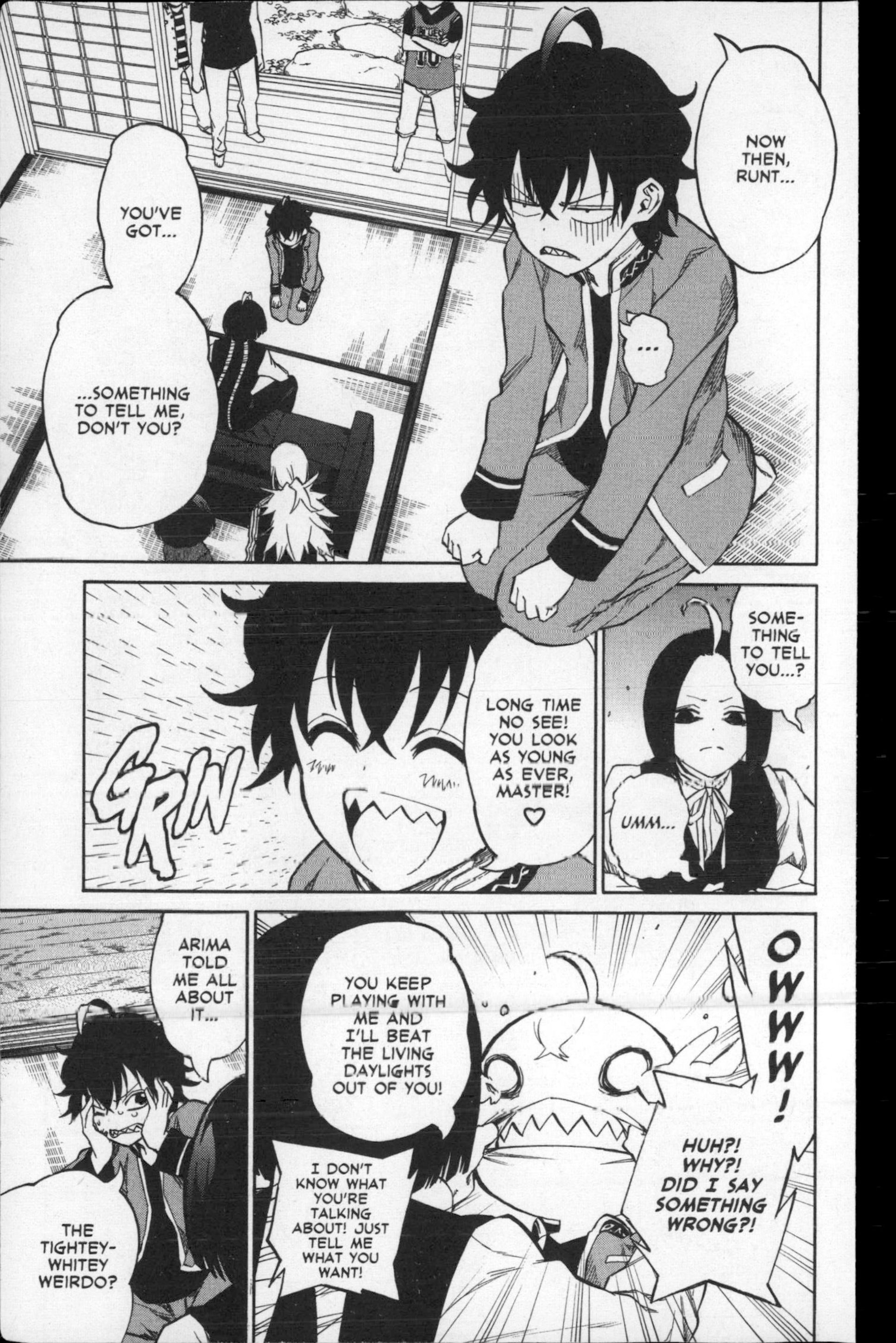
NOW THEN, RUNT...
YOU'VE GOT...
...SOMETHING TO TELL ME, DON'T YOU?
...
SOME-THING TO TELL YOU...?
UMM...
LONG TIME NO SEE! YOU LOOK AS YOUNG AS EVER, MASTER! ♡
GRIN
OWWW!
YOU KEEP PLAYING WITH ME AND I'LL BEAT THE LIVING DAYLIGHTS OUT OF YOU!
HUH?! WHY?! DID I SAY SOMETHING WRONG?!
I DON'T KNOW WHAT YOU'RE TALKING ABOUT! JUST TELL ME WHAT YOU WANT!
ARIMA TOLD ME ALL ABOUT IT...
THE TIGHTEY-WHITEY WEIRDO?

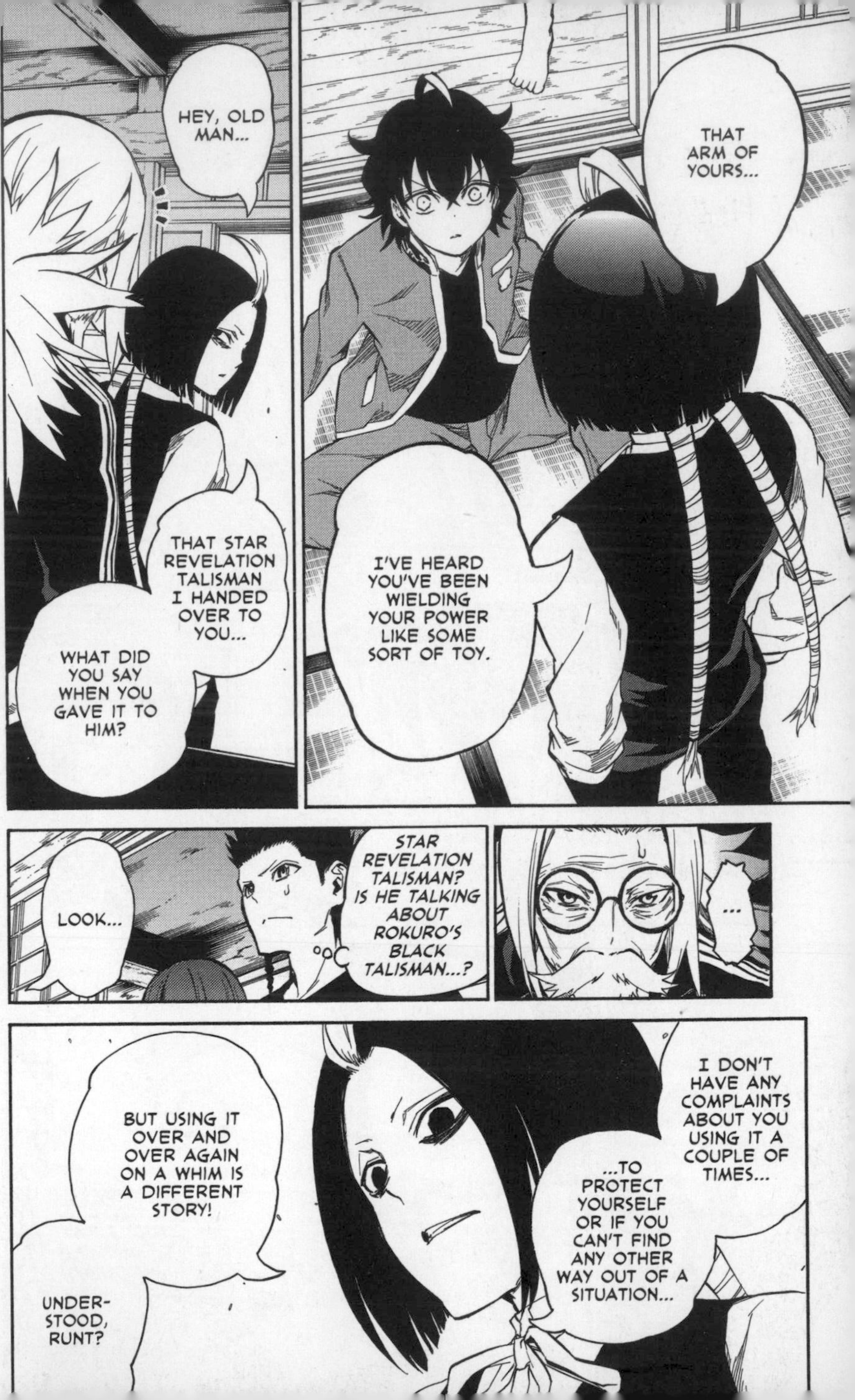
THAT ARM OF YOURS...
I'VE HEARD YOU'VE BEEN WIELDING YOUR POWER LIKE SOME SORT OF TOY.
HEY, OLD MAN...
THAT STAR REVELATION TALISMAN I HANDED OVER TO YOU...
WHAT DID YOU SAY WHEN YOU GAVE IT TO HIM?
...
STAR REVELATION TALISMAN? IS HE TALKING ABOUT ROKURO'S BLACK TALISMAN...?
LOOK...
I DON'T HAVE ANY COMPLAINTS ABOUT YOU USING IT A COUPLE OF TIMES...
...TO PROTECT YOURSELF OR IF YOU CAN'T FIND ANY OTHER WAY OUT OF A SITUATION...
BUT USING IT OVER AND OVER AGAIN ON A WHIM IS A DIFFERENT STORY!
UNDER-STOOD, RUNT?

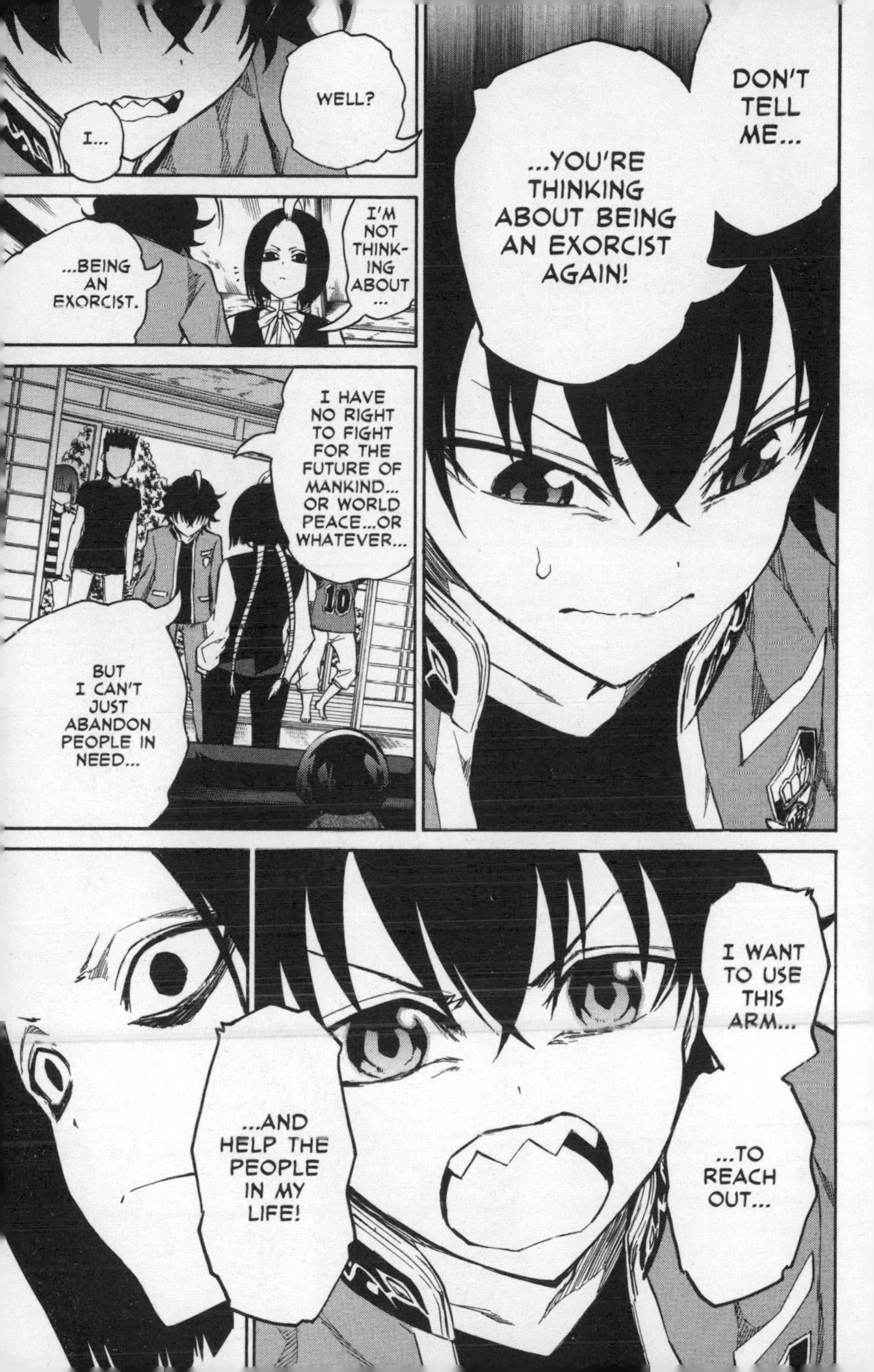
DON'T TELL ME...
...YOU'RE THINKING ABOUT BEING AN EXORCIST AGAIN!
WELL?
I...
I'M NOT THINKING ABOUT ...
...BEING AN EXORCIST.
I HAVE NO RIGHT TO FIGHT FOR THE FUTURE OF MANKIND... OR WORLD PEACE...OR WHATEVER...
BUT I CAN'T JUST ABANDON PEOPLE IN NEED...
I WANT TO USE THIS ARM...
...TO REACH OUT...
...AND HELP THE PEOPLE IN MY LIFE!

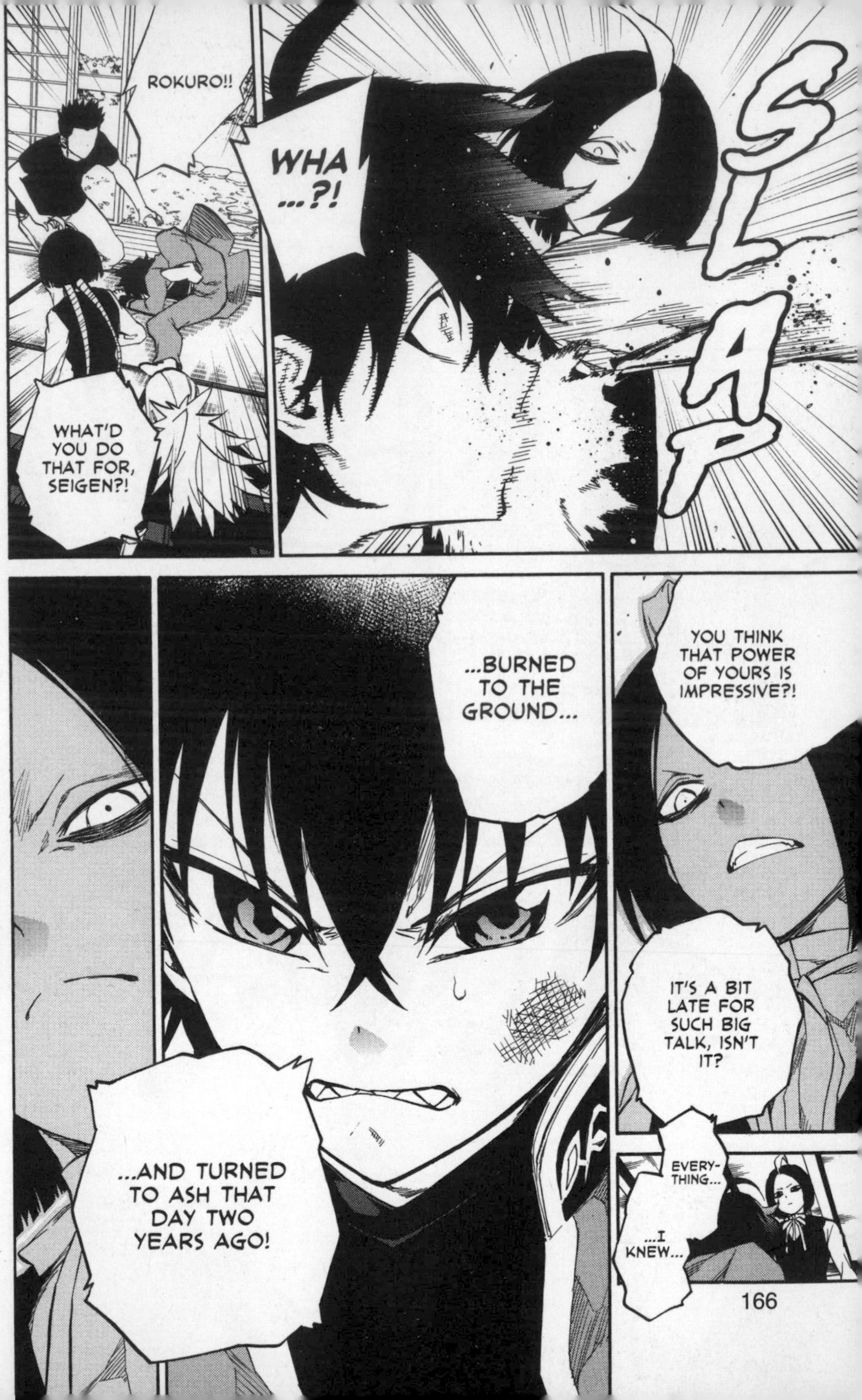
SLAP
WHA ...?!
ROKURO!!
WHAT'D YOU DO THAT FOR, SEIGEN?!
YOU THINK THAT POWER OF YOURS IS IMPRESSIVE?!
IT'S A BIT LATE FOR SUCH BIG TALK, ISN'T IT?
EVERY-THING...
...I KNEW...
...BURNED TO THE GROUND...
...AND TURNED TO ASH THAT DAY TWO YEARS AGO!

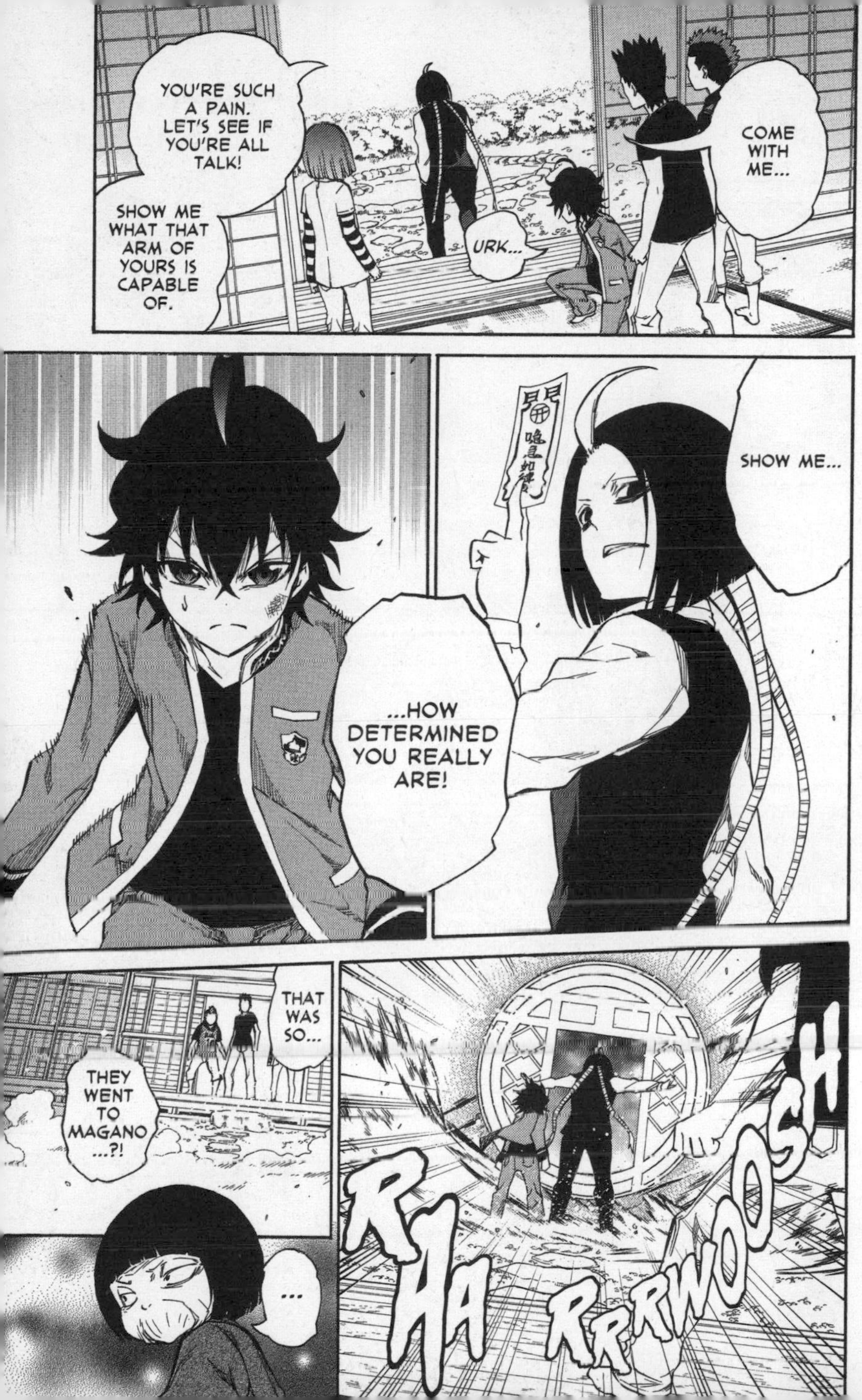
COME WITH ME...
URK...
YOU'RE SUCH A PAIN. LET'S SEE IF YOU'RE ALL TALK!
SHOW ME WHAT THAT ARM OF YOURS IS CAPABLE OF.
SHOW ME...
...HOW DETERMINED YOU REALLY ARE!
RHA RRRWOOSH
THAT WAS SO...
THEY WENT TO MAGANO...?!
...

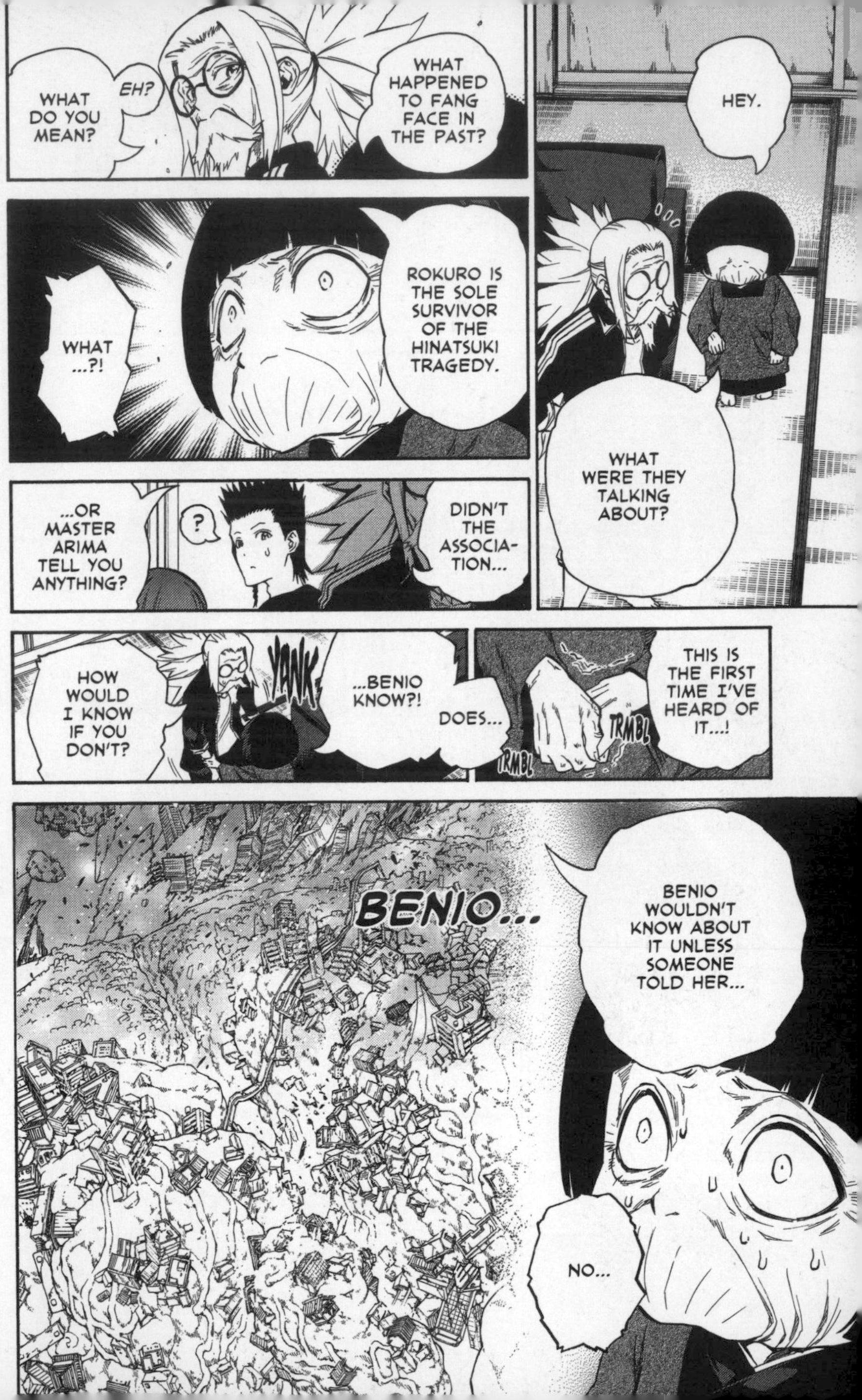
HEY.
WHAT WERE THEY TALKING ABOUT?
WHAT HAPPENED TO FANG FACE IN THE PAST?
EH?
WHAT DO YOU MEAN?
ROKURO IS THE SOLE SURVIVOR OF THE HINATSUKI TRAGEDY.
WHAT ...?!
DIDN'T THE ASSOCIATION...
...OR MASTER ARIMA TELL YOU ANYTHING?
?
THIS IS THE FIRST TIME I'VE HEARD OF IT...!
TRMBL
TRMBL
DOES...
...BENIO KNOW?!
YANK
HOW WOULD I KNOW IF YOU DON'T?
BENIO WOULDN'T KNOW ABOUT IT UNLESS SOMEONE TOLD HER...
BENIO...
NO...

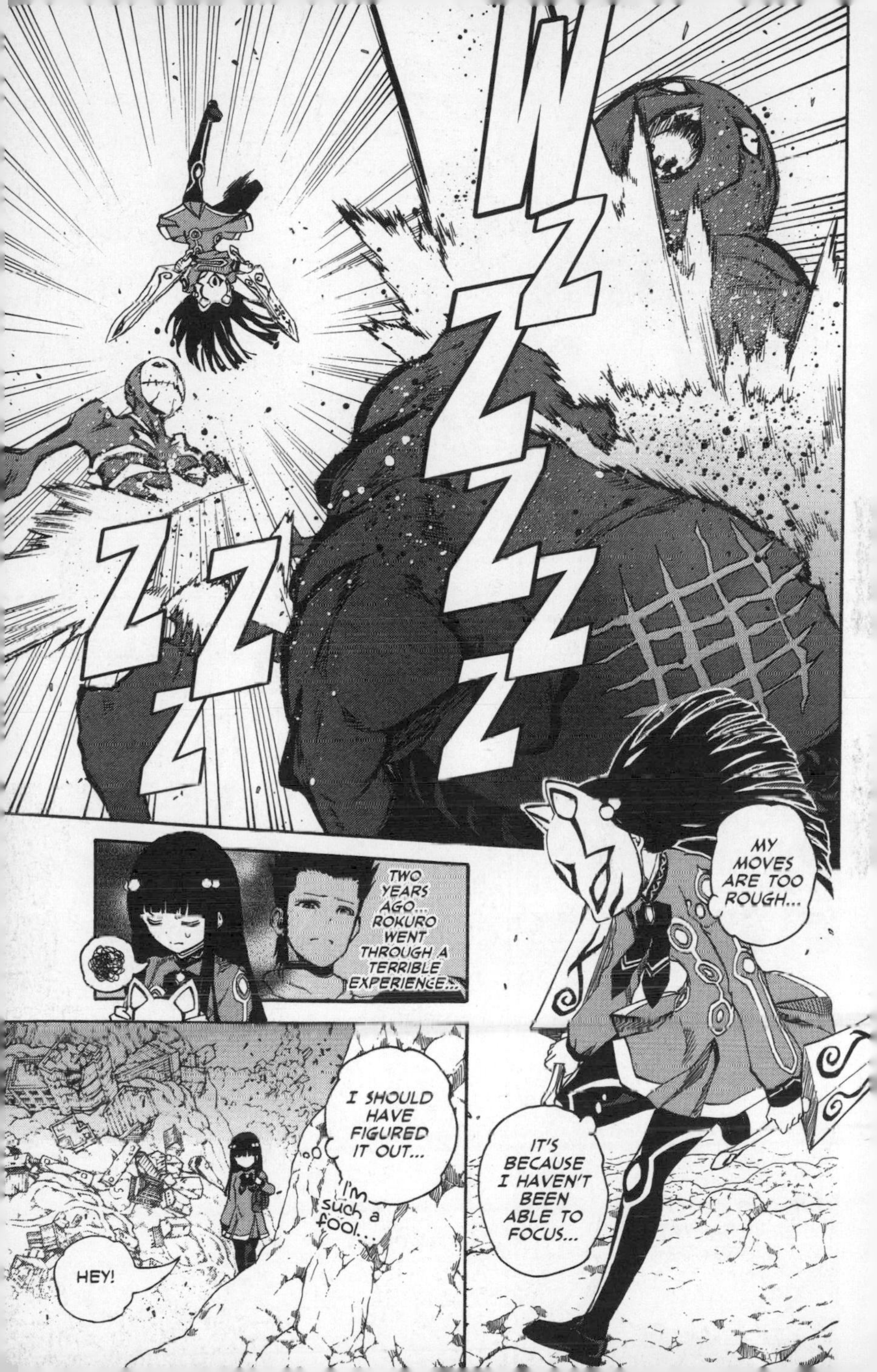
MY MOVES ARE TOO ROUGH...
IT'S BECAUSE I HAVEN'T BEEN ABLE TO FOCUS...
TWO YEARS AGO... ROKURO WENT THROUGH A TERRIBLE EXPERIENCE...
I SHOULD HAVE FIGURED IT OUT...
I'm such a fool...
HEY!

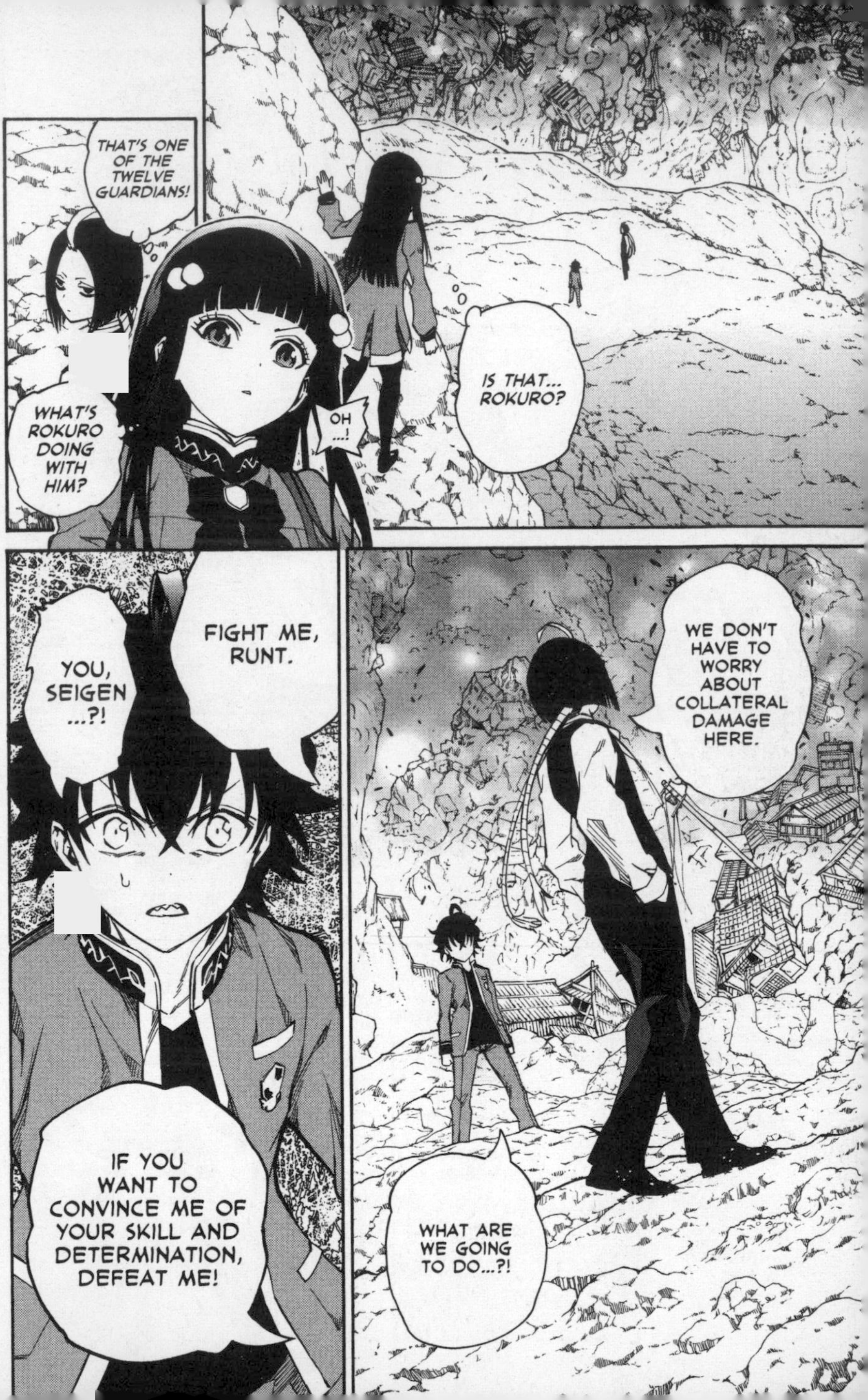
IS THAT... ROKURO?
OH ...!
THAT'S ONE OF THE TWELVE GUARDIANS!
WHAT'S ROKURO DOING WITH HIM?
WE DON'T HAVE TO WORRY ABOUT COLLATERAL DAMAGE HERE.
WHAT ARE WE GOING TO DO...?!
FIGHT ME, RUNT.
YOU, SEIGEN ...?!
IF YOU WANT TO CONVINCE ME OF YOUR SKILL AND DETERMINATION, DEFEAT ME!

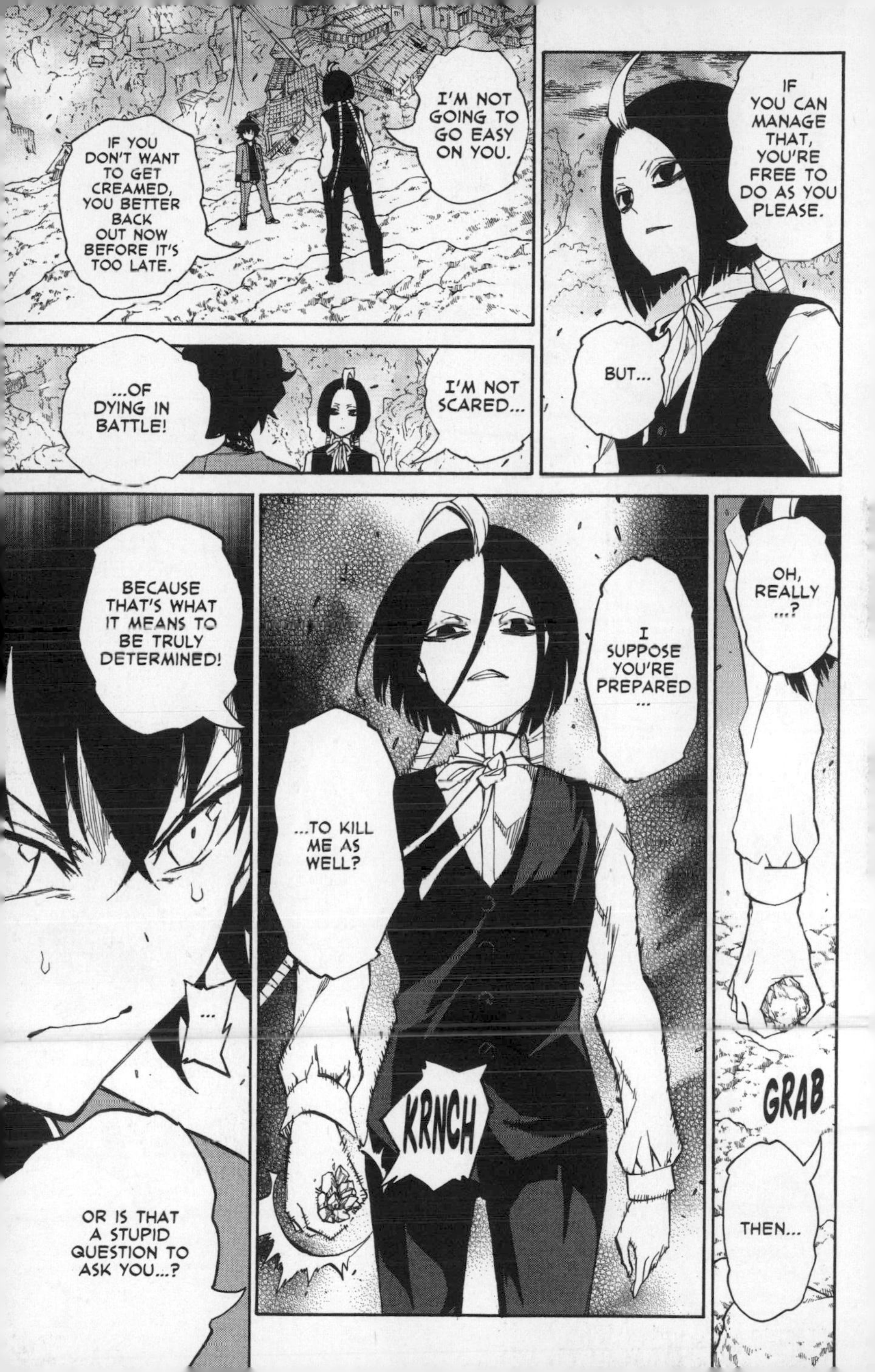
IF YOU CAN MANAGE THAT, YOU'RE FREE TO DO AS YOU PLEASE.
BUT...
I'M NOT GOING TO GO EASY ON YOU.
IF YOU DON'T WANT TO GET CREAMED, YOU BETTER BACK OUT NOW BEFORE IT'S TOO LATE.
I'M NOT SCARED...
...OF DYING IN BATTLE!
OH, REALLY ...?
GRAB
THEN...
I SUPPOSE YOU'RE PREPARED ...
...TO KILL ME AS WELL?
KRNCH
BECAUSE THAT'S WHAT IT MEANS TO BE TRULY DETERMINED!
...
OR IS THAT A STUPID QUESTION TO ASK YOU...?

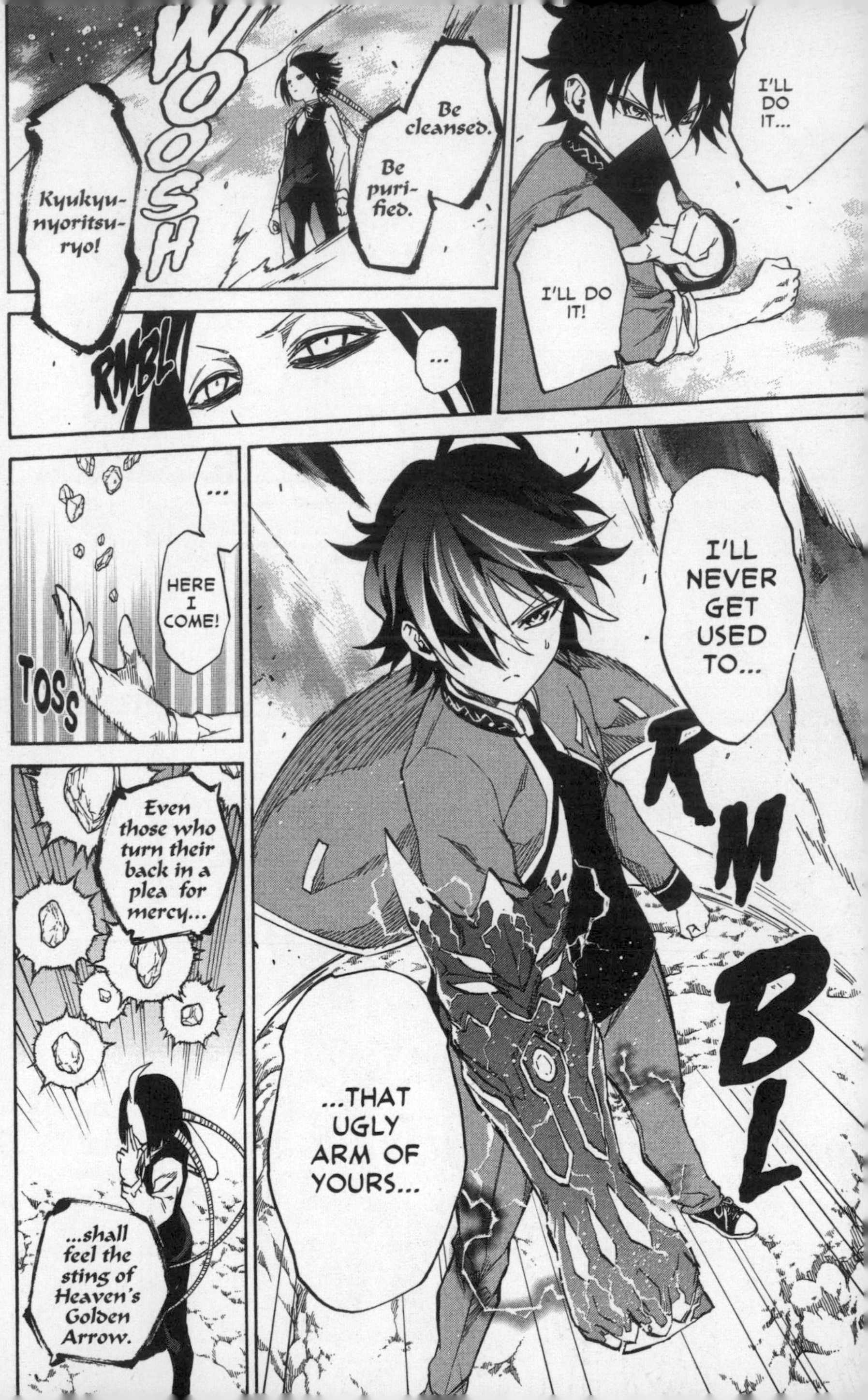
I'LL DO IT...
I'LL DO IT!
Be cleansed.
Be purified.
WOOSH
Kyukyunyoritsuryo!
...
RMBL
I'LL NEVER GET USED TO...
RMBL
...THAT UGLY ARM OF YOURS...
...
HERE I COME!
TOSS
Even those who turn their back in a plea for mercy...
...shall feel the sting of Heaven's Golden Arrow.

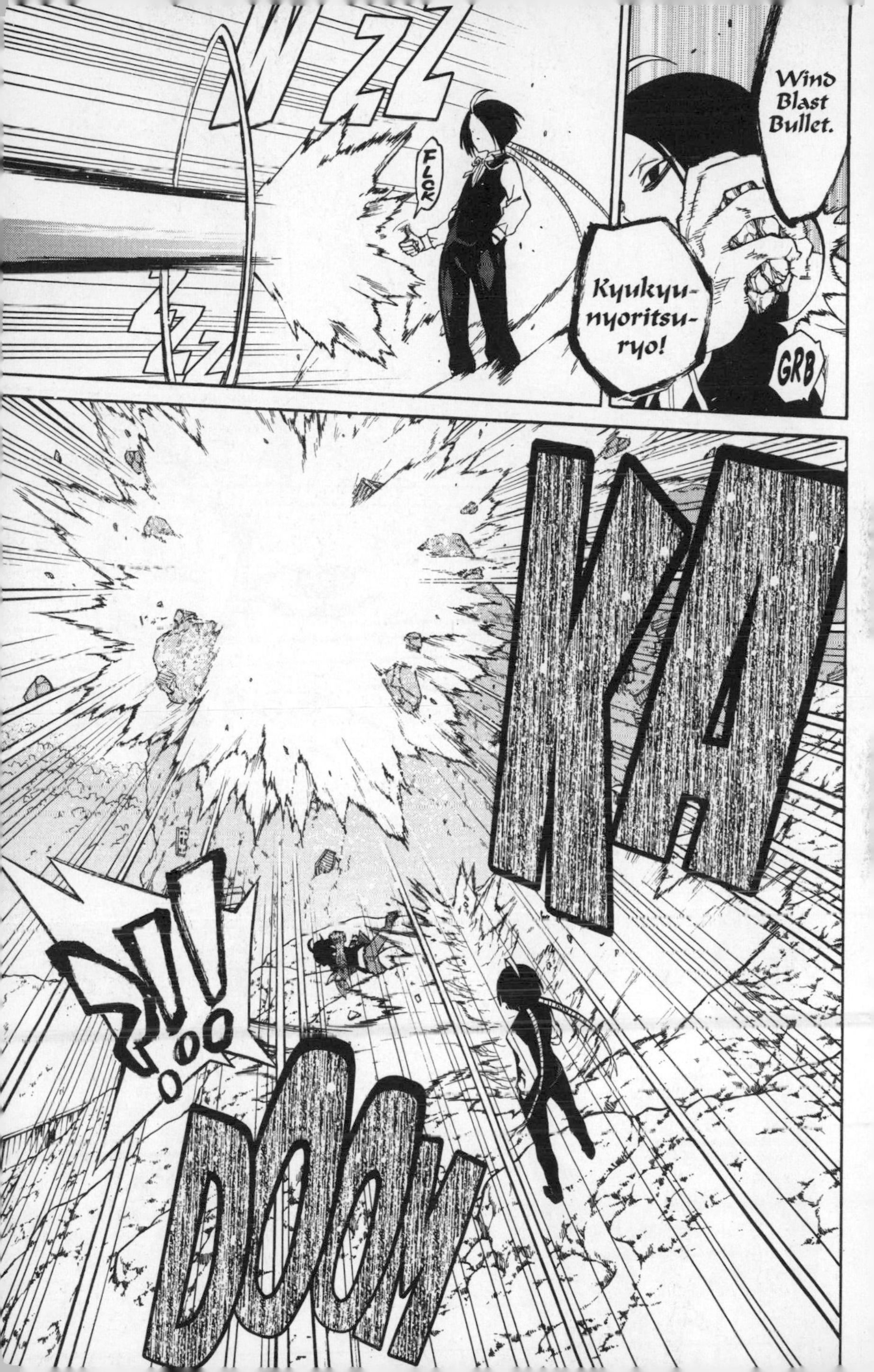
Wind Blast Bullet.
Kyukyu-nyoritsu-ryo!
GRB
FLCK

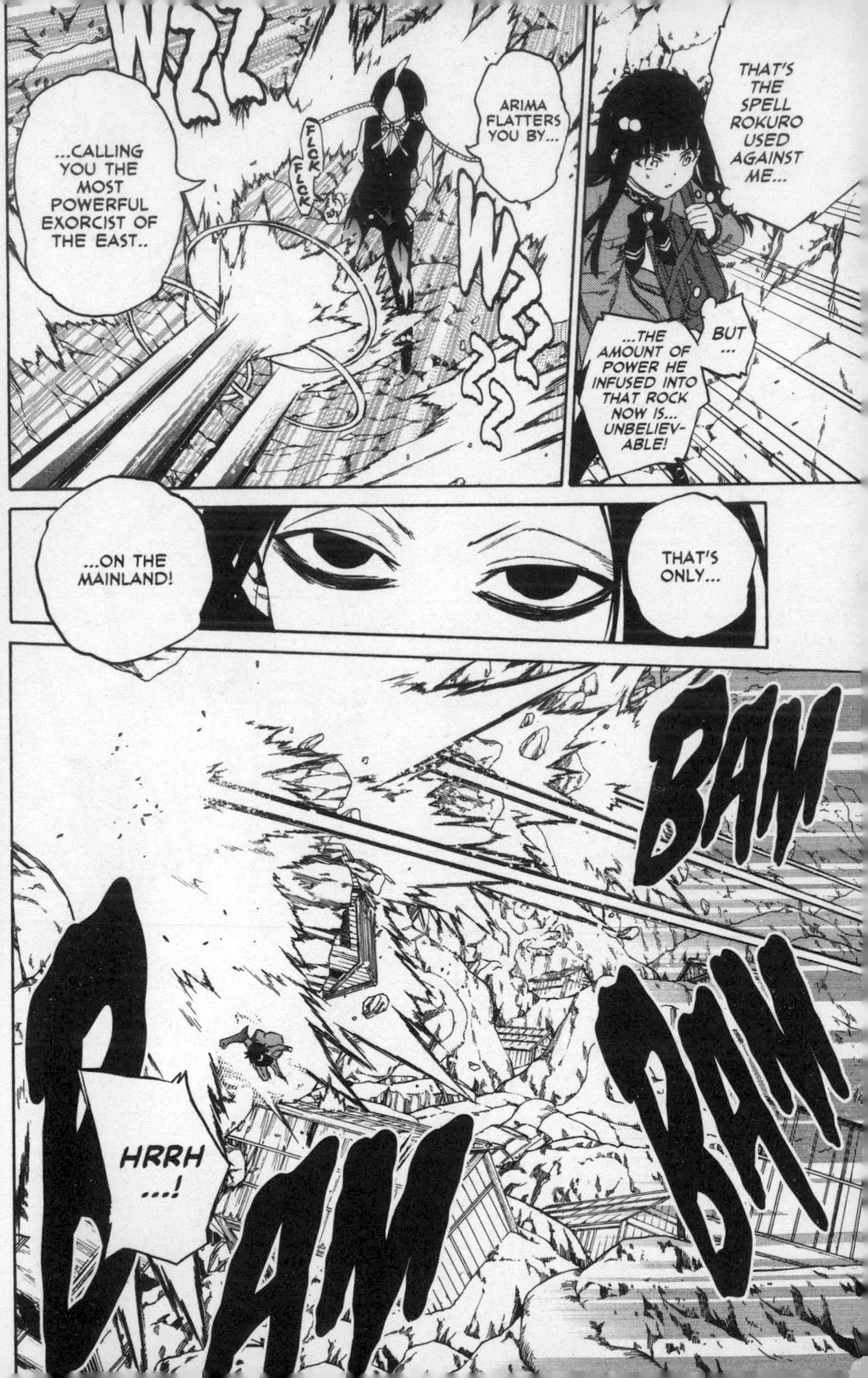
THAT'S THE SPELL ROKURO USED AGAINST ME...
BUT ...
...THE AMOUNT OF POWER HE INFUSED INTO THAT ROCK NOW IS... UNBELIEVABLE!
WZZ
ARIMA FLATTERS YOU BY...
FLCK FLCK
...CALLING YOU THE MOST POWERFUL EXORCIST OF THE EAST..
WZZ
THAT'S ONLY...
...ON THE MAINLAND!
BAM
BAM
HRRH ...!
BAM

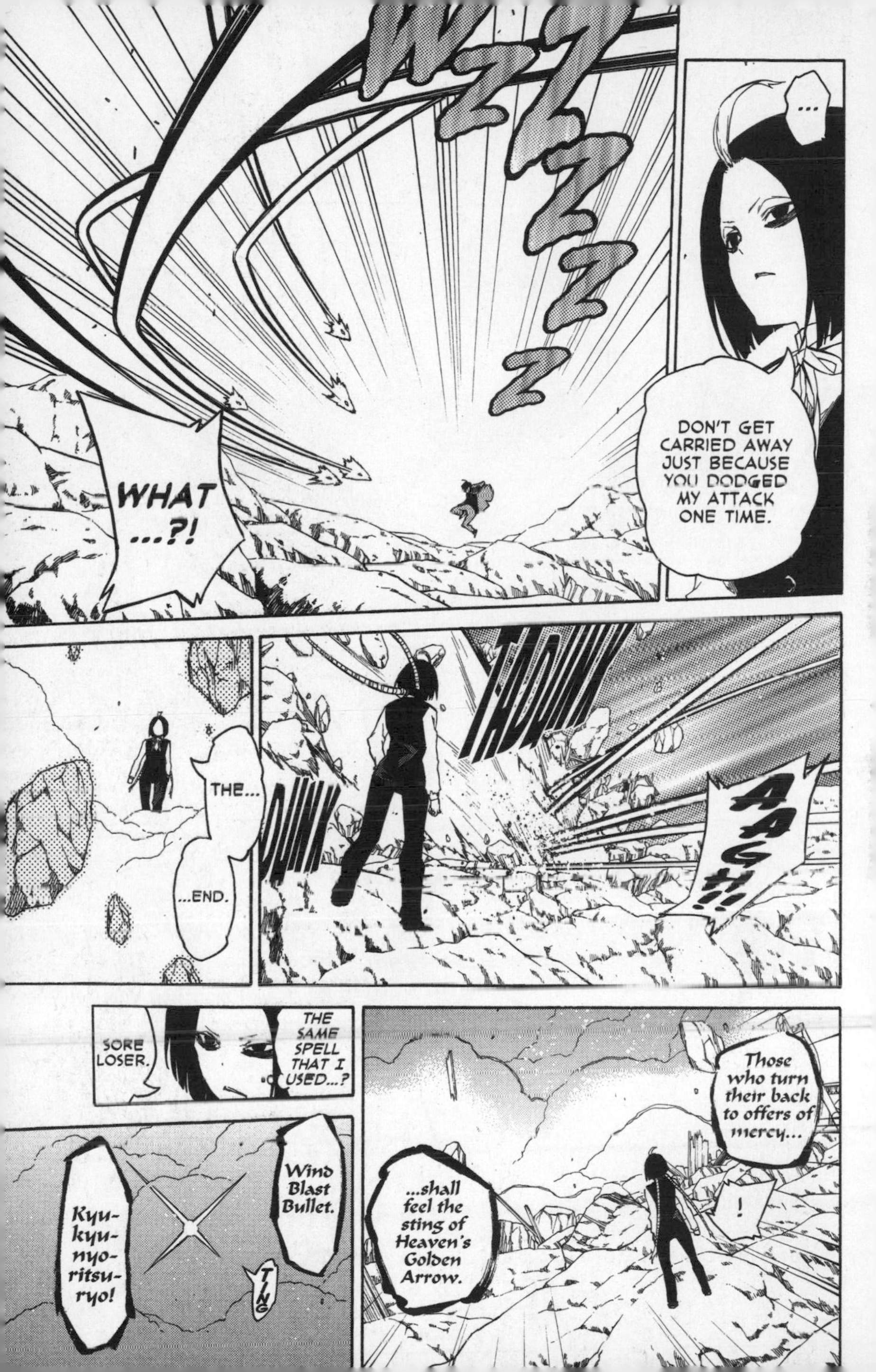
...
DON'T GET CARRIED AWAY JUST BECAUSE YOU DODGED MY ATTACK ONE TIME.
WZZZZZ
WHAT ...?!
THDUNK
DUNK
AAGH!!
THE...
...END.
Those who turn their back to offers of mercy...
...shall feel the sting of Heaven's Golden Arrow.
!
THE SAME SPELL THAT I USED...?
SORE LOSER.
Wind Blast Bullet.
Kyu-kyu-nyo-ritsu-ryo!
TING

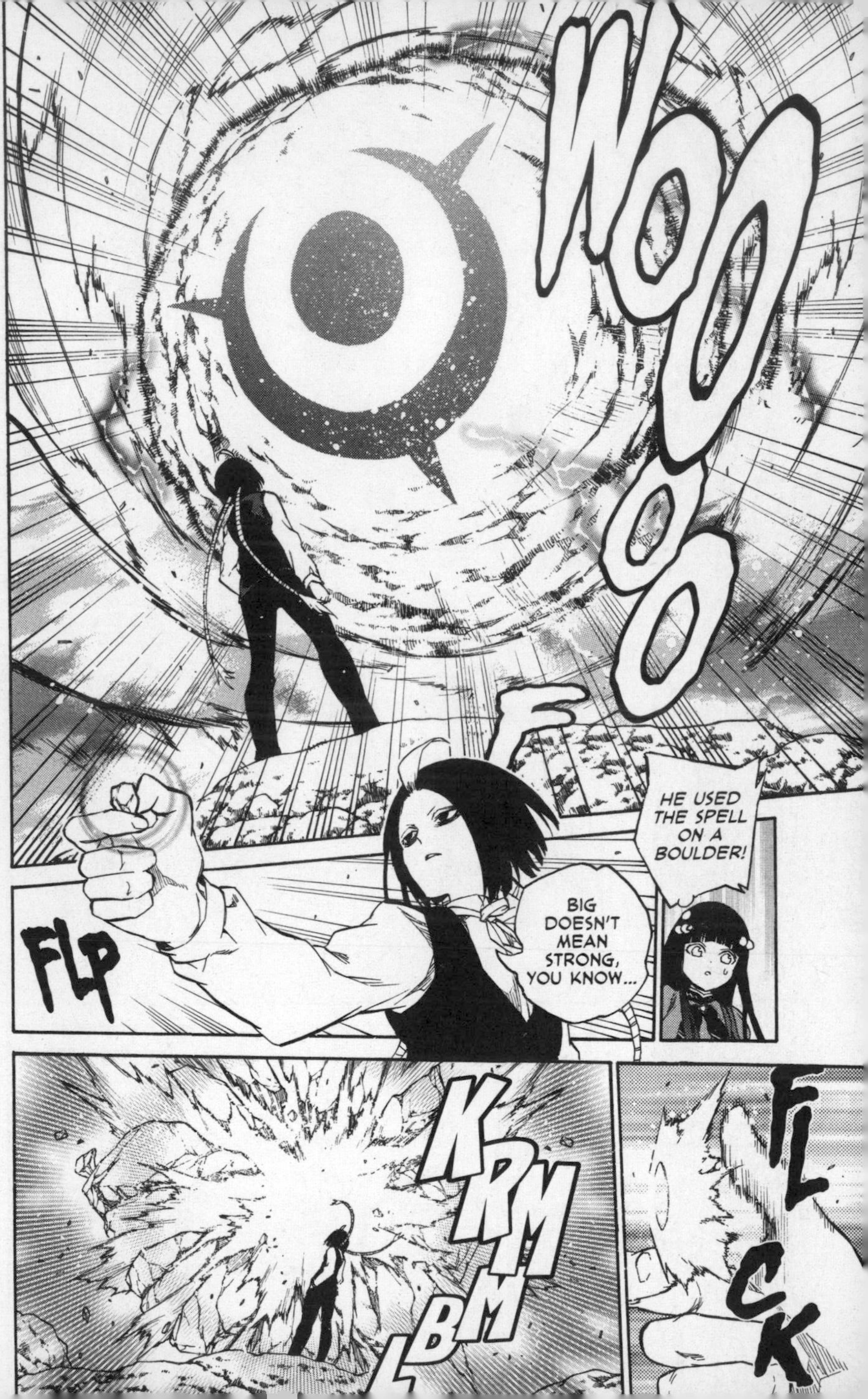
WOOOOOO
HE USED THE SPELL ON A BOULDER!
BIG DOESN'T MEAN STRONG, YOU KNOW...
FLP
FLICK
KRMMBML

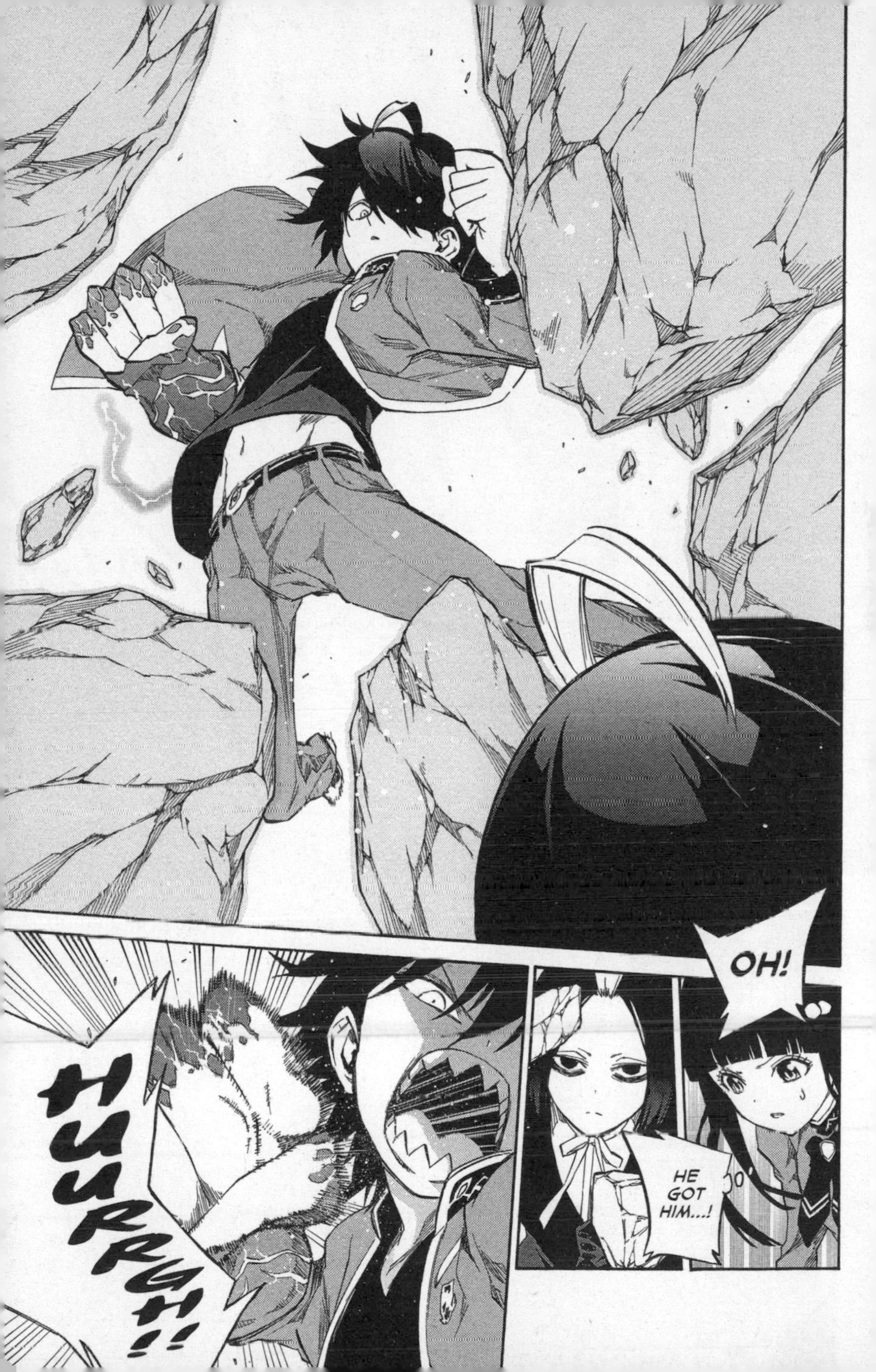
OH!
HE GOT HIM...!
HUURGH!!

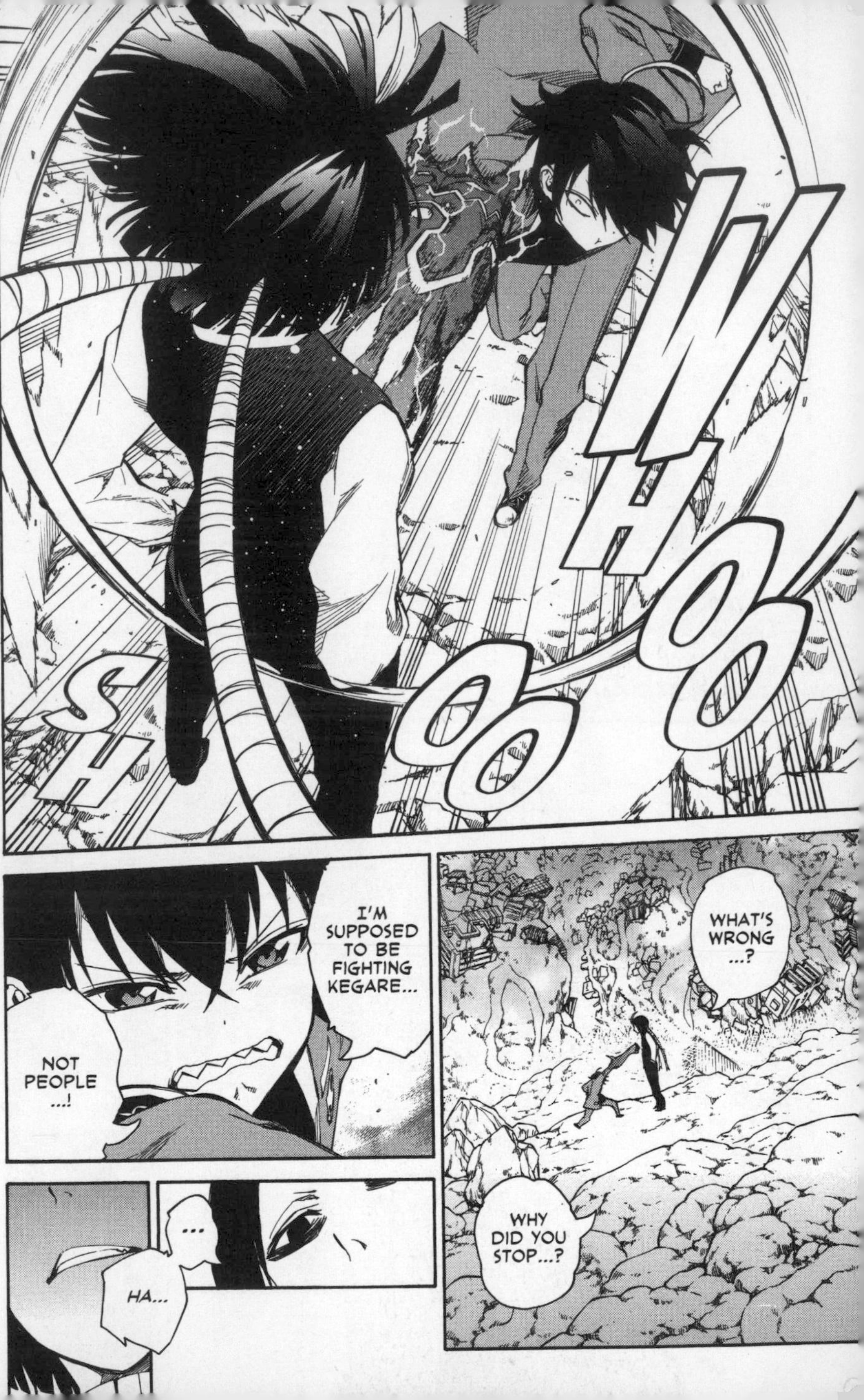
WHOOOOSH
WHAT'S WRONG ...?
WHY DID YOU STOP...?
I'M SUPPOSED TO BE FIGHTING KEGARE...
NOT PEOPLE ...!
...
HA...

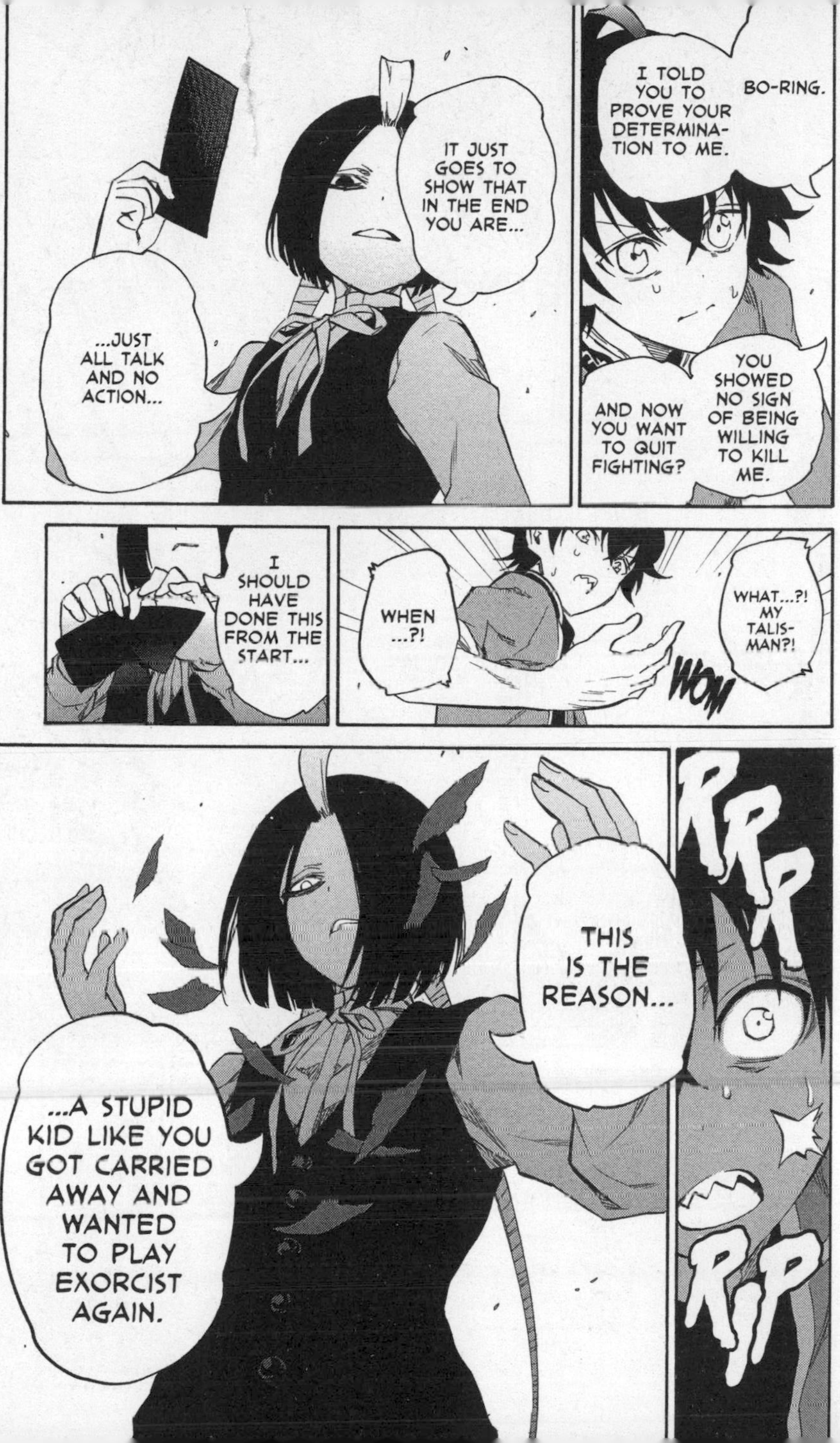
BO-RING.
I TOLD YOU TO PROVE YOUR DETERMINATION TO ME.
YOU SHOWED NO SIGN OF BEING WILLING TO KILL ME.
AND NOW YOU WANT TO QUIT FIGHTING?
IT JUST GOES TO SHOW THAT IN THE END YOU ARE...
...JUST ALL TALK AND NO ACTION...
WHAT...?! MY TALISMAN?!
WOM
WHEN ...?!
I SHOULD HAVE DONE THIS FROM THE START...
RIP
RIP
THIS IS THE REASON...
...A STUPID KID LIKE YOU GOT CARRIED AWAY AND WANTED TO PLAY EXORCIST AGAIN.

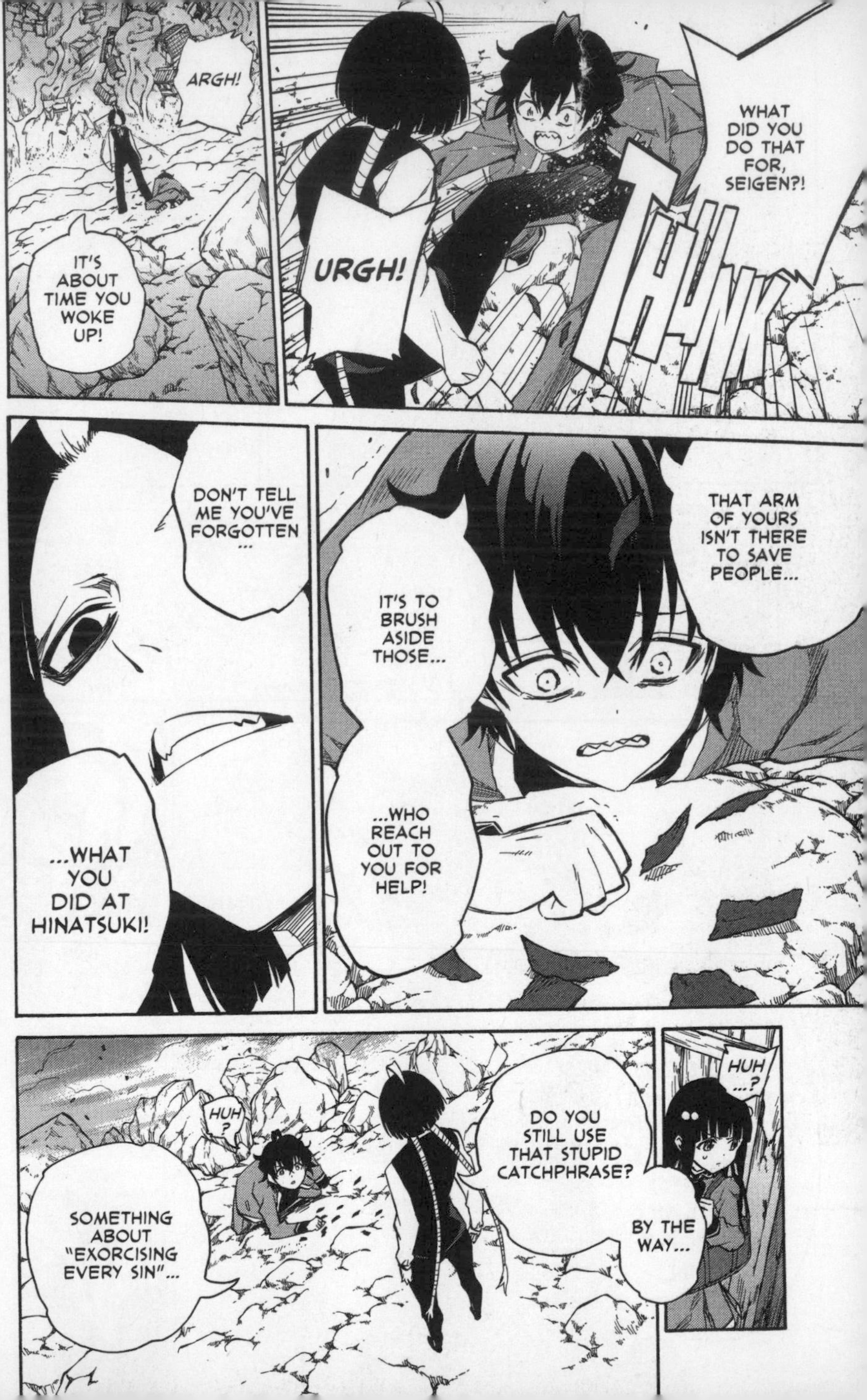
WHAT DID YOU DO THAT FOR, SEIGEN?!
THUNK
URGH!
ARGH!
IT'S ABOUT TIME YOU WOKE UP!
THAT ARM OF YOURS ISN'T THERE TO SAVE PEOPLE...
IT'S TO BRUSH ASIDE THOSE...
...WHO REACH OUT TO YOU FOR HELP!
DON'T TELL ME YOU'VE FORGOTTEN...
...WHAT YOU DID AT HINATSUKI!
HUH...?
BY THE WAY...
DO YOU STILL USE THAT STUPID CATCHPHRASE?
HUH?
SOMETHING ABOUT "EXORCISING EVERY SIN"...

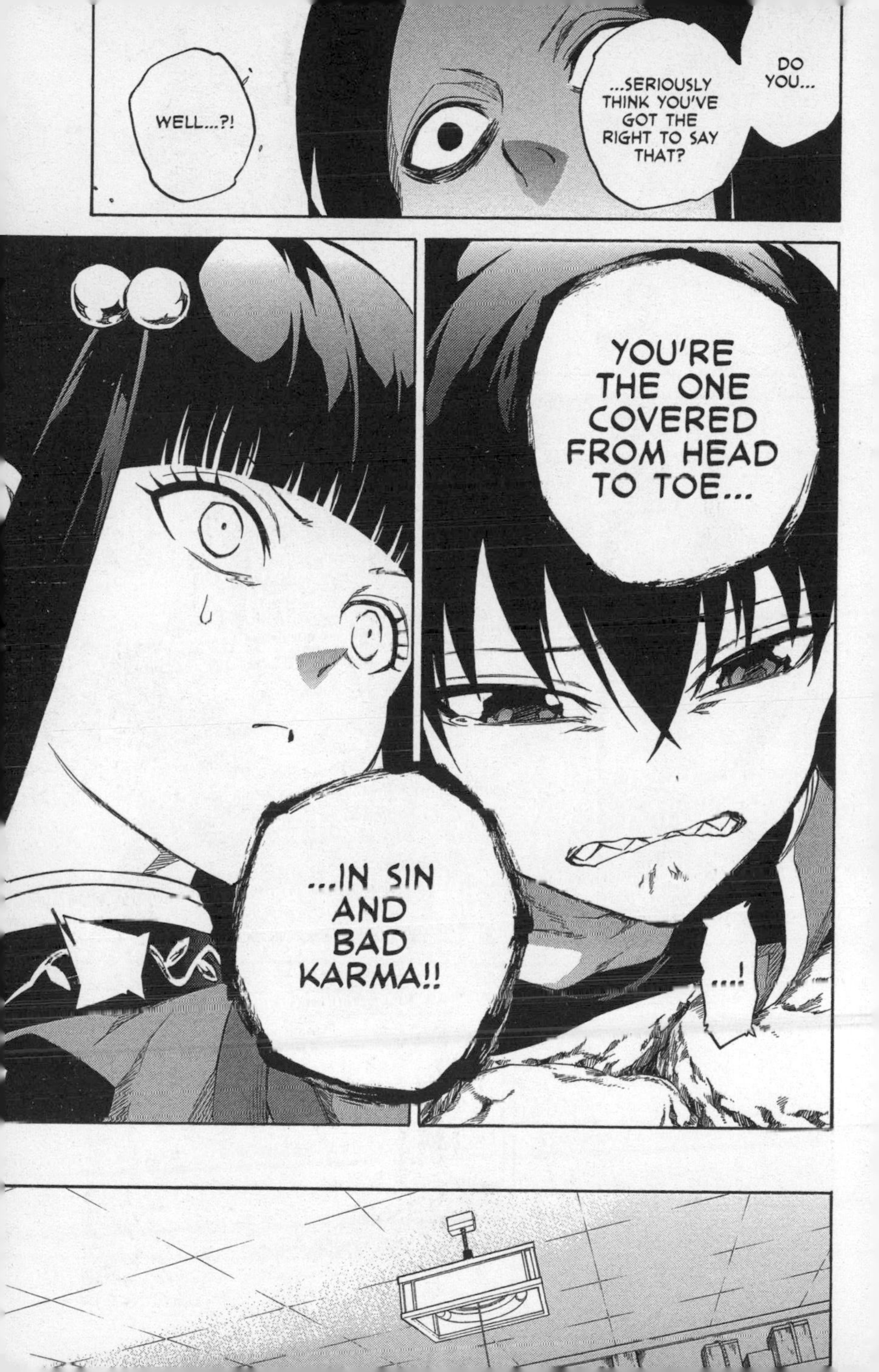
DO YOU...
...SERIOUSLY THINK YOU'VE GOT THE RIGHT TO SAY THAT?
WELL...?!
YOU'RE THE ONE COVERED FROM HEAD TO TOE...
...IN SIN AND BAD KARMA!!
...!

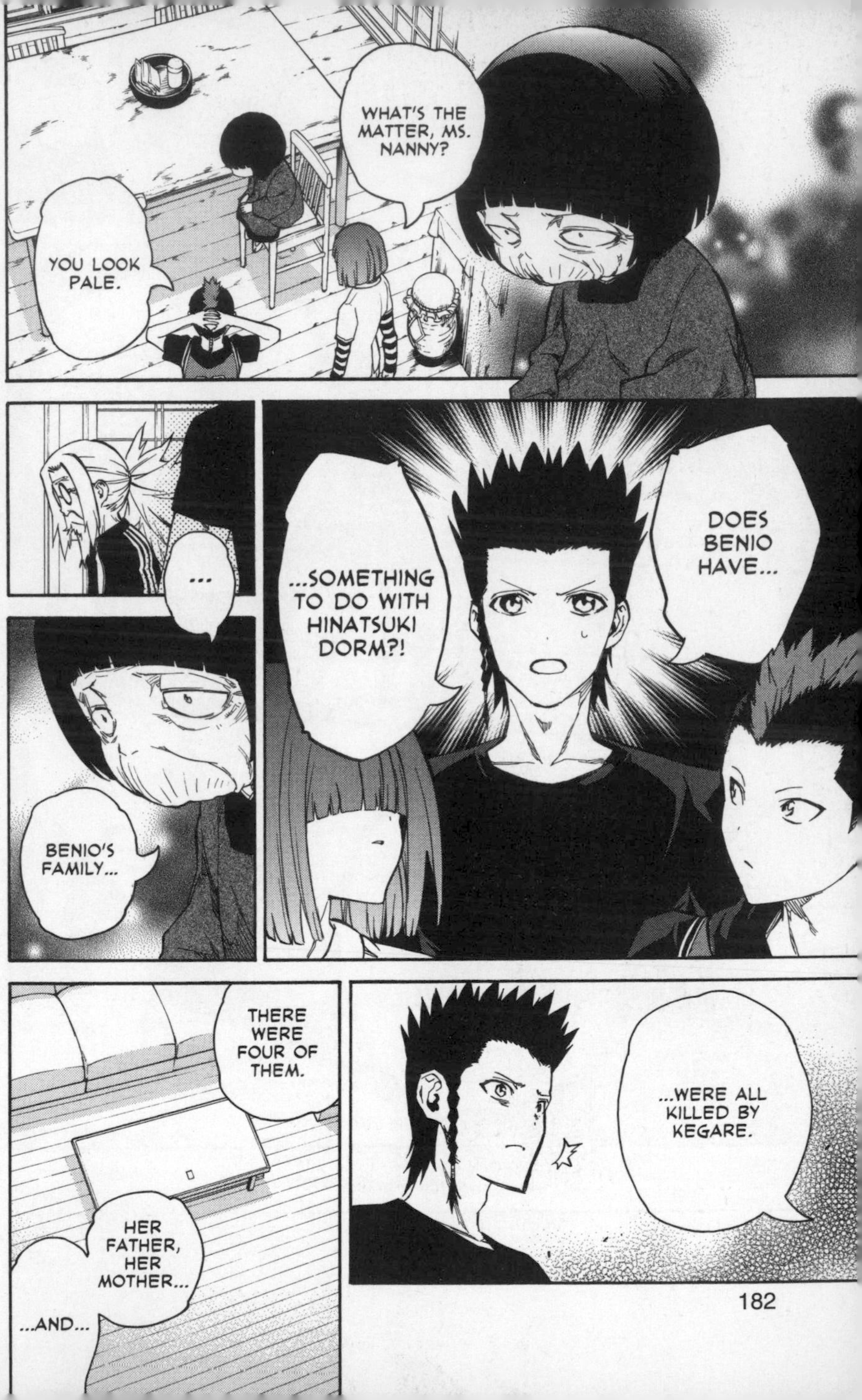
WHAT'S THE MATTER, MS. NANNY?
YOU LOOK PALE.
DOES BENIO HAVE...
...SOMETHING TO DO WITH HINATSUKI DORM?!
...
BENIO'S FAMILY...
...WERE ALL KILLED BY KEGARE.
THERE WERE FOUR OF THEM.
HER FATHER, HER MOTHER...
...AND...

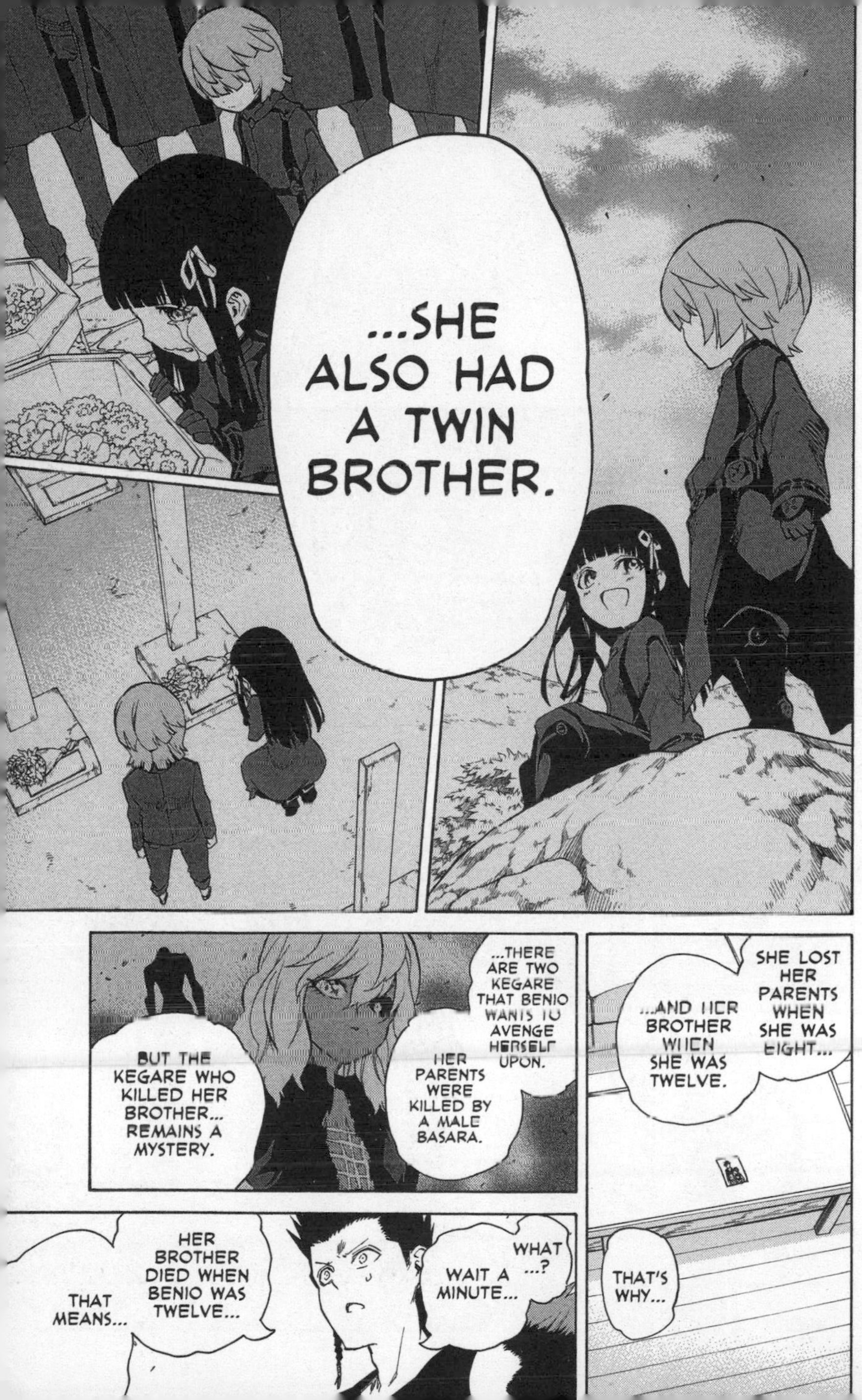
...SHE ALSO HAD A TWIN BROTHER.
SHE LOST HER PARENTS WHEN SHE WAS EIGHT...
...AND HER BROTHER WHEN SHE WAS TWELVE.
THAT'S WHY...
...THERE ARE TWO KEGARE THAT BENIO WANTS TO AVENGE HERSELF UPON.
HER PARENTS WERE KILLED BY A MALE BASARA.
BUT THE KEGARE WHO KILLED HER BROTHER... REMAINS A MYSTERY.
WHAT ...?
WAIT A MINUTE...
HER BROTHER DIED WHEN BENIO WAS TWELVE...
THAT MEANS...

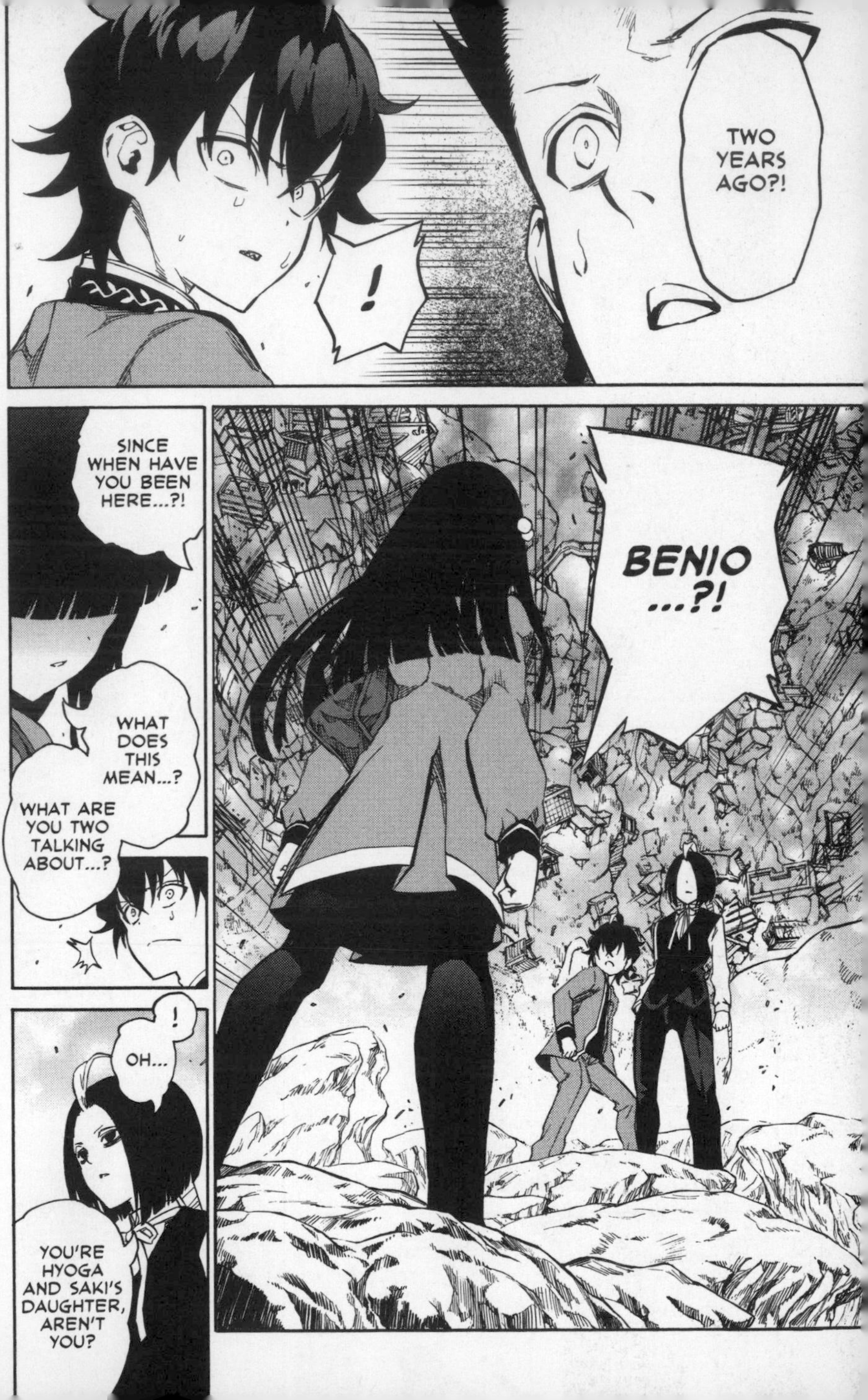
TWO YEARS AGO?!
!
BENIO ...?!
SINCE WHEN HAVE YOU BEEN HERE...?!
WHAT DOES THIS MEAN...?
WHAT ARE YOU TWO TALKING ABOUT...?
!
OH...
YOU'RE HYOGA AND SAKI'S DAUGHTER, AREN'T YOU?

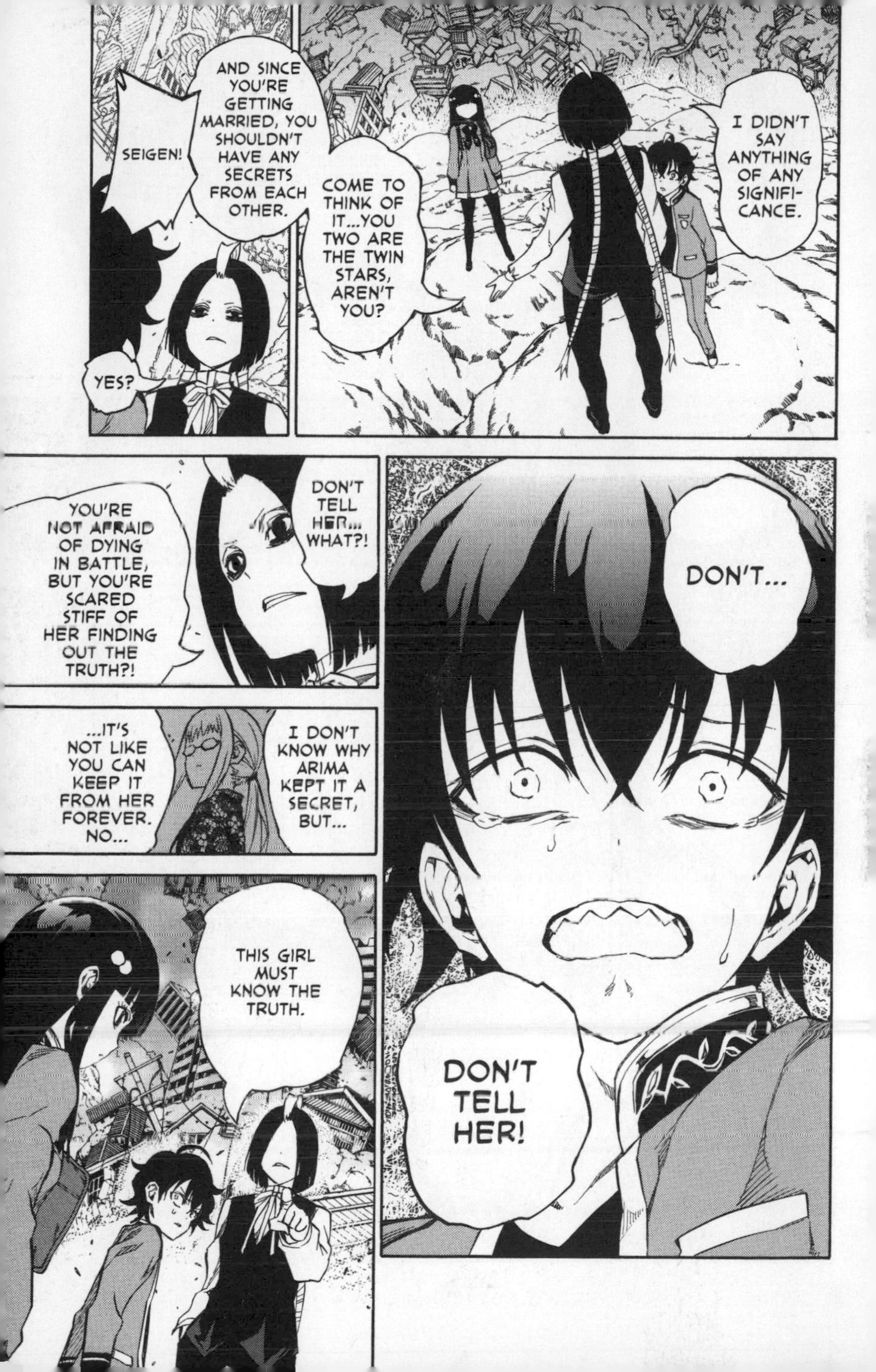
I DIDN'T SAY ANYTHING OF ANY SIGNIFICANCE.
COME TO THINK OF IT...YOU TWO ARE THE TWIN STARS, AREN'T YOU?
AND SINCE YOU'RE GETTING MARRIED, YOU SHOULDN'T HAVE ANY SECRETS FROM EACH OTHER.
SEIGEN!
YES?
DON'T...
DON'T TELL HER!
DON'T TELL HER... WHAT?!
YOU'RE NOT AFRAID OF DYING IN BATTLE, BUT YOU'RE SCARED STIFF OF HER FINDING OUT THE TRUTH?!
I DON'T KNOW WHY ARIMA KEPT IT A SECRET, BUT...
...IT'S NOT LIKE YOU CAN KEEP IT FROM HER FOREVER. NO...
THIS GIRL MUST KNOW THE TRUTH.

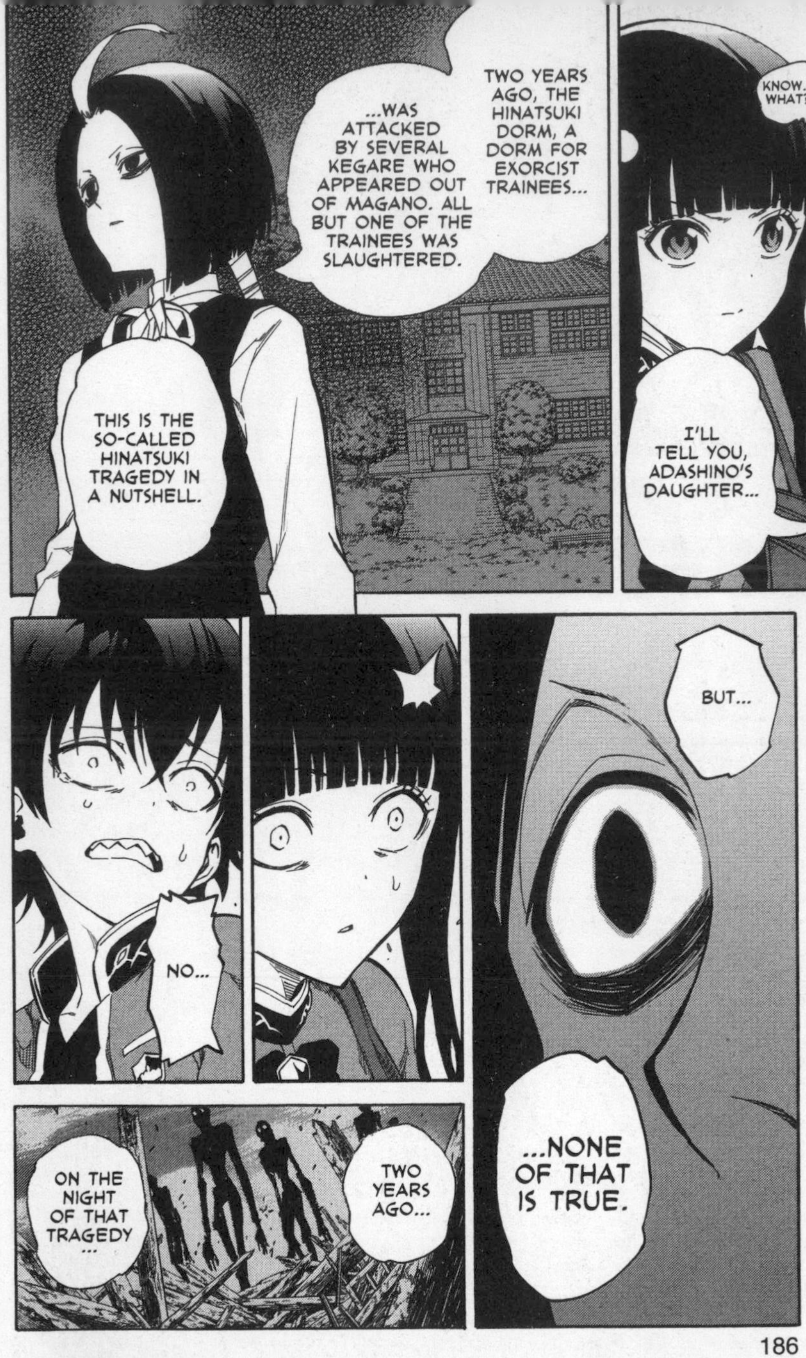
KNOW... WHAT?
I'LL TELL YOU, ADASHINO'S DAUGHTER...
TWO YEARS AGO, THE HINATSUKI DORM, A DORM FOR EXORCIST TRAINEES...
...WAS ATTACKED BY SEVERAL KEGARE WHO APPEARED OUT OF MAGANO. ALL BUT ONE OF THE TRAINEES WAS SLAUGHTERED.
THIS IS THE SO-CALLED HINATSUKI TRAGEDY IN A NUTSHELL.
BUT...
...NONE OF THAT IS TRUE.
NO...
TWO YEARS AGO...
ON THE NIGHT OF THAT TRAGEDY ...

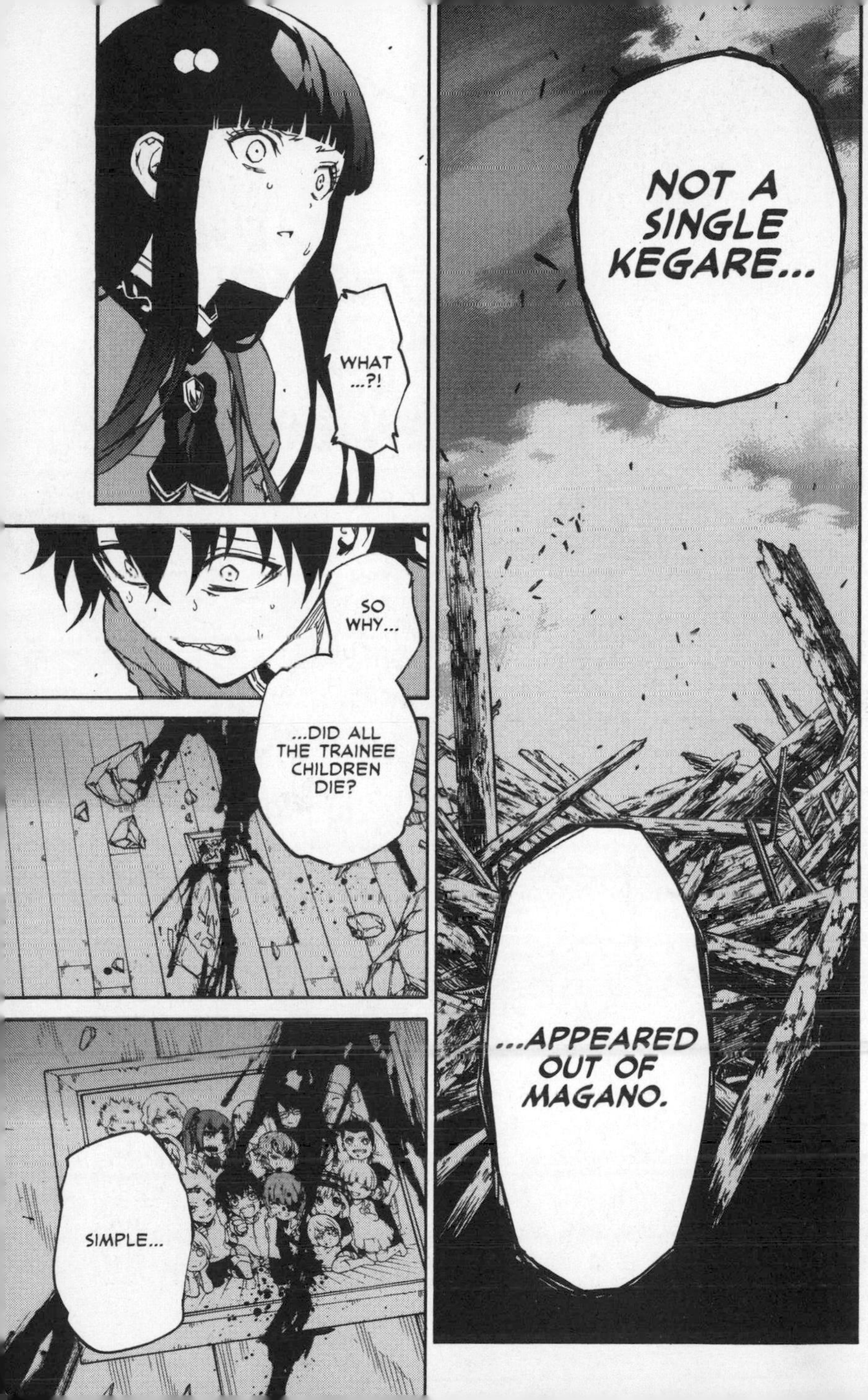
NOT A SINGLE KEGARE...
...APPEARED OUT OF MAGANO.
WHAT ...?!
SO WHY...
...DID ALL THE TRAINEE CHILDREN DIE?
SIMPLE...

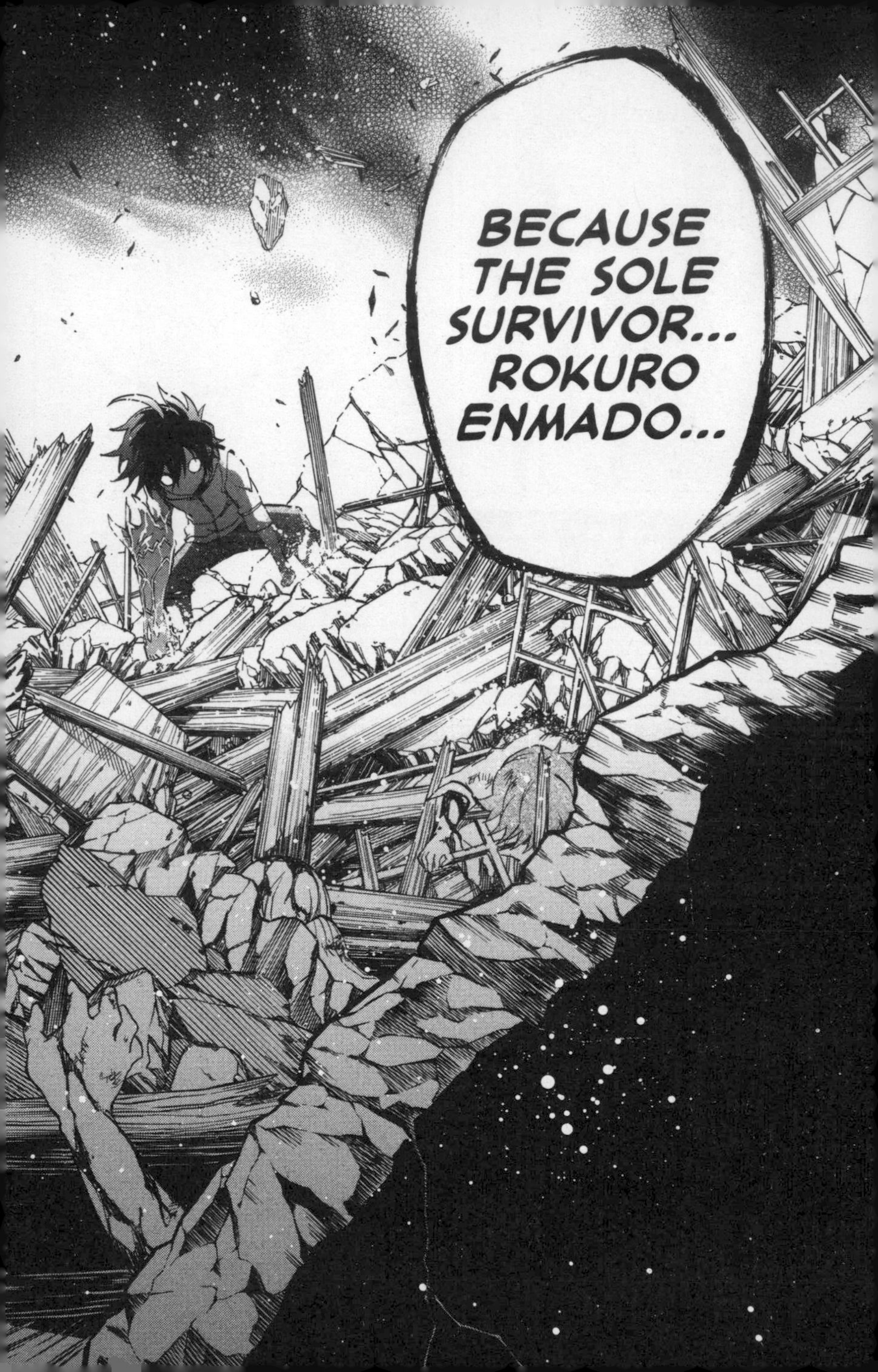
BECAUSE THE SOLE SURVIVOR... ROKURO ENMADO...

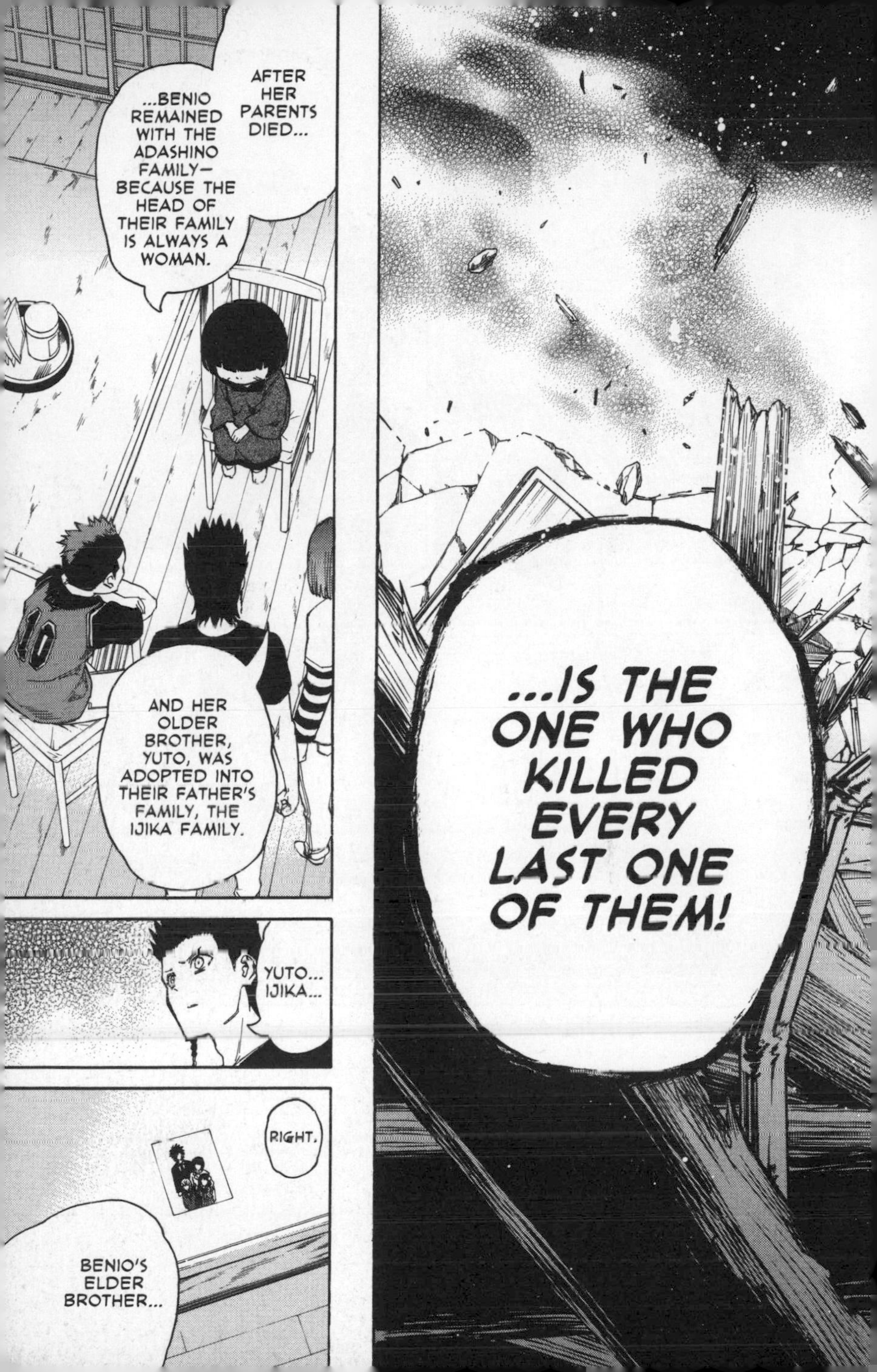
...IS THE ONE WHO KILLED EVERY LAST ONE OF THEM!
AFTER HER PARENTS DIED...
...BENIO REMAINED WITH THE ADASHINO FAMILY—BECAUSE THE HEAD OF THEIR FAMILY IS ALWAYS A WOMAN.
AND HER OLDER BROTHER, YUTO, WAS ADOPTED INTO THEIR FATHER'S FAMILY, THE IJIKA FAMILY.
YUTO... IJIKA...
RIGHT.
BENIO'S ELDER BROTHER...

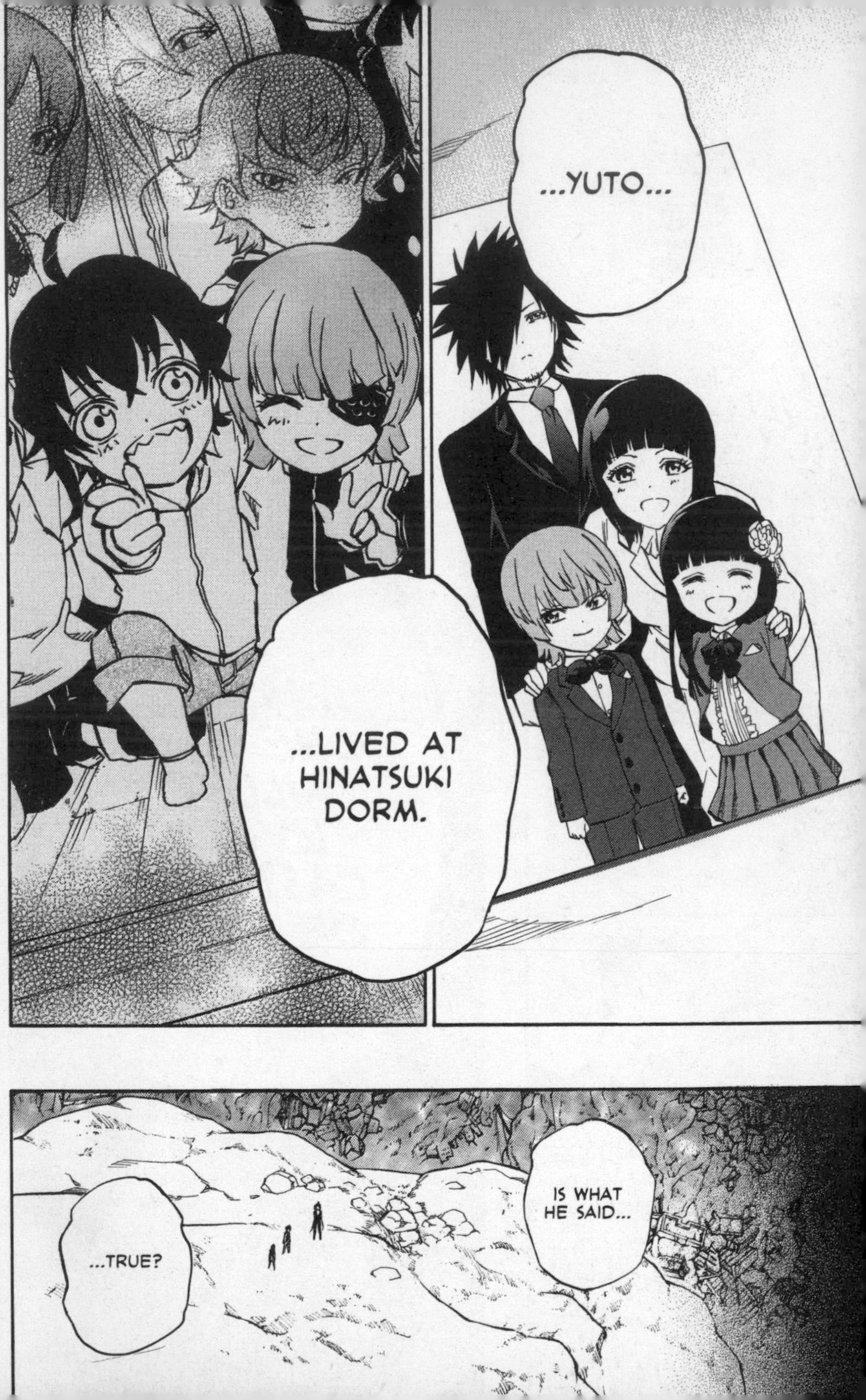
...YUTO...
...LIVED AT HINATSUKI DORM.
IS WHAT HE SAID...
...TRUE?

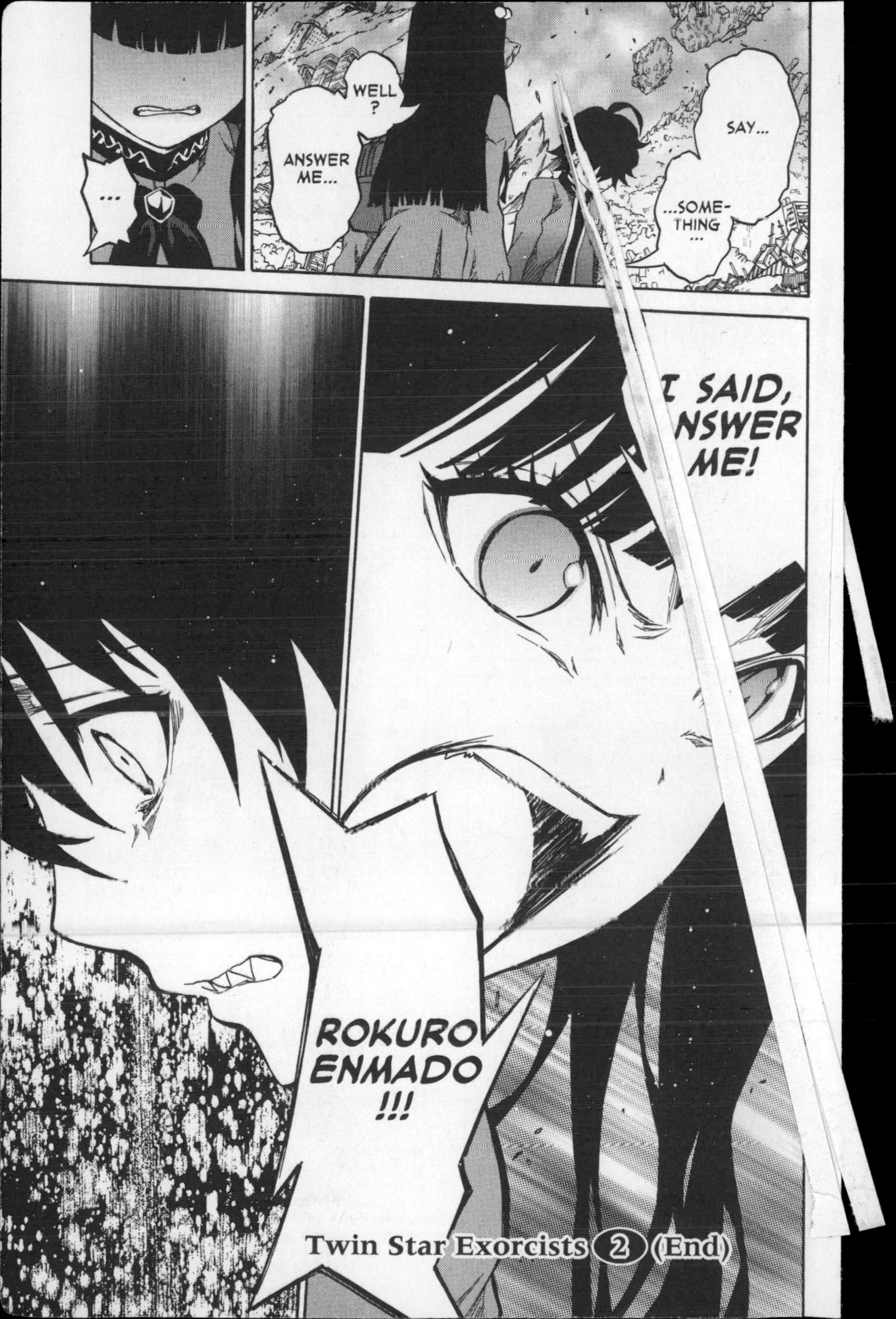
SAY... ...SOMETHING...
WELL? ANSWER ME...
...
I SAID, NSWER ME!
ROKURO ENMADO!!!

Twin Star Exorcists 2 (End)

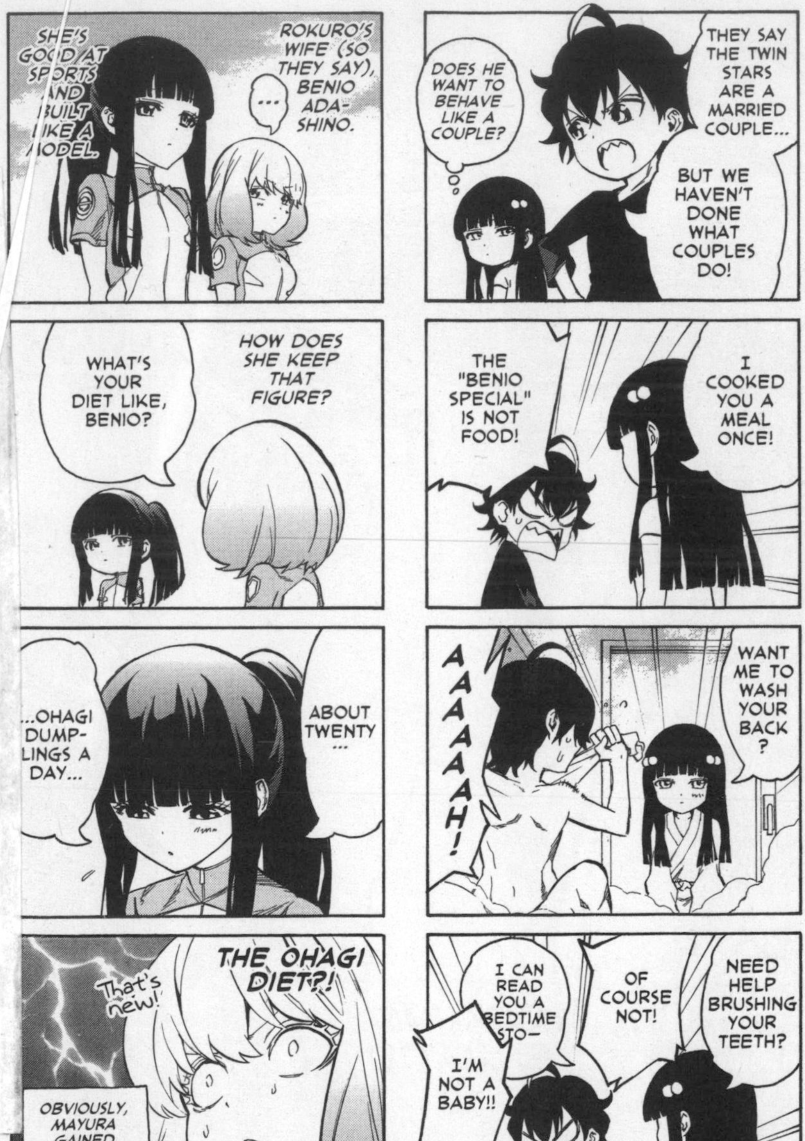
THEY SAY THE TWIN STARS ARE A MARRIED COUPLE...
BUT WE HAVEN'T DONE WHAT COUPLES DO!
DOES HE WANT TO BEHAVE LIKE A COUPLE?
I COOKED YOU A MEAL ONCE!
THE "BENIO SPECIAL" IS NOT FOOD!
WANT ME TO WASH YOUR BACK?
AAAAAAH!
NEED HELP BRUSHING YOUR TEETH?
OF COURSE NOT!
I CAN READ YOU A BEDTIME STO—
I'M NOT A BABY!!
ROKURO'S WIFE (SO THEY SAY), BENIO ADASHINO.
...
SHE'S GOOD AT SPORTS AND BUILT LIKE A MODEL.
HOW DOES SHE KEEP THAT FIGURE?
WHAT'S YOUR DIET LIKE, BENIO?
ABOUT TWENTY...
...OHAGI DUMPLINGS A DAY...
THE OHAGI DIET?!
That's new!
OBVIOUSLY, MAYURA GAINED WEIGHT AFTER ACTUALLY GIVING IT A TRY.

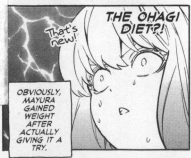

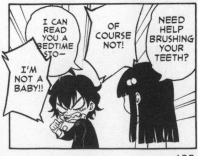

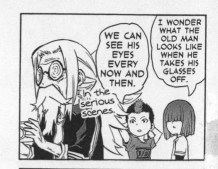

I WONDER WHAT THE OLD MAN LOOKS LIKE WHEN HE TAKES HIS GLASSES OFF.
WE CAN SEE HIS EYES EVERY NOW AND THEN.
In the serious scenes.
BUT I'VE NEVER SEEN HIM WITHOUT HIS GLASSES.
HE MIGHT ACTUALLY BE HANDSOME WITHOUT THEM.
HRM ...?
MY GLASSES ARE DIRTY.
OH!
HEY, THAT CAN'T BE RIGHT!!
RUB
RUB

Yukari Otomi (43)
She's the Old man's daughter! Seigen's ex-wife! And Mayura's mother!

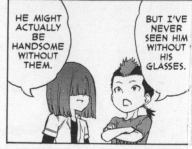

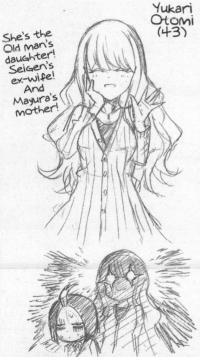

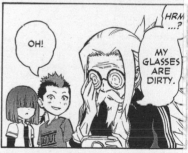

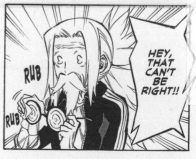

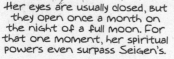

Her eyes are usually closed, but they open once a month on the night of a full moon. For that one moment, her spiritual powers even surpass Seigen's.

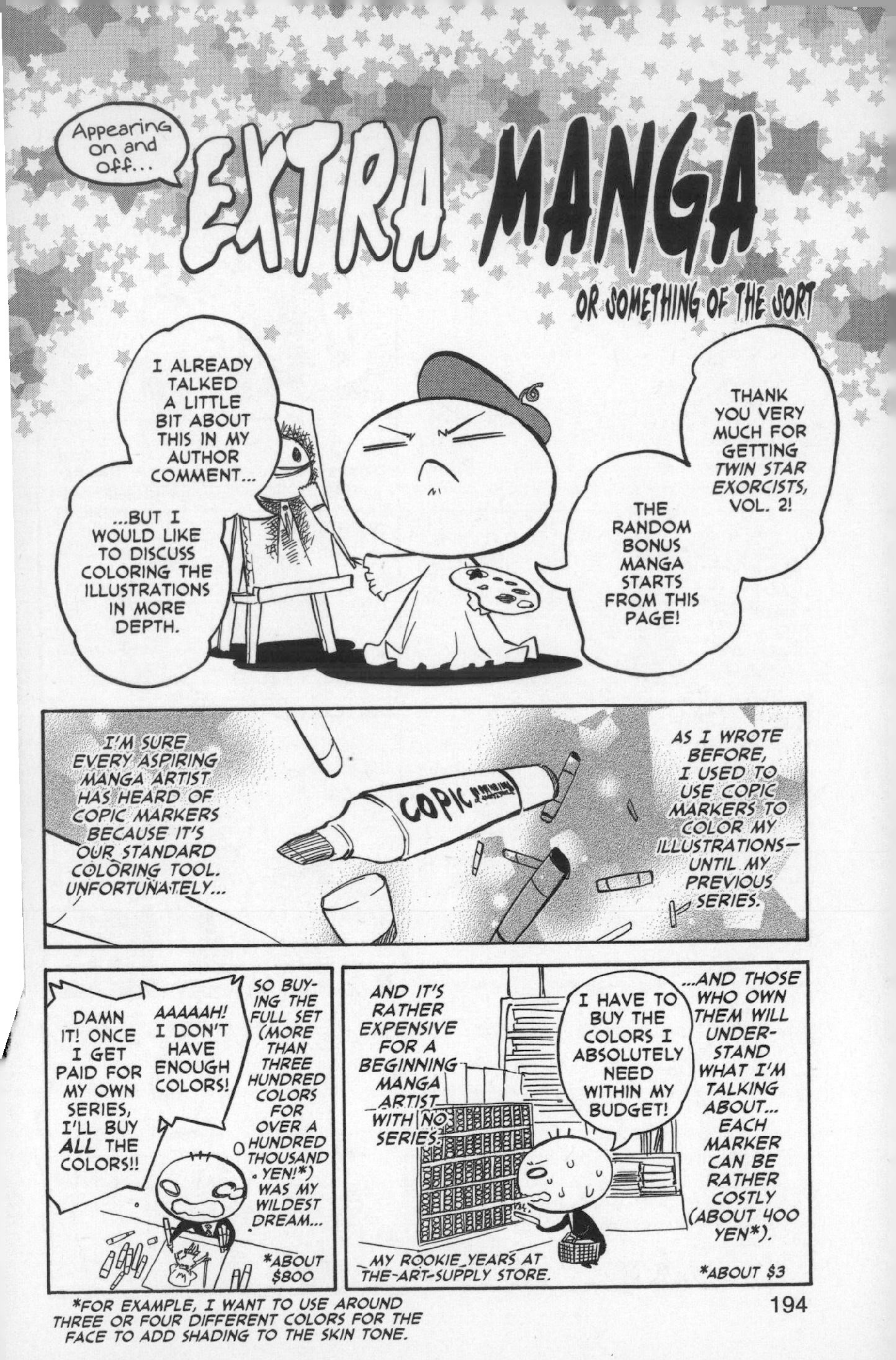

Appearing on and off...
EXTRA MANGA
OR SOMETHING OF THE SORT
THANK YOU VERY MUCH FOR GETTING TWIN STAR EXORCISTS, VOL. 2!
THE RANDOM BONUS MANGA STARTS FROM THIS PAGE!
I ALREADY TALKED A LITTLE BIT ABOUT THIS IN MY AUTHOR COMMENT...
...BUT I WOULD LIKE TO DISCUSS COLORING THE ILLUSTRATIONS IN MORE DEPTH.
AS I WROTE BEFORE, I USED TO USE COPIC MARKERS TO COLOR MY ILLUSTRATIONS—UNTIL MY PREVIOUS SERIES.
COPIC
I'M SURE EVERY ASPIRING MANGA ARTIST HAS HEARD OF COPIC MARKERS BECAUSE IT'S OUR STANDARD COLORING TOOL. UNFORTUNATELY...
...AND THOSE WHO OWN THEM WILL UNDERSTAND WHAT I'M TALKING ABOUT... EACH MARKER CAN BE RATHER COSTLY (ABOUT 400 YEN*).
I HAVE TO BUY THE COLORS I ABSOLUTELY NEED WITHIN MY BUDGET!
AND IT'S RATHER EXPENSIVE FOR A BEGINNING MANGA ARTIST WITH NO SERIES.
MY ROOKIE YEARS AT THE ART SUPPLY STORE.
*ABOUT $3
SO BUYING THE FULL SET (MORE THAN THREE HUNDRED COLORS FOR OVER A HUNDRED THOUSAND YEN!*) WAS MY WILDEST DREAM...
AAAAAH! I DON'T HAVE ENOUGH COLORS!
DAMN IT! ONCE I GET PAID FOR MY OWN SERIES, I'LL BUY **ALL** THE COLORS!!
*ABOUT $800

*FOR EXAMPLE, I WANT TO USE AROUND THREE OR FOUR DIFFERENT COLORS FOR THE FACE TO ADD SHADING TO THE SKIN TONE.

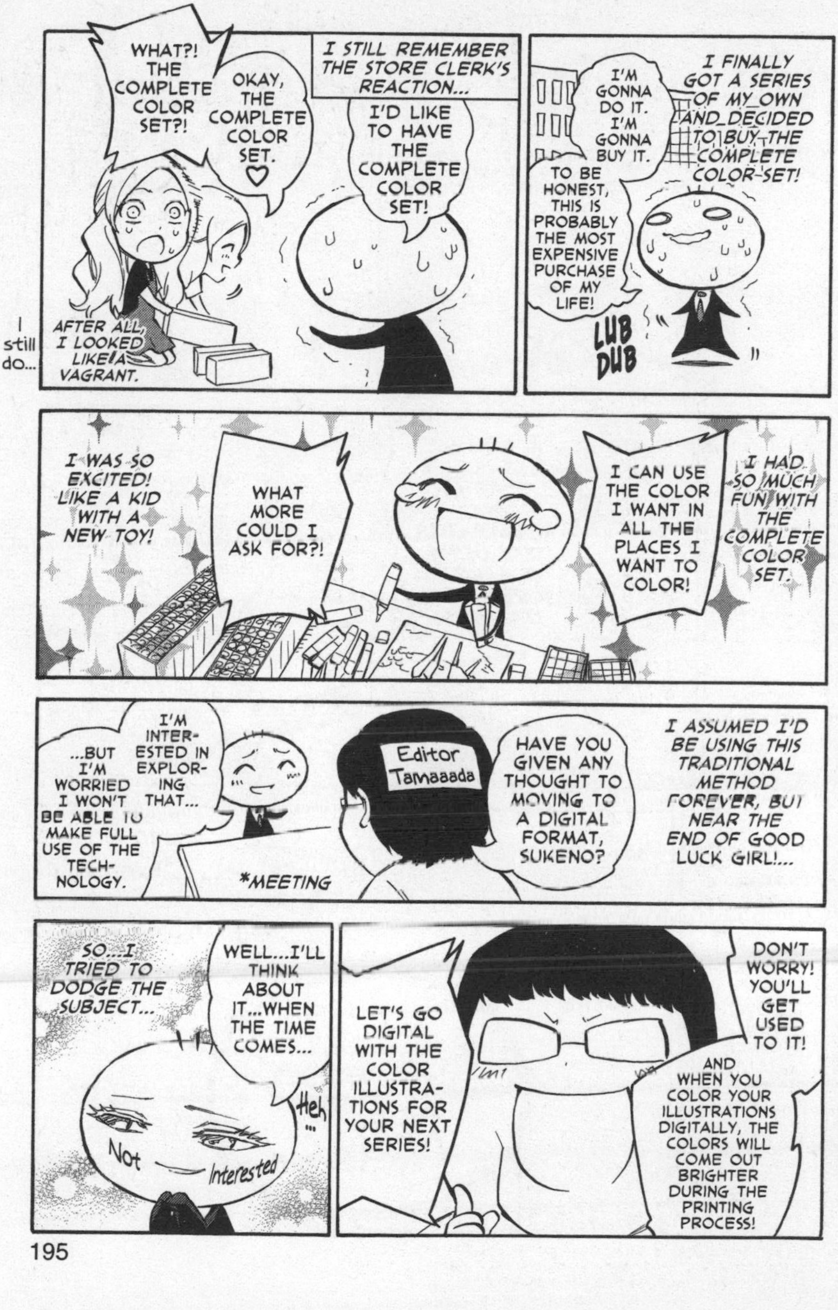
I FINALLY GOT A SERIES OF MY OWN AND DECIDED TO BUY THE COMPLETE COLOR SET!
I'M GONNA DO IT. I'M GONNA BUY IT.
TO BE HONEST, THIS IS PROBABLY THE MOST EXPENSIVE PURCHASE OF MY LIFE!
LUB DUB
I STILL REMEMBER THE STORE CLERK'S REACTION...
I'D LIKE TO HAVE THE COMPLETE COLOR SET!
OKAY, THE COMPLETE COLOR SET. ♡
WHAT?! THE COMPLETE COLOR SET?!
AFTER ALL, I LOOKED LIKE A VAGRANT.
I still do...
I HAD SO MUCH FUN WITH THE COMPLETE COLOR SET.
I CAN USE THE COLOR I WANT IN ALL THE PLACES I WANT TO COLOR!
WHAT MORE COULD I ASK FOR?!
I WAS SO EXCITED! LIKE A KID WITH A NEW TOY!
I ASSUMED I'D BE USING THIS TRADITIONAL METHOD FOREVER, BUT NEAR THE END OF GOOD LUCK GIRL!...
HAVE YOU GIVEN ANY THOUGHT TO MOVING TO A DIGITAL FORMAT, SUKENO?
Editor Tamaaada
I'M INTERESTED IN EXPLORING THAT...
...BUT I'M WORRIED I WON'T BE ABLE TO MAKE FULL USE OF THE TECHNOLOGY.
*MEETING
DON'T WORRY! YOU'LL GET USED TO IT!
AND WHEN YOU COLOR YOUR ILLUSTRATIONS DIGITALLY, THE COLORS WILL COME OUT BRIGHTER DURING THE PRINTING PROCESS!
LET'S GO DIGITAL WITH THE COLOR ILLUSTRATIONS FOR YOUR NEXT SERIES!
WELL...I'LL THINK ABOUT IT...WHEN THE TIME COMES...
SO...I TRIED TO DODGE THE SUBJECT...
Heh...
Not Interested

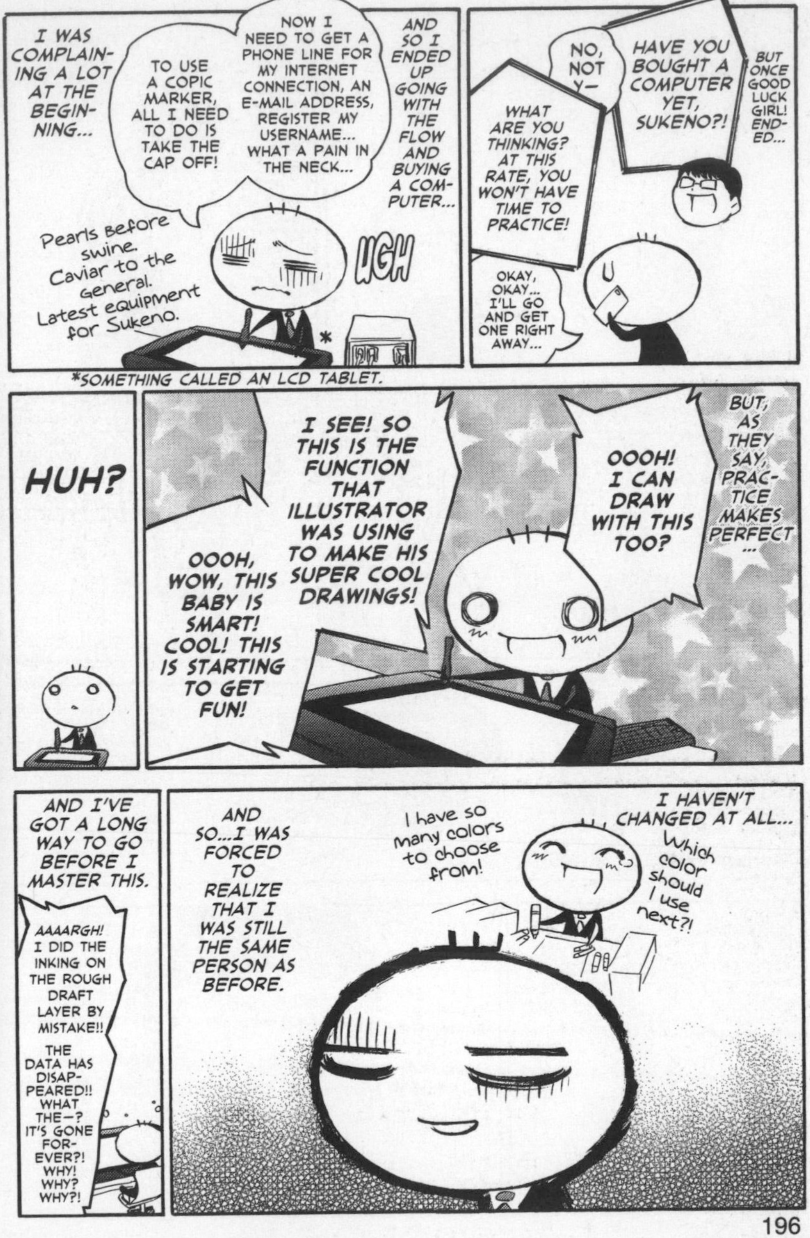
BUT ONCE GOOD LUCK GIRL! ENDED...
HAVE YOU BOUGHT A COMPUTER YET, SUKENO?!
NO, NOT Y—
WHAT ARE YOU THINKING? AT THIS RATE, YOU WON'T HAVE TIME TO PRACTICE!
OKAY, OKAY... I'LL GO AND GET ONE RIGHT AWAY...
AND SO I ENDED UP GOING WITH THE FLOW AND BUYING A COMPUTER...
NOW I NEED TO GET A PHONE LINE FOR MY INTERNET CONNECTION, AN E-MAIL ADDRESS, REGISTER MY USERNAME... WHAT A PAIN IN THE NECK...
TO USE A COPIC MARKER, ALL I NEED TO DO IS TAKE THE CAP OFF!
I WAS COMPLAINING A LOT AT THE BEGINNING...
UGH
Pearls before swine. Caviar to the general. Latest equipment for Sukeno.
*
*SOMETHING CALLED AN LCD TABLET.
BUT, AS THEY SAY, PRACTICE MAKES PERFECT...
OOOH! I CAN DRAW WITH THIS TOO?
I SEE! SO THIS IS THE FUNCTION THAT ILLUSTRATOR WAS USING TO MAKE HIS SUPER COOL DRAWINGS!
OOOH, WOW, THIS BABY IS SMART! COOL! THIS IS STARTING TO GET FUN!
HUH?
I HAVEN'T CHANGED AT ALL...
Which color should I use next?!
I have so many colors to choose from!
AND SO...I WAS FORCED TO REALIZE THAT I WAS STILL THE SAME PERSON AS BEFORE.
AND I'VE GOT A LONG WAY TO GO BEFORE I MASTER THIS.
AAAARGH! I DID THE INKING ON THE ROUGH DRAFT LAYER BY MISTAKE!!
THE DATA HAS DISAPPEARED!! WHAT THE—? IT'S GONE FOREVER?! WHY! WHY? WHY?!

—SHONEN JUMP Manga Edition—

STORY & ART **Yoshiaki Sukeno**

TRANSLATION **Tetsuichiro Miyaki**
ENGLISH ADAPTATION **Bryant Turnage**
TOUCH-UP ART & LETTERING **Stephen Dutro**
COVER & INTERIOR DESIGN **Shawn Carrico**
EDITOR **Annette Roman**

SOUSEI NO ONMYOJI © 2013 by Yoshiaki Sukeno
All rights reserved.
First published in Japan in 2013 by SHUEISHA Inc., Tokyo.
English translation rights arranged by SHUEISHA Inc.

The stories, characters and incidents mentioned in this
publication are entirely fictional.

Printed in the U.S.A.

Published by VIZ Media, LLC
P.O. Box 77010
San Francisco, CA 94107

10 9 8 7 6 5 4 3 2 1
First printing, October 2015

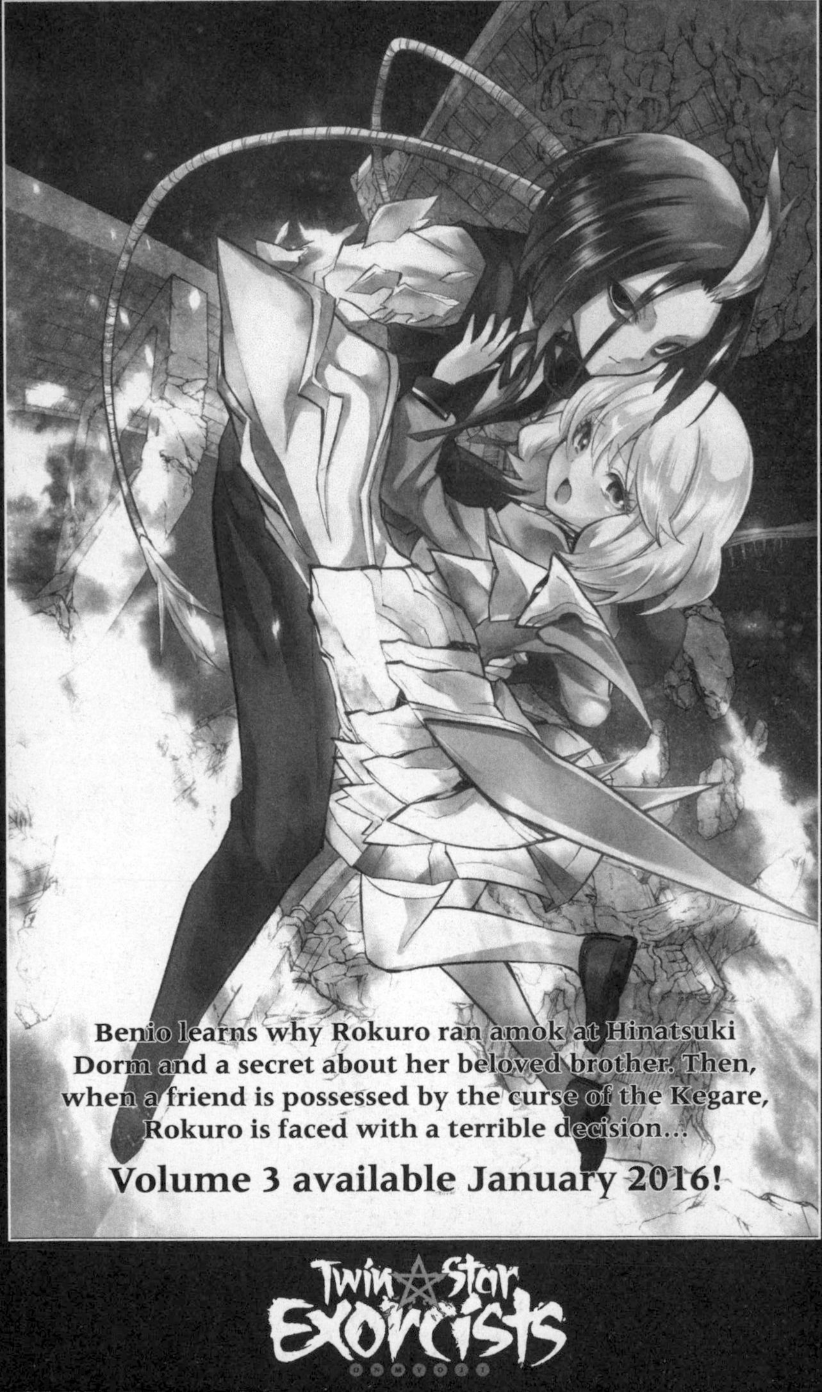
Benio learns why Rokuro ran amok at Hinatsuki Dorm and a secret about her beloved brother. Then, when a friend is possessed by the curse of the Kegare, Rokuro is faced with a terrible decision...
Volume 3 available January 2016!

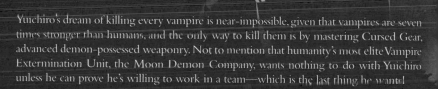

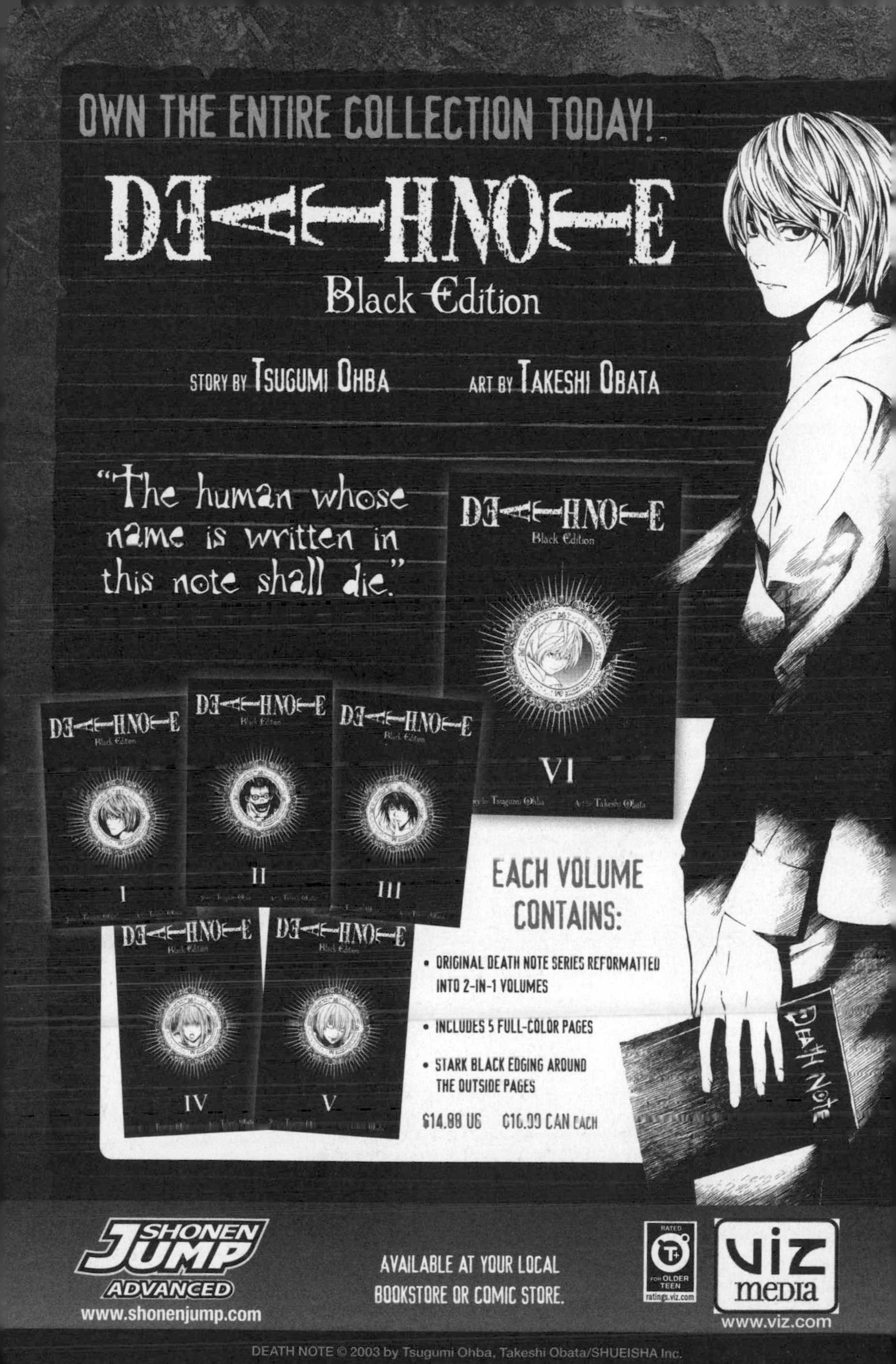
OWN THE ENTIRE COLLECTION TODAY!
DEATH NOTE
Black Edition
STORY BY TSUGUMI OHBA
ART BY TAKESHI OBATA
"The human whose name is written in this note shall die."
DEATH NOTE Black Edition VI
Story by Tsugumi Ohba Art by Takeshi Obata
DEATH NOTE Black Edition I
DEATH NOTE Black Edition II
DEATH NOTE Black Edition III
DEATH NOTE Black Edition IV
DEATH NOTE Black Edition V
EACH VOLUME CONTAINS:
• ORIGINAL DEATH NOTE SERIES REFORMATTED INTO 2-IN-1 VOLUMES
• INCLUDES 5 FULL-COLOR PAGES
• STARK BLACK EDGING AROUND THE OUTSIDE PAGES
$14.99 US $16.99 CAN EACH
DEATH NOTE
SHONEN JUMP ADVANCED
www.shonenjump.com
AVAILABLE AT YOUR LOCAL BOOKSTORE OR COMIC STORE.
RATED T+ FOR OLDER TEEN ratings.viz.com
viz media
www.viz.com

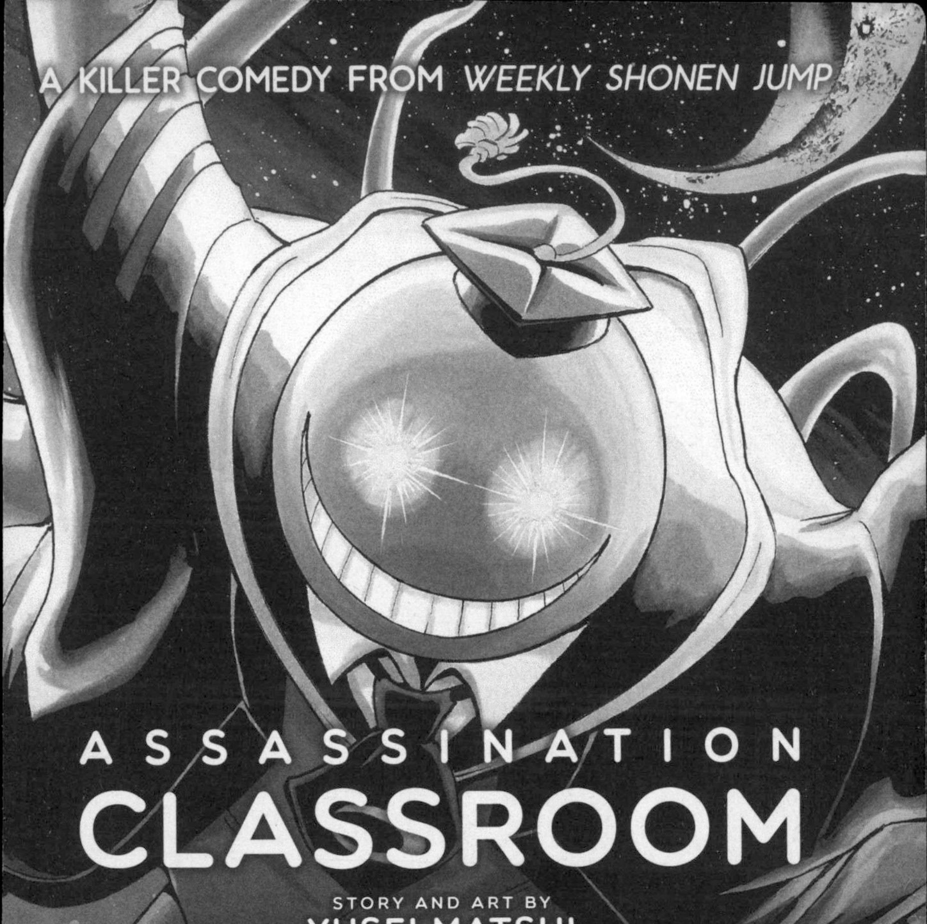
A KILLER COMEDY FROM *WEEKLY SHONEN JUMP*
ASSASSINATION
CLASSROOM
STORY AND ART BY
YUSEI MATSUI

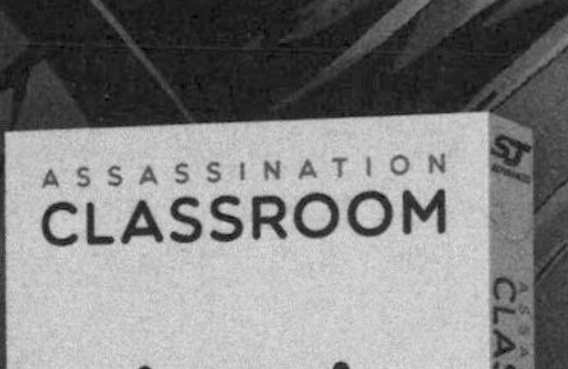
ASSASSINATION
CLASSROOM
STORY AND ART BY
YUSEI MATSUI
1
SHONEN JUMP ADVANCED

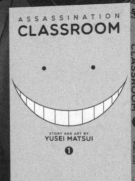

EYESHIELD 21

STORY BY RIICHIRO INAGAKI
ART BY YUSUKE MURATA

From the artist of *One-Punch Man!*

Wimpy Sena Kobayakawa has been running away from bullies all his life. But when the football gear comes on, things change—Sena's speed and uncanny ability to elude big bullies just might give him what it takes to become a great high school football hero! Catch all the bone-crushing action and slapstick comedy of Japan's hottest football manga!

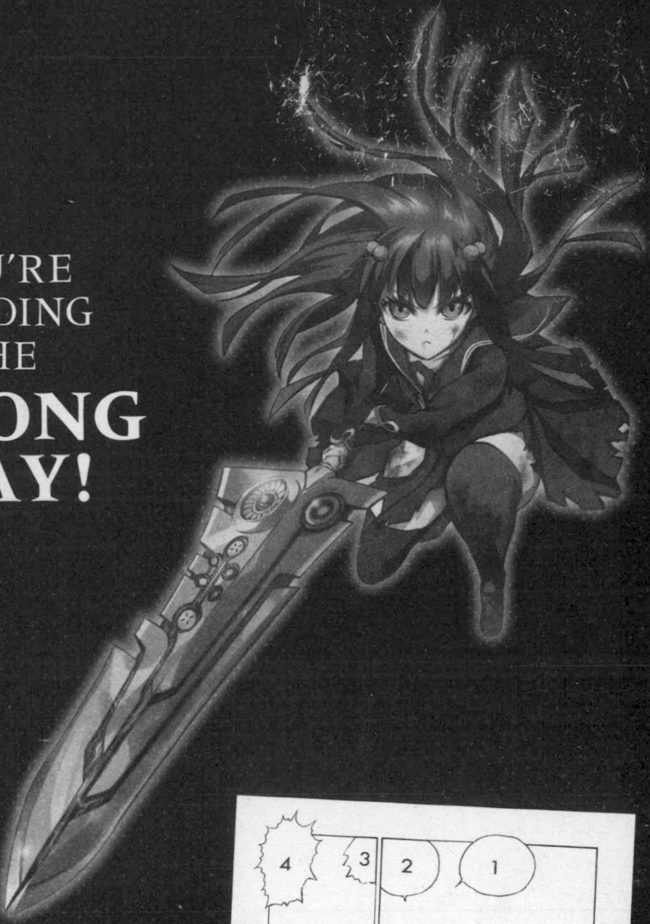

YOU'RE READING THE **WRONG WAY!**

Twin Star Exorcists reads from right to left, starting in the upper-right corner. Japanese is read from right to left, meaning that action, sound effects and word-balloon order are completely reversed from English order.

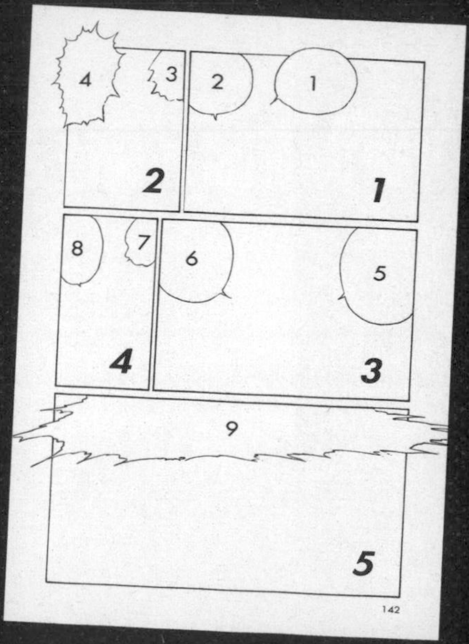
1
2
1
3
4
2
5
6
3
7
8
4
9
5
142